ISLAND AT WAR

CARIBBEAN
STUDIES
SERIES

Anton L. Allahar and Shona N. Jackson
Series Editors

ISLAND AT WAR

Puerto Rico in the Crucible of the Second World War

Edited by
Jorge Rodríguez Beruff
and José L. Bolívar Fresneda

University Press of Mississippi / Jackson

www.upress.state.ms.us

The University Press of Mississippi is a member
of the Association of American University Presses.

Copyright © 2015 by University Press of Mississippi
All rights reserved
Manufactured in the United States of America

First printing 2015

∞

Library of Congress Cataloging-in-Publication Data

Island at war : Puerto Rico in the crucible of the Second World War /
edited by Jorge Rodríguez Beruff and José L. Bolívar Fresneda.
  pages cm. — (Caribbean studies series)
Includes bibliographical references and index.
ISBN 978-1-62846-164-0 (cloth : alk. paper) — ISBN 978-1-62674-087-7
(ebook) 1. World War, 1939–1945—Puerto Rico. 2. Puerto Rico—Politics
and government—1898–1952. 3. Puerto Rico—Relations—United States.
4. United States—Relations—Puerto Rico. I. Rodríguez Beruff, Jorge,
editor. II. Bolívar, José L., editor.
  D742.P9I85 22015
 940.53'7295—dc23   2014042287

British Library Cataloging-in-Publication Data available

To our sadly deceased friends and contributors

*Fitzroy André Baptiste
A most distinguished and pioneer researcher
on the Caribbean during the Second World War*

*Michael "Mike" Janeway
Friend, renowned journalist, and historian on Puerto Rico
and United States relations; died while this work was in press*

Contents

ix   Acknowledgments

xi   Introduction

3   Rediscovering Puerto Rico and the Caribbean: US Strategic Debate and War Planning on the Eve of the Second World War
       Jorge Rodríguez Beruff

29   Puerto Rico: Headquarters of the Caribbean Sea Frontier, 1940–1945
       Fitzroy André Baptiste

61   War and Political Transition in Puerto Rico, 1939–1940
       Jorge Rodríguez Beruff

82   The Wartime Quartet: Muñoz Marín, Tugwell, Ickes, and FDR
       Michael Janeway

111   The War Economy of Puerto Rico, 1939–1945
       José L. Bolívar Fresneda

139   The German Blockade of the Caribbean in 1942 and Its Effects in Puerto Rico
       Ligia T. Domenech

169   Vieques: The Impact of the Second World War
       César J. Ayala Casás and José L. Bolívar Fresneda

188   The Anglo-American Caribbean Commission: A Socioeconomic Strategy Designed for Military Security, 1942–1946
       Mayra Rosario Urrutia

218 Geopolitics and Telecommunications Policy in Puerto Rico: ITT and the Porto Rico Telephone Company, 1942–1948
Luis Rosario Albert

245 What Did You Do in the War, Daddy? The Story of a Puerto Rican in the Second World War and Korea: Captain Harry Chabrán Acevedo, 1925–1986
Rafael Chabrán

261 Notes on Contributors

265 Index

Acknowledgments

We would like to thank above all the contributors who made this book such a special and valuable collection of research essays regarding the impact the Second World War on Puerto Rico. These are: Fitzroy André Baptiste, Ligia T. Domenech, Michael Janeway, César J. Ayala Casás, Mayra Rosario Urrutia, Luis Rosario Albert, and Rafael Chabrán.

A special thanks goes to Michael Janeway for taking the time to review the article by José L. Bolívar Fresneda and for providing such valuable and insightful suggestions. We deeply regret the passing away of this extraordinary colleague. He had a strong emotional and professional bond to Puerto Rico. It should also be mentioned that it has taken quite a few years for the excellent contribution by our other deceased contributor, Fitzroy André Baptiste, to be finally published. We know that he would have greatly enjoyed seeing this work as part of this collection. We dedicate this volume to these two outstanding scholars and fine human beings.

The editors would also like to thank the three anonymous readers who examined this collection for their very helpful suggestions and comments. They, as well as the editors at the University Press of Mississippi, helped us improve this volume. We would like to specially thank Craig W. Gill, assistant director and editor in chief of the University Press of Mississippi for guiding us through the arduous three-year process of publishing this book. Our thanks also go to Norman Ware, whose editing recommendations and corrections have made this a much more readable publication. Also, to John Langston, who has been so patient regarding our substitutions, as we can always find that perfect photograph that must be included. We have enjoyed working with all of you. We also wish to mention with gratitude Julio Quirós, director of the Fundación Luis Muñoz Marín, for his continued and unconditional support.

We would be amiss if we did not acknowledge the daily help and assistance we receive from our families. José L. Bolívar Fresneda thanks his wife, María de Lourdes Cervoni Ruíz; his son, Alejandro J. Bolívar Cervoni, a recent graduate of Duke University; and his daughter, Carolina S. Bolívar Cervoni, a sophomore at American University; words are not enough to thank you for your support. Jorge Rodríguez Beruff expresses his gratitude to Aura Muñoz Maldonado for her multifaceted support; and Iara, Diego, and Rosaura, my son and daughters, for their permanent inspiration.

Introduction

The Caribbean played an important military and strategic role during the Second World War that has not been sufficiently acknowledged in the countless studies of that global conflict. Such studies generally focus on the major theaters of combat, namely Europe and the Asia-Pacific region.[1] US strategic debate and war planning in the pre-1941 period underscored the importance of the entire Caribbean region to protect the continental United States from an attack from the south and to defend the Panama Canal. Thus, military preparations in the late thirties and early forties placed great emphasis on this vital geostrategic space. Puerto Rico became a major military enclave (together with Panama, Guantánamo in Cuba, and Trinidad), considered by the US military command to be a hub of its insular Caribbean defense system, as Fitzroy André Baptiste explains in his essay in this book, "Puerto Rico: Headquarters of the Caribbean Sea Frontier, 1940–1945." It became an "island at war," as we have entitled this book.

The course of the war in Europe, particularly after collapse of the British and French armies in France in the summer of 1940 and the uncertain fate of the British Isles, further enhanced the perception of an imminent threat to the "southern flank" of the United States. Some of President Franklin Roosevelt's and his military commanders' worst fears about German penetration of the Western Hemisphere, first entertained and war-gamed in 1938–1939, had become a looming possibility. Not only had France and Britain failed to contain Germany, but French and Dutch colonies in the Caribbean, several of them sources of oil and bauxite (among other strategic materials), could potentially aid the German war effort or even become enemy footholds in the Americas. During the Battle of Britain in early September 1940, Roosevelt signed the Destroyers for Bases Agreement with British prime minister Winston Churchill, which added a string of bases in British territories in the Atlantic and the Caribbean (Newfoundland, Bermuda, the Bahamas, Jamaica, Saint Lucia, Trinidad, Antigua, and British Guiana). The United States also

Joint Chiefs of Staff in Washington point out the location of Puerto Rico, highlighting its strategic and military importance during the Second World War, 1942; from left to right: H. H. Arnold, George Marshall, William Leahy, and Ernest King. (*Life* magazine, FDR Library)

obtained access to additional installations in independent countries of the Caribbean basin. It was during the Second World War that the Caribbean really became an "American Lake," to use the expression of noted geostrategist Captain Alfred Thayer Mahan.[2]

The Caribbean and the Gulf of Mexico were also important to Great Britain. The British relied on Mexico and Trinidad for aviation fuel, which had to be shipped through the U-boat-infested Gulf of Mexico and Caribbean, and they were also responsible for defending the numerous territories that Britain possessed in the area.[3] Only toward the end of 1942 did mounting German losses in the Atlantic and the Allied invasion of North Africa compel the German naval command to begin pulling its Atlantic naval forces homeward, thus gradually relieving the pressure in the Caribbean.

From 1939, the United States made major investments in Puerto Rico in the construction or expansion of large army, navy, and army air force bases and many smaller installations, as well as in the improvement of the infrastructure necessary for their operation. The considerable influx of funds for military construction and activities had an important impact on the island's economy. The enhanced strategic value ascribed to the island became evident in 1940 when the US Navy established in San Juan the Tenth Naval District, while the army created the Puerto Rico Department as a new command. The island was also a source of military manpower. About sixty-five thousand Puerto Ricans served in the US Armed Forces, mainly in the army, during the war years. Some of them were garrisoned in Panama and throughout the Caribbean. The Sixty-Fifth Infantry Regiment, a Puerto Rican unit, saw combat in the Europe during the last phases of the war. As in the United States, the population was mobilized for war through the educational system, the sale of war bonds, blackouts, propaganda, and a host of governmental and civic organizations. Local communities, such as those on the island of Vieques and many other places, were directly affected, positively or negatively, by military construction or activities.

Once the United States formally entered the war in December 1941, military operations focused on containing the German submarine offensive, known as the Second Happy Time, which, only in 1942, sank 181 ships in the Caribbean. Most of the shipping losses to the Allies—81 percent of all wartime losses—occurred during that critical year. The Battle of the Caribbean raged in Puerto Rican waters and across the region through 1942 and 1943. The submarines disrupted the Puerto Rican economy and severely affected the food supply. Anthony P. Maingot, the distinguished Caribbean scholar, has stressed the impact of the submarine war and concerns about fifth-column activities in the other countries in the region.[4]

The German naval offensive in the Caribbean, a theater of the larger Battle of the Atlantic, sought to block access to the Panama Canal, disrupt trade with Caribbean islands, and interrupt the maritime routes of the Gulf of Mexico, vital to the delivery of strategic supplies to European Allies. By the spring of 1942, the war was within sight of the beaches and rooftops of Puerto Rico itself. Then, German U-boats subjected the island to a stranglehold blockade. According to Rexford G. Tugwell, wartime governor of Puerto Rico: "The submarines invaded our sea. . . . For more than a year they would roam at will through the Caribbean passages and along our shores, obviously well-informed, sinking everything."[5] General George C. Marshall underscored on June 19, 1942, how much was at stake during this phase of the Second World War:[6]

> The losses by submarines off our Atlantic seaboard and in the Caribbean now threaten our entire war effort. The following statistics bearing on the subject have been brought to my attention. Of the 74 ships allocated to the Army for July by the War Shipping Administration, 17 have already been sunk. Twenty-two percent of the Bauxite fleet has already been destroyed. Twenty percent of the Puerto Rican fleet has been lost. Tanker sinkings have been 3.5 percent per month of tonnage in use.[7]

The Allied invasion of North Africa in November 1942, Operation Torch, was eventually followed by the invasion of Sicily and Italy. With the German submarine threat defeated, the war shifted its locus away from the Caribbean and across the Atlantic. Thus, by mid-1943, the frenzy of military construction practically came to a halt in Puerto Rico (with dire effects for the economy and the people of Vieques). However, the bonanza of Puerto Rican rum exports to the US market, created by the war, served to compensate for the reduction of military construction expenditures.

The impact of the war in the Caribbean was by no means circumscribed to its military aspects, as the essays of *Island at War* sustain. It also provoked or accelerated processes of change in all regional societies, with different outcomes. Great Britain's Caribbean colonies, and their relation to the seat of the British Empire, underwent their own profound evolution, while the French territories were subjected to military rule under the Vichy regime in the context of a military agreement with the United States. The war also conditioned US relations with Cuba and the Dominican Republic, as Roosevelt's administration sought to strengthen links with military strongmen Fulgencio Batista and Rafael Leónidas Trujillo. In both cases, enhanced military collaboration during the war created the conditions for close links in the postwar context. Roosevelt received Batista in Washington in December 1942 with great honors. With regard to the Dominican Republic, major financial concessions were made in the 1940 Hull-Trujillo agreement, which eliminated the country's external debt. In other words, all Caribbean societies were *involved* in the war in different ways, prompting interconnected economic, political, and societal changes. In this respect, it is relevant to quote the historian Gordon Wright on the character of modern war:

> Every modern war, someone has said, is also a revolution. It could hardly be otherwise; the stress and strain of total and protracted conflict unavoidably works profound changes in men and institutions. Some might argue that for the most part, these changes represent no drastic shift in direction, but only a speeding up of trends already under way in the prewar years. Yet even when existing processes are merely hastened, the unsettling impact may produce results equal to those of major revolutions.[8]

Wright's comment may seem to apply mainly to countries that suffered the direct brunt of war, but it is also fully applicable to a Caribbean society such as Puerto Rico. The British historian Arthur Marwick shared with Wright this broad approach to war, placing emphasis on institutional and social change.[9] Authors such as Bruce D. Porter,[10] Geoffrey Perret,[11] David Kennedy,[12] and Alan S. Milward[13] have also explored this perspective.

In the case of Puerto Rico, strategic considerations made the United States focus on the issue of social and political stability necessary for the implementation of extensive defense measures. This was an important impetus for a major shift in US policy toward the island that made possible the transformation of the internal political arrangement. The almost simultaneous removal of General Blanton Winship from the governorship and of Ernest Gruening from Washington policy making, and the subsequent decision, after the unexpected results of the 1940 election, to recognize Luis Muñoz Marín and his reformist Popular Democratic Party as the political force that would govern during the war, are evidence of this shift in policy. The new approach to Puerto Rico was confirmed when Rexford G. Tugwell, a left-wing member of Roosevelt's original Brain Trust group and effective reformist administrator, was named governor in 1941, shortly before the United States entered the war. Tugwell would manage the complex relationship with Muñoz Marín during the entire period of the war.

FDR would count on the full collaboration of the new Puerto Rican reformist wartime leadership. However, the war years witnessed a complex accommodation between the strategic concerns and aims of the Roosevelt administration and the reformist thrust of the Puerto Rican political leadership. The war economy, Tugwell's comprehensive reform of the government structure, and Popular Democratic Party social reforms combined to provoke major political, economic, and social changes. The Second World War was the context of a fast-paced, grand-scale shift from a sugar-based agricultural economy to an industrial and modernized society, together with a redefined political relationship with the United States. The foundations of postwar Puerto Rico were set during these critical years. *Island at War* aspires to shed light on this transformation of the island's socioeconomic and political structures in the crucible of the Second World War.

The impact of the Second World War in the Caribbean region has been studied by authors such as Anthony Maingot, Bernardo Vega, Fitzroy André Baptiste, Michael Anthony, Ken Post, Irwin F. Gellman, Eliane Sempaire, and Steven High.[14] We should note other works by US and Latin American scholars relevant to the Caribbean such as Blanca Torres Ramírez's study of Mexico, David G. Haglund's book on US strategy toward Latin America, and an anthology edited by Leslie Bethell and Ian Roxborough documenting the transition from the Second World War to the Cold War.[15] But perhaps the most important of these works still is the classic study by Fitzroy André Baptiste, *War, Cooperation, and Conflict: The European Possessions in the Caribbean, 1939–1945*. Baptiste's essay on Puerto Rico is published here, posthumously, for the first time. It is a scholarly paper he read on November 21, 1997, at a seminar on the Second World War held at the University of Puerto Rico, where he was invited by Humberto García Muñiz and Jorge Rodríguez Beruff.

Despite the importance of the topic, published scholarship on Puerto Rico's involvement in the global conflict and its domestic impact was scarce until

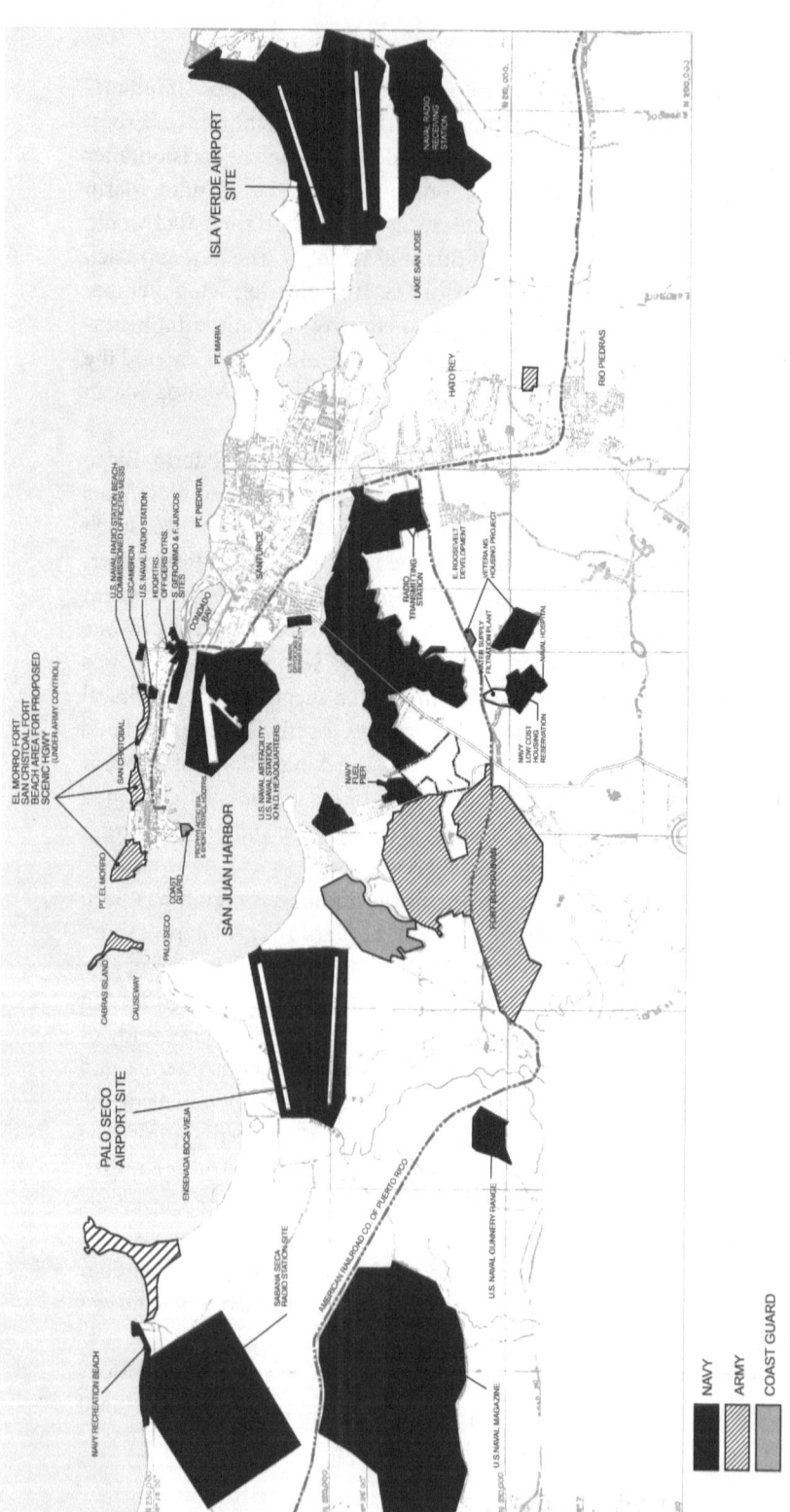

Map of the Puerto Rico Planning Board showing the locations of the military installations, 1948 (General Archives of Puerto Rico, Map Collection. Rendering courtesy of Francisco Rodríguez and Jorge Lizardi)

recently. But a new generation of scholars have been producing interdisciplinary research rich in fresh insights about the profound wartime changes.[16] Indeed, the editors believe that Puerto Rico's postwar transformation cannot be grasped without tracing its roots to the war years. However, most of this research has been published in Spanish and has not been readily accessible to English-language readers. This book, although not a history of the war years in Puerto Rico, aims to provide readers with important insights on the multifaceted impact of the war, while opening a window to recent scholarly research.

Island at War includes ten distinct topics written by nine distinguished academicians who have published in their fields of expertise. They represent such diverse institutions as the University of Puerto Rico, the University of California, Los Angeles, Whittier College, Columbia University, the University of the West Indies, and others. Their diverse provenance and institutional affiliation provides the book with many viewpoints, not only of scholars residing in Puerto Rico but also of outstanding researchers from the United States and elsewhere in the Caribbean. The editors have also aimed to provide an interdisciplinary comprehension of the Second World War's impact on Puerto Rico and accordingly have invited researchers from a variety of disciplines. Contributors include experts in the fields of history, political science, sociology, literature, journalism, communications, and engineering.

In "Rediscovering Puerto Rico and the Caribbean: US Strategic Debate and War Planning on the Eve of the Second World War," Jorge Rodríguez Beruff discusses the intensification of US strategic war planning related to the Caribbean between 1938 and 1941, in the face of European and Japanese expansionism. The author has published widely on political and military aspects of the war. Fitzroy André Baptiste's "Puerto Rico: Headquarters of the Caribbean Sea Frontier, 1940–1945," assesses the strategic significance of Puerto Rico to the overall war effort in the Caribbean. Baptiste, as we have mentioned, was the leading scholar on the consequences of the war for the European territories in the Caribbean. He made valuable research on the Vichy regime in Martinique and Guadeloupe. This broad background enables him to approach the military role of Puerto Rico from a regional perspective. Ligia T. Domenech's "The German Blockade of the Caribbean in 1942 and Its Effects in Puerto Rico" explores another military aspect in depth: the submarine war. The author, who has researched widely on this topic, explains how the German offensive in the Caribbean disrupted maritime traffic and almost provoked the collapse of the Puerto Rican economy.

"War and Political Transition in Puerto Rico, 1939–1940," also by Rodríguez Beruff, analyzes the political dynamics of the prewar period. It traces the transition from the stormy Puerto Rican governorship of General Blanton Winship to that of the far more able Admiral William D. Leahy during the opening days of the war. In "The Wartime Quartet: Muñoz Marín, Tugwell, Ickes, and FDR," Michael Janeway probes the relationship from 1941 forward between newly elected Senate president Luis Muñoz Marín and Rexford Guy Tugwell, the last continental appointed governor of Puerto Rico; and, between them and President Roosevelt and his powerful secretary of the interior, Harold Ickes. Janeway brings to bear in this essay his considerable research experience on US–Puerto Rico relations in the context of New Deal policies. Sadly, our good friend and contributor Michael Janeway will not be able to enjoy this publication; he died on April 17, 2014. José L. Bolívar Fresneda, a historian and engineer, assesses the impact of massive US military investment, the use of New Deal agencies for war purposes, and the fluke of the rum-revenue bonanza in "The War Economy of Puerto Rico, 1939–1945." Bolívar Fresneda is the author of the major study *Guerra, banca y desarrollo* on the Puerto Rican financial institutions and economy in the forties.[17] The economic consequences of the war are also explored in the essay "Vieques: The Impact of the Second World War" by César J. Ayala Casás and José L. Bolívar Fresneda. They are the authors of *Battleship Vieques*, a recent book about the fate of that island practically under control of the US Navy since the Second World War.[18] Ayala Casás and Bolívar Fresneda discuss in their essay the construction of a US naval base in Vieques, the navy's expropriation of two-thirds of the island, and the ensuing social and economic consequences. The navy's presence in Vieques was a legacy of the Second World War, and the matter was not resolved until 2003, when the navy withdrew from that island, leaving behind still lingering environmental and health issues. The US and British metropolitan governments' wartime responses to the newly reconfigured strategic importance of the Caribbean is analyzed by Mayra Rosario Urrutia in "The Anglo-American Caribbean Commission: A Socioeconomic Strategy Designed for Military Security, 1942–1946." This essay explains how policy toward Puerto Rico became part of a regional approach, not only militarily but also in economic and social policy. In "Geopolitics and Telecommunications Policy in Puerto Rico: ITT and the Porto Rico Telephone Company, 1942–1948," Luis Rosario Albert studies the conflicts surrounding the public telecommunications modernization plan in Puerto Rico between 1942 and 1948. The author, a filmmaker and academic researcher on communications, places developments in Puerto Rico, where the vast multinational corporation ITT originated, in a complex field of international power relations that embraces the Caribbean, the United States, and Europe. The final essay is Rafael Chabrán's moving personal account of the experiences of his father, a Puerto Rican military man, entitled "What Did You Do in the War, Daddy? The Story of a Puerto Rican in the Second World War and Korea: Captain Harry Chabrán Acevedo, 1925–1986." Chabrán, a noted Hispanist, through his family's (and his own) history throws light on how the war transformed the lives of many veterans.

The authors of *Island at War* approach the war years in Puerto Rico with emphasis on military, political, and economic aspects, but they also make reference to the relevance of cultural, social, and human aspects. The essays, although representing diverse perspectives, are closely interrelated. Taken together, they provide a broad view and valuable insights on the crucial importance of the Second World War for Puerto Rican history and US–Puerto Rico relations.

—Jorge Rodríguez Beruff and José L. Bolívar Fresneda

Notes

1. A case in point is the recently published and extensive account by Antony Beevor, *The Second World War* (London: Weidenfeld and Nicolson, 2012), which makes only a couple of cursory references to the Caribbean.

2. Jorge Rodríguez Beruff, "Cultura y geopolítica: un acercamiento a la visión de Alfred Thayer Mahan sobre el Caribe," *Op. Cit.*, Revista del Centro de Investigaciones Históricas, University of Puerto Rico, no. 11 (1999): 173–190.

3. For a contemporary account of the role of the Caribbean during the Second World War, see Department of State, *Caribbean Islands and the War: A Record of Progress in Facing Stern Realities* (Washington, DC: Government Printing Office, 1943).

4. Anthony P. Maingot, *The United States and the Caribbean: Challenges of an Asymmetrical Relationship* (Boulder, CO: Westview Press, 1994), esp. chapter 3. Other studies on the submarine war are César de Windt Lavandier, *La Segunda Guerra Mundial y los submarinos alemanes en el Caribe* (Santo Domingo: Editora Amigo del Hogar, 1997); and Gaylord T. M. Kelshall, *The U-Boat War in the Caribbean* (Annapolis, MD: Naval Institute Press, 1994).

5. Rexford G. Tugwell, *The Stricken Land: The Story of Puerto Rico* (Garden City, NY: Doubleday, 1946), p. 212.

6. Michael Gannon, *Operation Drumbeat: The Dramatic True Story of Germany's First U-Boat Attacks along the American Coast in World War II* (New York: Harper and Row, 1990), p. xvii.

7. Samuel Eliot Morison, *The Battle of the Atlantic, September 1939–May 1943*, vol. 1 of *History of United States Naval Operations in World War II* (Boston: Little, Brown, 1947), pp. 308–309.

8. Gordon Wright, *The Ordeal of Total War, 1939–1945* (New York: Harper Torchbooks, 1968), p. 234.

9. Arthur Marwick's contribution was monumental. It included books such as *The Deluge: British Society and the First World War* (London: Macmillan, 1991); *Women at War, 1914–1918* (London: Fontana and the Imperial War Museum, 1977); with Clive Emsley and Wendy Simpson, eds., *Total War and Historical Change: Europe, 1914–1955* (Philadelphia: Open University Press, 1971); and *War and Social Change in the Twentieth Century* (London: Macmillan, 1974).

10. Bruce D. Porter, *War and the Rise of the State: The Military Foundations of Modern Politics* (New York: Free Press, 1994).

11. Geoffrey Perret, *A Country Made by War* (New York: Random House, 1989).

12. David Kennedy, *Over Here: The First World War and American Society* (Oxford: Oxford University Press, 1992).

13. Alan S. Milward, *War, Economy and Society, 1939–1945* (Berkeley: University of California Press, 1979).

14. Maingot, *The United States and the Caribbean*; Ken Post, *Strike the Iron: A Colony at War*, 2 vols. (Atlantic Highlands, NJ: Humanities Press; The Hague: Institute of Social Studies, 1981); Michael Anthony, *Port-of-Spain in a World at War, 1939–1945* (Port of Spain: Ministry of Sports, Culture and Youth Affairs, 1983); Bernardo Vega, *Nazismo, fascismo y falangismo en la República Dominicana* (Santo Domingo: Fundación Cultural Dominicana, 1985); Fitzroy André Baptiste, *War, Cooperation, and Conflict: The European Possessions in the Caribbean, 1939–1945* (Westport, CT: Greenwood Press, 1988); Irwin F. Gellman, *Roosevelt and Batista: Good Neighbor Diplomacy in Cuba, 1933–1945* (Albuquerque: University of New Mexico Press, 1973); Eliane Sepaire, *La Guadeloupe en tan Sorin, 1940–1943* (Paris: Éditions et Diffusion de la Culture Antillaise, 1984); and Steven High, *Base Colonies in the Western Hemisphere, 1940–1967* (New York: Palgrave Macmillan, 2008).

15. Blanca Torres Ramírez, *México en la Segunda Guerra Mundial* (Mexico City: Colegio de México, 1983); David G. Haglund, *Latin America and the Transformation of U.S. Strategic Thought, 1936–1940* (Albuquerque: University of New Mexico Press, 1984); and Leslie Bethell and Ian Roxborough, eds., *Latin America between the Second World War and the Cold War, 1944–1948* (Cambridge: Cambridge University Press, 1992).

16. Without pretending to be comprehensive, we could mention the following studies and publications: Carlos I. Hernández Hernández, *Pueblo nómada: de la villa agrícola de San Antonio al emporio militar de "Ramey Base"* (Río Piedras, PR: Ediciones Huracán, 2006); Josefa Santiago Caraballo, "Guerra, reforma y colonialismo: Luis Muñoz Marín, las reformas del PPD y su vinculación con la militarización de Puerto Rico en el contexto de la Segunda Guerra Mundial" (Ph.D. diss., University of Puerto Rico, Río Piedras, 2005); Gerardo M. Piñero Cádiz, *Puerto Rico: el Gibraltar del Caribe* (San Juan: Editorial Isla Negra, 2008); José L. Bolívar Fresneda, "Un sueño irrealizado: el Banco de Fomento y la industrialización de Puerto Rico, 1942–1948" (Ph.D. diss., University of Puerto Rico, Río Piedras, 2007); Carlos I. Hernández Hernández, "Historia y memoria: inicio de la guerra en 'Europa'; pobreza, huracanes y recuerdos familiares," *Milenio: Revista de Artes y Ciencias* (University of Puerto Rico, Bayamón) 10 (2006): 219–232; Carlos I. Hernández Hernández, "Historia y memoria: representaciones de la Segunda Guerra Mundial en la ciudad señorial de Ponce" (Ph.D. diss., University of Puerto Rico, 2007); Jorge Rodríguez Beruff, *Strategy as Politics: Puerto Rico*

on the Eve of the Second World War (Río Piedras: University of Puerto Rico Press, 2007); Mayra Rosario Urrutia, "Detrás de la vitrina: expectativas del Partido Popular Democrático y política exterior norteamericana, 1942–1952," in *Del nacionalismo al populismo: cultura y política en Puerto Rico*, ed. Silvia Álvarez Curbelo and María de los Angeles Castro (Río Piedras, PR: Ediciones Huracán, 1993); José Collazo, *Guerra y educación: la militarización y americanización del pueblo puertorriqueño durante la Segunda Guerra Mundial, 1939–1945* (Santo Domingo: Editora Centenario, 1998); Norberto Barreto Velázquez, *Rexford G. Tugwell, el último de los tutores* (Río Piedras, PR: Ediciones Huracán, 2004); César J. Ayala Casás and José L. Bolívar Fresneda, *Battleship Vieques: Puerto Rico from World War II to the Korean War* (Princeton, NJ: Markus Wiener, 2011); Miguel Ángel Santiago Ríos, *Militarismo y clases sociales en Vieques, 1910–1959* (San Juan: Ediciones Huracán, 2007); Humberto García Muñiz, *La estrategia de Estados Unidos y la militarización del Caribe* (Río Piedras, PR: Instituto de Estudios del Caribe, University of Puerto Rico, 1988); Humberto García Muñiz and Rebeca Campo, "French and American Imperial Accommodation in the Caribbean during World War II: The Experience of Guyane and the Subaltern Roles of the Puerto Ricans," in *Colonial Crucible: Empire in the Making of the Modern American State*, ed. Alfred W. McCoy and Francisco A. Scarano (Madison: University of Wisconsin Press, 2009), pp. 441–452; Ché Paralitici, *No quiero mi cuerpo pa' tambor: el servicio militar obligatorio en Puerto Rico* (San Juan: Ediciones Puerto, 1998); Jorge Rodríguez Beruff, ed., *Las memorias de Leahy: los relatos del almirante William D. Leahy sobre su gobernación de Puerto Rico, 1939–1940* (San Juan: Fundación Luis Muñoz Marín, 2002); Jorge Rodríguez Beruff, *Strategy as Politics: Puerto Rico on the Eve of the Second World War* (Río Piedras: University of Puerto Rico Press, 2007); and José L. Bolívar Fresneda, *Guerra, banca y desarrollo: el Banco de Fomento y la industrialización de Puerto Rico* (San Juan: Fundación Luis Muñoz Marín; Instituto de Cultura Puertorriqueña, 2011).

17. Bolívar Fresneda, *Guerra, banca y desarrollo*.

18. Ayala Casás and Bolívar Fresneda, *Battleship Vieques*.

ISLAND AT WAR

Aerial view of Isla Grande Naval Base in San Juan, 1940 (Cultural Resources Division, San Juan Historic Site, National Park Service)

Rediscovering Puerto Rico and the Caribbean: US Strategic Debate and War Planning on the Eve of the Second World War

Jorge Rodríguez Beruff

During the period 1938 to 1941, an intense strategic debate took place in civilian and military circles regarding the defense policies the United States should adopt in view of impending (and, later, actual) war in Europe and Japanese expansionism in the Asia-Pacific region. This debate was, to a large extent, conducted in public. It signified the gradual waning of the pacifist and neutralist consensus of the pre-1938 period, during which intellectual and political critics of US participation in World War I had been extremely influential.[1] Opposition to war, a large military establishment, and "foreign entanglements" had brought together, since the 1920s, diverse and powerful political forces in Congress, academia, and the press, as well as a vast network of peace groups.[2] These forces were a formidable political obstacle to rearmament and decisive measures in preparation for war, as the sharp negative reaction to Franklin Roosevelt's Quarantine Speech of October 1937, in which the president called for an international quarantine of "aggressor nations," had demonstrated. Proposed military measures against Japan in the aftermath of the USS *Panay* incident also elicited a negative political response. This incident provoked a serious crisis in relations with Japan before the war. On December 12, 1937, Japanese forces attacked and sank the riverboat *Panay* patrolling the Yangtze River near Nanking, causing the deaths of three Americans and wounding forty-five others. Some naval circles called for retaliation, but Roosevelt preferred a diplomatic solution, with Japan paying $2.2 million in reparations the following year.

The Cuban Revolution of 1933, which brought down the dictatorial regime of General Gerardo Machado, was a major challenge to the new US regional approach. In that case, FDR used diplomatic and economic pressures to contain radical forces, rather than landing marines. US interventionist policies in Mexico, Central America, Panama, and the Caribbean after the Spanish-American War of 1898 had become a major issue that caused friction in relations with Latin America, particularly with emerging populist and nationalist movements. The improvement of overall US–Latin American relations, which required a redefinition of Caribbean policy, became increasingly urgent to the Roosevelt administration in view of the deteriorating situation in Europe and Asia. Under the rubric of the Good Neighbor policy, the Roosevelt administration abandoned overt military interventionism, continued the process begun by previous administrations of ending the direct administration of Caribbean countries (as in Haiti in 1934), and made certain measured concessions to nationalist demands such as renegotiating the Panama Canal treaties and abrogating the Platt Amendment to the Cuban Constitution, which had allowed for US intervention in that country. Many of these concessions were made in 1934.

In the 1930s, US military infrastructure in the Caribbean consisted of the bases and installations in Panama, Guantánamo (Cuba), San Juan Bay and Culebra (Puerto Rico), and Charlotte Amalie (Saint Thomas in the US Virgin Islands). It had not changed much since the beginning of the century and was considered adequate to ensure military control of the region and protect the Panama Canal and the US southern flank. The Great Depression, in fact, precluded any major military investment and provoked a relative military retrenchment. The perceived German naval threat had disappeared as a result of that country's crushing defeat in the First World War and subsequent arms limitations imposed by the Treaty of Versailles, while German rearmament and aggressive policies in central Europe, in the early thirties, were still incipient. In any case, the United States relied on Great Britain's naval supremacy and French land forces to contain Adolf Hitler's expansionist designs. None of the European countries with colonial possessions in the Caribbean—Great Britain, France, and the Netherlands—were considered potential military threats. They had been US allies in the First World War, and in particular a very strong alliance had been established since the beginning of the century with Great Britain. The United States had developed a growing commercial relationship with European colonies in the Caribbean, but its direct political and military presence in these territories was very limited. Its presence and interests were mainly confined to the larger islands to the north (Cuba, Hispaniola, and Puerto Rico),while providing a security umbrella to European possessions to the south. This arrangement would be radically transformed by the Second World War.

A new strategic debate began in 1938 that tended to underscore US military weakness and unpreparedness for both continental and hemispheric defense. Although the Caribbean had always figured prominently in US strategic thinking, its crucial importance for US defense plans was considerably magnified after 1938. The Caribbean became the subject of analysis in a deluge of articles and books. In fact, military control of Caribbean geostrategic space and its relationship to both continental and hemispheric defense plans became an almost obsessive preoccupation of strategic analysts. In prevalent discourse, many Caribbean islands suddenly became "Gibraltars," "Maltas," "bulwarks," "ramparts," "keys," "capstones," "strongholds," "sentinels," "watchdogs," "outposts," and "defense problems." Within the Caribbean, the geostrategic importance of the Puerto Rico–Virgin Islands zone was also greatly stressed. The Caribbean would no longer be perceived as region merely of exotic and paradisiacal islands, but also of vital strategic value to US defense preparations. Parallel to this intellectual and political discussion, war planning was revised also to reflect the renewed importance ascribed to the region. In many ways, the United States "rediscovered" Puerto Rico and the Caribbean during the period 1938 to 1941, but this rediscovery took place through "geostrategic eyes," to paraphrase the title of Mary Louise Pratt's book.[3]

Rediscovering the Caribbean

Among the strategic proposals that were publicly discussed in 1938, George Fielding Eliot's book *The Ramparts We Watch: A Study of the Problems of American National Defense*—which was in its sixth printing by 1939—had particular implications for military policy toward the Caribbean.[4] This book appeared in the context of the Sudetenland crisis and the Munich Agreement of September 29, 1938, which allowed Germany to annex parts of Czechoslovakia. The concessions made by Neville Chamberlain and Édouard Daladier to Hitler and Benito Mussolini were interpreted by FDR as signifying the lack of British and French resolve to contain German expansionism. It was at this critical juncture that the first steps toward US rearmament were taken. Eliot had previously written, with the noted military historian R. Ernest Dupuy, *If War Comes*, also dealing with international security issues.[5]

Eliot was a major of military intelligence reserve who published widely on military topics, including several books during the Second World War. He also contributed to magazines such *Life*, *Harper's*, *Current History*, and the *American Mercury*. In a broad analysis of US military security and strategy expounded in *The Ramparts We Watch*, he proposed a policy of "hemispheric security" based on a balanced expansion of naval and military forces, but placing great emphasis on the navy's role. He sharply criticized undue reliance on the expansion of air power, on which FDR placed great emphasis during this period.[6] It is interesting to note that the epigraph of the first chapter of Eliot's book is a quotation from an FDR speech on the deteriorating international situation, while the chapter on naval policy is headed by a statement by Admiral William D. Leahy, then chief of naval operations and later to become governor of Puerto Rico (1939–1940), on the importance of battleships.[7] Leahy was Roosevelt's personal friend and a key military adviser and collaborator throughout the 1930s and the Second World War period.

Regarding the Caribbean, Eliot's argument followed closely known tenets of Captain Alfred Thayer Mahan's geopolitical outlook, underscoring the vital importance of the Panama Canal, the need to ensure naval control of the entire region, and access to bases. Additionally, control of the Caribbean was considered essential to the defense of Brazil and the South Atlantic.[8] According to Eliot, Dutch, French, and British possessions in the region should not be allowed to fall under the control of a hostile power, while existing bases (Panama, Guantánamo, Puerto Rico, the Virgin Islands) should be developed and strengthened. He also called for the acquisition of additional bases and expressly mentioned Jamaica, Curaçao, Trinidad, Barbados, and Saint Lucia as possible sites, all European possessions. In this regard, he proposed considering a barter of the Philippines for the British Caribbean territories, or condoning the British and French war debts from the First World War in exchange for their Caribbean possessions, an old aspiration of some military sectors that had been rejected by FDR in 1936.[9]

Eliot placed great emphasis on the importance of the Puerto Rico–Virgin Islands area. In a map of the Caribbean region, he drew a square over the zone and named it the "Eastern Outpost."[10] The vital Mona and Anegada passages could be controlled from these islands and air and naval power projected toward the Atlantic and the Lesser Antilles:

> On the Mona passage we have Puerto Rico, a large island of considerable local resources with several good harbors, none of them unfortunately, able comfortably to accommodate battleships. There are no fixed defenses or even mobile heavy guns here, nor is there an air base. Just east of Puerto Rico and belonging to it is the islet of Culebra, whose Great Harbor is adequate for a fleet anchorage, though difficult to defend by fortification. A few miles further eastward, however, we possess a harbor of quite different characteristics. The island of Saint Thomas, one of the American Virgins, with its fine and easily protected port of Charlotte Amalie, is now our easternmost Caribbean possession. Together with Puerto Rico

and Culebra, it forms an outpost which extends the influence of Guantanamo 700 miles to seaward and it watches the Anegada Passage, 70 miles distant, which is the principal commercial route for European traffic directed upon Panama."[11]

He proposed augmenting the Puerto Rican garrison to about 1,500 men and providing it with coastal artillery.[12] With an additional base in Barbados or Trinidad and one or more auxiliary bases in the Lesser Antilles, the United States could seal all potential entry points to the Caribbean and project naval force toward the South Atlantic as far as the strategically important Brazilian "salient."[13] It is striking how closely actual US military planning followed Eliot's recommendations.

In late October 1938, *Life* magazine published an article entitled "America Gets Ready to Fight Germany, Italy and Japan," which included a half-page photo of Admiral Leahy standing in front of a world map. The map had a large arrow connecting the region of Dakar in West Africa with the Brazilian bulge and a caption that read "it is only 2,000 miles from Africa to South America." The article also included a map of the Caribbean indicating naval bases and maritime routes with the caption "Caribbean is strategic key to the Western Hemisphere" and indicated that "the region above is the part of his map which Admiral Leahy studies with most concern." It also said: "From the strategist['s] viewpoint, America's long soul-searchings over 'imperialism' in the Caribbean are sentimental twaddle. America *must* control the Caribbean or some other power may control America." *Life*'s article cited Eliot's books *The Ramparts We Watch* and *If War Comes* as authoritative sources on the Caribbean, emphasizing his recommendation for additional bases in several European possessions.[14]

It is also interesting that when a review of Eliot's *The Ramparts We Watch*, written by Walter Millis, was published in the *Washington Post* in November 1938, it was accompanied by a prominent photograph of Admiral William D. Leahy.[15] The fact that Millis, although calling Eliot a "militarist," sympathetically reviewed his book ("a brilliant clarification of our strategic problem"), is an indication of how broad the emerging consensus on defense policy was by late 1938. Millis was a leading critic of US expansionism and militarism and had published a widely read indictment of US participation in World War I.[16] Another article by the *Washington Star* on defense preparations cited both Leahy and Eliot as the main authorities on hemispheric defense, advancing quite similar proposals.[17] All this indicates the semiofficial character of Eliot's views, as well as Leahy's apparent support for his scheme.[18]

A host of other writers followed Eliot's lead. Wilbur Burton published an article in *Current History* in December 1938 entitled "Panama: Defense Problem No. 1." He argued that "isthmian connection between the Atlantic and the Pacific—whether via Panama, Nicaragua, or Tehuantepec—far transcends commerce: it is vital for national American well-being." According to the author, the main potential threat to the canal was "airplanes operating from floating carriers or from nearby land bases."[19] It is interesting to note that the vulnerability of the Panama Canal to a covert Japanese air attack from a secret airstrip on Panamanian soil provided the plot for a serialized story by Robert Carson that was published in the *Saturday Evening Post*. Humphrey Bogart's 1942 Warner Brothers film *Across the Pacific*, also starring Mary Astor and Sydney Greenstreet, was based on Carson's story. However, this cloak and dagger story, set on a Japanese ship and in Panama City, never achieved the fame of Bogart's next film: *Casablanca*.[20]

On the other hand, the military historian and geostrategic thinker Harold Sprout argued that the United States should aim, as a "minimum requirement," at the "indisputable military control of all marine approaches to North America and Northern South America out to a distance greater than the effective operating radius of a hostile fighting fleet or carrier based airplanes." He connected this strategic aim to the recommendation of the late 1938 Hepburn Board Report for bases in Puerto Rico and the Virgin Islands, noting that "the locus of the 1939 fleet maneuvers gave further emphasis to this new orientation."[21] He was referring to President Roosevelt's decision to hold the fleet maneuvers, Fleet Problem XX, for the first time entirely in the Caribbean in February 1939. Sprout had established in the late 1930s, together with Edward Mead Earle, the Institute for Advanced Study at Princeton University, considered one of the first strategic think tanks in the United States. At this time he was also collaborating with his wife, Margaret Sprout, on a major historical study of the US Navy.[22]

Norman J. Padelford developed a similar argument in "An Atlantic Naval Policy for the United States," published in the *U.S. Naval Institute Proceedings*, stressing the need for an Atlantic fleet, naval and air bases, and air power. He noted that:

> The Bahamas, the Greater and Lesser Antilles, and Venezuela are vital to the United States. Here lie the keys to the security of the Panama Canal and the Central American states. From here come indispensable petroleum, tropical foods, and raw materials required by American industry and consumers.[23]

This article was profusely illustrated with photographs of Santo Domingo, La Guaira, Cartagena, San Juan, la Citadelle in Haiti, and Guantánamo. Padelford, an internationalist, later published the influential book *The Panama Canal in Peace and War*, which went through several printings during the war years.[24]

Bombers over San Juan Bay, circa 1940 (Archivo Fundación Luis Muñoz Marín)

Puerto Rico: Gibraltar or Achilles' Heel?

"Puerto Rico: Gibraltar or Achilles Heel" is the title of a short article published by the journal *Hemisphere* in February 1940.[25] It encapsulates the dilemma the United States faced in Puerto Rico and the entire Caribbean due to the perceived potential for social and political instabilities that could undermine defense plans. At this time, defense preparations in Puerto Rico were gathering momentum with the building of major army bases in San Juan and Aguadilla, provoking concerns about widespread poverty and the capacity of the existing political arrangement to manage political conflicts and prevent a return to the violent incidents of the mid-1930s. This was also stressed in the article "Island Bulwarks," published in March 1940 by Colonel Cary I. Crockett of the US Marines, which reviewed the situation in Hawaii and Puerto Rico, underscoring the dire social and economic difficulties of the latter. This article was accompanied by several photographs of San Juan harbor, Spanish fortifications, and country scenes. A caption of a photograph of the Puerto Rican countryside read: "A crowded land brings social evils that may affect national defense"; while a town scene depicting *jíbaros* (peasants) riding donkeys elicited the comment: "An American scene in Puerto Rico, where hunger may grow into violent unrest."²⁶ In 1941, Lieutenant Commander Ephraim McLean wrote: "When all the new bases have been constructed and manned by units of our Army and Navy, Mahan's dream will have come true, for the Caribbean will then be an American lake."²⁷ The prolific and influential defense analyst and *New York Times* military affairs correspondent Hanson W. Baldwin also underscored the importance of Caribbean bases. He proposed, among other things, the deployment of long-range bombers in Puerto Rico.²⁸ An April 1939 article in *Harper's* magazine by Oswald Garrison Villard, calling for "sanity" in defense policy, appeared anachronistic amid the barrage of publications in favor of "preparedness."²⁹ Villard was a militant pacifist and anti-imperialist journalist who participated in the policy debate on Puerto Rico.

National Geographic, a reliable barometer of US geostrategic interests that played a major role in shaping public opinion on international issues,³⁰ also published long articles focusing on particular countries or subregions of the Caribbean. Laura Muñoz has analyzed the transformation of that journal's outlook on the region during the war:

> The transformation in the perception and representation of the islands is evident at first glance: from romantic and exuberant places they become bastions of Continental defense, especially of the Panama Canal "which divided the Continent but united the world."³¹

National Geographic's December 1939 cover story by E. John Long had the long-winded title "Puerto Rico: Watchdog of the Caribbean, Venerable Domain under American Flag Has New Role as West Indian Stronghold and Sentinel of the Panama Canal." The first section had the subheading "The Island's Strategic Location" and quoted the copilot of the Clipper plane that brought Long to Puerto Rico as saying, while pointing to a map of the Caribbean:

> Now do you see? About 1,000 miles to the Panama Canal, 1,000 miles to Miami, 700 to Bermuda, 550 to Caracas on the mainland of South America, 650 to Trinidad. This is the hub of a wheel. Put enough planes here, and enough land to guard your bases, and Puerto Rico becomes the "Gibraltar of the West Indies," or the "Hawaii of the Atlantic."³²

Interspersed with numerous photos of Puerto Rican scenery and everyday life, Long's article also included several photos of fortifications, battleships, bases, and military exercises. That *National Geographic* issue also contained a folded map of Mexico, Central America, and the Caribbean with a short note entitled "Heart of a Hemisphere," which stressed the vital strategic value of the entire region. The note was accompanied by a photo of General Edmund Daley, army commander in Puerto Rico, together with other officers, pointing at a large map of Puerto Rico.[33] Interestingly, a detailed analysis of the Puerto Rican situation by Earle K. James published just two years previously in *Foreign Policy Reports* had not referred to military questions.[34]

National Geographic also paid attention to the neighboring US Virgin Islands in an article published in September 1940, a critical period of the war in Europe. The article stressed that the islands had been purchased for their value as a naval base for the defense of the Panama Canal and intertwined descriptions of their exotic landscape, history, and progress under US administration, with references to the marine base in Charlotte Amalie.[35] The magazine devoted its January 1941 cover story to the British West Indies. Its title was "British West Indian Interlude." The map of the Lesser Antilles had the title "Like a Curving Shield, the West Indies Guard the Panama Canal," while the section with photographs read: "West Indies Links in a Defense Chain."[36] That article was followed, in the same issue, by a brief report by Edward T. Folliard on Martinique that discussed the French military presence in Martinique and Guadeloupe.[37] Other journals such as *Harper's*, *Survey Graphic*, *Hemisphere*, *Foreign Affairs*, and *Inter American Quarterly* were also stricken by the Caribbean fever.[38]

Books such as Carleton Beals's *The Coming Struggle for Latin America*, J. Fred Rippy's *The Caribbean Danger Zone*, and Walter Adolphe Roberts's *The Caribbean: The Story of Our Sea of Destiny*, as their titles suggest, were part of the debate.[39] For example, Beals's 1938 book, which went through several printings, dealt with the threat to US security posed by the growing fascist influence in Latin America and the Caribbean. He devoted attention to Puerto Rico, arguing that US policy toward the island undermined Roosevelt's claim to defend democracy in the hemisphere and exposed a weak flank to German propaganda. In this, he coincided with the arguments on Puerto Rico expounded by other liberals such as Oswald Garrison Villard.

> Puerto Rico is not considered part of Latin America except in Latin America itself. For Latin America, Puerto Rico is *terra irredenta*. What we do in Puerto Rico is ever sharply scrutinized by other countries.
>
> Actually the little island is ruled over by an appointed governor, safely protected, none ever quite so generally hated as the present Governor Winship. It is ruled over by American sugar companies, monopolizing the land in violation of the constitutional proviso limiting holdings to 500 acres. It is ruled over by a Congress made up mostly of lawyers and others representing the large American interests. It is ruled by a brutalized constabulary. . . .

Branded as "agitators" even by Secretary Ickes, harassed, jailed and murdered by the police, the Nationalists have retaliated, and violence has grown into violence, and bitterness into hatred. In this matter we have displayed the same dull colonial stodginess of any other imperialist power.

The head of the Nationalist Party, Pedro Albizú [sic] Campos (with whose partially medieval views I do not sympathize), has been railroaded to Leavenworth by a packed American jury.[40]

A 1940 book edited by William H. Haas, *The American Empire*, on the other hand, reviewed US policy toward all its overseas territories.[41] It underscored the acute problems and scant economic value of the US Virgin Islands and Puerto Rico. With regard to the former, the editor stated in the concluding chapter that "although their prospects for the present may prove disappointing, we have the assurance that no other nation can readily avail itself of their strategic features." Similarly, it highlighted the predominantly strategic military interests in continued US control over Puerto Rico: "Recent developments in Puerto Rico also point to its increasing military importance to the United States. For the present at least, this outweighs all other considerations." Haas ruled out both independence and autonomy as solutions to the island's problems, which he defined as overpopulation and poverty.[42] The chapter on Puerto Rico, written by Rafael Picó and William Haas, underscores the serious economic and social ills of the island and flatly stated "[t]hat autonomy or even complete independence would solve all Puerto Rican problems is far from true." It only advocated making elective the post of governor.[43] This is particularly illuminating given Picó's important political and technical role in the emerging Popular Democratic Party and in Rexford Tugwell's governorship of Puerto Rico.

Revising US War Plans

The revision of US war plans, which began in 1938, also reflected the growing importance assigned to the Caribbean and the Atlantic. Throughout the thirties, naval forces in the Caribbean-Atlantic region amounted to a few ships of the Training and Special Service Squadrons. War Plan Orange (war against Japan) only dealt with a possible threat to the Panama Canal from the Pacific. In November 1938, the Joint (Army-Navy) Board instructed the Joint Planning Committee to revise war plans in light of the new international circumstances.

The document drafted by Army Colonel Frank S. Clark and Navy Captain Russell S. Crenshaw, issued in April 1939, described a strategic situation very similar to that later used for Fleet Problem XX, the fleet maneuvers held in the Puerto Rico–Virgin Islands during February 1939: a fascist insurrection in a South American country supported by Germany and Italy. It thus placed great emphasis on the Caribbean as part of the hemispheric defense plans and already suggested the "Atlantic first" strategy followed by the United States during the war.[44]

The Joint Planning Committee also began working on the five crucial Rainbow Plans that were prepared during 1939 and 1940. Rainbow 1, the only plan completed during the first phase of war preparations, "envisioned a German-Italian violation of the Monroe Doctrine that would force a direct confrontation with the United States. German and Italian forces presumably would establish 'intermediate bases' in West Africa and Brazil, while American units concentrated in the Caribbean to interdict Axis lines of communication."[45] The lack of naval forces in the Pacific would trigger an attack on the Philippines and Guam. It was argued that the United States should concentrate on the unilateral defense of its own territory, the eastern Pacific and South Atlantic, and Latin America to latitude 10 degrees south (i.e., the Quarter Sphere concept). Donald Yerxa quotes a navy officer who claimed that "the crucial point in the Rainbow One concept is the Caribbean."[46] Rainbow 4 was similar to Rainbow 1, except that the United States would defend the entire hemisphere, while Rainbow 5 included the projection of military power to Africa or Europe.[47] Rainbow 4 was approved by FDR in mid-August 1940, and a revised version of Rainbow 5 was ready by November 1941.[48]

During this period, most existing war plans for the occupation of Latin American countries were abandoned, with the significant exceptions of Mexico (War Plan Green) and Brazil (War Plan Purple).[49] Understandably, defense planning for Puerto Rico gathered momentum during 1939. In July 1938, the commanding general of the army's Second Corps Area ordered the preparation of a defense plan for Puerto Rico. The Puerto Rico Defense Plan (code named Orange, not to be confused with War Plan Orange focused on Japan) was submitted on October 27, 1938. It provided only for the defense of the main island of Puerto Rico, excluding outlying islands. Immediately after the Fleet XX maneuvers (in May 1939), the Joint Planning Committee submitted to the Joint Board a statement on the Puerto Rico–Virgin Islands area, which placed great emphasis on their strategic value. It also recommended assigning this area the following missions:

1. Joint Mission: To defend the Puerto Rico–Virgin Islands area as an outlying base; to support the naval forces in controlling the Caribbean Sea and adjacent waters; and to support operations against shore objectives.
2. Army Mission: To hold Puerto Rico and the Virgin Islands against attacks by land, sea and air forces, and against hostile sympathisers; to install and operate required Army base facilities; to support the naval forces in controlling the Caribbean Sea and adjacent waters; and to support operations against shore objectives.
3. Navy Mission: To support the naval forces controlling the Caribbean area and adjacent waters; to control and protect the shipping in the coastal zone; to support the Army in the defense of Puerto Rico and the Virgin Islands; and to support operations against shore objectives.[50]

The Joint Planning Committee recommended that the army create a separate overseas department and the navy a new naval district in Puerto Rico. Within these parameters, the Joint Puerto Rico Coastal Frontier Defense Plan, the Puerto Rico Defense Project, and the revision of Plan White (against domestic disturbances) were drafted. This strategic planning process culminated in the comprehensive Puerto Rican Department Basic War Plan of February 19, 1941, and the Puerto Rican Defense Project of March 1, 1941.[51]

Puerto Rico in the Hepburn Board Report

The US Navy had not carried out a major study on base requirements since 1923, when the Rodman Board Report had been prepared. Naval war planning during the pre–World War I period had mainly focused on a possible German threat to US possessions in the Caribbean and to the Panama Canal. Germany, in fact, had elaborated a very detailed plan for the occupation of Puerto Rico.[52] Great Britain was also considered a potential enemy, but, given the extent of US-British collaboration, war with Britain was highly unlikely. During World War I, naval collaboration with Britain had been enhanced. Even the possibility of a major German naval attack in the Atlantic-Caribbean region was remote as long as Britain maintained naval supremacy in the North Sea. In such circumstances, Germany's naval operations would have to rely mainly on submarine warfare.

After World War I, the United States enjoyed a strategic environment that was more favorable than it was in 1938. Germany's naval power had been eliminated. Britain accepted US naval and military supremacy in the Caribbean, while the United States practically placed British and other European colonies in the region under its security umbrella. In addition, the Washington

Naval Conference (1921–1922) had placed strict limits on the size of the navies of the United States, Great Britain, Japan, France, and Italy.[53]

Thus, the presidencies of Warren Harding, Calvin Coolidge, and Herbert Hoover (known as the Republican Restoration) were characterized by great parsimony in naval expenditures. Also, strategic concern after World War I understandably shifted from the Atlantic back to the Pacific and to Japan's naval might.[54] It was FDR who began to reverse the trend in 1933 in the direction of renewed naval expansion. Dexter Perkins relates this "strategic vacuum" to changes in US Caribbean policy during the late twenties and early thirties.

> Per contra, it is significant that with the defeat of Germany, the Caribbean policy of the United States underwent a substantial revision. The sea power of the Reich had been destroyed; there was no European state that could or would challenge the position of the United States in the waters controlling the approaches to the Canal, and this fact explains why the Monroe Doctrine underwent substantial revision in late twenties and early thirties. The Roosevelt corollary was gradually abandoned.[55]

The Rodman Board Report reflected the post–World War I situation. It stressed the great strategic importance of the Panama Canal and the entire Caribbean geostrategic space. However, it did not consider that threats to the region warranted the construction of a major base for the US fleet. If eventually required, it could be constructed in Panama. Neither did it recommend a major expansion beyond the existing base system.[56]

The Hepburn Board was created by the Naval Expansion Act of May 17, 1938, in an entirely different context. The board consisted of two rear admirals, three captains, and one commander.[57] The report was submitted to the chief of naval operations, Admiral William D. Leahy, on December 1, 1938, and to Congress the following January 3 by Claude Swanson, secretary of the navy. It reflected the greatly enhanced strategic importance attached to Puerto Rico and the Caribbean in the ongoing strategic debate in the United States.

While agreeing with the strategic outlook contained in the Rodman Board Report, the Hepburn report stressed: (1) that the greatest need for additional bases was in the Atlantic-Caribbean region, given that "the United States Fleet has been based in the Pacific during recent years, when the expansion of the air force has been most rapid, the growth of air bases, to serve the fleet, has been almost wholly in that area"; and (2) that air and submarine bases were urgently required.[58]

Regarding Puerto Rico, the report stated:

In its study of the Caribbean the Board found only one site capable of being made into an air base suitable for the normal operation of patrol planes. This is at Isla Grande, in the harbor of San Juan, Puerto Rico.... In addition to its suitability for patrol planes, the site offers suitable area for the construction of a landing field and facilities for the training of one or more carrier groups. A base for patrol planes situated this far eastward in the Caribbean will be of major strategic importance. The Board understands that negotiations are in progress to have the site transferred by the insular government to the jurisdiction of the Navy.[59]

Consequently, the report recommended: "(a) Facilities for one carrier group (planned with a view to expansion to two carrier groups), (b) Facilities for two patrol-plane squadrons (original plans for this station must provide for immediate emergency expansion for at least four patrol-plane squadrons), (c) Facilities for complete engine overhaul, (d) Construction of breakwater at harbor entrance, [and] (e) Berthing at pier for one carrier."[60] Expansion or construction of air and naval facilities in Guantánamo and the US Virgin Islands were also proposed, but on a scale smaller to those of Isla Grande. Similarly, the board advised the creation of a submarine base at Isla Grande:

The Board previously in this report has recommended the establishment of an air base in San Juan. Necessary wharfage for submarines can be readily provided at the air base without interference with air activities.

The Board recommends that submarine berthing be provided at Isla Grande and that an adequate supply of fuel be established.[61]

The only two other sites in the Caribbean mentioned as possible submarine bases were Key West in Florida and the US Virgin Islands. However, new construction was recommended only in the case of San Juan.

The board prepared four lists of new bases: air, submarine, destroyers, and mines. Each list was further subdivided into Category A (for earliest completion) and Category B (for later completion). No Caribbean bases for destroyers or mines were proposed. In the lists for air and submarine bases, Isla Grande appeared in Category A. In the air bases list, Isla Grande appeared in fourth place of a total of fifteen, followed by Panama. In the submarine bases list, it occupied second place (after Guam) of five sites. Additionally, the Isla Grande project was the most costly, at $9.3 million, of all the base projects that were eventually approved by Congress in late February 1939.[62] The board left no doubt of the importance it ascribed to the San Juan bases. The final commentary of the report said:

> There are certain projects, however, which the Board has no hesitation in selecting because of their immediate strategic importance as being necessary for accomplishment at the earliest predictable date and without regard of the expansion contemplated by the Act of May 17, 1938. These items are: Kaneohe Bay, Midway Island, Wake Island, Guam, Johnston Island and Palmyra Island in the mid-Pacific area; Kodiak and Sitka in the Alaskan area; and San Juan, Puerto Rico, in the Atlantic area. In addition, the immediate increase of training facilities at Pensacola, Fla., is mandatory.[63]

The importance of Isla Grande was further enhanced by the congressional decision to reject major base construction in Guam.

The Isla Grande project, when considered in historical perspective, was the largest investment the United States had made in military infrastructure in Puerto Rico since it obtained control of the island in 1898. It placed the island firmly on the road of the ambitious defense plans that were rapidly implemented during the early 1940s and highlighted the prominent role that was being assigned to Puerto Rico in US Atlantic-Caribbean strategy. Ironically, it would be very rapidly superseded by naval demands for even more bases and installations on the island as a result of Fleet Problem XX. The army, and particularly the air corps, also had plans for the construction of major facilities in Puerto Rico.[64] The journal *Economic Review*, in an article of June 1939, took note of the rapid enlargement of military construction plans for Puerto Rico and their potentially favorable impact on the island's economy:

> Recent moves on the part of the military and naval authorities in Puerto Rico make the general outlines of the Government's plan clear enough. The notion that Isla Grande Airport, Pan American Airway's terminal, would be the center of operations, has gone into discard. It seems clear that the Army will locate its principal flying fields, shops and training quarters at some distance from the capital city and that the Navy will base no more than a squadron of reconnaissance planes at San Juan proper. It is also clear that the port of San Juan, regardless of where the military establishments are built, will be the heart of the military circulation system as far as supplies are concerned, and unquestionably the strategic moves of both the Army and Navy mean greatly increased tonnages at San Juan's docks. They also mean the establishment of considerable personnel at San Juan.[65]

The urgency for Caribbean bases is understandable in view of the intense strategic debate that was taking place in the United States, and the "lessons" derived from the fleet maneuvers of 1939.

Fleet Problem XX

Fleet Problem XX was specifically designed to identify naval and military requirements in the Caribbean and the Atlantic. In May 1938, Roosevelt, using the New York World's Fair (which opened to the public the following year) as a pretext, ordered the fleet to transit through the Panama Canal and visit eastern ports to await the coming maneuvers. The maneuvers were again discussed by FDR and Leahy during a November meeting in the White House.[66]

According to Fleet Problem XX's war hypothesis, a fascist revolt had occurred in Brazil (Green). Germany (White) dispatched a convoy across the Atlantic to aid the rebels. The United States (Black) issued a diplomatic note of protest and ordered its fleet to transit the Panama Canal and deploy in the waters between Cuba and Haiti. Black eventually declared war. Vice Admiral Adolphus Andrews was placed in command of the Black fleet, while the attacking White fleet was commanded by Admiral Edward C. Kalbfus.[67]

The scenario of the maneuvers was based on discussions on the international and Latin American situation by the State-War-Navy Standing Liaison Committee. The strategic problem had been posed by Undersecretary of State Sumner Welles during a meeting on November 14, 1938.

> On the same day (14 November) that Roosevelt asked for a tripling of the Army Air Corps, the Standing Liaison Committee was discussing the latest disquieting news from southern South America. Under Secretary of State Sumner Welles informed his counterparts from the War and Navy Departments, Chief of Staff Malin Craig and Chief of Naval Operations William Leahy, that State Department officers in Brazil were expecting German-instigated rebellions to occur soon in Uruguay, Argentina and Brazil—all "as part of a large Nazi movement to obtain control of those countries." What Welles wanted to know was, if these fears turned out to be real, would the navy be capable of heading off any "filibustering" activities on the east coast. Leahy thought so, assuming it could use Brazilian ports. For the next month, the administration studied Brazilian developments closely. According to Harold Ickes, the cabinet devoted much of its meeting of 16 December to the "very serious situation in Brazil. The Nazis there are up to mischief, undoubtedly with the encouragement, if not the active backing, of Hitler. They are also very active in Uruguay."[68]

This same scenario was again portrayed by Sumner Welles in January 1939, during another meeting of that committee.[69] It guided war planning toward Brazil (War Plan Purple) during the late 1930s and early 1940s.[70]

There was sharp concern in Washington during 1938 with the stability of the Getúlio Vargas government in Brazil due to fascist and German activities. In March, General Pedro Aurélio de Góes Monteiro, considered an ultraconservative officer and former fascist sympathizer, had called for Vargas's resignation. The Ação Integralista Brasileira, a fascist party that had backed Vargas's Estado Novo in 1937, unsuccessfully tried to carry out a coup and kill the president on May 10–11, 1938. US intelligence sources were informed that Germany had directly assisted in this ploy. Brazil was considered of particular strategic importance because, among other things, its northeast "bulge" could be reached by air from bases in northwest Africa. A German presence in Brazil was seen as directly threatening US interests in the Caribbean and the Panama Canal. The Chilean *nacistas* (Nazis), on the other hand, staged a bloody rebellion in September against the conservative government of Arturo Alessandri in Santiago. Fascist and Axis activities throughout Latin America became a major source of preoccupation in Washington during this period. The December 1938 Inter-American meeting in Lima, convened at the behest of the United States, had the purpose of counteracting perceived fascist subversion.[71]

Thus, Fleet Problem XX focused strategically on the interrelationship between the Brazilian bulge (the Natal area) and the South Atlantic on the one hand, and the Caribbean region on the other. The maneuvers, although mostly centered in the Puerto Rico–Virgin Islands zone, involved a large maritime area ranging from Cuba to the Lesser Antilles. Exercises took place in Marie-Galante, Guadeloupe; Guantánamo, Cuba; Saint Thomas and Saint Croix in the US Virgin Islands; Montserrat; Antigua; Samaná in the Dominican Republic; the Bahamas; and Mona, Ponce, Guayanilla, Rincón, Culebra, Vieques, and San Juan in Puerto Rico. Several air raids and naval attacks on San Juan harbor were staged. The Vieques Sound also saw much naval action. In the Dominican Republic, Samaná Bay was the site for air, naval, submarine, and mine laying exercises.[72] The ships *Raleigh*, *Reid*, and *Cummins* with three other ships and fifty planes were in Samaná in March.

It should be noted that the maneuvers also had a political dimension, because they were used to strengthen military and political ties to the Leónidas Trujillo regime in the Dominican Republic. The massacre of thousands of Haitians on the Dominican border in 1937 by Trujillo was no longer an obstacle to warm relations. Trujillo used the presence of the cruiser *Texas* and forty-two USMC planes to rename as "US Marine Corps" a section of Trujillo Avenue (an important waterfront avenue in Santo Domingo). He had earlier named another section of the thoroughfare "George Washington." This was done in a military ceremony in which two companies of marines, with their band, participated together with Dominican soldiers.

> At last, in February 1939, Brigadier General Upshur and Colonel Roy S. Geiger could visit Santo Domingo since they were participating in naval maneuvers near Puerto Rico. The cruiser *Texas* and about 42 planes came to Santo Domingo for the ceremony. A large number of marines were aboard the ship.[73]

Trujillo also decorated FDR's son, Colonel James Roosevelt, with a medal while the maneuvers were taking place.[74]

The Caribbean political situation—namely, that of Puerto Rico—made itself felt in other ways during Fleet Problem XX. The news summary for February 20 prepared on board the USS *Houston*, which carried FDR and Leahy, included the following dispatch as its main news item:

> Washington. The Government had a recommendation from the American Civil [Liberties] Union today for investigation of what were called "deplorable conditions" in Colonial Administration.
>
> The Civil Liberties group asked [for] a chance for Puerto Rico to vote on Independence and for both Puerto Rico and Hawaii to vote on Statehood.
>
> A new administration for Puerto Rico, citizenship for the natives of Samoa and Guam, extended native participation in the Virgin Islands Government and Native language schools for Guam, Samoa and Puerto Rico were other recommendations.[75]

On February 23, FDR received an invitation from Governor Winship to visit him in Puerto Rico, which he politely refused, on the grounds that his itinerary depended on the maneuvers.[76] The maneuvers ended on February 27 with a major naval battle about a hundred miles north of Puerto Rico. FDR reviewed the results of the maneuvers in Culebra with admirals Leahy, Kalbfus, Andrews, and Claude C. Bloch. He also observed a USMC landing exercise on Flamenco Beach on that island. Among the conclusions derived from the experience, it: (1) reaffirmed the importance of the Caribbean and the Atlantic, (2) underscored the need to enjoy air supremacy, and (3) emphasized the urgent need to obtain bases in the Caribbean.[77] Admiral Andrews, Black commander, informed the president that "some means . . . [must] be found to provide fortified and well-secured bases in this most important strategic area." He also recommended to Admiral Bloch, commander in chief of the fleet, that:

From left to right: General George Marshall; former admiral, now governor of Puerto Rico William D. Leahy; and Brigadier General Edmund L. Daley, at the governor's mansion, La Fortaleza, during a trip to Puerto Rico to inspect the progress of the construction of the military base and related infrastructure projects, 1939 (Colección *El Mundo*, University of Puerto Rico)

In view of the present world conditions, the importance of the West Indian area to our national defense, and the maintenance of our national policies, and the lack of bases therein, it is high time that corrective measures be taken. Not only should provision be made for suitable bases in areas now under American jurisdiction, but steps should be taken that would insure the availability of certain other harbors and facilities to our planes and vessels.[78]

As if further to underscore the existing national security consensus, on February 28 the State Department issued the following statement by Senator Morris Sheppard, chairman of the Military Affairs Committee, which was received on the *Houston*:

[Senator Sheppard] declared that to permit Panama, Hawaii, Puerto Rico or Alaska to fall to an enemy would jeopardize the security of the continental United States. He said: "A violation of the Monroe Doctrine would probably not occur as a sudden overt act. It could easily take the form of a step by step movement of a peaceful penetration by foreign nations until definite and powerful minorities would be established with the result that before military force replaced diplomatic negotiations hostile nations might already have a foothold in areas that would threaten the most important link in our entire system of defense, the Panama Canal."[79]

As we have seen, the urgency for an expanded and strengthened base structure in the Caribbean, including the construction of new facilities in Puerto

Rico and the Virgin Islands, had already been expressed in the Hepburn Board Report of December 1938.[80] The army and navy would use the juncture of the Fleet Problem XX maneuvers to make demands for additional bases and resources considered vital for the defense of Puerto Rico and the Caribbean. According to Patrick Abbazia, Fleet Problem XX placed FDR firmly on the road to the destroyers-for-bases agreement with Great Britain.[81] At the conclusion of the exercise, Roosevelt also informed his chief of naval operations, William D. Leahy, that he would be named governor of Puerto Rico to succeed the aging and problematic General Blanton Winship. It would be one of Leahy's major tasks as governor of Puerto Rico to oversee war preparations on that island, the hub of the envisaged regional naval and military arrangement, from a military and, particularly, from a political perspective.

This crucial period was a watershed in US policy not only toward Puerto Rico but toward the entire Caribbean region. Traditional military enclaves in Panama, Cuba, and Puerto Rico were consolidated and expanded. The relationship with the military strongmen Fulgencio Batista and Leónidas Trujillo in Cuba and the Dominican Republic, respectively, was strengthened. FDR even mended fences with Mexican president Lázaro Cárdenas despite his nationalization of the oil companies in 1938. The acquisition of bases in British territories in the Atlantic and the Caribbean, as well as an enhanced US role vis-á-vis the French and Dutch territories, expanded US political and cultural influence, as the Trinidadian writer V. S. Naipaul brilliantly described in his novel *Miguel Street*.[82] The entire region became an "American Mediterranean," as Alfred Thayer Mahan had proposed just before the Spanish-American War.

David Haglund, among others, has analyzed how the concern with fascist subversion and Axis activities in Latin America shaped US hemispheric policy during the prewar period.[83] However, potential threats in the Caribbean were perceived as particularly menacing due to its adjacent geographical position and the critical importance assigned to the Panama Canal. Not only did the debate on the strategic importance of the Caribbean serve to legitimize an expanded presence in the region, but it was probably also a factor in creating an internal consensus in the United States in favor of military preparations in general and of forging a closer relationship with Great Britain in particular.

Notes

This essay is a revised version of "Puerto Rico and the Caribbean in US Strategic Debate on the Eve of the Second World War," *Revista Mexicana del Caribe* 1, no. 2 (1996): 55–80.

1. Among the abundant literature that reflected the views of the antiwar movement are Harry Elmer Barnes, *The Genesis of the World War: An Introduction to the Problem of War Guilt* (New York: Alfred A. Knopf, 1926); C. Hartley Grattan, *Why We Fought* (New York: Vanguard Press, 1929); Harold D. Lasswell, *Propaganda Technique in the World War* (New York: Alfred A. Knopf, 1927); Sir Arthur Ponsonby, *Falsehood in War-Time* (London: Allen and Unwin, 1928); Walter Millis, *The Road to War: America, 1914–1917* (Boston: Houghton Mifflin, 1935); Helmut C. Engelbrecht and F. C. Haninghen, *Merchants of Death: A Study of the International Armaments Industry* (New York: Dodd, Mead, 1934); Charles A. Beard, *The Devil Theory of War* (New York: Vanguard Press, 1936); Charles C. Tansill, *America Goes to War* (Boston: Little, Brown, 1938); Alice M. Morrissey, *The American Defense of Neutral Rights, 1914–1917* (Cambridge: Harvard University Press, 1939); and Horace C. Peterson, *Propaganda for War: The Campaign against American Neutrality, 1914–1917* (Norman: University of Oklahoma Press, 1939).

2. Donald F. Drummond, *The Passing of American Neutrality, 1937–1941* (Ann Arbor: University of Michigan Press, 1955), chapter 1.

3. Mary Louise Pratt, *Imperial Eyes: Travel Writing and Transculturation* (London: Routledge, 1992).

4. Major George Fielding Eliot, *The Ramparts We Watch: A Study of the Problems of American National Defense* (New York: Reynal and Hitchcock, 1938).

5. R. Ernest Dupuy and George Fielding Eliot, *If War Comes* (New York: Macmillan, 1937); see also George Fielding Eliot, *Defending America* (Foreign Policy Association, World Affairs Pamphlets, new series, no. 4, 1939).

6. The notion that rearmament should mainly be based on the massive development of air power was advanced by Roosevelt toward the end of 1938 and opposed by both the navy and the army, who wanted a balanced expansion. Apparently, Roosevelt saw air power as an alternative to a large army, as well as an effective means of supporting the European allies.

7. Eliot, *The Ramparts We Watch*, pp. 1, 193.

8. The author has discussed Mahan's outlook on the Caribbean in his "Cultura y geopolítica: un acercamiento a la visión de Alfred Thayer Mahan sobre el Caribe," *Op. Cit.*, Revista del Centro de Investigaciones Históricas, University of Puerto Rico, no. 11 (1999): 148–157.

9. Ibid., pp. 154–157.

10. Ibid., p. 148.

11. Ibid., pp. 152–153.

12. Eliot, *The Ramparts We Watch*, p. 259.

13. Rodríguez Beruff, "Cultura y geopolítica," pp. 154–155.

14. "America Gets Ready to Fight Germany, Italy and Japan," *Life* 5, no. 18 (October 31, 1938). Emphasis in the original.

15. Walter Millis, "Anatomy of National Defense," *Washington Post*, November 13, 1938.

16. Millis, *The Road to War*. See also Walter Millis, *The Martial Spirit* (Cambridge, MA: Literary Guild of America, 1931) on the Spanish-American War; and his "Arms and the Men," *Fortune* 9 (March 1934): 53. He also published a critical appraisal of US military history, *Arms and Men: A Study in American Military History* (New York: G. P. Putnam's Sons, 1956).

17. Joseph S. Edgerton, "Defense of Neighbors Held Essential to Safety of the U.S., Continental Plan Advocated to Make Sure Enemy Would Not Seize Weak Country for Basis of Attack," *Washington Star*, November 27, 1938.

18. *The Ramparts We Watch* was also received in Latin America as an authoritative source ("an eminent military authority") of US military policy and strategic thinking. It is significantly cited as the sole source of US strategic thinking regarding the need to internationalize the Panama Canal in a 1939 article by Víctor Raúl Haya de la Torre, the influential Peruvian politician. The article is reproduced under the title "Should the Panama Canal be Internationalized" in Robert J. Alexander, ed., *Aprismo: The Ideas and Doctrines of Víctor Raúl Haya de la Torre* (Kent, OH: Kent State University Press, 1973), pp. 335–341.

19. Wilbur Burton, "Panama: Defense Problem no. 1," *Current History* (December 1938): 34–36.

20. Cloak and dagger stories regarding Panama were not entirely off the mark. Documents obtained after the war demonstrated that Germany had established the intelligence operation "Project 14" as early as 1938, designed to gather information on the vulnerabilities of the canal. See Ladislas Farago, *The Game of the Foxes* (New York: David McKay, 1971), chapter 4.

21. Harold Sprout, "Strategic Considerations in Hemisphere Defense," *Quarterly Journal of Inter-American Relations* 1 (October 1939): 21–29.

22. Harold and Margaret Sprout, *Toward a New Order of Sea Power: American Naval Policy and the World Scene, 1918–1922* (Princeton, NJ: Princeton University Press, 1940).

23. Norman J. Padelford, "An Atlantic Naval Policy for the United States," *U.S. Naval Institute Proceedings* 66, no. 6 (September 1940): 1304.

24. Norman J. Padelford, *The Panama Canal in Peace and War* (New York: Macmillan, 1943).

25. "Puerto Rico: Gibraltar or Achilles Heel," *Hemisphere* (February 1940): 3–4.

26. Colonel Cary I. Crockett, "Island Bulwarks," *U.S. Naval Institute Proceedings* (March 1940): 372–383.

27. Lieutenant Commander Ephraim R. McLean Jr., "The Caribbean: An American Lake," *U.S. Naval Institute Proceedings* (July 1941): 952.

28. Hanson W. Baldwin, *United We Stand! Defense of the Western Hemisphere* (New York: Whittlesey House, 1941), pp. 105, 165, 217–218, 328–332; Hanson W. Baldwin, "America Rearms," *Foreign Affairs* 16, no. 3 (April 1938): 430–444; Hanson W. Baldwin, "Our New Long Shadow," *Foreign Affairs* 17, no. 3 (April 1939): 465–476; and Hanson W. Baldwin, "The Naval Defense of America," *Harper's* 183 (April 1941): 449–463.

29. Villard argued that armamentism would take the United States down the road of fascism. See Oswald Garrison Villard, "Wanted: A Sane Defense Policy," *Harper's* 178 (April 1939): pp. 449–456.

30. Catherine A. Lutz and Jane L. Collins, *Reading National Geographic* (Chicago: University of Chicago Press, 1993).

31. Laura Muñoz, "Bajo las barras y las estrellas, el Caribe en tiempos de guerra y sus representaciones en National Geographic (1939-1944)," in *Caribe imaginado, visiones y representaciones de la región*, ed. Laura Muñoz and María del Rosario Rodríguez (Morelia, Mexico: Universidad Michoacana and Instituto Mora, 2009), p. 68. Author's translation.

32. E. John Long, "Puerto Rico: Watchdog of the Caribbean, Venerable Domain under American Flag Has New Role as West Indian Stronghold and Sentinel of the Panama Canal," *National Geographic* 76, no. 6 (December 1939): 697. For an analysis of *National Geographic* articles on Puerto Rico, see Jorge L. Crespo Armáiz, "De la prosperidad a la resistencia: la representación de Puerto Rico en la revista *National Geographic* (1898-2003)," unpublished manuscript.

33. Crespo Armáiz, "De la prosperidad a la resistencia."

34. Earle K. James, "Puerto Rico at the Crossroads," *Foreign Policy Reports* 13, no. 15 (October 15, 1937): 182–192.

35. This article is analyzed in Muñoz, "Bajo las barras y las estrellas," pp. 70–71.

36. Anne Rainey Langley, "British West Indian Interlude," *National Geographic* 79, no. 1 (January 1941): 1–46.

37. Edward T. Folliard, "Martinique: Caribbean Question Mark," *National Geographic* 79, no. 1 (January 1941): 47–55.

38. See, for example, "Puerto Rico: Gibraltar or Achilles Heel," 3–4; Lawrence and Sylvia Martin, "Outpost No. 2: The West Indies," *Harper's* 182 (March 1941): 359–368; James K. Eyre, "Martinique: A Key Point in Hemisphere Defense," *Inter American Quarterly* (October 1941): 82–88; and Charles Taussig, "The Caribbean," *Survey Graphic* (March 1941): 146–148, 198–200.

39. Carleton Beals, *The Coming Struggle for Latin America* (Philadelphia: J. B. Lippincott, 1938); J. Fred Rippy, *The Caribbean Danger Zone* (New York: G. P. Putnam's Sons, 1940); and Walter Adolphe Roberts, *The Caribbean: The Story of Our Sea of Destiny* (Indianapolis: Bobbs-Merrill, 1940). Beals also published *America South* (Philadelphia: J. B. Lippincott, 1938). For the many books that were published on the Caribbean and Latin America from a security angle, see Hines Calvin Warner, "United States Diplomacy in the Caribbean during World War II" (Ph.D. diss., University of Texas at Austin, 1968), pp. 431–432.

40. Beals, *The Coming Struggle*, pp. 239–240.

41. William H. Haas, ed., *The American Empire: A Study of the Outlying Territories of the United States* (Chicago: University of Chicago Press, 1940).

42. Ibid., pp. 378–380.

43. Ibid., p. 90.

44. Donald A. Yerxa, "The United States Navy and the Caribbean Sea, 1914-1941" (Ph.D. diss., University of Maine, 1982), pp. 339–343.

45. Ibid., p. 341.

46. Ibid., p. 342.

47. Ibid., p. 341; see also John Child, "From 'Color' to 'Rainbow': U.S. Strategic Planning for Latin America, 1919-1945," *Journal of Interamerican Studies and World Affairs* 21, no. 2 (May 1979): 247–249.

48. Marion D. Francis, "War Plans and Defense Measures Prior to Organization of the Caribbean Defense Command (1 July 1939–29 May 1941)," section 2, chapter 1 of *History of the Antilles Department*, Historical Section, Adjutant General's Office, Antilles Department, San Juan, October 1945, p. xv.

49. Child, "From 'Color' to 'Rainbow,'" pp. 239–247.

50. Francis, "War Plans and Defense Measures," pp. 5–6.

51. Ibid., pp. 9–73.

52. Holger Herwig and David Trask, "Naval Operations Plans between Germany and the USA, 1898–1913: A Study of Strategic Planning in the Age of Imperialism," in *The War Plans of the Great Powers, 1880–1914*, ed. Paul Kennedy (Boston: Allen and Unwin, 1985), pp. 39–74; and María Eugenia Estades, *La presencia militar de Estados Unidos en Puerto Rico, 1898–1918: intereses estratégicos y dominación colonial* (Río Piedras, PR: Ediciones Huracán, 1988), pp. 65–73.

53. The treaties signed on February 6, 1922, established a ratio of 5:5:3, respectively, for US, British, and Japanese battleship and carrier tonnage, allotted 1¾ to France and Italy, prohibited the construction of new battleships for a ten-year period, and limited their maximum tonnage. Samuel Eliot Morison, *The Two-Ocean War: A Short History of the United States Navy in the Second World War* (Boston: Little, Brown, 1963), p. 6.

54. In 1924, the director of the navy's War Plans Division concluded that Japan was a more likely enemy than Britain and that strategy should be "Pacific-first." By 1927, the General Board was of the opinion that there almost no possibility of war with Britain. Yerxa, "The United States Navy and the Caribbean Sea," p. 245.

55. Dexter Perkins, *The United States and Latin America* (Baton Rouge: Louisiana State University Press, 1961), p. 24.

56. Ibid., pp. 256–257.

57. Rear Admiral Arthur J. Hepburn (senior member), Rear Admiral E. J. Marquart, Captain James S. Woods, Captain Arthur L. Bristol Jr., Captain (Civil Engineering Corps) Ralph Withman, and Commander William E. Hilbert (recorder).

58. *Report on the Need of Additional Naval Bases to Defend the Coasts of the United States, Its Territories and Possessions*, H.R. Doc. no. 76-65, pp. 4–15.

59. Ibid., p. 16.

60. Ibid.

61. Ibid., p. 30.

62. "La Cámara aprobó la base naval para Puerto Rico," *El Mundo* (San Juan), February 24, 1939, p. 1.

63. Ibid., p. 36.

64. "As early as January 1939, the Panama Canal Department recognized the urgent need for bases in other parts of the Caribbean region. These bases would permit advance warning of an enemy attack and would enable the Army Air Corps to engage hostile aircraft before they could strike the Canal. Nature has favored the Caribbean by providing a chain of islands extending from Cuba southeast to the northern coast of Venezuela. These islands offered natural sites for air bases to guard the Caribbean approaches to the Panama Canal."

Herman Hupperich, "The Caribbean: Vital Link in Western Hemisphere Air Defense during World War II," in *Militarists, Merchants, and Missionaries: United States Expansion in Middle America*, ed. Eugene R. Huck and Edward H. Moseley (Tuscaloosa: University of Alabama Press, 1970), pp. 131–132. For the economic impact of these defense projects and defense spending in general in Puerto Rico, see José L. Bolívar Fresneda, *Guerra, banca y desarrollo: el Banco de Fomento y la industrialización de Puerto Rico* (San Juan: Fundación Luis Muñoz Marín; Instituto de Cultura Puertorriqueña, 2011).

65. "Puerto Rico Sees Bright Future as Major Defense Area in Caribbean," *Economic Review* 4, no. 3 (June 1939), pp. 25–32, 65.

66. Henry H. Adams, *Witness to Power: The Life of Fleet Admiral William D. Leahy* (Annapolis, MD: Naval Institute Press, 1985), p. 100.

67. For a general description of the maneuvers, see Patrick Abbazia, *Mr. Roosevelt's Navy: The Private War of the U.S. Atlantic Fleet, 1939–1942* (Annapolis, MD: Naval Institute Press, 1973), chapter 3, "A Mirror to War: Fleet Problem XX."

68. David G. Haglund, *Latin America and the Transformation of U.S. Strategic Thought, 1936–1940* (Albuquerque: University of New Mexico Press, 1984), p. 99.

69. Child, "From 'Color' to 'Rainbow,'" p. 249.

70. "The President has directed the preparation of a war plan *PURPLE*, under the following assumptions: . . . GERMANY joined by ITALY has successfully conducted a war against ENGLAND and FRANCE. The British and French fleets have been destroyed or dissipated and are no longer a factor to be considered. British and French colonies and dominions in the Western Hemisphere are no longer under British and French protection and their final disposition is awaiting the action of a peace conference. CANADA, BRITISH and FRENCH GUIANA and NEWFOUNDLAND have proclaimed their independence and have asked the UNITED STATES for protection under the Monroe Doctrine. The British and French Islands in the Caribbean area are still nominally under British and French control. The 1st and 6th Divisions, U.S. Army (full peace strength) have reinforced the garrison at Porto Rica [sic]. . . . A civil war exist in BRAZIL. Federal Forces (north) are opposed to rebel forces (south) along a general line east and west through SAO PAULO. GERMANY and ITALY have established bases of operations in the CAPE VERDE and CANARY ISLANDS off the African coast. They are reinforcing the rebel front by furnishing men and munitions in such quantities and under such conditions as to constitute a definite economic and political penetration of the SOUTH AMERICAN continent and a violation of the Monroe Doctrine. ARGENTINA has aligned itself with the Rebel forces. Other South American countries are neutral but are sympathetic to the aims and purposes of the United States. JAPAN is intensely engaged in the expansion of her interests in the Western Pacific." Major A. H. Rogers, "War Plan Purple, Oral Presentation," May 20, 1940, course at the Army War College, 1939–1940, War Plans, Formulation of War Plans Period, Report of Staff Group no. 3, pp. 6–7, US Military History Institute, Carlysle Barracks, PA.

71. Haglund, *Latin America and the Transformation of U.S. Strategic Thought*, pp. 82–99; see also Alton Frye, *Nazi Germany and the American Hemisphere, 1933–1941* (New Haven, CT: Yale University Press, 1967), chapters 7, 8.

72. For the itinerary of the maneuvers, see "Memorandum, Subject: Chronological Record of Contacts and Events," FDR Library, FDR Papers, OF 200, Container 49, Folder 200-MMM; see also "Hostile Planes Raid Puerto Rico," *New York Times*, February 26, 1939.

73. Bernardo Vega, *Trujillo y las fuerzas armadas norteamericanas* (Santo Domingo: Fundación Cultural Dominicana, 1992), p. 228.

74. For the rapprochement with Trujillo during Fleet Problem XX, see ibid., pp. 228–230.

75. *USS Houston Evening Press News* (February 20, 1939), FDR Library, FDR Papers, OF 200, Container 49, Folder 200-MMM.

76. "Naval Aide to the President, a: Blanton Winship" (February 25, 1939), FDR Library, FDR Papers, OF 200, Container 48, Folder 200-III.

77. For a more detailed description of the maneuvers, see Abbazia, *Mr. Roosevelt's Navy*, chapter 3; and Yerxa, "The United States Navy and the Caribbean Sea," pp. 335–339.

78. Yerxa, "The United States Navy and the Caribbean Sea," p. 339.

79. *State Department Bulletin*, no. 48 (February 28, 1939), p. 4, FDR Library, FDR Papers, OF 200, Container 49, Folder 200-MMM.

80. Among the priority recommendations of the Hepburn Board were the construction of a secondary naval air base with berthing facilities at San Juan. It also called for an expansion of the Saint Thomas naval air base and the retention of a submarine facility there. This was followed by the more ambitious and sweeping recommendations for new base facilities contained in the Greenslade Report of January 1941. Yerxa, "The United States Navy and the Caribbean Sea," pp. 336, 355.

81. Abbazia, *Mr. Roosevelt's Navy*, p. 49.

82. V. S. Naipaul, *Miguel Street* (1959; repr., New York: Vintage Books, 2002).

83. Haglund, *Latin America and the Transformation of U.S. Strategic Thought*.

Puerto Rico: Headquarters of the Caribbean Sea Frontier, 1940–1945

Fitzroy André Baptiste

These are ominous days—days whose swift and shocking developments force every neutral nation to look to its defenses in the light of new factors. The brutal force of modern offensive war has been loosed in all its horror....

The element of surprise which has ever been an important tactic in warfare has become the more dangerous because of the amazing speed with which modern equipment can reach and attack the enemy's country....

The Atlantic and Pacific Oceans were reasonably adequate defensive barriers when fleets under sail could move at an average speed of five miles an hour.... Later, the oceans still gave strength to our defense when fleets and convoys propelled by steam could sail at fifteen or twenty miles an hour.

But the new element—air navigation—steps up the speed of possible attack to two hundred, to three hundred miles an hour.

Furthermore, it brings the new possibilities of the use of nearer bases from which an attack or attacks on the American Continent could be made. From the fiords of Greenland it is 4 hours by air to Newfoundland; 5 hours to Nova Scotia, New Brunswick and Quebec; and only 6 hours to New England.

The Azores are only 2,000 miles from parts of our eastern seaboard and if Bermuda fell into hostile hands it is a matter of less than 3 hours for modern bombers to reach our shores.

Caricature drawn by the locally famous artist Carmelo Filardi in *El Mundo*, 1944 (Archivo General de Puerto Rico)

From a base in the outer West Indies, the coast of Florida could be reached in 200 minutes.

The islands off the west coast of Africa are only 1,500 miles from Brazil. Modern planes starting from the Cape Verde Islands can be over Brazil in 7 hours.

And Para, Brazil, is but 4 flying hours to Caracas, Venezuela; and Venezuela but 2½ hours to Cuba and the Canal Zone; and Cuba and the Canal Zone are 2½ hours to Tampico, Mexico; and Tampico is 2½ hours to St. Louis, Kansas City and Omaha.

On the other side of the continent, Alaska, with a white population of only 30,000 people, is within 4 or 5 hours of flying distance from Vancouver, Seattle, Tacoma and Portland. The islands of the southern Pacific are not too far removed from the west coast of South America to prevent them from becoming bases of enormous strategic advantage to attacking forces....

An effective defense by its very nature requires the equipment to attack an aggressor on his route before he can establish strong bases within the territory of American vital interests.[1]

The above are extracts of an emergency message dated May 16, 1940, to the US Congress by President Franklin D. Roosevelt. The *casus* of the message was the sweeping victory of the Nazi German war machine in western Europe in the hot summer of 1940, and the geopolitical threat that this posed to the security of the United States and the Western Hemisphere.

In the context of this essay, however, the president's speech holds significance in pinpointing the role that one "new element"—the airplane—played in revolutionizing global strategy and warfare by the outbreak of the Second World War. Another "new element," not mentioned by the president but of which he was aware, was the submarine. By introducing long-range and rapid-movement capabilities and thus a greater combat radius to warfare, the airplane and the submarine together threatened to alter adversely the global balance of power held by the Anglo-Saxon powers (Great Britain and the United States). As a 1941 think tank at Balliol College, Oxford, observed insightfully, a determined enemy power or group of powers could now challenge the long-standing dominance of the Anglo-Saxon powers, which were based on sea power, by deploying a combination of air power, sea power, and land power in order to control "certain strategically crucial narrow seas" of the globe. The "strategically crucial narrow seas" included:

> (1) the Mediterranean and Aegean area, which would give him [the enemy] access to Africa and South-Western Asia; (2) the Indonesian archipelago, which would bring Australia within striking distance and would open the way to command of the Western Pacific; (3) the Bering Sea, the narrowest sea-passage between the European-Asiatic land-mass and North America; (4) ... the Caribbean [which] would only be available to a European aggressor if he had already succeeded in establishing himself in the South American continent ... (5) the "Straits of Dakar," between West Africa and the Bulge of Brazil, by way of which he might be able to gain and maintain a foot-hold in Latin America [and] (6) in the Northern Atlantic ... a series of "stepping stones"—the Faroes, Iceland, Greenland—between Northern Europe and Canada. A power which was relatively weak on the sea but strong in the air might succeed in seizing and holding these "stepping stones," and would then be in a position to cut the communications between North America and Great Britain.[2]

With some bearing on our discussion, too, the territories in most of these crucial narrow seas were owned then by continental European powers. In the Indonesian archipelago, there were the Dutch East Indies and Portuguese Timor; in the western and eastern Mediterranean, the possessions of France, Spain, and Italy; the Faroes, Iceland, and Greenland were Danish possessions; and, astride the "Straits of Dakar," Senegal with its capital Dakar was a French colony in West Africa, while the Atlantic "stepping stones" of the Azores, Madeira, the Canaries, and the Cape Verde Islands shared ownership between Spain and Portugal. Finally, the territories of the Caribbean and its fringe such as British, Dutch, and French Guiana were owned predominantly by Britain, Denmark, France, the Netherlands, and (until 1898) Spain.[3]

In sum, "all [these] odds and ends of territory"[4] in the narrow seas of the globe came to have a geostrategic significance out of proportion to their size. Moreover, that significance was enhanced by the First World War, when the Dutch East Indies, the eastern Mediterranean/Middle East, and the circum-Caribbean emerged as sources of petroleum and bauxite, two raw materials basic to the operationalization of the airplane, the submarine, and a host of other new war instruments.[5]

The United States, "an insular nation,"[6] was forced into a series of responses to the threats posed to her security by the advent of the airplane and the submarine. One response, diplomatic, was the *Angelsachsentum*,[7] or Anglo-Saxon Grand Alliance, with Great Britain particularly and Canada to a lesser extent; US and British strategic planners had viewed each other as mutual principal enemies as recently as the outbreak of the First World War.[8] The *Angelsachsentum* was intended to counter the threat by two new perceived enemies: Germany in the Atlantic sea frontier and Japan in the Pacific sea frontier.

Two other related responses were the development of naval aviation and the establishment of bases advanced far to the front of the continental United States into the Caribbean, Atlantic, and Pacific[9]: a "Sea Maginot Line," or several.[10] We discern the elements of these responses in the First World War. On the assumption that hostile, meaning German, cruiser submarines of great radius posed, or were likely to pose, a threat to the inner Caribbean and the Atlantic and Gulf coasts of the United States, the following actions were taken:

(1) Denial of *permanent* or *temporary* bases to the enemy "in that tract of water bounded by the South American and Central American Coast, and the islands of the Caribbean fringe";
(2) Acceleration of submarine construction and assembly in the United States;
(3) The provision of convoys inclusive of naval escort for merchant shipping;
(4) A district defense system, including the placement at "essential focal points" of a "few single powerful guns"; "purely defensive mine fields of limited area and nets"; air patrols and listening stations; "adequate sweeping service"; the retention of nine destroyers to aid "very limited district escort out for shipping by chaser and destroyer"; and the deployment of "a few coast guard [vessels] or yachts" in order "to answer rescue calls";

(5) Control of warnings, including the quickest transmission possible of reports of sightings of enemy craft and information about enemy activity (in code and not in English);[11]
(6) Scanning "most carefully" lists of people shipping goods to ports in Cuba, Haiti, Colombia, Venezuela, Central America, Mexico, and Curaçao;
(7) Considering "most carefully" the chartering of ships to persons trading in the area in (6) above, "paying particular attention to sailing vessels";
(8) Watching "most carefully" the character and quantity of goods shipped within the defined zone: fuel oil, foods (especially tinned foods), electrical supplies, metals (especially copper), rubber, cotton, and "materials used in the manufacture of high explosives";
(9) Careful monitoring of ports in which trading vessels clear, "bearing in mind the fact that ships trading with the enemy might discharge some portion of their cargo before entering the port for which cleared, claiming marine disaster for any portion of a deck load, but more likely trading through a third intermediary party";
(10) Surveillance of "the character of the crews shipped or any passengers carried on vessels trading within *the dangerous area*"; and
(11) Placement, where suspicion existed, of "a secret agent on the suspected vessel."[12]

These precautions were taken during the First World War, presaging the more elaborate construct of World War II. The developments led Lieutenant Commander Virgil Baker, US Navy district communication superintendent at Puerto Rico, to write this in 1919:

> That theory of strategy which provides that Naval bases necessary for the outposts of naval battle lines shall be advanced as far as possible to the front has been strengthened by the facts brought out by the European war and by the wide development of the means and the increase in the efficiency of naval scouting. It has become almost an axiom that there is no other consideration so formidable and serious to an invading fleet as that of a securely defended and well-equipped Naval base possessed by the country to be invaded and situated at a position well advanced to the front beyond the objective of the invading fleet.[13]

Enmeshed in the abovementioned First World War defensive-offensive scheme against hostile cruiser submarines in the Caribbean and adjoining land-sea region were the Panama Canal Zone (PCZ), Guantanamo Bay in Cuba, Saint Thomas in the US Virgin Islands (newly acquired from Denmark), and Puerto Rico. They were the arches of a first line termed the "American Lake" by John Child.[14]

The PCZ was the main arch of the original "American Lake." It was located within the confines of a new Central American republic that was carved out of the national territory of Colombia by the United States largely for reasons of US national interest. The other components of the formative "American Lake" were Guantanamo Bay in Cuba; Puerto Rico, with the adjacent Culebra and Vieques Islands; and the US Virgin Islands. Puerto Rico and her neighboring isles were an outright acquisition by the United States from Spain in the 1898 Spanish-American War. A byproduct of the same conflict was Cuba's independence from Spain. However, the new Cuban republic was imposed on from the outset by a series of unequal treaties, which, inter alia, gave the United States base rights in perpetuum at Guantanamo Bay. As stated above, the US Virgin Islands was a new acquisition by purchase from Denmark in 1917, partly to forestall German acquisition of the islands.

Guantanamo Bay, Puerto Rico, and the US Virgin Islands figured in a series of surveys conducted by the United States on its base needs in the Caribbean and Pacific during and after World War I. For example, a 1917 survey, "Naval Base Sites in the Antilles" by civil engineer L. M. Cox of the US Navy's Bureau of Yards and Docks, had the following to say about Guantanamo Bay:

> Of our present possessions in the Caribbean, Guantanamo Bay offers the best site for a fully equipped and defended main base, capable of taking care of all the requirements of a fleet in war.[15]

Additionally, Cox recommended, in order of priority, two other sites as secondary bases, capable of defense against cruiser raids in the temporary absence of the fleet and capable of development as submarine and destroyer bases. The two sites were:

> Culebra Island, with dredging and enlargement of Great Harbor entrance and anchorage and enlargement of boat canal between Great Harbour and Target Bay. Advanced base defensive equipment.
>
> St. Thomas Island, Harbor of Charlotte Amalia [sic], to be defended by permanent batteries against cruiser and raider attack and facilities afforded in the harbor itself for destroyers, submarines and other small craft held temporarily in advance of the Culebra advance base.[16]

Endorsing Cox's recommendations, Admiral Charles J. Badger cited a 1916 report by the General Board of the Navy on the "value of these [Danish West Indian] islands as a naval base," in conjunction with "the Culebra Region":

Boy walking with a bicycle in a small town outfitted with the flags of the Allies: the Soviet Union, Great Britain, the United States, France, and China (Archivo Fundación Luis Muñoz Marín)

What may be called the Culebra Region or the Virgin Island Region should be considered as a whole as a base in that part of the West Indies rather than to consider that Culebra Island or the Danish West India Islands, or any one of them, as such a base. With this view, the Danish W.I. Islands will be a distinct acquisition to the present resources of a base in the Virgin Islands. They will extend the jurisdiction of the United States in a favorable direction strategically, and they offer some possible advantages in the way of giving favorable sites for batteries. They do not offer any particular advantages as regards protection from the elements, but they do, of course, add the harborage of St. Thomas Harbor and also of Hurricane Hole in St. John Island to the other harborage that now is under the jurisdiction of the United States.[17]

Reports by Commander W. R. White of 1917 and Lieutenant Commander Virgil Baker of 1919 spelled out the assets of "Porto Rico" as a naval base of the United States.[18] Those assets included its capital, San Juan, with an estimated population of seventy thousand, served by five regular steamship lines and two cables, and having freight-handling facilities, two large foundries, three well-equipped repair shops, and "general commercial equipment."[19]

Its human assets were described as a "white native labor" force that was "loyal" and mostly "skilled and intelligent." Moreover, they had the potential for development into skilled mechanics and all the other skilled trades necessary to a naval base, "under proper instruction and training, and under better living and social condition." These Puerto Rican human assets contrasted starkly with those of Samaná Bay in Santo Domingo, where the only available labor force was "the most ignorant negro type . . . not skilled nor trained, nor . . . capable of being trained in the mechanical or other skilled trades," and with the surrounding population "unfriendly."[20]

Above all else were Puerto Rico's assets as a naval base in association with Narragansett Bay in the continental United States. By Puerto Rico was meant "a general strategic area which includes Eastern Puerto Rico, Culebra, the Virgin Islands and Vieques Island, together with the body of water which these islands bound." Narragansett Bay was defined as "the acres of Long Island Sound, Block Island Sound, Vineyard Sound and Massachusetts Bay" on the Atlantic coast of the United States: a collective front of 1,400 miles.[21]

Writing in the eighteenth century, George Brydges Rodney, the great British naval strategist, said that the nation that controlled Puerto Rico and Narragansett Bay would thereby dominate the Atlantic coast of North America.[22] Baker was of the view that, since Rodney's time, "the truth of that statement (by Rodney) has been continually strengthened by the advance and development of naval armament and tactics and by the lessons of the European war."[23]

Two sites in the western part of Vieques Sound, it was concluded, were the only locations in those parts of the West Indies under US control that met the requirements of a first-class naval base, with little or no dredging. The sites were:

> The area bounded by the eastern coast of Porto Rico and the Cordilleras Reefs and extending from Cape San Juan as far south as Pineros Island, and by a breakwater to be built in comparatively shallow water in a northerly direction over Lavandera Rocks and Largo Shoals and extending to Little Palominos Island.

> The area bounded by Pineros Island, Point Puerca, Cabras Island, the shoal southeast of Point Cascajo, and Arenas Bank, and by Vieques Island as far east as Caballo Point, from where the breakwater should be built in a northwesterly direction along the reefs and shallow water toward Descubridor Rock or to South Chinchorro Shoal.[24]

A first-class naval base should be capable of housing the following military and naval forces:

(a) Super-dreadnoughts and battle cruisers
(b) Scout cruisers and destroyers
(c) Submarines and submarine chasers

(d) Small cruisers and gunboats
(e) Auxiliary vessels, such as repair ships, supply ships, fuel ships, ammunition ships, hospital ships, mine layers, transports, etc.
(f) Aircraft of all classes
(g) The defending garrisons, and the industrial population employed in the manufacturing and repairs shops. These might total from 50,000 to 100,000 men.[25]

To that end, a first-class naval base should command a number of "principal requisites," as follows:

(a) Protection against the sea, so as to provide smooth water and good anchorages
(b) Location near the probable objectives
(c) Security against attack by land and against bombardment from the sea
(d) Moderately deep water of large area
(e) Two or more entrances or exits well protected by shore batteries in order to make deployments safe
(f) Reliable cable and radio communication
(g) Good lines of operation and of communication
(h) Plenty of fresh water and fresh foods
(i) Naval stores, metals, and fuels
(j) A sufficiently large area of ground for shops, store-houses, barracks, and aircraft hangars, as well as for drill grounds for the defending garrisons
(k) Electric power, from water-falls, if possible
(l) A plentiful supply of loyal and intelligent skilled and unskilled labor
(m) Excellent sanitary conditions
(n) Hard bottom for torpedo practice.[26]

The two sites could easily be defended against attack by sea by locating batteries of the highest caliber of guns in the high hills west of them and close to the coast. Moreover, an invading army, even if it succeeded in gaining a foothold in the western part of Puerto Rico, was likely to find an advance to the east coast "almost impossible" on account of the topography west of Fajardo and the east coast. Advance would be along the coast via two steep passes that could be defended successfully by a force equivalent to one-half that of the attacker. Also, Fajardo was connected to San Juan by railroad, thereby enabling the quick movement of auxiliary forces in a contingency.[27]

In addition to its other assets, San Juan's small but well-protected harbor could provide backup assets to the projected first-class naval base in the form of "an excellent small auxiliary base for such small craft as submarines, submarine-chasers, and, possibly, air-craft."[28] Finally, the naval base was proximate to the iron ore of Cuba; to the coal of Charleston, South Carolina; and to the oil fuel of Texas and Mexico.²⁹ Hence, the value of Puerto Rico as a first-class naval base for the United States was a foregone conclusion:

> Neither in the West Indies nor in any other part of the world has Nature provided all requisites of a first-class Naval base. All possible locations in the West Indies are lacking in the metals, fuels, and ships' stores that a Navy requires. Also, whatever site is chosen, the building of long and more or less expensive breakwaters will be necessary.³⁰

In retrospect, Puerto Rico–Culebra and Guantanamo Bay first came to be regarded as key points on an "American Lake" in about 1918, serving as fronts to both the PCZ and the Atlantic and Gulf coasts of the United States. In turn, they interlocked with a similar Pacific perimeter. By Executive Order no. 1613 of September 23, 1912, Great Harbor in Culebra, Guantanamo Naval Station in Cuba, Pearl Harbor in Hawaii, Kiska in the Aleutian Islands, Guam, Subic Bay in the Philippines, and the Tortugas in Florida were declared harbors prohibited to commercial, noncommercial, and public foreign vessels without special authorization from the US Navy Department.

In 1930, following the establishment of the PCZ as the United States' first Airspace Reservation Area in 1929, the seven abovementioned harbors were accorded similar status by Executive Order no. 5281. Although the Tortugas later lost that status by Presidential Proclamation no. 2112 of January 4, 1935, the other six maintained their joint status as Airspace Reservations *and* Protected Harbors into the early years of Second World War. Indeed, the Airspace Reservation status of Culebra Island and Guantanamo Bay were enhanced by Executive Orders no. 8684 of February 14, 1941, and no. 8749 of May 1, 1941, respectively. Similar status was bestowed on Kodiak in Alaska; Kaneohe Bay in Hawaii; Palmyra, Johnston, Midway, and Wake Islands and Kingman Reef in the central Pacific; Guam; and Tutuila Island in American Samoa between November 18, 1940, and April 2, 1941.

Likewise, the status of Defensive Sea Area, sometimes called "Naval Defensive Sea Area," was bestowed on Culebra and Guantanamo Bay by the same Executive Orders nos. 8684 and 8749 of February 14 and May 1, 1941, in respect of Airspace Reservation. Similar status was granted to Pearl Harbor, Kiska and the Unalaska Islands, Kaneohe Bay, Palmyra, Guam, and Honolulu between May 26, 1939, and December 20, 1941. In all, thirty-seven such Defensive Sea Areas were established within and outside the United States from 1918 through 1942.³¹

A 1938–1939 report by Rear Admiral Arthur J. Hepburn on the "Need of Additional Naval Bases to Defend the Coasts of the United States, Its

Territories and Possessions"[32] ranked Isla Grande and San Juan, Puerto Rico; Coco Solo, PCZ; Saint Thomas, US Virgin Islands; and Guantanamo Bay in its priorities for airbase and submarine base developmental projects with war looming, as follows:

Air Bases
Category A (for earliest completion):
    Chesapeake Bay (Hampton Roads, Virginia)
    Southeastern base (Jacksonville, Florida)
    Pensacola, Florida
    Puerto Rico (San Juan)
    Coco Solo, Canal Zone
    Seattle (Sand Point), Washington
    Sitka, Alaska
    Kodiak, Alaska
    Pearl Harbor (Ford Island), Hawaii
    Kaneohe Bay (Oahu), Hawaii
    Midway Island
    Wake Island
    Johnston Island
    Palmyra Island
    Guam

Category B (for later completion):
    Northeastern base (Quonsett Point, Rhode Island)
    Quantico, Virginia
    Corpus Christi, Texas
    Guantanamo Bay, Cuba
    Virgin Islands (Saint Thomas)
    San Diego, California
    Alameda, California
    Unalaska Island, Alaska
    Canton Island (Phoenix Islands)
    Rose Island, Rhode Island

Submarine Bases
Category A (for earliest completion):
    Guam
    Puerto Rico (San Juan)
    Canal Zone (Balboa)
    Unalaska Island, Alaska

Midway Island
Wake Island

Category B (for later completion):
New London, Connecticut
Hampton Roads, Virginia
San Francisco (Treasure Island), California
Kodiak, Alaska[33]

Indeed, the projects at San Juan in the Caribbean; Kaneohe Bay, Midway Island, Wake Island, Guam, Johnston Island, and Palmyra Island in the mid-Pacific area; and Kodiak and Sitka in the Alaskan area were termed as "necessary of accomplishment at the earliest possible date" on account of "their immediate strategic importance." Another site earmarked for a 50 percent increase in facilities for training pilots was Pensacola, Florida. It was termed "mandatory."[34]

The overall climate led to the passage by Congress of H.R. 9218, "an Act to establish the composition of the United States Navy, to authorize the construction of certain naval vessels, and for other purposes," or, more commonly, the Naval Expansion Act of 1938. In addition to previous tonnages agreed to and established by treaties in Washington on February 6, 1922; in London on April 22, 1930; and authorized by Congress on March 27, 1934, and amended on June 25, 1936, the measure provided, inter alia, for the following as the United States' "war arsenal" geared up for the Second World War:

> (a) Capital ships, one hundred and five thousand tons, making a total authorized underage tonnage of six hundred and thirty thousand tons: *Provided*, That vessels of tonnages in excess of thirty-five thousand tons each may be laid down if the President determines with respect to the tonnage of capital ships being built by other nations that the interests of national defense so require, in which event the authorized composition of the United States Navy of capital ships is hereby increased by one hundred and thirty-five thousand tons, making a total authorized underage tonnage of six hundred and sixty thousand tons;

> (b) Aircraft carriers, forty thousand tons, making a total authorized underage tonnage of one hundred and seventy-five thousand tons;

> (c) Cruisers, sixty-eight thousand seven hundred and fifty-four tons, making a total authorized underage tonnage of four hundred and twelve thousand five hundred and twenty-four tons;

(d) Destroyers, thirty-eight thousand tons, making a total authorized underage tonnage of two hundred and twenty-eight thousand tons;

(e) Submarines, thirteen thousand six hundred and fifty-eight tons, making a total authorized underage tonnage of eighty-one thousand nine hundred and fifty-six tons.

The President of the United States is hereby authorized to undertake such construction, including replacements, as is necessary to build the Navy to the total authorized underage composition as provided for in section 1 of this Act.

The President of the United States is hereby authorized to acquire or construct additional naval airplanes, including patrol planes, and spare parts and equipment, so as to bring the number of useful naval airplanes to a total of not less than three thousand.

The President of the United States is hereby further authorized to acquire and convert or to undertake the construction of the following auxiliary vessels:

(a) Three destroyer tenders, a total of twenty-seven thousand tons light displacement tonnage;

(b) Two submarine tenders, a total of eighteen thousand tons light displacement tonnage;

(c) Three large seaplane tenders, a total of twenty-five thousand tons light displacement tonnage;

(d) Seven small seaplane tenders, a total of eleven thousand five hundred and fifty tons light displacement tonnage;

(e) One repair ship of nine thousand five hundred tons light displacement tonnage;

(f) Four oil tankers, a total of thirty-two thousand tons light displacement tonnage;

(g) One mine layer of six thousand tons light displacement tonnage;

(h) Three mine sweepers, a total of two thousand one hundred tons light displacement tonnage; and

(i) Two fleet tugs, a total of two thousand five hundred tons light displacement tonnage.

There is hereby authorized to be appropriated, out of any money in the Treasury of the United States not otherwise appropriated, such sums as may be necessary to effectuate the purposes of this Act, which purposes shall include essential equipment and facilities at navy yards for building any ship or ships herein or heretofore authorized.

There is hereby authorized to be appropriated, out of any money in the Treasury not otherwise appropriated, the sum of $150,000,000 to be expended at the discretion of the President of the United States for the construction of experimental vessels, none of which shall exceed three thousand tons standard displacement, and the sum of $3,000,000 to be expended at the discretion of the President of the United States for the construction of a rigid airship of American design and American construction of a capacity not to exceed three million cubic feet either fabric covered or metal covered to be used for training, experimental, and development purposes.[35]

Within this macroprogram, the Hepburn Board prioritized the development of a secondary air base at Isla Grande in San Juan harbor, with facilities for one carrier group and with plans for another; facilities for two patrol plane squadrons, within original plans for at least four such squadrons; pier berthing for one carrier; and facilities for complete engine overhaul. Most importantly, a breakwater was to be built at the harbor entrance, given the fact that "the wide harbor mouth permits the entrance of ocean swells into the area needed for patrol-plane take-off." The result was that such operations were "dangerous." Additionally, Isla Grande was to be provided with berthing space and fuel storage for submarine operations in the Caribbean.[36]

US naval aviation in general, and the facilities at the Canal Zone, Guantanamo Bay, Puerto Rico–Culebra–Isla Grande, and Saint Thomas in particular, had come a long way from the uncertain time before the First World War to the Hepburn Board Report and the 1938 Naval Expansion Act. Its pioneers included navy men such as Bradley A. Fiske and Washington Irving Chambers. They were instrumental in effecting the technologization of the conservative US naval establishment, evidenced by the establishment of the Office of the Chief of Naval Operations and the Bureau of Aeronautics in 1915 and 1921, respectively. Moreover, they were among the fathers of US naval aviation. Chambers, as head of a navy board, got the board to recommend that naval aviation must attain the ability to serve the fleet throughout the world. This would be best achieved "away from the coast" of the United States, namely at bases far offshore.[37]

Working with well-known civilian aviators such as Eugene Ely and Glenn Curtiss, these naval officers pioneered experiments in integrating naval aviation with the fleet, especially the development of the attack aircraft carrier. The Flying Beat, the hydro-aircraft, and the catapult—all essential mechanisms in the process of harnessing aviation for sea operations—began to take shape in the model basin of the Washington Navy Yard and at sea.

As early as 1913, the USS *Mississippi* was assigned to work out exclusively "the problems relating to the use of the aircraft with the Fleet." An aircraft station was established at Pensacola in Florida for the purpose of training officers and men for the navy's Air Service and for conducting experiments "to develop the aircraft that can operate with our Fleet across the open sea." By 1916, a new experimental battleship, the USS *North Carolina*, was already using aircraft and kite balloons; was fitted with catapults; and had on board the latest four types of aircraft developed for sea operations. In addition, eight other armored cruisers were in the process of being fitted out, while scout cruisers were being designed to carry aircraft.[38]

Not without opposition from the old battleship-first-of-the-line school of Alfred Thayer Mahan and the air-power-first school of William Mitchell, the turning point for the acceptance of naval aviation as an adjunct to the naval force and sea power came between 1926 and 1935. The USS *Lexington* and *Saratoga* were commissioned as aircraft carriers. The Bureau of Aeronautics also acquired in 1930 a thousand planes that had been authorized in 1926. Instrumental in effecting these and other developments was William Pratt, who became chief of operations in 1930. Between January 23 and 27, 1929, Pratt commanded the so-called Black Fleet in an attack on the PCZ in war gaming. The highlight was the role of the USS *Saratoga*. It demonstrated successfully the concept of the Fast Carrier Task Force in naval warfare.[39] This set the stage for the encounters in the Pacific against Japan during the Second World War. The laboratory for these war games in the interwar period was the Caribbean Sea near the PCZ, Guantanamo Bay, Saint Thomas, and Puerto Rico.

Puerto Rico as Headquarters of the Caribbean Sea Frontier in the Second World War[40]

It was during the Second World War that Puerto Rico attained its apogee as the headquarters of a sea area called the Caribbean Sea Frontier (CSF). Moving "away from the coast" of the United States, the CSF was the first of three concentric rings. The second was the Hemispheric Ring, defined in a US war plan called Rainbow 5; and the third was the Global Ring, elaborated in a plan known as ABC-1. To position Puerto Rico and the CSF in context, it is first necessary to establish the second and third perimeters of Rainbow 5 and ABC-1.

As I have shown in *War, Cooperation, and Conflict*, two important reports on strategic options, one British and the other American, formed the immediate background to ABC-1. The British report was handed to the first sea lord in early September 1940 by a committee headed by Admiral Sir Sidney Bailey, a high-ranking admiralty officer. The Bailey Committee report formed the basis of a fresh round of talks on war planning in London during September and October 1940 with a visiting team of US special advisers sent by Roosevelt. The team was headed by Admiral Robert L. Ghormley, assistant chief of naval operations.

The second strategic assessment was a memorandum on national defense policy presented to Roosevelt by Admiral Harold Rainsford Stark, chief of naval operations, in November 1940. It advanced the Plan Dog concept—the basic strategy that the Allied powers adopted against the Axis powers from 1941 onward. The work of many minds, the Stark document was the most comprehensive analysis of US national military policy since the earlier "Basis for Immediate Decisions Concerning the National Defense" drafted in the hot summer of June 1940 regarding the European theater. It also incorporated the latest information from the Anglo-American staff talks in London.

In a second round of meetings held in Washington from the end of January to the end of March 1941, British and American representatives, not without different emphases, held fast to the overall strategic analyses of the Bailey Committee report and of Admiral Stark. The result was the ABC-1 agreement.

ABC-1 concluded that, in the event the United States entered the war, "the paramount territorial interests of the United States" would dictate a Western Hemisphere–first defense. Accordingly, the United States had at all times to maintain such dispositions of its forces as would "prevent the extension in the Western Hemisphere of European or Asiatic political or Military power." It was agreed that efforts should also be made in general to ensure that the United States would have access to the territorial waters and land bases of the Latin American republics for purposes of hemispheric defense. With defense of the Western Hemisphere ensured, the broad objective would be the defeat of Germany as "the predominant member of the Axis powers" and the maintenance of the security of the United Kingdom.

The Atlantic-European area, therefore, was to be the decisive theater. There, the principal task of US naval forces would be to secure the sea communications of the Allies. This effort was to be centered in the North Atlantic, particularly in the northwestern approaches to the British Isles. Under that concept, the United States' naval effort in the Mediterranean would initially be of secondary importance, although efforts would be directed to prevent the extension of Axis control in that sea area as well as in North Africa. As for Japan, all reasonable steps would be adopted to avoid its intervention in the conflict. If those failed, the policy would be to wage a defensive war in the Pacific theater.

The ABC-1 report contained annexes, two of which were particularly important and related. The first, Annex II, defined the principles of command that were to operate in various delineated theaters. The other, Annex III, was a "United States–British Commonwealth Joint Basic War Plan" that prescribed Atlantic and Pacific areas within which US and British forces would assume the major responsibility for defense. In Annex II, the decisive Atlantic theater was divided into four areas: the United Kingdom and British Home Waters, the North Atlantic, the Western Atlantic, and the South Atlantic. The limits of the first area were described as the "waters to the westward of Longitude 30° West and to the northward of Latitude 43° North and the land areas bordering on, and the islands in, the above ocean area." It was envisaged that a northwestern escort force and the US Navy's Submarine Force Three operating from bases in Halifax, Iceland, and the British Isles would participate in ocean escort and trade protection in the sea lanes between North America and the United Kingdom. In support, US Army land and air forces would be moved to Iceland and Northern Ireland to relieve British forces, while army air units and a token army-reinforced infantry regiment would be established in Britain itself. The army commitments in the British Isles and in Iceland were to be undertaken after September 1, 1941. The British, however, were to provide the major naval, air, and land forces.

Great Britain was given responsibility for the North Atlantic and South Atlantic areas. In the North Atlantic, Force H (Gibraltar) of the Royal Navy was to carry the major burden of defense. This would consist of one battleship, one battle cruiser, one aircraft carrier, one six-inch cruiser, and eight destroyers, assisted by a special Gibraltar and Straits force of seven destroyers and land and air forces of the British Army and Royal Air Force in that sector. Their main task was to protect the sea communications of the associated powers in and around the western Mediterranean and the Atlantic bounded to the north by latitude 43 degrees north; to the south by latitude 20 degrees north; to the west by longitude 40 degrees west; and to the east by the coastline of Spain, Portugal, and West Africa by longitude 5 degrees west.

In fulfillment of this objective, however, the plan provided for an initial commitment of a US naval force of ten old submarines at Gibraltar, with provision for an additional seven by July 1, 1941. Moreover, after September 1, 1941, a US Gibraltar force comprising three battleships, one carrier, four eight-inch cruisers, thirteen destroyers, and twelve patrol-type seaplanes, together with the abovementioned submarine contingent, was to relieve the British naval forces in this area by transfer from the Pacific. That, however, would be contingent on the overall situation in the Pacific and the Atlantic closer to that time.

In contrast, the US commitment to the defense of the South Atlantic continued to follow peacetime conditions. It was apparently made contingent on the acquisition of suitable bases there, presumably in northeastern Brazil. The South Atlantic zone was delimited as the area between latitudes 20 degrees north and 25 degrees south, and between longitudes 74 degrees west and 33 degrees east, together with the islands and land areas contiguous thereto. It was to be covered primarily by the South Atlantic forces of the Royal Navy, whose strength consisted of one carrier, one seaplane carrier, five eight-inch cruisers, seven six-inch cruisers (two of them old), fourteen armed merchant cruisers, six corvettes, and six sloops.

The area of primary US responsibility, corresponding to the definition of the zone as one of "paramount territorial interests," would be the western Atlantic. It was defined as the Atlantic Ocean area, together with islands and contiguous continental land areas, north of latitude 25 degrees south and west of longitude 30 degrees west, except the area between latitudes 20 degrees north and 43 degrees north that lies east of longitude 40 degrees west.

Within this defined Western Hemisphere, US naval forces were to operate from their own territories as well as from British/Canadian territory and British territory in the western Atlantic and Caribbean, to protect the sea communications of the associated powers. Also, they were to protect the territory of the associated powers and to prevent the projection of enemy power into the Western Hemisphere via the Atlantic-Caribbean "stepping stones." To that end, they were to be ready to occupy the Portuguese Azores and Cape Verde Islands.

The plan proposed certain dispositions of US naval forces, with assistance from those of the associated powers, chiefly Britain and the Netherlands. Depending on the Pacific war front, a US naval force was carded to strengthen the western Atlantic forces by July 1, 1941. That force would consist of three eight-inch cruisers and six destroyers of the 1,850-ton type for ocean escort; four six-inch cruisers for the hunting force; three old submarines for the submarine force; and twelve patrol-type seaplanes for general assignment.

ABC-1 also assigned certain tasks to the US Army, assisted by the naval forces of the United States and her allies. The army was to help repel any external and internal attack on the Western Hemisphere by the enemy. Such help was to include engaging in the "Secret War" against enemy agents. Finally, the army was to build up its United States forces in anticipation of an eventual transatlantic offensive against Germany.

Total US Army strength in the continental United States consisted of two cavalry divisions, two armored divisions, and twenty-seven infantry divisions, with appropriate army, corps, and General Headquarters reserves. Of those, a reinforced corps of three infantry divisions was normally maintained as a reserve for the support of overseas garrisons and of the Latin American republics. The principal overseas garrisons were at the Panama Canal, Puerto Rico, and Newfoundland, with estimated force strengths on April 1, 1941, of twenty-three thousand, twelve thousand, and one thousand troops, respectively. Finally, the plan called for a maximum of four infantry divisions and two armored divisions to be trained and equipped by September 1, 1941, to effect, together with the land forces of the associated powers, the overseas responsibility of the Allies in the western Atlantic area.

Although the details were not finalized until about mid-1941, ABC-1 envisioned a US-dominant command structure over all areas in the Atlantic and Pacific, particularly in the western Atlantic. This was spelled out in the US plan, Rainbow 5. This plan was one of five US war plans dating back to 1938–1939. They reflected to some extent a push by US planners to stretch the "American Lake" lines of Guantanamo Bay–Puerto Rico–Saint Thomas to embrace territories owned by European powers in the Caribbean. This stretching of the strategic line was referred to as the Quarter-Sphere. Ultimately, however, the planners envisaged an even wider stretching to include other territories owned by Denmark, Spain, and Portugal.

In 1918, the US Navy's General Board had identified British-owned Bermuda, the Bahamas, and Jamaica; French-owned Martinique and Guadeloupe; and Dutch-owned Curaçao as potentially valuable for acquisition by the United States, or for the United States to resist any change of ownership to a different European power.[41] Of these, Curaçao was a refinery point for petroleum originating from Venezuela. So, too, was British-owned Trinidad, which herself had petroleum resources of some significance. The United States had included both of these islands in her First World War scheme and was prepared to protect them against any attack by German cruiser submarines.[42]

Between 1918 and 1939, the United States' gilt-edged assessment of the British- and Dutch-owned Caribbean shot up when British Guiana and Dutch Guiana emerged as world-class producers of bauxite, and important suppliers of this commodity for aircraft production to the United States.[43]

In the run-up to World War II, the United States achieved a first lodgment in the European-owned Caribbean when Britain "secretly" leased her base facilities in Bermuda, Saint Lucia, and Trinidad, in connection with an unneutral scheme to establish a "Neutrality Patrol" in the Caribbean and western Atlantic on the eve of war. With the outbreak of hostilities, the patrol was implemented not only for the inner Caribbean but for a wider hemisphere.[44] Puerto Rico, Saint Thomas, Guantanamo Bay, and the PCZ were involved in all of this. Indeed, the patrol exposed the deficiencies of Guantanamo as a first-class base in the Caribbean and pointed out the need for a suitable alternative. Samaná Bay, Vieques Sound, and Trinidad were among the alternatives suggested, with Trinidad rated as the best "from a standpoint of location and ultimate possibilities."[45]

Developments in the war in Europe from May–June 1940 into early 1941 provided the United States with opportunities to lodge herself in both the British territories and the French ones. The "secret" leases in respect of Bermuda, Saint Lucia, and Trinidad were expanded into the well-known Destroyers for Bases Agreement of September 1940 and March 1941. Britain, in return for some old US destroyers from World War I that were badly needed to counter the Axis blitzkrieg, gave the United States the right to construct naval and air bases in a "stepping-stone" series of eight British transatlantic territories: Newfoundland, Bermuda, the Bahamas, Jamaica, Antigua, Saint Lucia, Trinidad, and British Guiana.[46]

The coming to power of the pro-German Vichy regime after the fall of France led the United States to establish a virtual protectorate over Martinique, Guadeloupe, and French Guiana under an agreement of November 1940 with Admiral Georges Robert, Vichy's man-on-the-ground. Of vital importance to the United States, the agreement anaesthetized some US$250–$300 million of Bank of France gold and some French warships, including the *Béarn*, an aircraft carrier, that had ended up in Martinique in June 1940.[47]

Another victim of the German victories in Europe in the summer of 1940 was the Netherlands, the colonial power in oil-refining Curaçao and Aruba and in bauxite-rich Dutch Guiana (Surinam). By mid-1941, US-Dutch talks were in a preparatory stage, and they were to conclude in a formal US lodgment in these territories in late 1941–early 1942.[48]

Rainbow 1 anticipated such a US lodgment in the British, French, and Dutch Caribbean, as well as in Natal and other points on or adjacent to Brazil's bulge; in Samaná Bay; and on the Caribbean coast of Colombia and Venezuela. The plan assumed that in the event of aggression in Europe by the Axis powers, the democracies of western Europe, mainly Great Britain and France, as well as the republics of Latin America, would remain neutral and that the United States would be left alone to resist an external attack. In such a scenario, the plan stated that the United States should adopt a "Quarter-Sphere"

Headquarters of the Caribbean Sea Frontier

Aerial photographs of the Tenth Naval District in San Juan, 1942 (Archivo General de Puerto Rico)

strategy, deploying its forces from base facilities in American-owned and non-American-owned territories primarily in the circum-Caribbean area.[49]

Rainbows 4 and 5 were really extensions of Rainbow 1. Rainbow 4 called for US defense of the entire Western Hemisphere, including the Caribbean Sea and western Atlantic Quarter-Sphere defined by Rainbow 1. Contemplating the classic situation of World War I in which the United States would again have to link up with Britain and France in war against a common enemy, Rainbow 5 not only called for everything in Rainbow 1 and 4 to be done, but ultimately for the United States to intervene militarily in "either or both of the African or European continents in order to effect the defeat of Germany, or Italy, or both." This was the nucleus of the "Europe-first" strategy that was laid down in ABC-1 in March 1941 before the United States entered the war.[50]

Although the Caribbean Sea Frontier, with Puerto Rico as its headquarters, was formally promulgated on February 26, 1942, in the heat of the Battle of the Caribbean against German U-boats, its conception dated back to Rainbow 5 of May 29 and June 2, 1941, and even earlier.

Puerto Rico had been the headquarters of the US Tenth Naval District since January 1, 1940. The district's boundaries then embraced all island possessions of the United States in the Puerto Rico–Culebra–US Virgin Islands area and all waters between the seventeenth and twentieth parallels of north latitude and between longitude 63-18 west and the western meridian of longitude of the Mona Passage, *exclusive of foreign territorial waters*. On January 8, 1941, and again on July 1, 1941, the limits were redefined to include the leased bases in the British transatlantic territories, except Bermuda and Newfoundland.[51]

By secret directive, Serial 071912 of July 1, 1941, under Rainbow 5, the chief of naval operations brought into being the Caribbean Naval Coastal Frontier (CNCF).[52] The term "Coastal Frontier" designated areas that were geographically contiguous and in which command could be shared between the navy and army. The naval division was called the Naval Coastal Frontier, and the army division the Defense Command. Puerto Rico was the base for the navy and Panama that for the army. Accordingly, the terminologies reflected a tension between the navy and army as to who should have overall command. That was decided in favor of the navy in that it was a naval officer who was given the rank of commander, Caribbean Naval Coastal Frontier, based in Puerto Rico.[53]

In turn, the CNCF was divided into three sectors: Guantanamo, Puerto Rico, and Trinidad. The limits of the Guantanamo sector were west of a line passing through Cape Isabela and Beata Point, Hispaniola, extended to cut the northern and southern coastal frontier boundaries.[54] The sector also embraced the Naval Defensive Sea Area and Airspace Reservations created by Executive Order no. 8749 of May 1, 1941, to wit:

> The airspace over the Guantanamo Naval Reservation and over the territorial waters within Guantanamo Bay between high-water mark and the sea in and about the entrance channel within a line bearing true south extending three nautical miles from the shore line of the eastern boundary of Guantanamo Naval Reservation, as laid down in the Agreement between the United States of America and the Republic of Cuba signed by the President of Cuba on 16 February, 1903, and by the President of the United States on 23 February, 1903, a line bearing true south extending three nautical miles from the shore line of the western boundary of the said Naval Reservation, and a line joining the seaward extremities of the above two bearing lines.[55]

The Puerto Rico sector's limits were east of the eastern boundary of the Guantanamo sector and northward of the fifteenth parallel of north latitude.[56] Here, too, the limits encompassed the Naval Defensive Sea Area and Airspace Reservation for Culebra, established by Executive Order no. 8684 of February 14, 1941. This joint area was defined as "the airspace over the island of Culebra, Puerto Rico and over the territorial waters between the extreme high-water mark and the three-mile marine boundary surrounding it."[57] The third sector, Trinidad, was delimited to the area lying east of the eastern boundary of the Guantanamo sector and south of the fifteenth parallel of north latitude.[58]

Under Rainbow 5, the CNCF was one of four interlocking Coastal Frontiers established on July 1, 1941. The others were the North Atlantic Coastal Frontier, divided into New England, New York–Philadelphia and the Chesapeake Bay, and British-leased Newfoundland and Bermuda; the Southern Coastal Frontier, divided into the Carolinas, Florida, and the Gulf of Mexico and including the British-leased Bahamas; and the Panama Coastal Frontier, with fronts on both the Pacific Ocean and the Caribbean Sea.[59]

Following the Japanese attack on Pearl Harbor and in response to the German U-boat offensive against US, Allied, and neutral shipping in United States and Caribbean waters in early 1942, the CNCF was redesignated the Caribbean Sea Frontier (CSF) on February 26, 1942, with the same three sectors of Puerto Rico (headquarters), Guantanamo, and Trinidad.

With US forces stationed in the British and Dutch Guianas by then, the boundary was demarcated as

> a line running westwards on the 25th parallel of north latitude to the Meridian of 72 degrees west longitude, thence to a point on the north coast of Cuba in

approximately latitude 2247 north, longitude 7947 west, thence westerly around the shore of Western Cuba and easterly along the shore to Cienfuegos Light in latitude 3203 north, longitude 8072 west (this placed the entire land area of Cuba, Isle of Pines, and other small islands [coastal] of Cuba in the Caribbean Sea Frontier), thence south to a point in latitude 1805 north, longitude 8027 west, thence to Punto de Gallinas, Colombia, latitude 1228 north, longitude 7140 west, thence along the international boundaries to include all of Venezuela, British Guiana, Surinam, and French Guiana to and including the eastern boundary of French Guiana. No eastern limit was given.[60]

Following the entry of US forces into oil-important Aruba and Curaçao on February 11, 1942, a virtual fourth sector of the CSF was established in the form of the Command All Forces, Aruba and Curaçao, or CAFAC, on April 1, 1942. The boundaries of the CAFAC were defined "as a circle of 200 miles radius, centered on a point between Aruba and Curaçao at latitude 1225 north, longitude 6930 west, including the South American continent."[61] A final adjustment to the CSF cleared up an anomaly in which French Martinique and Guadeloupe, under Vichy rule, were split between the Trinidad and Puerto Rico sectors, respectively. By directive 181520 dated April 19, 1942, Admiral Ernest J. King, commander in chief of the US Fleet and chief of naval operations, placed both French islands within the Puerto Rico sector.[62]

With further minor adjustments, the preceding defined the boundary of the CSF until its declaration as a noncombat zone on May 28, 1945. Until then, the CSF, with Puerto Rico as headquarters, interlocked with the hemispheric system of Rainbow 5 and the global ABC-1.[63] Among the naval and civilian personnel who helped shape Puerto Rico's centrality in the CSF and its wider rings during World War II were Vice Admiral John W. Greenslade, Rear Admiral Raymond A. Spruance, Vice Admiral John H. Hoover, and Charles W. Taussig.

A monograph is badly needed about the former three, although Hoover is the subject of an oral manuscript in the US archival system.[64] Also, we learn a bit about him from Vice Admiral Jesse B. Oldendorf's orally based history, "As Seen from the Bridge: Glimpses along the Sea Road to Tokyo as Seen by an Admiral Enroute."[65]

Born in Ohio in 1880, Greenslade graduated from the US Naval Academy in 1899, seeing action in both the Spanish-American War and the Philippine insurrection between 1898 and 1902. From World War I to his retirement in December 1945, he assumed what became a dual career: naval man-of-action combined with naval administration and training. The former path took him through the ranks to that of vice admiral in 1938, a rank he held until his retirement. The latter saw him as secretary and treasurer of the US Naval Institute, 1915–1917, where he authored several articles and addresses on naval subjects; head of the Department of Ordinance and Gunnery in 1917; inspector of ordinance in charge of the US Naval Proving Ground and the Powder Factory in Maryland and Virginia from 1920 to 1923; head of operations at the Naval War College, Newport, Rhode Island, from 1926 to 1928; aide to the secretary of the navy in 1930; and member of the General Board of the United States Navy in 1931–1932, 1934–1936, and 1939–1941.

As a senior member of the General Board of the Navy, Greenslade helped negotiate the US-Vichy Agreement of November 1940 that virtually neutralized the French Caribbean territories, until the removal of the local Vichy authorities under Admiral Robert in the middle of 1943. Next, he led a US team of experts that selected the actual sites for the US bases to be built in the British transatlantic territories, under the Destroyers for Bases Agreement of September 1940. He also figured in the ensuing complex Anglo-American negotiations that pinned down the terms of the leases in March 1941. By then, he was heading a board that was reevaluating US needs for shore establishments, pursuant to the Hepburn Report of 1938. Via these activities, Greenslade and his associates had input in defining the CSF and its interlock with Rainbow 5 and ABC-1.[66]

Spruance, first as captain and then as rear admiral, headed the Tenth Naval District at Puerto Rico between February 26, 1940, and July 31, 1941. He laid the foundations for the establishment of the CNCF on July 1, 1941, and of the CSF in early 1942.[67]

Spruance's successor at Puerto Rico from August 1, 1941, to the end of the war was John H. Hoover. He was the first commander of the CNCF and its successor, the CSF. From Oldendorf, his subordinate in the Trinidad sector and the CAFAC during 1942, we learn that he was "not a particularly small man, but ... slight of build." He was "shy"; he had gray hair and dark, piercing eyes; he read a good deal; and he could outplay his younger staff in tennis.[68]

From his Joint Operations Center in a bomb-proof structure in a moat at Fort San Cristóbal in San Juan, Hoover coordinated the war effort of the CSF in the Battle of the Caribbean of 1942–1943.[69] To better wage that battle as well as to protect the secrecy of Operation Torch, the Allied landing in Vichy- and German-controlled Morocco in November 1942, he put the squeeze on the Vichy French Caribbean territories from February 1942 to early 1943. A freeze was imposed on the movement of French commercial shipping between the United States and the French territories, as well as within Caribbean waters. Also aided by the Allied "theft" of copies of a new Vichy cryptosystem from the French embassy in Washington in June 1942, Hoover and his superiors were able to monitor the cyphers of the Vichy Caribbean authorities in this critical 1942–1943 period.[70]

Finally, with the tide of the war moving in favor of the Allies by mid-1943, Hoover was instrumental in easing Admiral Robert and his *Vichyites* out of Martinique, Guadeloupe, and French Guiana.[71] At every stage, he had plans to invade the French possessions if their authorities did not comply with Allied security demands.[72]

Hoover and his superiors were gracious, too. Admiral Robert and his party were routed through Puerto Rico on their way back to France. Hoover helped Robert undergo an operation at the Naval Hospital in Puerto Rico during his stay.[73] Also, the French admiral and his party were given some US$10,000 toward living expenses soon after their arrival in Puerto Rico on July 16, 1943.[74] Additionally, the State Department paid Robert $2,240, equivalent to his salary and cash allowances as high commissioner of the French Antilles, from July 1 to November 1, 1943. The sum was to help Robert meet his San Juan expenses and incidental expenses during his repatriation voyage. Likewise, Robert's aide, Lieutenant de Vaisseau P. de Boutiny, was given $1,220.[75]

Playing a vital complementary role to these naval men in the CSF was a civilian, Charles W. Taussig. He was instrumental in establishing the Anglo-American-Canadian Caribbean Commission in the heat of the Battle of the Caribbean, on March 9, 1942. Historically, Taussig is remembered for building the Caribbean Commission into a postwar regional agency of Great Britain, France, the Netherlands, and the United States to manage "economic democracy" and decolonization in the dependent Caribbean.[76] However, the commission was forced into being in March 1942 as part of the effort of the CSF to turn back the determined German U-boat warfare.[77]

To this end, the commission and the CSF collaborated to structure a remarkable land-sea "bridge" through the Caribbean area. The "bridge" provided for the establishment of an emergency food cache to supply the numerous islands of the Caribbean in case of need due to enemy action. The governments of Cuba, Haiti, and the Dominican Republic as well as the colonial authorities of the Allies cooperated in this project.

Although more expensive than the regular route, the wartime land-sea "bridge"

> was both a military asset and a help to the Navy; it eliminated between 700 and 800 miles of water travel; [and] it permitted the use of schooners and small vessels, not available for long hauls, to transport supplies across the Florida Strait, the Windward Passage, the Mona Channel, and the Virgin Islands Passage. Water

transportation tied in with the railroad haul from Havana to Santiago de Cuba, and truck haul from Port-au-Prince, Haiti, across the Hispaniola Road to the eastern tip of Santo Domingo.[78]

Needless to say, the Puerto Rico–Culebra–US Virgin Islands link was part of the bridge. So, too, was the chain of British and Dutch territories within the CSF. From the onset of operations in mid-1942 to January 16, 1943, the United States–Cuba–Hispaniola–Puerto Rico–Jamaica tier moved the following cargoes:[79]

	Long Tons
Merchandise passed through Santiago stock pile	22,948
Merchandise moved from Florida to Havana	13,097
Merchandise moved from Baltimore and Mobile to Santiago de Cuba	7,822
Merchandise moved from Santiago to Puerto Rico	6,158
Merchandise moved from Santiago to Jamaica	4,575
Merchandise moved from Santiago to Port-au-Prince	304
Merchandise moved from San Pedro de Macoris to Puerto Rico	1,086

The carriers of the above included ten Cuban, seven Jamaican, six Dominican, and two Canadian crafts of an aggregate capacity of 9,226 tons. Between July 1942 and October 23, 1943, some 32,808 short tons of supplies moved across the above bridge, over 57 percent of it to Puerto Rico and the US Virgin Islands.[80] Likewise, in the two years up to late 1945, the Schooner Pool of the Eastern Caribbean, with its headquarters in Barbados, pulled together 120 vessels to carry another 250,000 tons of freight between the smaller West Indies islands.[81]

Thus, small and big actors alike played their part in the CSF-led war effort in the Caribbean in World War II. Today, the region covered by the CSF is part of the hemispheric Organization of American States and the North Atlantic Treaty Organization. In retrospect, the First World War and the ensuing years saw the first stage of this eventual interlock, consequent on the advent of the airplane and submarine. The next stages occurred during the Second World War, with Puerto Rico holding center stage as the headquarters of the Caribbean Sea Frontier.

Notes

1. Foreign Office (F.O.) 371/24239, Release to the press and other media of May 16, 1940, of the text of the president's message to Congress by Stephen Early, secretary to the president.

2. F.O. 371/30505, A1022/320/51, "The Strategic Significance of the Overseas Possessions of Continental European States for British-American Sea and Air Power," Balliol College, Oxford, December 30, 1941, pp. 1–4, 5, 2–6.

3. Ibid., pp. 2–7.

4. For the expression, see General Board of the US Navy (GBN) 414.3:780, January 24, 1918, "Ownership of Islands and Reefs Pending in Pacific Ocean and Elsewhere," pp. 2–3. The document was sent by Admiral Charles J. Badger, the GBN's senior member present to the navy secretary, Josephus Daniels. Attached to the document are three enclosures dated October 13, 1917, by Rear Admiral Albert P. Niblack of Division One, Battleship Force, US Atlantic Fleet, USS *Alabama* (flagship). See also National Archives, GBN 414-3, August 6, 1917, "Sovereignty and Control over Certain Islands and Harbours in Caribbean Panama."

5. Fitzroy André Baptiste, *War, Cooperation, and Conflict: The European Possessions in the Caribbean, 1939–1945* (Westport, CT: Greenwood Press, 1989), pp. 29–32 (petroleum), 115–117 (bauxite).

6. F.O. 371/24255, "Findings of a U.S. Senate Committee," John H. Godfrey, British director of naval intelligence, section 2 for the expression.

7. For the term *Anglesachsentum*, see Holger H. Herwig, "Prelude to Weltblitzkrieg: Germany's Naval Policy toward the United States of America, 1939–1941," *Journal of Modern History* 43, no. 4 (December 1971): 649–668. Although used in the context of the Second World War, the term is relevant to the First World War and its antecedents.

8. J. A. S. Grenville, "Diplomacy and War Plans in the United States, 1890–1917," *Transactions of the Royal Historical Society*, 5th ser., 2 (1961): 1–21.

9. Lester Brune, *The Origins of American National Security Policy: Sea Power, Air Power, and Foreign Policy, 1900–1941* (Manhattan: MA/AH Publishing, Kansas State University, 1981), pp. 1–30.

10. The Maginot Line was the land-based French system built to deter Nazi Germany prior to World War II, although it wasn't of much use.

11. National Archives, Record Group (R.G.) 80, Box 64 (PD 170-3 to 170-10), papers on the defense system against cruiser hostile submarines covering the period February to June, 1918.

12. National Archives, R.G. 80, Box 64 (PD 170-10), letter op. 28, December 27, 1917, from the navy secretary to the secretaries of state, treasury, commerce, and labor and to the chairman of the War Shipping Board and War Trade Board. Regarding the Panama Canal Zone, see the following documents issued by President Woodrow Wilson: "Protection of Panama Canal: Rules and Regulations for Regulation, Management and Protection of Panama Canal and Maintenance of Its Neutrality: A Proclamation," May 23, 1917 (US Official Bulletin, no. 18, p. 5); and "Executive Order Establishing Defensive Areas for Panama Canal Terminal Ports," August 27, 1917 (US Official Bulletin, no. 99, p. 8). National Archives.

13. Mat. 7 E/3/19, 4405-127, March 20, 1919, J. S. McKenn, acting chief of naval operations, to the General Board, Naval War College and Bureau of Yards and Docks, enclosing a report dated March 6, 1919, from Baker, US Naval Radio Station, San Juan (hereafter Baker Report). The report referred to a number of charts of Puerto Rico and the Virgin Islands: C. & G.S. Charts nos. 904, 920, 922, and 948.

14. John Child, "From 'Color' to 'Rainbow': U.S. Strategic Planning for Latin America, 1919–1945," *Journal of Interamerican Studies and World Affairs* 21, no. 2 (May 1979): 233–259; and John Child, "Strategic Concepts of Latin America: An Update," *Inter-American Economic Affairs* 34 (1980): 61–82.

15. GBN 404:707, May 25, 1917, p. 2. The report was sent to the navy secretary by Admiral Charles Badger of the General Board. In turn, the navy secretary returned it to the General Board for filing on April 5, 1917 (Op-17-BM 288690-57, 2nd endorsement). Note, too, that Cox proposed the acquisition of Samaná Bay in the Dominican Republic "in the present emergency and to deny it to an enemy." He described Samaná Bay as "an excellent harbor with ample anchorage for the fleet in operations in the Eastern Caribbean," p. 2. National Archives.

16. GBN 404:707, May 25, 1917, p. 3.

17. Ibid., pp. 3–4, citing GBN 427:605, para. 7, of November 1, 1916.

18. Baker Report. The Oliver Report, the essentials of which were incorporated into the Baker Report, is at GBN 404, "White, USS *Vixen* at 'A Port in the West Indies,'" November 1, 1917, to navy secretary (via chief of operations and General Board), with C. & G.S. Chart no. 917 enclosed (hereafter White Report); Commandant James H. Oliver to navy secretary (via the same channels) no. 42-3, November 5, 1917; W. V. Pratt, acting chief of naval operations, no. 8616-3, Op. 23, November 17, 1917, to GBN; and F. L. Sandoz, secretary, GBN, to navy secretary, December 29, 1917 (2nd endorsement). The 1917 and 1919 documents used the spelling "Porto Rico." National Archives.

19. Baker Report, p. 4-16.

20. Ibid., pp. 3-13 (Puerto Rico), 5-21 (Samaná Bay).

21. White Report, pp. 2-7, 2-8; and Baker Report, pp. 2-5, 2-6, including the 1,400-mile front.

22. White Report, p. 1-5.

23. Baker Report, p. 1-2.

24. Ibid., p. 3, 12(a) and 12(b). See also White Report, p. 3, 15(a) and 15(b).

25. Baker Report, p. 2-9; and White Report, p. 2-11.

26. Baker Report, pp. 2–3, 10; and White Report, pp. 2–3, 12. Regarding aircraft, White noted in 1917 that "the developments of later years seem to indicate that soon aircraft will be able, in one flight, to reach from the northeast corner of the Carriban [sic] Sea as far as Colon, Key West or Narragansett Bay."

27. Baker Report, p. 4-15.

28. Ibid., p. 4-16.

29. Ibid., p. 4-14.

30. Ibid., p. 3-11.

31. For this, see Brunson MacChesney, *International Law Situation and Documents, 1956: Situation, Documents and Commentary on Recent Developments in the International Law of*

the Sea, Naval War College, NAVPERS 15031, vol. 46 (Washington, DC: Government Printing Office, 1957), pp. 156–207. According to MacChesney, Great Harbor, Culebra, and Guantanamo Bay were declared closed harbors in 1904 and 1912, pp. 156–157. The same Executive Order of September 23, 1912 (no. 1613), also declared the two to be Airspace Reservation Areas, pp. 194–200.

32. GBN papers, for copy submitted by the navy secretary to the speaker of the House of Representatives by letter dated December 27, 1938. It was printed as H.R. Doc. no. 76-65, January 3, 1939. The survey was authorized by an act of May 17, 1938, Pub. L. no. 528, 75th Cong., National Archives.

33. H.R. Doc. no. 76-65, January 3, 1939, pp. 25–36, 150, with cross-reference to pp. 16–17, 51–61.

34. Ibid., pp. 36, 151, for the quotations.

35. Ibid., pp. 37–38. H.R. no. 9218 was coded Pub. L. no. 528, 75th Cong., chapter 243.

36. Ibid., pp. 15–16, 53–54.

37. Brune, *The Origins of American National Security Policy*, n. 9, for the quotation.

38. Desmond P. Wilson, "Evolution of the Air Attack Carrier: A Case Study in Technology and Strategy" (Ph.D. diss., Michigan Institute of Technology, 1966), chapter 2; and Vincent Davis Jr., *The Politics of Innovation: Patterns in Navy Cases* (Denver: University of Denver Press, 1967), chapter 5, pp. 43–47. Josephus Daniels examines the roles that he and Franklin D. Roosevelt played as navy secretary and assistant navy secretary, respectively, during World War I, in the history of US naval aviation in his study *The Wilson Era* (Chapel Hill: University of North Carolina Press, 1944, 1946), vol. 1, pp. 288–296; vol. 2, pp. 122–123, 253, 567–570. On the USS *North Carolina*, see National Archives, R.G. 45, Box 164 (June 8–September 15, 1916), file for June 16–22, 1916, letter dated June 19 from the commanding officer to the navy secretary.

39. Brune, *The Origins of American National Security Policy*, pp. 73–74; Wilson, "Evolution of the Air Attack Carrier," pp. 27–28, 41; and Davis, *The Politics of Innovation*, pp. 46–47.

40. Unless otherwise stated, this discussion is based on Baptiste, *War, Cooperation, and Conflict*, chapter 7, pp. 75–83.

41. GBN 414.3:780, January 24, 1918, "Ownership of Islands and Reefs Pending in Pacific Ocean and Elsewhere," pp. 8, 17(a). Also evaluated as possible US acquisitions were Samaná Bay in the Dominican Republic; the Isle of Pines in Cuba; Magdalena Bay, Mexico, in a swap to Mexico for a US naval station at Pichilinque Bay, Baja California; Serrana Bank (or Serrana Key), including Southwest Cay, North Cay, Narrow Cay, South Cay, and East Cay on San Andrés and Providencia Islands, Colombia; Serranilla Bank (or Keys), the ownership of which was said to be unclear; Cocos Island, Costa Rica; La Orchila, Venezuela; and the Pearl Islands (Gulf of Panama) and Shepherd Island (Almirante Bay) in Panama, pp. 8–19. In addition to the Mariana, Caroline, and Marshall Islands, the Pacific evaluation included Agnes Island (just off the coast of Queensland, Australia); Johnston Island; Gente Hermosa (Swains) Island; Howland Island; Baker Island; Jarvis Island; Christmas Island (Kirimati); Washington Island; Palmyra Island; Clipperton Island; and the Galapagos Islands, pp. 5–8, 10–16, 10 (g–h).

42. National Archives, R.G. 80, Box 64 (PD 170-3 to 170-10).

43. Fitzroy André Baptiste, "The Exploitation of Caribbean Bauxite and Petroleum, 1914–1945," *Social and Economic Studies* (Institute of Social and Economic Research, University of the West Indies, Mona) 27, nos. 1–2 (March–June, 1988): 107–140. Special issue on Caribbean economic history, edited by Barry Higman.

44. Baptiste, *War, Cooperation, and Conflict*, pp. 3–5, 17–20.

45. Ibid., p. 27.

46. Ibid., pp. 51–62.

47. Ibid., pp. 63–74.

48. Ibid., pp. 29–38, 115–140.

49. Ibid., pp. 5–6.

50. Ibid., p. 6.

51. Ibid., p. 104.

52. Ibid.

53. Ibid., p. 80.

54. Ibid., p. 82.

55. MacChesney, *International Law Situation and Documents*, pp. 205–206, 163.

56. Baptiste, *War, Cooperation, and Conflict*, p. 82.

57. MacChesney, *International Law Situation and Documents*, pp. 205, 162.

58. Baptiste, *War, Cooperation, and Conflict*, p. 82.

59. Ibid., pp. 80–81.

60. Ibid., p. 147.

61. Ibid., pp. 148–149.

62. Ibid., p. 148.

63. Ibid., p. 215.

64. John H. Hoover, "The Reminiscences of Admiral John H. Hoover," as told to John T. Mason Jr., interviews 3, 4, and 28, October 1963 and December 2, 1963, Oral History Research Office, Columbia University, New York, and deposited in Operational Archives, Washington Navy Yard, Washington, DC.

65. Jesse B. Oldendorf, "As Seen from the Bridge: Glimpses along the Sea Road to Tokyo as Seen by an Admiral Enroute," as told to Hawthorne Daniel, Oral History Research Office, Columbia University, New York, and deposited in Operational Archives, Washington Navy Yard, Washington, DC.

66. Baptiste, *War, Cooperation, and Conflict*, pp. 72–74, 85, 171–172, 176, 178, 190 (US-Vichy agreement known as the Robert-Greenslade Agreement), 85–93, 101, 105, 116, 218 (board of experts to select the base sites), 79–83, 86, 103–105, 218 (Shore Establishment Board Report).

67. Ibid., pp. 104–105, 108, 177.

68. Oldendorf, "As Seen from the Bridge," p. 14. For Oldendorf's comments about Spruance, see p. 2.

69. Baptiste, *War, Cooperation, and Conflict*, pp. 141–169; and Gaylord T. M. Kelshall, *The U-Boat War in the Caribbean* (Port of Spain: Paria Publishing Company, 1987).

70. Baptiste, *War, Cooperation, and Conflict*, pp. 180–190. The author supervised a Caribbean Studies paper by Jacqueline Plummer, a Martinican student, at the University of the

West Indies, Saint Augustine (Trinidad). The student tapped both oral and written French-language sources.

71. Baptiste, *War, Cooperation, and Conflict*, pp. 191–214.

72. Ibid., pp. 183, 185, 186 (Plans Bungalow, Decanter, Frap, Frigid, Mudbath, and Package of 1942), 211 (Plan Guadeloupe of 1943).

73. Victor Braegger, Swiss consular agent, Puerto Rico, letters dated August 30 and September 7, 1943, to his Washington, DC, legation; sent by A. B. Cook, commander, CSF, to the vice chief of naval operations, September 21, 1943, as CCSF/EF 28-21, Serial 0871; Operational Archives, Washington Navy Yard, Washington, DC. Although Hoover had demitted his command on August 12, 1943, he helped facilitate Robert's operation.

74. James Forrestal, acting navy secretary, to secretary of state, 087713 (SC) EF28-21, op-13/eah, July 7–8, 1943 (arrival of Robert and party); and James Forrestal, acting navy secretary, to secretary of state, 091712 (SC) EF28-21, op-13A/eah, August 12, 1943 (recommendation to pay the money on Hoover's last day in his comment; it was approved).

75. Ralph A. Bard, acting navy secretary, to secretary of state, 0124013 (SC) EF28-21, op. 13-B/hjm, October 15–16, 1943. Again, Hoover had a hand in this before his departure.

76. Fitzroy André Baptiste, "The Federal Process in the West Indies as Seen by the United States, 1947–1960," paper presented at the symposium to commemorate the fiftieth anniversary of the 1947 conference to launch the federal experiment at Montego Bay, Jamaica; University of the West Indies, Mona, November 6, 1997, pp. 5–8.

77. Baptiste, *War, Cooperation, and Conflict*, pp. 152–153.

78. R.G. 844.00/6-445, Box 6042, Folder 2, State Department internal memo dated June 4, 1945, taken from a report of the War Food Administration, Office of Distribution, March 1944, entitled "Report of Operations of the Caribbean Emergency Program, July 1942 to December 1943," testimony of Colonel R. W. Olmstead, deputy director, Office of Distribution, War Food Administration, March 14, 1944, before the Subcommittee on Insular Affairs, House of Representatives, 78th Congr., 2nd sess. The information was compiled into a booklet, "Investigation of Political, Economic, and Social Conditions in Puerto Rico," covered in hearings on "the Land-Water Route" before the congressional committee on March 14, 15, 21, and 23, 1944. National Archives.

79. Ibid.

80. Ibid.

81. R.G.844.00/10-2445, Box 6042, folder 3; American Consulate, Saint George's, Grenada, to secretary of state, dispatch 354, October 24, 1945, with enclosures of photographs of the schooners and seamen, "traffickers" and stevedores, involved in the pool. The Grenada consulate had collected the data with a view to getting the authorization of the State Department to publish the story in *National Geographic*; the author cannot say whether this happened.

War and Political Transition in Puerto Rico, 1939–1940

Jorge Rodríguez Beruff

Robert Hayes Gore was Franklin Delano Roosevelt's first nominee for governor of Puerto Rico. Gore was a successful Florida newspaperman who had devised an ingenious fund-raising scheme named Shareholders in America, which promoted small contributions to FDR's 1932 presidential campaign and also provided the candidate with valuable publicity. Gore thus financed FDR's campaign in Florida and the US Virgin Islands. After the election, he actively sought the post of commissioner of the Internal Revenue Service. It seems, however, that he disqualified himself by making a controversial and embarrassing statement during a social event in Havana in January 1933 that elicited the response of the city mayor. He told the group of Cuban functionaries and notables that FDR would send an "army" to Cuba if the government did not put the house in order. He was referring to the embattled authoritarian regime of Gerardo Machado, which fell just a few months later. His nomination to the Puerto Rican governorship was a second best, at a time when other attractive patronage posts were being filled by the administration.[1]

Apart from his role in the election, Gore had no other known qualifications for the post, as he had no previous knowledge of Puerto Rico or the Caribbean, or administrative experience in government. His attitude to the governorship is reflected in a letter he wrote to FDR on April 22, 1933, expressing his interest in the job.

> I do want to be Governor General of Porto Rico. I have a reason. I go to Florida each winter because I cannot stand the cold dry atmosphere of the north due to a rhinitis condition of my throat and nose. Moreover, I have nine children and

President of the Senate Luis Muñoz Marín, 1940s (Archivo Fundación Luis Muñoz Marín)

six of them are still in school, and I want them to have the opportunity to learn Spanish, which I believe is important in view of our possibilities in South and Central America.

Almost as an afterthought, Gore added that he would also have "the opportunity to do some real constructive work for this country and for the people of those islands."[2]

His brief governorship was a resounding failure. Under his administration, the worsening economic situation resulted in heightened social and political turmoil. He totally aligned himself with the Coalición, an electoral alliance made up of the Union Republican and Socialist Parties that had won a plurality in the 1932 election, while alienating Antonio R. Barceló, the leader of the Liberal Party, the single largest party in Puerto Rico. Luis Muñoz Marín, another prominent leader of the Liberal Party, waged an unrelenting and effective campaign against Gore in Washington and Puerto Rico. Gore made provocative statements in favor of mass migration of Puerto Ricans to Florida, endorsing statehood, proposing cockfighting as a "national sport," and reestablishing English as the medium of instruction in public schools.³ With regard to this last point he dismissed José Padín, a capable commissioner of instruction, generating a political storm.

Powerful political and economic interests, particularly those linked to the sugar industry, demanded that a strong-handed governor be named to replace Gore. James Beverley, Gore's predecessor, explicitly recommended a former military officer and mentioned retired general Blanton Winship. It was in this context of a perceived breakdown of order in Puerto Rico that Winship, a former judge advocate general of the army, was named governor in late 1934.⁴

Winship studied at Mercer University in Macon, Georgia, later earning a law degree at the University of Georgia. He entered the army in 1898 and made a colonial career in the Philippines, Cuba, and Mexico and in Europe. He served in the Philippines from 1899 until 1902. He was in Cuba after the military intervention ordered by Theodore Roosevelt in 1906 that imposed the provisional administration of Charles Magoon, serving from 1906 to 1909 on the advisory commission to revise Cuban laws presided over by Colonel Enoch Crowder. From 1912 to 1916, he was with General Frederick Funston during the US intervention at Veracruz, Mexico, as Funston's officer in charge of civil affairs. Winship was in France from 1917 to 1923 and was awarded the Distinguished Service Cross for extraordinary heroism in Lachausee, France.

After the conclusion of hostilities in November 1918, Winship was made director general of services for the settlement of all claims in Europe arising out of US military activities. He was in Washington in November 1925, when he was named a member of the military court that court-martialed Brigadier General William (Billy) Mitchell for insubordination. (Ironically, Mitchell received many honors following his death in 1936.)

In May 1927, Winship was appointed military aide to President Calvin Coolidge, in which capacity he served until January 1928, when he was relieved of his detail in order to comply with orders designating him as legal advisor to the governor-general of the Philippines. General Winship was appointed judge advocate general on March 1, 1931, with the rank of major general. He retired on November 30, 1933, before then coming to Puerto Rico.⁵

He came to Puerto Rico with Colonel Elisha Francis Riggs (a close acquaintance of the powerful senator Millard Tydings), who took over the direction of the Puerto Rican police. Riggs was also a veteran of the First World War; he had served in the US Embassy in Petrograd during the Russian Revolution and had experience in military intelligence. Riggs had served in Nicaragua in the campaign against Augusto César Sandino.⁶ General Winship and Colonel Riggs promptly undertook to fulfill the role for which they had been chosen—to forcefully restore order. From late 1935, a violent confrontation developed between the Winship administration and the radicalized Nationalist Party, led by Pedro Albizu Campos. In retaliation for a police attack on Nationalists in Río Piedras that left four Nationalists dead, Riggs was assassinated by two young Nationalists in February 1936, escalating the conflict even further. On March 21, 1937, the police attacked an unarmed Nationalist march in Ponce that left nineteen dead and more than one hundred wounded. This incident, known as the Ponce Massacre or the Palm Sunday Massacre, was the bloodiest act of political violence in Puerto Rico's recent history. An American Civil Liberties Union (ACLU) report issued shortly after the event placed the blame on Winship's administration, particularly on the governor himself.[7] The Ponce Massacre had major repercussions in Washington and San Juan. Roosevelt, against the advice of Harold Ickes, the secretary of the interior, decided not to sponsor an official investigation of this bloody incident.

It should be noted that policy toward Puerto Rico was not based only on strong-arm measures taken by Winship to repress the Nationalist Party. It also consisted of federal relief initiatives to address dire social conditions and rising unemployment provoked by the Great Depression. For this purpose, the Puerto Rico Emergency Relief Administration (PRERA) was created in 1933, and, subsequently, the Puerto Rico Reconstruction Administration (PRRA) under the direction of Ernest Gruening, a powerful functionary of the Department of the Interior. The PRRA was established as a substitute for the PRERA, but it had a wider role and a bigger budget. Control over the PRRA, and direct access to FDR, gave Ernest Gruening considerable influence in Puerto Rican affairs, a fact that Harold Ickes, formally his superior, strongly resented. After the Riggs assassination, Gruening, whose relationship with Luis Muñoz Marín had always been rocky, finally broke with him and established a close liaison with Winship and the *coalicionista* leadership. The federal administration also partially endorsed a reformist blueprint proposed by a Puerto Rican committee, known as the Plan Chardón, but its main recommendations were not implemented due to the entrenched opposition of the sugar industry and the Coalición.

The repression of the Nationalist Party and the apparent reestablishment of order in Puerto Rico were Winship's main claims of success. However, his governorship had been seriously undermined by the events in Ponce and faced major challenges in 1938, including a prolonged dock workers strike and the resurgence of Nationalist violence. On July 25, 1938, the governor organized a parade in Ponce, where the Ponce Massacre had occurred, to commemorate the fortieth anniversary of the arrival of US troops in Puerto Rico. A small group of Nationalists attacked the reviewing stand where Winship was positioned, surrounded by government functionaries and Coalición politicians. A total of thirty-six persons were wounded. National Guard colonel Luis Irrizary and Nationalist Ángel Esteban Antongiorgi were killed. The incident was a major security disaster and a blow to Winship's credibility. The recurrence of Nationalist violence was not the only factor contributing to political instability. The policy of excluding Muñoz Marín and the proindependence and reformist wing of the Liberal Party after Riggs's assassination in the process of forming a new political movement was also an element in the political equation. In addition, Winship's Puerto Rican political allies, the ruling Coalición, had clearly fallen out of grace with important political functionaries in Washington, mainly with Harold Ickes.

The deteriorating situation in Europe, underscored by the Munich crisis in September 1938, soon posed the Roosevelt administration with the dilemma of whether to retain the problematic General Winship as governor of Puerto Rico during a period that would require social and political stability to provide a favorable environment for defense preparations, or replace him with a more effective functionary. The strategic debate intensifying in the United States regarding the military importance of the Caribbean placed great stress on the need to ensure stability in all regional societies. The governor knew of the defense plans for the Caribbean and Puerto Rico that were beginning to be formulated, and he sought to present himself as the right man to oversee their implementation.[8] However, he was dismissed in 1939, and his replacement by Roosevelt's closest naval adviser, Admiral William D. Leahy, was not merely a change of functionaries but part of a broader redefinition of Washington's approach to Puerto Rico that created conditions for major political changes in the island's politics.

The transition from the governorship of General Blanton Winship to that of Admiral William D. Leahy in the opening days of World War II was a complex and drawn-out process that really began in 1938. By March 1, 1939, President Roosevelt had informed Admiral Leahy, then chief of naval operations, that he would be appointed governor of Puerto Rico once he passed into retirement. FDR gave Leahy the unexpected news of his new assignment while cruising near San Juan aboard the USS *Houston* at the conclusion of the Fleet Problem XX naval maneuvers that were being held in the Caribbean at the time.[9] More than six months would elapse before Leahy took the oath of office in San Juan in early September 1939. Winship, closely allied with the governing Coalición, resisted all attempts to obtain his resignation until he was unceremoniously dismissed by Roosevelt.

Roosevelt's choice of Admiral Leahy was by no means casual. Apart from holding the country's highest naval post, he was a trusted friend and close adviser. They had met in 1913 when Roosevelt was assistant secretary of the navy and Leahy a young officer in the Personnel Division. In 1915, Leahy's command of the USS *Dolphin*, the secretary's personal dispatch ship, brought him into closer contact with Roosevelt and his family. During the 1930s, Leahy's naval career, which had brought him to the post of chief of naval operations, was promoted by the president. Although Leahy had only visited Puerto Rico briefly in 1921, he had considerable experience in the Caribbean. He was a veteran of the decisive Battle of Santiago de Cuba during the Spanish-American War, served in Panama during the construction of the canal, and took part in the 1912 intervention in Nicaragua. In 1916, he participated in the military interventions in Haiti and the Dominican Republic under Rear Admiral William B. Caperton. According to Leahy, Roosevelt informed him that he would be recalled from Puerto Rico in case he needed him for other tasks related to the war. This was precisely what happened when he was removed from the governorship and named to the delicate post of ambassador to Vichy France. Later during the Second World War he occupied high posts such president of the Joint Chiefs of Staff and the Combined Chiefs of Staff.[10]

President Roosevelt announced at a press conference on May 12, 1939, that he would name Admiral William D. Leahy to the governorship of Puerto Rico. The following day, *El Mundo*, the local San Juan newspaper with the island's largest circulation, carried the news in bold letters as the main front-page story with a photograph of Leahy and a brief biographical sketch. The story mentioned his interest in Puerto Rico's strategic value and that he would be taking office in July.[11] In a brief letter to Ruby Black, Jesús T. Piñero, the president of the Association of the Sugar Cane Industry, claimed that a cablegram was handed to a visibly surprised Winship while he was taking a siesta, informing him of his dismissal. The Coalición reacted to the loss of such an important ally by interrupting the legislative caucus in order to "mourn" the decision with Winship at La Fortaleza, the governor's official residence.[12]

Winship's "Resignation"

On May 14, *El Mundo* followed up on the story by reporting that the decision to dismiss Winship had been based on the "need to eliminate all sources of dissension" due to the "growing importance of Puerto Rico in national defense."[13] It also reported that more than $30 million would be devoted to defense preparations in 1940 and a total of $200 million would be invested over the coming five years (1940–1945). Leahy would "head and coordinate the enormous national defense projects."[14] It was claimed that the base construction program was part of a broader and ambitious plan to "industrialize" Puerto Rico, and for this purpose the staggering amount of one billion dollars would be assigned over the next twenty years![15] The US press also attributed Leahy's nomination to strategic military considerations regarding defense plans for Puerto Rico and the Caribbean.[16]

As Vito Marcantonio, an influential left-wing congressman for New York, argued, the surprise announcement was equivalent to dismissal, since Winship had not resigned despite Ickes's considerable armtwisting.[17] Winship's letter of resignation is dated June 3 and says that he had been thinking about resigning for about a year but "for different reasons had postponed the request."[18] This letter received a polite reply from the president two days later, thanking him for his "long and distinguished career in the service of [his] government" and for his "most arduous task" in the governorship of Puerto Rico.[19] Ickes recorded in his diary Winship's stonewalling on the issue of his resignation:

> I cabled on Thursday Governor Winship, asking him to send in his resignation so as to take effect in time for Admiral Leahy to take over as Governor on September 1. I had not received any reply from Governor Winship before I left Washington late Friday afternoon. Neither have I received an acknowledgement of the earlier radiogram that I sent him, telling him that Admiral Leahy would be prepared to take over on September 1.[20]

Ickes had been insistently trying since April 1939 (a month before Roosevelt's announcement of his intention to name Leahy) to obtain Winship's resignation. Ickes met Winship on April 27 to discuss Puerto Rican affairs. When the issue of his resignation came up, Winship defended his record in "a long recital." He argued that he was willing to resign but still had "to dispose of a large number of bills." Ickes then requested that he should still hand in his resignation effective on the date when he estimated that pending matters would be settled. But Winship was adamant and said that he would like to discuss the issue with the president. Winship also attacked Puerto Rico's attorney general, Benigno Fernández García, for his handling of the Capitol Racket scandal. Consequently, Ickes called the president and asked him to stand firm on Winship's resignation.[21]

On May 3, Roosevelt received a memorandum from his personal secretary about Winship's reluctance to resign, noting that "Secretary Ickes is very anxious that this be accomplished in this definite manner" (i.e., before the governor returned to Puerto Rico). The memo also said that Leahy had to be confirmed before Congress adjourned for the summer, in order to be able to draw his governor's salary.²² Another memorandum of that day said: "Secretary Ickes has just phoned me that General Winship is in town. Secretary Ickes told the General that his resignation was desired, and suggested that he resign effective as of a future date at which time he could clear up everything of an urgent nature there."²³

Winship met Roosevelt the following day. On that day, prominent Puerto Rican politicians of the governing *Coalición* alliance Rafael Martínez Nadal and Miguel Angel García Méndez, and entrepreneur Alfonso Valdés, all cabled Roosevelt expressing their support for the governor.²⁴ Resident commissioner Santiago Iglesias also wrote praising Winship and requesting that he should continue in his post, to which Roosevelt answered on May 12, saying that "some time ago I determined to make Admiral Leahy Governor of Puerto Rico when he went on the retired list."²⁵ During his meeting with Roosevelt, Winship apparently managed to persuade him that it was inopportune to resign while under fire from Representative Vito Marcantonio.

In a letter to Roosevelt dated April 27—the same day that Ickes was meeting Winship—Marcantonio had accused Winship of corruption in the awarding of a $75,000 contract to Frederick R. Graves, a friend of the governor, for the design of the plans for a dry dock to be built in San Juan. Marcantonio claimed, among other things, that the plans were practically a copy of a set of plans drawn four years earlier in the office of the commissioner of the interior.²⁶ He also gave a speech at the Confederation of Puerto Rican Societies in New York calling for Winship's immediate removal.²⁷ Roosevelt referred Marcantonio's letter to Ickes on May 11 instructing him to investigate the charges. The following day, he proceeded to announce that he would be replacing Winship.

Ickes was incensed at Roosevelt's incapacity to extract an immediate resignation from Winship during his meeting of May 4: "I resent the fact that the President authorized me to ask for Winship's resignation and then refused to back me up." He blamed Marcantonio's anti-Winship campaign for Roosevelt's reticence.²⁸ But he did not let up in his pressure on the governor, making public on May 5 that Puerto Rico had lost $2,735,000 earmarked for the Las Garzas hydroelectric project due to the refusal of the *coalicionista* legislature to approve the required legislation.²⁹ In his press release, Ickes blamed the legislature for sacrificing social and economic development and the potential employment of thousands of workers.³⁰

Winship, on the other hand, felt that he had won another round in his fight with Ickes. The day after he met the secretary, *El Mundo* quoted the governor as saying that rumors about his possible resignation were "foolish."³¹ On May 9, *El Mundo* again reported on the issue of the resignation, saying that

Admiral William D. Leahy and Governor Blanton Winship share a lively moment at the New York World's Fair, circa 1934. (Colección *El Mundo*, University of Puerto Rico)

Winship had decided to retain the governorship "indefinitely" and that, consequently, Marcantonio had decided to attack him on the floor of the House.[32] Thus, Roosevelt's statement of May 12 replacing Winship with Leahy was generally interpreted as a major victory of Marcantonio's attacks on Winship during April and early May. These attacks could have precipitated events, but Winship's fate had been sealed at least since the president's conversation with Leahy aboard the *Houston* on March 1, 1939.

The decision, however, was based on broader considerations such as the perceived continued instability of Puerto Rican politics, the corruption scandals and growing political difficulties with the Coalición, the negative impact of US policy toward Puerto Rico on US and Latin American public opinion, and the consequent urgent need to revise colonial policy in view of strategic and national defense considerations. The existing arrangement, strongly conditioned by the need to contain Nationalist and proindependence militancy in the early and mid-1930s, was no longer considered a desirable framework for the implementation of the ambitious defense plans that were being formulated in late 1938 and early 1939. According to Leahy, FDR's instructions included taking measures for an improvement of social conditions and overseeing defense preparations in the Caribbean. In his memoirs, Leahy was extremely critical of Rafael Martínez Nadal and the Puerto Rican elite he allegedly represented.[33]

Winship's close alignment with the Coalición, his reputation as a repressive colonial administrator, the insistent accusations of corruption, and his evident reluctance to follow instructions emanating from Washington, particularly from Harold Ickes, not only disqualified him as an acceptable agent for a change in policy but also transformed him into a political liability. To Ickes, who never liked him, the envoy had become too "creolized" and was acting as a "puppet" of the real strongman: Rafael Martínez Nadal, president of the Puerto Rican Senate and main leader of the Union Republican Party.[34] President Roosevelt was fully cognizant of the Puerto Rican political situation, which he had closely followed since his first term, and of Winship's difficulties, when he offered the governorship to Admiral Leahy.

Reactions to Winship's Removal

Understandably, the leadership of the Coalición interpreted Winship's removal as a major political blow engineered by the hated secretary of the interior that could foreshadow a major and negative shift in Washington policy. Another important setback was FDR's almost simultaneous decision to remove Ernest Gruening from Puerto Rican policy making by naming him governor of Alaska. Rafael Martínez Nadal's recent controversial declaration regarding "fascist control" over Puerto Rico by the United States, published by the *New York Times* on March 27, could be interpreted as an outburst not against US colonial control in general, but against the undesired meddling of the secretary of the interior.[35] It is interesting that in his tirade, which compared US policy to that of the Russian czars and the German Nazi leaders, Martínez Nadal said that it had been the practice of the Americans to construct new leaders when the old ones were no longer useful to the colonial regime.[36] Army intelligence took due note both of Martínez Nadal's statement and of the fact that it was extensively quoted in an April 11 Radio Berlin broadcast, a summary of which was published by *El Mundo*.[37]

The displeasure of the Coalición was evident. After his return from Washington, Winship, following instructions received during his trip, called an extraordinary session of the legislature just as the White House announced his removal from the governorship. It had the purpose of approving financial aspects of the Las Garzas hydroelectric project, restoring several posts at executive agencies eliminated by the legislative majority as retaliation for the Capitol Racket investigation, and securing cuts of about 10 percent in the budget.[38] However, only eight senators attended the session, and it was reported that it would conclude without any action.[39]

The large Las Garzas project was part of the restructuring of hydroelectric and power facilities promoted by Ickes since the mid-1930s with the government's acquisition of the Ponce Electric Company. In late 1938, Martínez Nadal had refused to sign a letter to Ickes making a commitment to approve the required legislation.⁴⁰ An important bone of contention was the jurisdiction over the project by the Consultative Board for Emergency Measures (Junta Consultiva de Medidas de Emergencia) created by the legislature. In February 1939, in response to a point in Winship's address to the legislature, Martínez Nadal again reiterated his refusal to eliminate the Consultative Board from the legislation.⁴¹ Unlike the Senate president, House speaker Miguel Ángel García Méndez signed the letter, and the House of Representatives approved legislation in a form acceptable to Ickes. The Senate refused to go along and approved a law without the required provisions. The Las Garzas project was reportedly related to "national defense plans," and Washington functionaries had threatened to have Congress approve a "little TVA in Puerto Rico" in case the Puerto Rican legislature did not approve the required legislation.⁴²

On the other hand, on February 14 the Justice Department under Benigno Fernández García concluded its investigation of the Capitol Racket and submitted its findings to Secretary Ickes. The investigation had been carried out by Assistant Attorney General Enrique Campos del Toro. Since October 1938, he had faced all sorts of obstacles in the course of his inquiry.⁴³ After being interrogated by Campos del Toro, Antonio Pomalles, Martínez Nadal's secretary, committed suicide. The report revealed blatant irregularities in the administration of the legislature, among which was that only about 100 of the body's 356 employees actually worked. The top Coalición leadership—including Bolívar Pagán and Alfonso Valdés—were mentioned in the report as responsible for the scandal, and a Socialist senator, Sixto A. Pacheco, was charged as liable to criminal prosecution.⁴⁴

The Coalición responded by launching a legislative investigation of the Justice Department and stepping up its attacks on Fernández García and Campos del Toro.⁴⁵ During the hearings at the legislature, Campos del Toro refused to submit himself to questioning by Bolívar Pagán. They came close to a physical encounter as Pagán charged that the accused legislators were "more decent" than some functionaries in the Justice Department, while Campos del Toro refused to obey Pagán's order to take a seat.⁴⁶ Campos del Toro subsequently demanded that Winship take action against "administrative and political immorality" or he would travel to Washington to report on the situation.⁴⁷ The *Liberales* decided to boycott the rest of the legislative session because of the attack on the Justice Department.⁴⁸ The scandal continued to attract political attention throughout April 1939 as the Coalición legislature decided not to appropriate funds for a large number of posts in the Justice Department and even eliminated the post in the Lottery of Puerto Rico occupied by Socialist senator Epifanio Fiz Jiménez's wife.⁴⁹ It was Epifanio Fiz Jiménez, a dissident of the majority political formation, who first blew the whistle in 1938 on legislative corruption and later published his charges in a book.[50]

Parallel to the Capitol Racket scandal, Representative Marcantonio continued his attacks on corruption by Winship and Treasurer Leslie A. McLeod even after the announcement of the former's removal. On August 5, in a long speech in the US House of Representatives entitled "Five Years of Tyranny in Puerto Rico," he called the governor the "Nero of the Caribbean." The speech's title possibly made reference to a February speech by Bolívar Pagán entitled "Five Years of Governor Blanton Winship in Puerto Rico" that said, among other things, "Mr. Winship . . . friend No. 1 of our island and our people." Pagán's speech, which sharply contrasted with Marcantonio's view of things, had been inserted in the *Congressional Record* by Santiago Iglesias, Puerto Rico's resident commissioner in Washington.[51] In his speech, Marcantonio denounced Winship's repressive record, reiterated his charges regarding Frederick R. Graves, and claimed that the governor had five official automobiles (compared to one for the governor of New York) and had used over $225,000 in public funds for personal patronage while there were no funds for school lunches.[52]

Government corruption thus became, in 1938 and 1939, a crucial issue that would plague the Coalición in the campaign for the 1940 elections. The Popular Democratic Party (Partido Popular Democrático, PPD) effectively exploited the issue in its campaign, stressing corrupt electoral practices, particularly the buying of votes. It also insistently claimed that there was no fundamental difference between the Coalición and Tripartismo (Tripartite Union).[53] The latter was a new political formation made up of the dissident factions of the Coalición parties and the anti-*muñocista* wing of the Liberal Party, which was seen by Washington, particularly by Harold Ickes, as an acceptable and preferred alternative to the governing Coalición.

House Speaker García Méndez's speech of July 4, 1939, calling for the "union of the Puerto Rican family" was, among other things, designed to distance himself from charges of corruption and indirectly place the blame on the other leaders of the Coalición. Contemporary observers interpreted the emergence of the Tripartismo (of which García Méndez was already unofficially a key actor) as a response to rampant corruption. Luis Muñoz Marín (founder of the PPD) observed in his memoirs that "[t]he stated purpose of what was called *Tripartismo* was to moralize [*adecentar*] Puerto Rican life. The word itself had a certain superficial tone of neat *señoritos* with regard to certain political and administrative procedures, alien to demands for [a] profound social transformation."[54]

On May 17, Martínez Nadal again reacted to the adverse political developments by stating that Puerto Ricans were being treated as "puppets" of US policy.[55] Two days later, the Coalición bestowed honors on Winship, officially declaring him an "adoptive son of Puerto Rico" in a legislative resolution that also emphasized Puerto Rico's strategic importance.[56] The University of Puerto Rico, also controlled by the Coalición, decided to grant the outgoing governor an honoris causa doctorate.[57] San Juan's "high society" honored Winship as a hero at several receptions and cocktail parties: at Colonel Manuel Font's residence, the Lion's Club, the Berwind Country Club, the YMCA, and so on. Manuel González, a wealthy Galician businessman, also organized a farewell party at the Condado Hotel, which he owned.[58] He later became a close friend of Winship's successor.

As a further act of defiance, the legislature approved a resolution demanding statehood, despite the fact that the proposal of Santiago Iglesias, the Coalición's resident commissioner in Washington, to make Puerto Rico an incorporated territory had not progressed in Congress.[59] There were also clear signs that the Roosevelt administration did not wish the "status" question to be posed at all in the context of the rapidly deteriorating international situation.[60] On June 26, Iglesias introduced legislation in Congress entitled "To Enable the People of Puerto Rico to Form a Constitution and State Government and Be Admitted into the Union on an Equal Footing with the States."[61] Winship also defiantly joined the chorus in favor of statehood during a meeting of a statehood association at the Escambrón Beach Club, one of the many events organized in his honor.[62] He promised to promote from private life "complete membership" of Puerto Rico in the United States.[63]

The official *Liberales* and the *Populares*, on the other hand, welcomed Winship's removal. José Ramírez Santibáñez, Antonio R. Barceló's successor as head of the Liberal Party, publicly expressed satisfaction. A change in the governorship would clearly create a more favorable environment for the opposition Tripartista political formation that he was building. Enrique Bird Piñero, a Liberal who subsequently became a close collaborator of Muñoz Marín, described the reception of Leahy's nomination by the *Liberales*:

> The best news arrived several months later: Winship had been relieved of the governorship and would return to Washington to await a new assignment to an important post. He would be succeeded in the governorship by Admiral William D. Leahy.... The implications of the news could not be more positive for us the Liberals: Washington was notifying the Coalición, by removing its great crony Winship, that good times were over. With the Coalición discarded and Muñoz Marín far afield talking to the peasants [*jíbaros*] about independence, the message

was apparently clear: Mr. Ramírez Santibáñez, rally the decent people of the country to the Partido Liberal, and you may win the 1940 elections![64]

To Luis Muñoz Marín, the change in the governorship ended a long struggle that had begun soon after Winship's inauguration in 1934. The general had proven to be a harder nut to crack than his predecessor, Robert Gore. Although Muñoz's strategy for the 1940 elections did not emphasize obtaining Washington's support or making political pacts at the summit of power, a new governor opened the possibility of discussing crucial electoral issues. In 1937, Muñoz had written to Arthur Garfield Hays, the prominent civil liberties lawyer, that "[l]ittle changes in governors or other officials would be simply small change. Little flatteries, such as appointing a Puerto Rican governor, would be like shooting at Madrid with cap pistols. . . . Give us sovereign, irrevocable powers, either as a state or an independent republic—and let us make the choice between those two ourselves."[65]

Muñoz carefully framed his reaction to Leahy's inaugural speech of September 11. He said that the message "merits the approval and sympathy of our people. Leahy can not offer more to our people than what he has offered in his inaugural speech . . . an impartial and friendly attitude toward the different points of view regarding Puerto Rican problems that may be presented to him." He noted his disagreement with Leahy's stance on the application of the Fair Labor Standards Act but added that he was sure that "we will be in agreement with him in many of his objectives" and pledged the support of the Partido Popular.[66] In its October issue, *El Batey*, the official party biweekly, extensively covered a meeting between Muñoz Marín and Admiral Leahy:

> Mr. Muñoz Marín said after his interview with Governor Leahy that he felt this governor was a sensible man and had good intentions to improve the conditions of our people.
>
> *El Batey* advises its readers to have a spirit of sympathy and understanding toward the efforts of the new governor to improve the situation of our people and counsels all to give their cooperation to the governor in the efforts he proposes to undertake for the welfare of Puerto Rico.[67]

Two months after Leahy's inauguration, Muna Lee, Muñoz's wife, wrote to Ruby Black, who was Muñoz's unofficial representative in Washington and a major source of information on federal affairs, that "[i]t is less depressing now than formerly with Governor Leahy . . . really making one feel that he cares about law and order and the Constitution and such things. . . . Luis seems to think that so far Leahy is the best governor the Island has ever had."⁶⁸ By January 1940, initial support by Muñoz of the new governor had become hyperbolic praise:

> Let me tell you something about Governor Leahy. I think he has been by far the best governor that has been sent to Puerto Rico since the beginning of the American Regime. He is the only one that I know who knows how to deal with this situation.⁶⁹

However, the US liberals with whom Muñoz had developed a close relationship of collaboration received the nomination of Admiral Leahy with great misgivings. They were glad to be rid of Winship but had expected a progressive civilian to be named to the post. Instead, to their chagrin, Roosevelt had named a high-ranking naval officer of conservative inclinations. On May 15, the Committee for Fair Play to Puerto Rico, associated with the ACLU, issued a statement criticizing the decision to name a naval officer to a post that dealt with "strictly civilian" matters of "extreme difficulty." The statement also made reference to the exploitation for propaganda purposes of the Puerto Rican situation by the "Nazi press" and the need to name a highly qualified civilian administrator for the governorship.⁷⁰ This statement was the only critical reaction to Leahy's nomination that was reported in the US press, and several conservative newspapers editorialized strongly in favor of Roosevelt's decision.⁷¹

In a letter to Ruby Black, Robert W. Claiborne privately expressed concerns similar to those contained in the ACLU statement. Claiborne was a labor lawyer entrusted by the Roosevelt administration with enforcement of the Fair Labor Standards Act in Puerto Rico and was involved in a sharp confrontation with the Winship government. Politically, he was close to Luis Muñoz Marín, and Ruby Black had lobbied strongly in favor of his nomination to the post of administrator of the Wages and Hours Division of the US Department of Labor in Puerto Rico.⁷² Shortly before the letter was written, Santiago Iglesias had denounced in the US House of Representatives Claiborne's links to Vito Marcantonio and Muñoz.⁷³

> Dear Ruby:
> Thanks to you and the others Winship is out.
> But why the continued "occupation"? A naval Administration is out of the frying pan into the fire.
> The Faschists [sic] are celebrating, for "for the sake of peace and military reasons" they will be protected in their exploitations.

> Loyalty of a frustrated, unsatisfied people quickly switches to anyone that comes along. You have an Ireland here, which in the next war will be a serious problem to the U.S.
>
> How could Roosevelt have failed to send a liberal thinker, and a young man? Guam is being transferred from Navy to Interior, and we get a Naval Officer for Governor, one who however fine his points is of an older school than even Winship, and a damn right stronger, because not feeble mentally.
>
> Is this only an interim appointment, while Roosevelt can be looking for a civilian.[74]

Oswald Garrison Villard, an anti-imperialist journalist who closely followed US policy in Puerto Rico, once again voiced his criticisms in an article in the *Nation* meaningfully entitled "Puerto Rico S.O.S." While saying that he had met Leahy and found him "open-minded and eager to learn," he argued that his nomination to the governorship created the impression that Puerto Rico was not part of the US and "merely a military satrapy." He also commented with irony that "the President thought it would do no harm to have it known in Berlin that an admiral has been put in charge of the Island."[75] The meeting with Leahy to which Villard makes reference was not recorded by the former as a happy one.

> I also received, during this period, a visitation by Mr. Oswald Garrison Villard, a self-styled "liberal" magazine writer, who told me it was wrong to appoint a military man over liberty loving people who wanted only the privilege of self government, and that his group of Liberals would oppose my appointment.
>
> When I related Governor Winship's account of the assassins he said that much could be said in justification of their being only patriots.
>
> I then assured Mr. Villard that if any of the "patriots" attempted to assassinate me they would have no further trouble in this world because they would be dead before they could move their feet. He expressed horror at this barbarous attitude of mine saying that he did not believe an American could so deliberately dispense with the due process of law.[76]

The way the political forces in Puerto Rico reacted to the new governor was prescient of the lines of political conflict during Leahy's brief but crucial period in La Fortaleza. Soon, frictions with the Coalición had become an all-out confrontation as the November 1940 elections approached. It became evident that one of the Admiral's objectives was to end the control over Puerto Rican politics of the ailing caudillo, Rafael Martínez Nadal. Leahy, and quite possibly Ickes, would have preferred to see the Tripartista leader Miguel Angel

García Méndez as Nadal's substitute, but he was an electoral fiasco. It would be Luis Muñoz Marín and the Popular Democratic Party, who were not considered serious political contenders, who would reap the benefits of the conflict. In many ways it was ironic that it was a conservative naval officer, with little sympathy for Muñoz, who would carry out the task of placing Puerto Rico on the path of reformist politics that characterized the war period.

Notes

1. Paul A. Gore, *Past the Edge of Poverty: A Biography of Robert Hayes Gore, Sr.* (Fort Lauderdale, FL: R. H. Gore Company, 1990), chapter 7.

2. Ibid., p. 103.

3. The troubled administration of Gore is discussed in Thomas Mathews, *La política puertorriqueña y el Nuevo Trato* (Río Piedras: University of Puerto Rico Press, 2007), chapter 3.

4. Ibid., p. 111.

5. Biography of Blanton Winship, n.d., personal library of José L. Bolívar Fresneda.

6. Sonia Carbonell Ojeda, "Blanton Winship y el Partido Nacionalista" (master's thesis, University of Puerto Rico, 1984).

7. Jorge Rodríguez Beruff, *Strategy as Politics: Puerto Rico on the Eve of the Second World War* (Río Piedras: University of Puerto Rico Press, 2007), p.178.

8. Blanton Winship, "The Status of Puerto Rico: An Address by General Blanton Winship over the Columbia Broadcasting System from Washington, D.C., March 25, 1939," Puerto Rico Trade Council, Washington, DC, 1939.

9. For Leahy's account of this conversation and of his governorship, see Jorge Rodríguez Beruff, ed., *Las memorias de Leahy: los relatos del almirante William D. Leahy sobre su gobernación de Puerto Rico, 1939–1940* (San Juan: Fundación Luis Muñoz Marín, 2002).

10. Rodríguez Beruff, *Strategy as Politics*, chapter 2.

11. "Almirante Leahy Gobdor. de Pto. Rico," *El Mundo* (San Juan), May 13, 1939, p. 1. See also "Nombramiento de Leahy relacionado con defensa nacional," *El Mundo* (San Juan), May 13, 1939, p. 1; and "Leahy to Succeed Governor Winship," *New York Times*, May 13, 1939, p. 1.

12. Jesús T. Piñero to Ruby Black, May 15, 1939, Ruby Black Collection, Box 4, Folder 13, Document 105, Historical Research Center, University of Puerto Rico, Río Piedras.

13. "Nombramiento de Leahy trata de eliminar fuentes de disensión," *El Mundo* (San Juan), May 14, 1939, p. 1.

14. "Emplearán en la isla más de $30,000,000 en el próximo año," *El Mundo* (San Juan), May 15, 1939, p. 1.

15. "Hay planes para industrializar a Puerto Rico," *El Mundo* (San Juan), May 19, 1939, p. 1.

16. See press clippings on Leahy's nomination in Leahy's scrapbook, William D. Leahy's Papers, Manuscript Division, Library of Congress.

17. "Marcantonio insiste en que Winship fue destituído," *El Mundo* (San Juan), May 12, 1939, p. 5.

18. Blanton Winship, Governor, to the president, June 3, 1939, FDR Library, FDR Papers, OF 400, Container 25, Folder P.R.

19. Franklin D. Roosevelt to Honorable Blanton Winship, Governor, June 5, 1939, FDR Library, FDR Papers, OF 400, Container 25, Folder P.R.

20. Harold L. Ickes, *The Secret Diary of Harold L. Ickes*, vol. 2, *The Inside Struggle, 1936-1939* (New York: Simon and Schuster, 1954), p. 641.

21. Harold L. Ickes, "Secret Diary," Saturday, April 29, 1939, p. 3401, Manuscript Division, Library of Congress. This entry was deleted in the published version of Ickes's diary, *The Secret Diary of Harold L. Ickes*.

22. E. M. W., "Memorandum for the President," May 3, 1939, FDR Library, FDR Papers, OF 400, Container 25, Folder P.R.

23. Ibid.

24. "Cablegrafían dándole respaldo al gobernador Blanton Winship," *El Mundo* (San Juan), May 4, 1939, p. 1; "El cablegrama que dirigió Martínez Nadal a Roosevelt," *El Mundo* (San Juan), May 5, 1939, p. 1; see also *New York Times*, "Winship's Friends Urge His Retention, Believe Sec. Ickes Is Trying to Force Him Out," May 5, 1939, p. 8.

25. Franklin D. Roosevelt to Hon. Santiago Iglesias, May 12, 1939, FDR Library, FDR Papers, OF 400, Container 25, Folder P.R. See also "Nombramiento de Leahy decidido hace algún tiempo," *El Mundo* (San Juan), May 15, 1939, p. 1.

26. Vito Marcantonio to Franklin Delano Roosevelt, April 27, 1939, FDR Library, FDR Papers, OF 400, Container 25, Folder P.R.

27. See translation of article appearing in *La Voz*, May 1, 1939, "Marcantonio Says Winship Should Be Removed," FDR Library, FDR Papers, OF 400, Container 25, Folder P.R.

28. Ickes, "Secret Diary," p. 3417.

29. "Puerto Rico pierde una asignación de $2,945,000," *El Mundo* (San Juan), May 6, 1939, p. 1.

30. "Interior Department Press Release," May 5, 1939, Ruby Black Collection, Folder 13, Document 97, Ruby Black Collection, Historical Research Center, University of Puerto Rico, Río Piedras. The Spanish translation is included in Reece B. Bothwell González, *Puerto Rico: cien años de lucha política*, vol. 3 (Río Piedras: University of Puerto Rico Press, 1979), pp. 195-196.

31. "Blanton Winship calificó de 'tontos' en Nueva York los rumores que circulan en cuanto a que renunciaría como gobernador," *El Mundo* (San Juan), April 28, 1939, p. 1.

32. "Winship decide retener gobernación indefinidamente," *El Mundo* (San Juan), May 9, 1939, p. 1. The *New York Times* carried a similar report that same day (p. 5).

33. Rodríguez Beruff, *Las memorias de Leahy*, pp. 70-71.

34. It should also be noted that, since 1936, Ickes had been somewhat sidelined in terms of Puerto Rican policymaking as Roosevelt had chosen to support the hard-line course drawn by Ernest Gruening and Winship; but a change in the governorship could help him regain a greater degree of control over Puerto Rican policy making.

35. "Sen. Martínez Nadal Charges U.S. with Fascist Control," *New York Times*, March 27, 1939, p. 4; also "Que Puerto Rico está esclavo dijo ayer Martínez Nadal," *El Mundo* (San Juan), March 25, 1939, p. 1.

36. Resident Commissioner Santiago Iglesias inserted Martínez Nadal's controversial speech in the *Congressional Record*. See *Congressional Record Appendix*, April 10, 1939, pp. 5637–5638, Ruby Black Collection, Box 4, Folder 13, Document 77, Historical Research Center, University of Puerto Rico, Río Piedras.

37. Colonel John W. Wright, Commander, Sixty-Fifth Infantry Regiment, "Weekly Summary of Certain Political Activities," March 29 and April 12, 1939, R.G. 165, Military Intelligence Division (MID), 1917–1941, Box 3112, National Archives.

38. "El Gobernador trajo instrucciones de Washington," *El Mundo* (San Juan), May 12, 1939, p. 1.

39. "Hay planes para terminar mañana sesión legislativa," *El Mundo* (San Juan), May 12, 1939, p. 4.

40. Eliseo Combas Guerra, *En torno a La Fortaleza, Winship* (San Juan: Biblioteca de Autores Puertorriqueños, 1950), pp. 242–244.

41. "Martínez Nadal no contribuirá a aprobar ninguna ley que le arrebate facultades al pueblo de un modo indirecto," *El Mundo* (San Juan), February 18, 1939, p. 1.

42. "El gobernador trajo instrucciones de Washington," *El Mundo* (San Juan), p. 1; Combas Guerra, *En torno a La Fortaleza*, pp. 243–246; and Blanton Winship, Governor, to the president, June 3, 1939, FDR Library, FDR Papers, OF 400, Container 25, Folder P.R.

43. Combas Guerra, *En torno a La Fortaleza*, p. 209.

44. Epifanio Fiz Jiménez, *El racket del capitolio (Gobierno de la Coalición repúblicosocialista)* (San Juan: Editorial Esther, 1944); and "Justicia tiene y prácticamente decidido acusar," *El Mundo* (San Juan), April 22, 1939, p. 1.

45. See, for example, "Martínez Nadal le escribe a Gruening que habrá demostraciones si nombran a Fernández García Gobernador interino," *El Mundo* (San Juan), June 9, 1939, p. 1; and "Washington quiere retener a Fernández García," *El Mundo* (San Juan), June 10, 1939, p. 1.

46. "Justicia rechazará hoy ultimatum del Comité legislativo," *El Mundo* (San Juan), April 12, 1939, p. 1; and "Se temió un grave encuentro entre Campos y Bolívar Pagán," *El Mundo* (San Juan), April 13, 1939, p. 1.

47. "Campos del Toro proyecta salir hacia Washington," *El Mundo* (San Juan), April 14, 1939, p. 1.

48. "Los Liberales se retiran de la legislatura," *El Mundo* (San Juan), April 14, 1939, p. 1; and "Winship no logró Liberales volvieran a legislatura," *El Mundo* (San Juan), April 15, 1939, p. 5.

49. "En el Senado se enmienda presupuesto . . .," *El Mundo* (San Juan), April 23, 1939, p. 1.

50. Fiz Jiménez, *El racket del capitolio*.

51. *Congressional Record Appendix*, February 15, 1939, Ruby Black Collection, Box 4, Folder 13, Document 32, Historical Research Center, University of Puerto Rico, Río Piedras.

52. The Spanish version of this important speech is reproduced in Félix Ojeda Reyes, *Vito Marcantonio y Puerto Rico* (Río Piedras, PR: Huracán, 1978), pp. 67–94. See also "Marcantonio Hails Winship Dismissal," *New York Daily Worker*, May 22, 1939, p. 1.

53. "Informe a los campesinos de Puerto Rico sobre el alegado 'racket'—o robalete—del Capitolio," *El Batey* 1, no. 3 (April 1939): 1; and "La nueva Alianza," *El Batey* 1, no. 6 (August 1939): 6.

54. Luis Muñoz Marín, *Memorias, 1898–1940* (San Juan: Inter American University Press, 1982), pp. 185–186. Author's translation.

55. "Aquí somos unos muñecos, dice Martínez Nadal," *El Mundo* (San Juan), May 17, 1939, p. 1.

56. "Winship declarado hijo adoptivo de Puerto Rico," *El Mundo* (San Juan), May 19, 1939, p. 10.

57. "Winship to Get a Degree, Puerto Rico University Adds Governor to Honors List," *New York Times*, May 24, 1939, p. 3.

58. *Puerto Rico Ilustrado*, July 1–18, 1939, photo section.

59. "La asamblea legislativa acordó solicitar estadidad," *El Mundo* (San Juan), May 20, 1939, p. 1; and "Estadidad a la mayor brevedad posible y en el interim gobernador electivo," *El Mundo* (San Juan), June 1, 1939, p. 10.

60. For an analysis of the status proposals presented in Congress during this period, see José Trías Monge, *Historia constitucional de Puerto Rico*, vol. 2 (Río Piedras: University of Puerto Rico Press, 1981), pp. 218–234. He notes that neither Resident Commissioners Santiago Iglesias nor Bolívar Pagán were able to get any action from Congress apart from some minor amendments to the Jones Act (p. 233).

61. "To Enable the People of Puerto Rico to Form a Constitution and State Government and Be Admitted into the Union on an Equal Footing with the States," H.R. 6986, 76th Cong., 1st Ses., June 26, 1939; Ruby Black Collection, Box 4, Folder 13, Document 119, Historical Research Center, University of Puerto Rico, Río Piedras.

62. A huge banner placed above the stage read "Puerto Rico 49th State"; *Puerto Rico Ilustrado*, July 1, 1939, photo section.

63. "Puerto Rico Is Toasted by Winship as 49th State," *New York Times*, June 20, 1939, p. 44.

64. Enrique Bird Piñero, *Don Luis Muñoz Marín, el poder de la excelencia* (San Juan: Fundación Luis Muñoz Marín, 1991), pp. 78–79. Author's translation.

65. Luis Muñoz Marín to Arthur Garfield Hays, June 14, 1937, Ruby Black Collection, Box 3, Folder 11, Document 115, Historical Research Center, University of Puerto Rico, Río Piedras.

66. "Muñoz Marín comenta el discurso de Leahy, la cooperación que ofrece el Partido Popular al gobernador," *El Mundo* (San Juan), September 12, 1939, p. 6.

67. "Muñoz Marín conferencia con el nuevo gobernador Leahy," *El Batey* 1, no. 8 (October 1939): 4. Author's translation.

68. Muna Lee to Ruby Black, November 8, 1939, Ruby Black Collection, Box 4, Folder 12, Document 151, Historical Research Center, University of Puerto Rico, Río Piedras.

69. Luis Muñoz Marín to Ruby Black, January 8, 1940, Ruby Black Collection, Box 5, Folder 14, Document 2, Historical Research Center, University of Puerto Rico, Río Piedras.

70. The statement was signed by Oswald Garrison Villard, president, Professor William L. Nunn, vice president, Earl P. Hanson, Carleton Beals, Arthur Garfield Hays, Representative Vito Marcantonio, Rockwell Kent, Walter McK Jones, Vilhjalmur Stefansson, Charlotte Leeper, David Rein, Gifford Cochran, and Mr. and Mrs. Bourne. See "Press Statement," American Civil Liberties Union, May 15, 1939, Ruby Black Collection, Box 4, Folder 13, Document 103, Historical Research Center, University of Puerto Rico, Río Piedras.

71. See, for example, "Governor Leahy," *Providence Bulletin*, May 16, 1939; "Liberties Union against Leahy" (editorial), *Miami Herald*, May 16, 1939; and "Changing Governors in Puerto Rico," *New York Herald Tribune*, May 16, 1939.

72. See the numerous letters of recommendation for this post, among them those of Ruby Black and Luis Muñoz Marín, Ruby Black Collection, Box 4, Folder 12, Documents 70–111, Historical Research Center, University of Puerto Rico, Río Piedras.

73. See comments by Santiago Iglesias, May 11, 1939, Ruby Black Collection, Box 4, Folder 13, Document 101, Historical Research Center, University of Puerto Rico, Río Piedras.

74. Robert W. Claiborne to Ruby Black, May 13, 1939, Ruby Black Collection, Box 4, Folder 13, Document 102, Historical Research Center, University of Puerto Rico, Río Piedras.

75. Oswald Garrison Villard, "Puerto Rico S.O.S.," *Nation*, June 21, 1939, pp. 728–729. See also Villard's previous article, "Liberty and Death in Puerto Rico," *Nation*, April 3, 1937, pp. 371–373.

76. William D. Leahy, "Sailor's Adventure in Politics: Puerto Rico, 1939–1940," p. 4, William D. Leahy's Papers, State Historical Society of Wisconsin. See also Rodríguez Beruff, *Las memorias de Leahy*.

The Wartime Quartet: Muñoz Marín, Tugwell, Ickes, and FDR

Michael Janeway

The relationship that took hold in 1941 between newly elected Senate president Luis Muñoz Marín and Rexford Guy Tugwell, the last continental-appointed governor of Puerto Rico, has by now drawn around itself a wreath of conventional wisdom, affording only a limited measure of objectivity.[1]

This wartime linkup was a timely but sometimes bumpy alliance between Muñoz Marín, having just led his new Partido Popular Democrático (PPD) to a narrow margin of control over the Puerto Rican legislature, and Rex Tugwell, the only inspired appointment as governor of the island the United States ever made. A brilliant academic economist, leading light of Franklin D. Roosevelt's Brain Trust in his 1932 campaign for the presidency, and undersecretary of agriculture in his first term, Tugwell orchestrated the New Deal's reform farm policies in the pit of the Great Depression. In Washington, political horse trading got the better of Tugwell's innovative reforms; agribusiness came out on top. Puerto Rico was for him a second shot at fundamental reform of agricultural ownership, management, economics, and social effect. In 1941 as in 1933, Tugwell was "a man with a plan"; a reformer on a grand scale possessed of dramatic good looks and a vibrant personality; in Muñoz's own words many years later, "as audacious as myself"—a high compliment indeed.[2]

For our purposes, it's important to understand Tugwell's place in the New Deal scheme of things, and in Franklin Roosevelt's long-term estimation. One of the preeminent historians of the New Deal, Arthur M. Schlesinger Jr., rated Tugwell "chief presidential confidant" in the second year of the Roosevelt Administration, "perhaps the least pliant of the Roosevelt intimates . . . a sort

Luis Muñoz Marín relaxes with Puerto Rican soldiers stationed in Cuba during the Second World War. (Archivo Fundación Luis Muñoz Marín)

of conscience." Such intimacy (and such a personal background) guaranteed that Tugwell would become the ripest of targets for conservatives in Congress and the press, who tagged him early on as an arrogant radical. In one outlandish reactionary caricature, Tugwell was the nefarious Lenin (or Stalin) looming behind FDR's acquiescent Alexander Kerensky in "the Roosevelt Revolution."[3]

In March 1934, Tugwell took an Agriculture Department fact-finding team to Puerto Rico. The mission coincided with a trip by Mrs. Roosevelt to examine the island's social and economic plight; it was a happy accident in that it helped ensure the president's solid support for fast, remedial action. Backed by the White House, Tugwell collaborated then with freshman senator Muñoz Marín and a close circle of Puerto Rican reformers on an ambitious New Deal reconstruction plan that recognized the island's unique victimization in the Great Depression. (The failure of the ensuing Puerto Rican Reconstruction Administration [PRRA] is another story.)[4]

As for the Tugwell-Roosevelt relationship, the president remarked in late 1936, as Tugwell prepared to leave Washington under reactionary fire, "that no one connected with [himself] or the Administration had been subjected to such criticism as Rex has. Yet Rex has never whimpered or asked for sympathy or run to anyone for help. He has taken it on the chin like a man." Those words had strong roots, and a future as well.[5]

Beyond Clichés

Clichés crowd out more significant themes in the accepted narrative of Tugwell's years as governor of Puerto Rico (1941–1946). Tugwell was (as conventional wisdom emphasizes) preoccupied with fighting off Muñoz Marín's constant pressure for political patronage. Muñoz, in turn, chafed at Tugwell's lack of sympathy for the maneuvering he deemed necessary for the PPD to hold its thin margins of power in the first years of its primacy at the *Capitolio* in San Juan.[6]

Of course, the strong glue between the two men is acknowledged, if at times diplomatically, in their respective memoirs. "Controversies with Muñoz," Tugwell mused in his postwar account of his governorship, *The Stricken Land*,[7] "were a kind of technical difference of opinion. We were in fundamental agreement" about a New Deal–style agenda focused on agricultural reform and public ownership of utilities, despite Muñoz's view that "I was always bucking his political judgment." In addition, arriving in Puerto Rico in March 1941, Tugwell was frankly awed by Muñoz's sophistication about the threat of fascism on the march. By comparison, he acknowledged, "until it was just next to too late," he himself had been party to American liberal opposition to involvement in the oncoming war on grounds that, as in 1917, it would be a death knell for domestic reform. "In the Spring of 1941 Muñoz saw [these issues] more clearly than most of my friends in the States," Tugwell wrote in 1946. "He obviously had the outlook of a statesman."[8]

With similar politesse, Muñoz wrote in his *Memorias* in the 1970s that "Tugwell had administrative experience of great quality at high levels of one of the most complicated governments in the world. Among us, in the Popular Party [of Puerto Rico], there was scarcely anyone" who had a semblance of such expertise in governance. Among the professor-*gobernador*'s gifts to Puerto Rico, Muñoz adds benignly, was his demonstration that "to do good work," government required not only dedicated, technocratic public servants but professionalized budgeting and, above all (Tugwell's great passion), government planning. Graciously, Muñoz touched on his kinship with Tugwell in being "a radical . . . in the sense of [being] a person who digs deep into the roots of specific and general problems."[9]

None of this was untrue. But left there, even with pungent anecdotes added in, we have only pieces of a much larger picture. From those fragments, leading historians of modern Puerto Rico have tended to sum up the successes of the Muñoz-Tugwell alliance in limited terms, balancing out which of the two gets the most credit.[10]

The Quartet

The wartime relationship between Muñoz and Tugwell can be properly understood only by stepping back and widening the lens—as Jorge Rodríguez Beruff has done in demonstrating the extent to which Muñoz Marín's march to power in 1939–1941 was a subset of a larger historical drama: the unfolding of US national security strategy for the coming of World War II, and, in particular, Washington's anticipation of the Battle of the Atlantic.[11]

For the deeper one looks, the Tugwell-Muñoz team-up was not just a duet. It was half of a quartet, a sometimes raucous square dance. President Franklin D. Roosevelt and his formidable secretary of the interior, Harold L. Ickes—the tiger of the New Deal—were the ultimate decision makers (for once, usurping Congress in that role) in easing the inertia that had effectively frozen US–Puerto Rican arrangements for more than four decades. I shall argue here that Muñoz's and Tugwell's ability to achieve any results at all during World War II were in great part a function of the nature and depth of their respective personal relationships with President Roosevelt and Secretary Ickes, as well as with each other.[12]

In widening the frame, however, we must also note that Ickes, a straight shooter, and the often devious Roosevelt dealt with each other in large part by means of spirited combat (which included periodic resignations in protest by Ickes; FDR always refused them). Ickes was persistent and ingenious in contesting the president's technique of setting up his administrators as rivals as a means of retaining control over a government rapidly expanding in size and scope, and over policy disputes Roosevelt was not ready to decide.[13]

Some of their feuds were long term; they quarreled over the governance of Puerto Rico for five years. In 1934, Roosevelt moved oversight for Puerto Rico from the colonial-minded War Department to Interior—a promising initiative. He promptly undermined Secretary Ickes's control of his fresh turf by handpicking Ernest Gruening as director of Interior's new Division of Territories and Island Possessions, and then of the PRRA, and assigning him a line of direct report to the White House, right around an infuriated Ickes. This was not a recipe for healthy rivalry, especially after 1936, when Gruening, a longtime anticolonial reformer, switched sides against a backdrop of mounting violence, aligning himself with bullheaded Governor Blanton Winship and the conservative Puerto Rican establishment that dominated the legislature. Muñoz, leader of the New Deal forces on the island, had enjoyed Gruening's patronage ever since a journalistic collaboration between them had sprung up in the 1920s. That patronage was the first casualty of Gruening's angry turnabout. The president—moved by events more than by Gruening—followed suit.[14]

At times, the turmoil of 1936–1939 found Ickes and Roosevelt at bitter odds as to whether any semblance of New Deal socioeconomic reforms in Puerto Rico remained an administration priority or whether they were trumped by "law and order" imperatives. This lasted until Ickes succeeded in getting Gruening moved to the quietude of the governorship of Alaska in 1939. But, as we shall see, Ickes and Roosevelt took up a subsequent quarrel in 1941 over control of Caribbean policy. One connecting thread through it all was that Ickes had found a raw nerve in Roosevelt, taunting him over the years as to whether his Good Neighbor Policy and anticolonialism (a switch from his brash imperialism as assistant secretary of the navy under Woodrow Wilson) were substantive, or merely rhetorical. For, as Tugwell observed: "There was an admiral concealed somewhere in Roosevelt."[15]

FDR and Tugwell

Another cliché affixed to the narrative examined here is that Tugwell had, supposedly, fallen from presidential favor by the end of the first Roosevelt administration (more or less as doors in Washington began slamming shut against Muñoz), and that he was rescued from "exile" for the 1941 Puerto Rican gubernatorial appointment as an act of charity—or, alternatively, to further remove him from public view. In fact, FDR and Tugwell corresponded warmly and confidentially after 1936, and met periodically at the White House for extremely candid talks, the subjects of which included 1940 presidential politics and the onset of World War II. As a business executive and then chairman of the New York City Planning Commission under Mayor Fiorello H. La Guardia (a high-maintenance ally of FDR's; Tugwell was the mediator), Tugwell also ran some missions for the president (including a significant one to the Caribbean).[16]

In November 1939, FDR sent word to Tugwell that he wanted him back in the government. (Tugwell replied: "The President ought to know that ever since I enlisted [in the 1932 campaign] I have been in the army.") Some weeks before that, as Germany, Great Britain, and France went to war, Ickes told his diary independently, "this Administration owes it to Tugwell to get him back again."[17]

After flurries of correspondence about jobs that didn't quite fit, Ickes queried Tugwell in New York: Would he take charge of the Division of Territories and Island Possessions, the job Ernest Gruening had botched? Ickes thought

Gruening such a bad administrator that the "able and resourceful" Tugwell could handle it with time left over to take on other weighty assignments from him and the president. Moreover, as the US possessions involved were on the edge of international war zones, the importance of the Territories job had just escalated. Tugwell was interested, but he would have had to take a substantial pay cut. He decided tentatively: not the right move.[18]

Nevertheless, what ensued reflects the tight bonds uniting the three men, even when Ickes and FDR were in the grip of a ferocious feud. That intimacy sprang from several sources. At president-elect Roosevelt's Manhattan townhouse in February 1933, it was then–Professor Tugwell who ushered Ickes, the noisy reformer from Chicago whose name FDR could not yet pronounce correctly, into their first meeting, during which Roosevelt offered Ickes the secretary of the interior job. Tugwell and Ickes were close friends ever after. It was to Ickes that Roosevelt made his comments about Tugwell's uncomplaining loyalty late in 1936—perhaps for effect on his querulous cabinet officer.[19]

The most powerful of the links among the three men was their shared passion for land, forest, and resource conservation: for the protection and planned, scientific use of the nation's natural assets and treasures. FDR, Ickes, and Tugwell were the most committed of the preeminent New Dealers to what today would be called the environmental agenda. For reasons of space, only a few anecdotes must serve to convey the depth of feeling involved. To begin at the end, Roosevelt was a man who, several weeks before his death in April 1945, near victory in a raging world war, fighting against great odds to hold the wartime alliance together and build a postwar United Nations, his health and energies collapsing, could still write out directions for that year's Hyde Park tree farm spring planting.[20] ("The chestnut trees are to go as fill-ins among the trees which did not do well just east of the gravel bank...")[21]

Early in their association, Tugwell remarked of the conservation-based core of his budding relationship with Roosevelt: "I was thus able to meet him on ground foreign to the others of our [Brain Trust] group." As Tugwell prepared for his introductory trip to Puerto Rico back in 1934, he conferred with the president and was struck by the quality of detail FDR brought to the subject of the island's troubled agricultural economy. In fact, they disagreed about what Tugwell judged to be Roosevelt's out-of-date attachment to homestead family farming as the way to break up the island's sugar monoculture, but did get "from him some really valuable ideas." To counter overreliance on the cheapest food on the market, rice, "he thought more could be done with protein-high legumes. He talked about other resources which he thought strangely unexploited. There were hardwoods and bamboos, insecticides, spices and essential oils, for instance."[22]

Once, as agriculture undersecretary during the first Roosevelt administration, Tugwell brought the officer in charge of the national forests to meet with the president for an hour and a half to debate a question bothering FDR: should timber be treated as "a natural resource such as coal or oil," or as an agricultural crop? From San Juan, in the grim weeks after Pearl Harbor, Tugwell wrote FDR urging him to reserve time at Hyde Park to "look at your trees. I know what about three days of that does for you—even at the worst of times." They'd ridden through them together on forest trails, Roosevelt at the custom-made hand controls of his bouncing Ford convertible.[23]

Harold Ickes's passion for conservation rivaled that of Roosevelt and Tugwell in fervor. But, given the pugilistic nature of the Roosevelt-Ickes relationship, it was accompanied by perhaps the bitterest, longest running of their feuds: Ickes's unrequited lust for transfer of the US Forest Service to Interior from the Department of Agriculture, liberating it in the process from timber industry influence. Ickes had been a crusading Progressive Republican; one of his goals, encouraged by FDR, was to exorcise the stink the "regular Republicans" had cast on the Interior Department in the Teapot Dome oil-leasing scandal under the Warren Harding administration. Ickes vowed to make Interior a true "Department of Conservation," glowing with integrity. Control of the Forest Service was essential to that dream. Ickes was happy to trade lesser Interior Department bureaus over to Agriculture in exchange. Not surprisingly, conforming to the New Deal fabric of set-piece rivalries, agriculture secretary Henry A. Wallace opposed Ickes's design adamantly.[24]

Although he was Wallace's deputy until 1937, Tugwell was sympathetic to the Ickes plan. He became the permanent mediator in this New Deal struggle without end. In 1934, with FDR's tacit support, Ickes tried hard to lure Tugwell to move to Interior as undersecretary in charge of all conservation issues—bringing the Forest Service with him. Then, late in 1939, the president, Ickes, and Tugwell began negotiating anew a variation on such a plan. At one point—July 1940—with his third-term campaign and emergency aid to Britain demanding his full attention, FDR found time to beseech Tugwell to take the Forest Service job, and together they'd build it into an overarching public lands agency, wherever it wound up on the federal landscape. He was tired of the squabbling over it. "*I want you to do my forestry for me.* You know I love the forests and want to do the right thing. So do you" (emphasis added). But, for a larger pileup of reasons than usual, the other key player, Ickes, was just then on the worst of terms with the president and talking resignation with a vengeance. So Roosevelt's entreaty to Tugwell that day took this turn:

Meanwhile, see Harold. Hold his hand. . . . I am not sure that he is speaking to me. Be nice to him.²⁵

This roundelay about public lands management was still in progress in December 1940, when Ickes changed the subject with his call to Tugwell for help on Puerto Rico. The US Supreme Court's March 1940 reinforcement of the widely ignored 1900 ban on corporate ownership of more than five hundred acres of Puerto Rican land was the cover for the mission. But Ickes had larger concerns (shared by FDR): first, what to make of Muñoz Marín's unexpected return to center stage in Puerto Rico's elections, featuring his trade-in of *independentista* leanings for a 1940 election campaign stance maintaining that, for the present, the island's constitutional status was not an issue. And second, how to assess the Puerto Rican situation as German naval penetration of the South Atlantic became ever more threatening. Tugwell arrived in San Juan in March 1941. The prevailing winds sped his own conversion from prewar liberal isolationism to an appeal to Ickes in April that, as "our first line of defense" against Hitler, the United States should put in place a "Caribbean Protectorate" of all the islands.²⁶

Through 1941, public attention was focused on bringing off Tugwell's dual appointments as chancellor of the University of Puerto Rico and governor of Puerto Rico (a scheme concocted collaboratively by Muñoz and Tugwell, encouraged by Ickes and FDR, which quickly backfired). Nevertheless, the president, the interior secretary, and the new governor kept up an active back-and-forth about their "Tugwell-as-public-lands-czar" project. They were still at it in 1942.²⁷

Muñoz on the Outs

The nature and depth of the relations among the four protagonists—FDR, Ickes, Tugwell, and Muñoz—was just cited as decisive. Strictly speaking, that should read "depth—or lack of it." For one of the links was afflicted by lasting mistrust. Neither Roosevelt nor Ickes ever fully overcame the disenchantment with Luis Muñoz Marín that took hold in Washington in 1936 in the thick of infighting for domination of the PRRA, and the explosion of *nacionalista* violence highlighted by the assassination of an able police chief popular in San Juan and influential in Washington. That was the spur to Ernest Gruening's hard-line turn from "reform" to "law and order," pulling the president behind him.

For his part, Harold Ickes had come to loathe Gruening, increasingly defiant and imperious as Territories Division director. Certainly he opposed

FDR's acquiescence as Gruening and Winship steered the insular government in the direction of a police state. Yet, amid the confusion, Gruening managed to persuade Ickes as well as FDR that Muñoz's drive for patronage control in Puerto Rico, plus his ambivalence about the administration's state-of-siege response to the *nacionalista* violence, proved him to be a self-promoting, undependable, "rule-or-ruin" politico; definitely not a team player.[28]

There were early warnings. As support for Muñoz in Washington began to slip away in 1936, Ruby Black, his wired-in press representative and de facto ambassador there, wrote to him and his first wife, Muna Lee, that

> While Luis is [still] most highly regarded, everything he says is taken in the White House with a grain of salt because he is considered a politician with a political purpose for himself and his party. That is nothing against him; FDR is a politician too. But it causes them to take more trouble to verify what he reports.

In February 1937, Ickes remarked to his diary that, on the basis of Ruby Black's coverage of Muñoz for the Puerto Rican press,

> it would appear that Munos Marin [sic] has the entree at all times, not only to my office but to Mrs. Roosevelt and to [Assistant Secretary of the Interior Oscar] Chapman, especially the latter. Of course Munos Marin is trying to make himself appear to be the big man in Puerto Rico on account of his supposedly close relationship with officials here. As a matter of fact the President distrusts Munos Marin and I have never taken him in full faith. Gruening used to do so but they are now on the outs. Chapman apparently has been seeing altogether too much of him and I wrote him a memorandum yesterday cautioning him not to be so generous in granting [Muñoz] interviews and not to give or accept social favors.[29]

The same week, Eleanor Roosevelt, Muñoz's "secret weapon" in securing New Deal entrée since 1933, sought to ward off a meeting with Muñoz that Black was trying to arrange (as she had effectively in the past). The first lady explained, "I think it is better for me not to see Mr. Marin [sic] at the present time, as it always creates the impression that he has an inside hold on the administration, which, of course, is not true."[30]

Rodríguez Beruff documents the Roosevelt administration's cautious decision to "recognize" Muñoz as the new Puerto Rican "caudillo" in the days after the 1940 election, based on a one-vote PPD margin in the Senate and outgoing governor William D. Leahy's terse view that the election results were "OK." (The results, in fact, were confusingly mixed: the Coalición had won a plurality of the vote and elected its candidate for resident commissioner, the hyperbolic

Bolívar Pagán.) But the PPD's upset election advantage did not restore Muñoz to the prized "New Deal golden boy" position within the Roosevelt administration he'd enjoyed between 1933 and the start of 1936, or elevate him anywhere near the status he would enjoy across official Washington after 1948.[31]

Ickes noted in his diary for December 7, 1940, that Leahy "recognized that Muñoz Marín is unstable but believes that he will be inclined to go along with the [Roosevelt] administration whenever he can." But in August 1941, the interior secretary could not contain his distaste at Muñoz's appearance to his eyes when Governor-Designate Tugwell brought him in for a visit: Muñoz "used to be a very handsome man of a tall, well-set swarthy type"; now he "looked fat and sloppy and dirty." Still, "he did a good job in overturning the old political crowd that used to control Puerto Rico."[32]

Early in 1942, the president went so far as to write Governor Tugwell that the Coalición's resident commissioner, Bolívar Pagán, was "wholly a politician," while Muñoz was "far more disinterestedly working for the good of the people of Puerto Rico." In such a private aside, as in his famous declaration at Hyde Park on Labor Day weekend, 1941, that the *Presidente del Senado* was "what we might call the Prime Minister of Puerto Rico," Roosevelt would from time to time bestow upon Muñoz what Tugwell later called a "bouquet of words." But after 1936, FDR delivered not much of substance to Muñoz personally. Far-reaching presidential largesse for Puerto Rico came instead, from 1938 forward, in the form of the mammoth US military buildup—overridingly a matter of national self-interest.[33]

The exception was the 1943 President's Committee on Reform of the 1917 Organic Act defining the terms of US possession of Puerto Rico. This body set a course toward elective governorship for the island, from which much more liberalization followed. (We shall come to Muñoz's view that the 1943 proposal was grossly inadequate.) That arduous journey began with a personal appeal from Tugwell to FDR in March 1942 noting that the disastrous war news from the Pacific revealed the brittle weakness of British and Dutch colonial policy. One lesson, he argued, was that it was time "that we abjure colonialism not in words but by a deed," by moving Puerto Rico toward self-governance. Roosevelt responded immediately with a request to Tugwell to spell out what he had in mind.[34]

Tugwell, in a 1958 meditation on Muñoz's strengths and flaws,[35] much more sympathetic to Muñoz on a grand scale than he was in *The Stricken Land* twelve years earlier, concluded that over the long haul Roosevelt and Muñoz "had distrusted each other completely." Tantalizingly, Tugwell wrote that "whether this had been due to a lingering imperial taint in the Roosevelt blood or to *merely a distaste for being used in another's game*" (emphasis

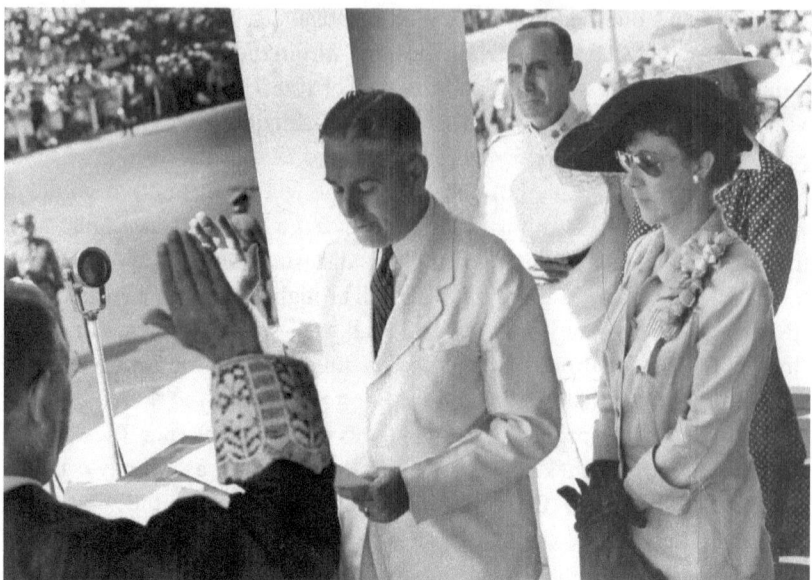

Rexford G. Tugwell takes the oath as governor of Puerto Rico accompanied by his wife, Grace, September 19, 1941. (Archivo Fundación Luis Muñoz Marín)

added), the president's view of Muñoz reflected a grand seigneur's protection of his prerogatives. This is a significant insight: Roosevelt *never* liked, or tolerated for long, even an especially favored subordinate presuming on his territory or crossing a boundary in acting in the president's name. And Tugwell was correct: in a sequence of proclamations in Puerto Rico invoking FDR's name and words since 1933, Muñoz—really a self-proclaimed Roosevelt acolyte—had demonstrated such presumption.[36]

A wartime example of the syndrome is a cable exchange between Muñoz and the president in December 1941, a week after Pearl Harbor. That August, FDR had met with Winston Churchill on a warship off Newfoundland; there they issued their Atlantic Charter, their shared vision for the postwar world. At Roosevelt's insistence, one of the provisions affirmed "the right to self-determination of peoples." Meeting with Muñoz three weeks later at the White House (days after anointing him "prime minister" at Hyde Park), the president confided in him that he could assume that the provision covered Puerto Rico. Muñoz cabled FDR in December that it would boost morale on the island, and "have [a] very good effect" across Latin America, if Roosevelt would "authorize" him to repeat the gist of their conversation in an upcoming radio address. FDR was sweetly evasive in response: "[W]e are all avoiding discussion at this time of specific details of the broad policy" in order to keep tensions with the British and other allied colonial governments at a minimum. "However you would be right of course in referring to the general policy initiated at [the] Atlantic conference."[37]

Ruby Black had been an amazingly effective intermediary for Muñoz in the thick of Washington crossfire at a time when he was in full favor at the White House and the Interior Department.[38] But over time, because of Muñoz's impaired line of personal credit with Roosevelt and Ickes, he would need an ambassador with more direct clout than Black had held. In charge on the island in 1941 with the electoral base he'd lacked in the 1930s, Muñoz was resolved to push key elements of the PPD 1940 campaign agenda swiftly through the legislature no matter what Washington thought about it. As the drama played out, the current of strength on the Washington–San Juan channel arose from the idiosyncratic, enduring links between Tugwell and FDR, and on their own track, between Tugwell and Ickes. Muñoz was something of a bystander to that traffic.[39]

Caribbean Policy Intrigue

In order to grasp the full scope of Tugwell's role as governor of Puerto Rico, we must note in passing one more battle royal Ickes was waging with Roosevelt in 1941, and with the State Department for good measure. The United States had no consular service in the Caribbean at this time, no basis for securing reliable information. In pace with the mounting US military presence in the region flowing from FDR's destroyers-for-bases deal with Churchill in August 1940, the State Department was preparing to launch a new Caribbean Division. Moreover, Roosevelt and the State Department had deployed a behind-the-scenes envoy to conduct quiet diplomacy in the West Indies and with Great Britain about respective Caribbean interests.[40]

He was Charles Taussig, a sugar industry magnate and New Dealer who had inherited the New York–based American Molasses Company, with extensive Caribbean operations. (It was Taussig who had invited Tugwell to come aboard American Molasses as his executive vice president upon his departure from the Roosevelt administration at the start of 1937, and before he joined Mayor La Guardia's team.) Taussig and the State Department were also pushing a plan for what became the Anglo-American Caribbean Commission (AACC), with an emphasis on postwar planning for the region. Tugwell, who remained friendly with Taussig, knew some of this. Ickes, however, had been kept in the dark. For FDR was once again stage managing a cutthroat competition, this one for control of an urgent piece of US policy.[41]

This pot boiled over in 1941 when Tugwell learned (from Taussig), and Ickes began to get word as well, that a report from Taussig to the president, backed by the State Department, included the piquant notion of an outright raid on Ickes's domain. The idea was to move the entire Division of Territories and Island Possessions (at the very least, its oversight for Puerto Rico and the Virgin Islands) out of the Interior Department and either replant it at the State Department or set it up as an independent agency. Ickes cried foul, charging policy incoherence, the appearance of "setting up of colonial empire," and treachery on the part of "this busybody Taussig" and his State Department sponsors. He commenced a string of memos designed, as he put it, to "disturb the peace of mind of the President."[42]

Someone acceptable to Ickes had to mediate his feud with Taussig and the State Department. That was Tugwell, who, as governor of Puerto Rico, representing the Interior Department, became the second-ranking US member of the AACC upon its creation in 1942; Taussig and Britain's colonial secretary were the cochairs. Along the way, Tugwell had to deal with a firestorm of anxiety in Puerto Rico that the AACC was a cover for a diabolical Plan Caribe or Plan Taussig that would submerge the island in a federation dominated by the British West Indies, outside US tariff protection, and secretly profiting Taussig (and Tugwell).[43]

Early in November 1941 Tugwell wrote to Roosevelt from San Juan confiding just how deeply he'd wound up in the middle of the Interior–State Department mess ("Taussig and Ickes heartily detest each other, as you probably know") and suggesting that the president needed to assure Puerto Ricans that their interests were not threatened by the AACC; quite the opposite. "Yours of November third clears the air for me and I heartily agree," FDR wrote back, penning the word "Private" at the top of his letter. He added, "I will try to make the Caribbean situation clear . . ." Here the dots connected: Tugwell's AACC role, and ability to mediate the Ickes-Taussig shootout, reinforced his push for reform of the status in which the United States held Puerto Rico. For all the infighting, Tugwell, Taussig, Ickes, and FDR agreed that the less they did to make Puerto Rico self-governing, the less credible their pressure on Winston Churchill would be to yield in his role as HM's Protector of the British Empire, around the world as well as in the West Indies.[44]

Tugwell under Fire

Coalición resident commissioner Bolívar Pagán had no credibility whatsoever with Roosevelt or Ickes. But he was tireless in feeding anti-Tugwell and anti-Muñoz fodder to the San Juan–Washington alliance of conservative and sugar lobby irreconcilables, in league with New Deal haters in Congress (whose ranks swelled in the 1942 elections). Because this cabal fueled a constant buzz of rumor that Tugwell was about to quit or be fired, some federal bureaucrats, even midlevel officials at Interior, found it politic to take their cues from the establishment Puerto Rican "powers that be" rather than to back up Tugwell and the unpredictable Muñoz. Ickes was too consumed by his added wartime duties as petroleum coordinator (or "Fuels Czar") to catch up with all this mischief. But his able deputy after 1942, interior undersecretary Abe Fortas, was quick to fill the space.[45]

Early in February 1942, Ickes made a statement of all-out support for Tugwell against "petty" charges by "the political party which lost control of the [insular] government" in the 1940 elections (that is, the Coalición), "fighting to regain that control by attempting to bludgeon and embarrass the President's appointee into supporting discredited policies." The stakes rose as the war came to the Caribbean that season. German submarines shelled Aruba and sank six tankers in February 1942; by April the U-boats were everywhere, and shipping losses meant shrinkage of food and oil supplies. No matter how hard Tugwell labored in Washington for shipping and supply sustenance, and he did, it was easy for his and Muñoz's enemies to lay the blame at the door of La Fortaleza.[46]

In March 1942, when the White House's access to intelligence abroad was still chaotic (the OSS had not yet come into existence), an unnamed continental with some knowledge of the scene in San Juan sent one of FDR's freelance intelligence agents in Washington a seven-page report giving Tugwell credit for good intentions but faulting him on performance: his policy agenda was unrealistic, he was much too dependent on Muñoz Marín, and he was too aloof in personal style. Roosevelt sent the document to Ickes with instructions to show it to no one else and return it promptly, adding: "It sounds to me as if the writer ... had been misled against Rex."

What followed reflects the tenor of unusual personal links rather than bureaucratic routine. Ickes read the report judiciously, acknowledging that Tugwell's personal style could get in his way. (At the same time, Ickes did not fail to note: "From the very first you and I have not thought much of Munoz Marin. He was too sleek, too plausible.") On balance, Ickes was supportive, especially of the Tugwell-Muñoz agricultural reforms. (Whatever his doubts about Muñoz, Ickes was dedicated to displacing the sugar "plantocracy" exploitation of Puerto Rico.) Ickes posed, then knocked down, the notion of running a covert check on what was going on in Puerto Rico, adding, "*Rex has been such a good friend of both of us* that I feel a distaste at the very thought ..." (emphasis added).

Responding to Ickes, Roosevelt signed off on the exchange in a trusting spirit: "I think we can let Rex rock along for while. You and I still have high hopes." Tugwell never heard a word of this go-round. Roosevelt shortly followed up by asking Congress for $15 million for a Puerto Rican food production project.[47]

Tugwell had a much closer call just a few months later. By the summer of 1942, German U-boats had effectively blockaded Puerto Rico. Insular conservatives and merchant profiteers directed civil discontent at Tugwell. But the governor was effectively cultivating the US military commanders, who in turn confided that they'd been approached by Chamber of Commerce plotters seeking collaboration in a de facto overthrow of Tugwell and Muñoz. (This would-be junta, which included some continentals, mistakenly assumed that the military wanted to take charge.) Tugwell obtained from Ickes and Fortas agreement that he would retain civil authority as governor if *he* chose to declare martial law—and so informed the head of the US Army command in Puerto Rico.[48]

In this unstable situation, Charles Taussig, based on much communication with Tugwell but acting bizarrely on it, dreamed up a convoluted scheme whereby Tugwell (whom Taussig claimed wanted to quit) would be called back to Washington, and Justice Martín Travieso, a pillar of the Puerto Rican political establishment, would be dispatched from the capital bearing a Fourth of July message from Ickes to Puerto Ricans that would lift the curtain on the proposal for an elective governorship by 1944. (Implicitly, Travieso would be poised to take charge on the island.) All this was supposed to calm Puerto Rico down. But US censors caught up with a conspiratorial account of the plot and sent it to Ickes's deputy, Abe Fortas. That was sufficient to poison Ickes's mind against Travieso, with an extra helping for Charles Taussig ("There is no reason why [Taussig] should be butting in on this anyhow"). Taussig's motives were indeed murky. Ickes recorded in his diary that his own motive had been to protect Tugwell ("I did not want him to be the objective [sic] of any riotous mob nor would I want to have to pull him out under fire").[49]

Stormy times got stormier. In November 1942, as the first of two congressional investigating committees prepared to descend on Puerto Rico, Tugwell sent through Interior Department channels an all-purpose letter stating that "if conditions make my resignation desirable, it is always available." Ickes immediately took the matter to Roosevelt and wrote back a week later that the president "was concerned about the Puerto Rican situation but quite firm" that the administration would stand behind Tugwell. Roosevelt, wrote Ickes, seems to have no question about this. With this view I fully concur. If we allow the mob to have its way with you, there wouldn't be any use in sending another Governor of Puerto Rico at all.

Such candid reassurances, even when Tugwell hit potholes in Washington as well as in San Juan, became the pattern.[50]

FDR to the Rescue

One episode of presidential solace for Tugwell stands out. At a break in the Organic Act reform talks in Washington in July 1943, the president's commission, led by Fortas and Tugwell on the administration side and by Muñoz and insular opposition leaders on the Puerto Rican side, were summoned to the White House. FDR dealt with the commission summarily. (Tugwell: "They were not asked to sit down and not asked to express any opinions.") The president signaled that Fortas had briefed him on disagreement within the commission about how far reforms ought to go for the time being. That was all: best wishes; out they went.[51]

Evident to the others was that Roosevelt wanted Tugwell to stay when the group exited. Tugwell's account of their talk that day was that "[i]t was as though I had last gone out [of FDR's office] the day before"—as had been the custom in 1932–1935.

> Nothing was changed. There was the same assumption that I could be told anything and that anything I said or did was at least rightly meant. There was the same assumption —hardly justified now—that I knew everything that is going on and need not be brought up to date.

FDR (the "admiral" within revealing himself) wanted limits on self-governance to be granted; rampant insular election corruption was on his mind. Tugwell pushed back on the need to acknowledge Puerto Rican *dignidad* and work in good faith for reform of corrupt practices. Roosevelt, who himself was frank in predicting that self-government across all island colonies was likely to be "bad" at first, was persuaded. Then,

> as to the various [congressional] investigating committees and their embarrassment to him, [FDR] said that did not exist and not to worry about it for a minute. He said that his only concern had been the fear that I might get sick of it and quit.

As to that he said that if he could stand the Hearst Press [and other anti–New Deal newspapers], I ought to be able to stand *El Mundo*. Anyway, he pointed out, they always go too far and lose public support.[52]

Through 1944, Tugwell kept Washington updated on agitation by the conservative alliance aimed at calling off the 1944 insular election. (PPD preregistration of voters indicated that Muñoz was headed for a major victory.) FDR, Ickes, and Fortas all responded with messages of concern about these antics (they also alerted the Justice Department), and of support for Tugwell. In March 1944, topping off one round in this flurry, with anti-Tugwell vituperation rampant in the legislature, Ickes cabled the Puerto Rican Senate: "Governor Tugwell has the complete confidence of the President and myself. He has conducted himself like a statesman."[53]

In July 1944, with his health markedly failing, Roosevelt told Tugwell of a hysterical plea from Bolívar Pagán that the president remove the governor to ensure fair elections that fall; Pagán further threatened that if Tugwell remained, the Coalición would boycott the elections. Roosevelt related: "I told [Pagán] that was the most un-American suggestion I had ever heard, and wrote him a scorching reply." This time there was a presidential grace note for Muñoz (if only another "bouquet of words"). Weary (although not as weary as Roosevelt), his wife ailing, Tugwell retreated to see his parents at their farm in upstate New York. From there he wrote to Muñoz ("Dear Luis") by hand about his musings and wish for

> a quieter life. Meeting with the President about it, however, I got no encouragement. He wants us to go on. I say us, because you were prominent in the conversation. It was a good talk.... He was as solid and determined as ever. He knew about many machinations that I only found in detail in Washington and he has written a couple of stinging letters which I notice have not been publicized by certain gentlemen who received them [including Bolívar Pagán]. I assured him of our continued enthusiasm and our willingness to go on if we had his confidence.[54]

Muñoz and Tugwell

There were plenty of displays of mercurial temperament between the governor and *el Presidente del Senado*, because life on the Puerto Rican political firing line was a constant push and pull. Tugwell would threaten Muñoz with the consequences of failure to stick close to him. An early demonstration of this syndrome came as the UPR chancellorship half of the bargain the two of them had struck in mid-1941 blew up that fall, accelerated by a barrage of protest against it from the opposition press. Tugwell found Muñoz in rooms he'd taken at the Escambrón Beach Club.

> I was furious and I told him so. I said I had been a target [of protest] since the day that I arrived. . . . He had sat around and said, "Well, that's the kind of fight it is." . . . I said I was his opportunity and that of the people of Puerto Rico and the only one he had. If I went home he would be through and the next step would be a military government.

Muñoz, shaken, secured a temporary cease-fire from *El Mundo*. That didn't put the UPR deal back together, but it clarified the terms on which they were working together.[55]

Those terms were various indeed. At times it was Tugwell who undertook the backroom wheeling and dealing to prop up the fragile PPD legislative majority, as one or another swing-vote legislator joined or severed allegiance to it. For his part, in sincerity as well as out of self-interest, Muñoz repeatedly mustered backing for Tugwell that exceeded the call of duty. The best-known incident, with Tugwell under brutal attack on the island and in Congress in 1942, was when Muñoz secured a petition of *respaldo a Tugwell* with 314,000 signatures, and cabled the results to the president, Mrs. Roosevelt, and Ickes.[56]

Less known were disarmingly brazen impulses by Muñoz to put Tugwell's credibility with FDR and Ickes to his own political use. In May 1943, with hope for an elective governorship in time for the 1944 election still flickering, Muñoz took Tugwell to Ponce to meet with some local PPD leaders. "Had from them," Tugwell noted in his diary, "the startling suggestion that I should be the [PPD] candidate for Governor" in 1944. "Said no, but they said what if you were nominated anyway." As on many occasions, Tugwell made plain his view that Muñoz should prepare to trade in his behind-the-scenes caudillo role and become governor. (A day or so later Muñoz remarked to Tugwell that something or other he'd done was "unbecoming in a candidate.")[57]

Muñoz had subsequent brainstorms along these lines, and he did get Tugwell designated chairman of the Puerto Rican delegation to the 1944 Democratic National Convention. (For their own complex reasons, FDR and Ickes blocked that move.)[58]

Ambassador Tugwell

But another pattern emerges. I have noted in passing that Tugwell, too often stereotyped as an arrogant political misfit, was the mediator of choice between top Roosevelt administration figures snarling at each other, between the president himself and Ickes, Ickes and Wallace, Ickes and Taussig, FDR and Mayor La Guardia; there were others. As the San Juan–Washington quartet played on, it became clear to those on the inside that one of Tugwell's greatest contributions was his supple skill as a transformative ambassador between the chronically distracted triad of FDR, Ickes, and Abe Fortas in Washington, and Muñoz under a swirl of pressures in Puerto Rico.[59]

The Roosevelt team, after all, was at least and at last at work on reform (however inchoate) of Puerto Rico's colonial bondage. On the other hand, as late as 1945, FDR, Ickes, and even Tugwell were unclear as to what Muñoz's actual desired outcome had evolved into, from his prewar *independentista* position and his 1940 campaign statements that constitutional status was on hold. Did he want a subsidized independence (or, as Undersecretary of State Sumner Welles put it, "divorce with alimony")? One or another form of generously supported autonomy? Down the road, statehood?[60]

It was Tugwell who brought Washington around to the fact that for Muñoz to have credibility in steering Puerto Ricans (especially the *independentistas* who constituted the vast majority of the PPD ranks) to the transitional self-governing status then achievable, and to be able to negotiate for more in a postwar environment, he had to be as independent as possible of administration summonses and pressures. A sampling of such interventions:

Muñoz balked repeatedly at participating in the 1943 President's Committee to recommend reform of the Organic Act: why go to the congressional well without pushing for much more than an elected governor? Tugwell was successful in persuading Roosevelt, Ickes, Fortas, and Sumner Welles at the State Department that the context for Muñoz's reluctance was his need to deter "his *independentista* gang" in the PPD from charging that he'd caved in to Washington. It was Tugwell who handled the subtle psychodrama in the proceedings of the committee that enabled Muñoz to press his demands in a way that educated Washington about the duality of Puerto Rican aspirations—more autonomy, but more US support as well—without forcing a break.[61]

By May 1944, Muñoz was fighting a two-front political battle on the island (to his left, against escalation of *independentista* sentiment in the PPD, and to the right, against Coalición intrigue to get the elections for that year called off). To clarify what remained murky to them (and, to a lesser extent, to Tugwell) about Muñoz's postwar goals, FDR, Ickes, and Fortas wanted Muñoz to come to Washington for consultations. But, Congress having shelved for the moment the elective governorship project, Tugwell argued: "[N]o Puerto Rican *politico* can afford to go to Washington just now without bringing something home." He urged instead that Fortas come to the island.[62]

In December 1944, the elections safely won, Tugwell sorted out a replay of the administration effort to get Muñoz to Washington, this time with a fresh agenda item: FDR wanted the State Department to arrange for Muñoz "to visit a few Latin American countries with the thought that it might be beneficial to our relations there." Far from taking "the President's project" as a compliment, Tugwell warned, it would, "at this moment"—with so little to show in the way of Organic Act reform, and with his fight with PPD *independentistas* headed for a showdown—"put Muñoz in a most embarrassing position." Muñoz indeed resisted, and Tugwell's counsel prevailed.[63]

Tugwell and Muñoz quarreled more fiercely than ever when, in 1943, Muñoz began to deal in secret with International Telephone and Telegraph mogul Sosthenes Behn about blocking Tugwell's plan to bring the Puerto Rican Telephone Company (PRTC) under state control. (In exchange, Behn was promising Muñoz major ITT investment on the island.[64]) But, furious as Tugwell was with Muñoz about the covert PRTC negotiation, he was quick to perceive, and explain to Ickes and Fortas, that it was "the result on a shrewd political mind" of the administration's inability to counter the worst of conservative congressional hostility. If, as was undeniable, the life was going out of the New Deal, and if the Republicans were poised to kill it off entirely, Muñoz needed anchors to the right.[65]

Tugwell's Crucial Contribution

Tugwell's adroitness at governing (which even so dedicated a conservative critic as Republican US senator Robert Taft came round to appreciating), his effective relations with the Puerto Rican–based US military, his diplomacy in Washington, and the caliber and constancy of support he received from Roosevelt, Ickes, and Fortas when the going got rough in Puerto Rico, merit a sharp reevaluation upward. Without these strengths, the fierce campaign by the enemies of social and economic reform on the island, the sugar lobby, and Muñoz's other conservative enemies intent on "win[ning] in Washington what they have already lost" in Puerto Rico (as Tugwell put it in a letter to Ickes at the end of 1943) might well have succeeded. The disintegrating Coalición and its bedfellows might have done even better than they did in prompting investigative mischief in Congress and fomenting labor and civil unrest on the island, to the extent of bringing on what Tugwell, Ickes, and Fortas managed (with difficulty) to fight off between 1942 and 1944: martial law followed by the return of some form of military occupation.[66]

And Muñoz might well have had a much tougher time holding his own with the Truman administration, especially after Congress went Republican in 1946. As it was, before the 1946 elections, conservative opposition and Washington politics very nearly blocked Muñoz (backed by Tugwell) in putting across the PPD's Jesús Piñero as Tugwell's successor; the choice very nearly went to conservative General Pedro del Valle, or to a mainland Democratic Party hack, as in 1933. Tugwell put the case for effective (never mind progressive) governance of Puerto Rico in colloquial fashion to Julius Krug, Ickes's unsophisticated successor as secretary of the interior, in April 1946: "Munoz is the big shot and the only one who can actually be dealt with."[67]

As wartime governor of Puerto Rico, Tugwell paved the way for Muñoz to recover what *he* had lost in 1936–1937, and not fully regained even with his electoral success in 1940 and 1944—full legitimacy, trust, and stature in Washington's estimation. Arguably, without Tugwell's instrumental finesse within the Wartime Quartet, the grand advances Muñoz was able to achieve for Puerto Rico from 1946 forward would have been at the least delayed; at worst, derailed.

Notes

1. I will focus here on relationships at the top of the Puerto Rican government, and between it and Washington, to the exclusion of policy, political, and military issues covered elsewhere in this collection.

2. The New Deal's "domestic allotment plan," which Tugwell orchestrated, subsidized farmers to cut back on production in order to raise collapsed farm prices. A processing tax on middleman producers would finance the subsidies, as well as modernization and conservation in agricultural techniques. The result would restore farmers' buying power, raise poorer farmers' living standards, and stabilize markets. Thus it was complementary to the New Deal strategy for recovery and reform of the US industrial economy. See Elliot A. Rosen, *Hoover, Roosevelt, and the Brains Trust: From Depression to New Deal* (New York: Columbia University Press, 1977), pp. 156–160, 175–182; Arthur M. Schlesinger Jr., *The Crisis of the Old Order, 1919–1933* (Boston: Houghton Mifflin, 1957), pp. 403–405, 424; Arthur M. Schlesinger Jr., *The Coming of the New Deal* (Boston: Houghton Mifflin, 1958), pp. 36–39; Kenneth S. Davis, *FDR: The New York Years* (New York: Random House, 1979), pp. 268–272, 362–364; Sarah T. Phillips, *This Land, This Nation: Conservation, Rural America, and the New Deal* (New York: Cambridge University Press, 1977), p. 65–70; Rexford G. Tugwell, *Roosevelt's Revolution: The First Year, A Personal Perspective* (New York: Macmillan, 1977), pp. 48–52; and Luis Muñoz Marín, *Memorias, 1940–1952* (San Juan: Fundación Luis Muñoz Marín, 1980), p. 71.

3. Schlesinger, *The Coming of the New Deal*, pp. 361, 549–550; Bernard Sternsher, *Rexford Tugwell and the New Deal* (New Brunswick, NJ: Rutgers University Press, 1964), pp. 230, 347, 352–353; Davis, *The New York Years*, pp. 471–475.

4. There are many accounts of Tugwell's involvement in 1934–1935 in what became the PRRA. Thomas H. Mathews's *Puerto Rican Politics and the New Deal* (Gainesville: University Press of Florida, 1960), pp. 155–165, 185–186, is especially detailed and reliable. See also James L. Dietz, *Economic History of Puerto Rico: Institutional Change and Capitalist Development* (Princeton, NJ: Princeton University Press, 1986), pp. 149–154; Rexford G. Tugwell, *The Stricken Land: The Story of Puerto Rico* (Garden City, NY: Doubleday, 1946), pp. 44–59; and Rexford G. Tugwell, *The Diary of Rexford G. Tugwell: The New Deal, 1932–1935*, ed. Michael V. Namorato (New York: Greenwood Press, 1992), pp. 95–102, 119, 123, 151, 160–161, 178, 187.

5. Harold L. Ickes, *The Secret Diary of Harold L. Ickes*, vol. 1, *The First Thousand Days, 1933–1936* (New York: Simon and Schuster, 1953), p. 692.

6. Tugwell, *The Stricken Land*, pp. 297, 342–343; A. W. Maldonado, *Luis Muñoz Marín: Puerto Rico's Democratic Revolution* (Río Piedras: University of Puerto Rico Press, 2006), p. 275.

7. Reissued in 2010 in translation, edited by Jorge Rodríguez Beruff as *La Tierra Azotada: memorias del ultimo gubernator estadounidense de Puerto Rico*, and published by the Fundación Luis Muñoz Marín and Fundación Rafael Hernández Colón.

8. Tugwell, *The Stricken Land*, pp. 93–94, 171–172.

9. Muñoz Marín, *Memorias*, pp. 75–76.

10. For example, in key passages, Charles Goodsell and Raymond Carr credit Tugwell and Muñoz more or less equally, whereas Arturo Morales Carrión and Gordon Lewis weight the scale in Muñoz's favor. Lewis, a shrewd (and fair-minded) skeptic about Muñoz, claims that the "'revolution of 1940' was written, not by Governor Tugwell, but by the *Populares* and their impressive leader." Lewis concludes: "They had shaped its vital center, the agrarian reform law, long before [Tugwell's] arrival." Charles T. Goodsell, *Administration of a Revolution: Executive Reform in Puerto Rico under Governor Tugwell, 1941–1946* (Cambridge: Harvard University Press, 1965), pp. 205–206; Raymond Carr, *Puerto Rico: A Colonial Experiment* (New York: New York University Press, 1984), pp. 65–66; Arturo Morales Carrión, *Puerto Rico: A Political and Cultural History* (New York: W. W. Norton, 1984), pp. 253–254; and Gordon K. Lewis, *Puerto Rico: Freedom and Power in the Caribbean* (New York: Harper Torchbooks, 1963), p. 107.

11. In so doing, Rodríguez Beruff brings the straightforward Admiral William D. Leahy, FDR's replacement for conservative Governor Blanton Winship in 1939, to the front rank of players. Leahy, a conservative who also happened to be the man in uniform Roosevelt trusted more than any other, having judged in 1940 that it was impossible to work with the right-wing Coalición and that the breakaway centrist Tripartismo had failed to seize the day, concluded (not without ambivalence) that Muñoz and the PPD deserved to take what they'd won fairly. Leahy's balanced view was good enough for the top officials of the Roosevelt administration, all of them similarly ambivalent about the Puerto Rican election results. See Jorge Rodríguez Beruff, *Strategy as Politics: Puerto Rico on the Eve of the Second World War* (Río Piedras: University of Puerto Rico Press, 2007); and Jorge Rodríguez Beruff, ed., *Las*

memorias de Leahy: los relatos del almirante William D. Leahy sobre su gobernación de Puerto Rico, 1939–1940 (San Juan: Fundación Luis Muñoz Marín, 2002).

12. Certainly there were other important factors, dealt with elsewhere in this volume, such as Puerto Rico's unexpected wartime rum tax revenue, freeing it from the tight purse strings held by Congress.

13. Tugwell in particular was sophisticated about these techniques of Roosevelt's, because he and the other principal 1932 campaign Brain Trusters had been caught in the middle of them at various times in the year before FDR took office as president. Schlesinger, *The Coming of the New Deal*, pp. 527–528, 541–542, 583–584; and Robert Dallek, *Franklin D. Roosevelt and American Foreign Policy, 1932–1945* (New York: Oxford University Press, 1979), pp. 28–31.

14. T. H. Watkins, *Righteous Pilgrim: The Life and Times of Harold L. Ickes, 1874–1952* (New York: Henry Holt, 1990), pp. 512–527; Morales Carrión, *Puerto Rico*, pp. 229–239; Mathews, *Puerto Rican Politics*, pp. 313–315; and Ickes, *Secret Diary*, vol. 1, p. 594.

15. An example: In June 1937, for densely complicated reasons (including the coincidental timing of a *nacionalista* attempt on the life of the federal judge based in Puerto Rico and the climax of Roosevelt's attempt to "pack" the US Supreme Court), Roosevelt reversed his support of Ickes's demands for an independent, government-sponsored investigation of Governor Winship's blunderbuss handling of the Ponce massacre earlier that year (supplementing the dramatic inquest conducted by the American Civil Liberties Union). Thus, FDR—overnight—joined Gruening behind Winship and the conservative Coalición. Ickes, who had been trying to remove Winship for many months, wrote the president in cold fury: "I am not particularly interested in what may happen to Governor Winship." What concerned him was "the record that your Administration will leave for justice and fair play in our Possessions," not to mention the potential for damage to US "prestige" in Puerto Rico, on the mainland, and across Latin America, "especially where the issue of civil liberties"—at the center of the Ponce massacre storm—was involved. See Watkins, *Righteous Pilgrim*, pp. 519–527; Franklin D. Roosevelt to Harold L. Ickes, June 9, 1937, and Ickes to Roosevelt, June 10, 1937 (both in Ickes Papers, Box 257, Library of Congress, Washington, DC); Ickes to Roosevelt, June 2, 1941, and Roosevelt to Ickes, June 16, 1941 (both in FDR Library, FDR Papers, PSF Box 55); and Rexford G. Tugwell, *The Art of Politics, as Practiced by Three Great Americans: Franklin Delano Roosevelt, Luis Muñoz Marín, and Fiorello H. La Guardia* (New York: Doubleday, 1958), pp. 148–149.

The link between the events in Puerto Rico and FDR's court packing bill included the obstructive lead role played by the conservative Democratic senator Millard Tydings of Maryland in both affairs. See Jeff Shesol, *Supreme Power: Franklin Roosevelt vs. the Supreme Court* (W. W. Norton, New York, 2010), pp. 323, 424–426; Nelson Lichtenstein, *The Most Dangerous Man in Detroit: Walter Reuther and the Fate of American Labor* (New York: Basic Books, 1995), pp. 74–80; and Harold L. Ickes, *The Secret Diary of Harold L. Ickes*, vol. 2, *The Inside Struggle, 1936–1939* (New York: Simon and Schuster, 1954), pp. 91, 95, 149.

16. See, for example, Rexford G. Tugwell and Charles Taussig to Franklin D. Roosevelt, July 21, 1937, Tugwell to Roosevelt, August 26, 1937, Tugwell to Roosevelt, December 23, 1937, and Roosevelt to Tugwell, December 27, 1937 (all in FDR Library, FDR Papers, PSF Box 167); Tugwell to Roosevelt, August 10, 1937, Roosevelt to Tugwell, August 12, 1937, and Tugwell to Roosevelt, December 14, 1937 (all in FDR Library, FDR Papers, PSF Box 564); Rodríguez

Beruff, *Strategy as Politics*, p. 368; Tugwell, *The Stricken Land*, pp. 64–69; and Rexford G. Tugwell, unpublished diary, February 6, 1940, FDR Library, Tugwell Papers, Box 32.

17. Adolf A. Berle to Rexford G. Tugwell, November 15, 1939, and Tugwell to Berle, November 16, 1939 (both in FDR Library, Tugwell Papers, Box 3).

18. Harold L. Ickes to Rexford G. Tugwell, September 18, 1939, Tugwell to Ickes, September 21, 1939, and Ickes to Tugwell, September 25, 1939 (all in FDR Library, Tugwell Papers, Box 23); Harold L. Ickes, *The Secret Diary of Harold L. Ickes*, vol. 3, *Lowering Clouds, 1939–1941* (New York: Simon and Schuster, 1954), pp. 6, 33–34, 427; and Rexford G. Tugwell, unpublished diary, November 17, 1939, FDR Library, Tugwell Papers, Box 32.

19. Phillips, *This Land, This Nation*, pp. 65–66, 204–205; Watkins, *Righteous Pilgrim*, pp. 469–494; and Ickes, *Secret Diary*, vol. 1, p. 692. For the first encounters of Roosevelt and Ickes (and Ickes and Tugwell) with one another other, see Frank Freidel, *Franklin D. Roosevelt: Launching the New Deal* (Boston: Little, Brown, 1973), pp. 154–155; Raymond Moley, *The First New Deal* (New York: Harcourt, Brace and World, 1966), pp. 93–95; Watkins, *Righteous Pilgrim*, p. 279; Ickes, *Secret Diary*, vol. 1, p. 240; and Jeanne Nienaber Clarke, *Roosevelt's Warrior: Harold L. Ickes and the New Deal* (Baltimore: Johns Hopkins University Press, 1996), pp. 26–27.

20. Scientifically planned, at its peak it held 550,000 trees.

21. Interview with David Hayes, National Park Service program manager, Roosevelt-Vanderbilt National Historic Sites, September 28, 2009, Hyde Park, NY; and Brian Black, "The Complex Environmentalist: Franklin D. Roosevelt and the Ethos of New Deal Conservation," in *FDR and the Environment*, ed. Henry L. Henderson and David B. Woolner (New York: Palgrave Macmillan, 2005), p. 32.

22. Rexford G. Tugwell, *In Search of Roosevelt* (Cambridge: Harvard University Press, 1972), p. 124; and Tugwell, *The Stricken Land*, p. 35.

23. Rexford G. Tugwell, *To the Lesser Heights of Morningside: A Memoir* (Philadelphia: University of Pennsylvania Press, 1982), pp. 92, 95; Phillips, *This Land, This Nation*, pp. 7–15; Tugwell, *The Diary of Rexford G. Tugwell*, p. 173; Franklin D. Roosevelt to Rexford G. Tugwell, February 3, 1942, and Tugwell to Roosevelt, February 11, 1942 (both in FDR Library, Tugwell Papers, Box 23); and Tugwell, *The Stricken Land*, pp. viii, 208.

24. Ickes, *Secret Diary*, vol. 1, pp. 240–241, 303. The president was always willing to back Ickes in principle in this vision, and entertained it himself. But the time was never right, or influential conservationists were split on the matter, or a swing-vote US senator close to the timber industry, which liked the status quo, needed to be placated.

25. This extraordinary mediation on Tugwell's part is attested to by Ickes in his private diary as well as by Tugwell. The hottest ember on the fire at that moment was FDR's selection of agriculture secretary Henry Wallace as his 1940 running mate. Ickes viewed his rival Wallace as naïve and incompetent, and, for good measure, thought that he had a shot at the vice presidential nomination himself. Rexford G. Tugwell, unpublished diary, July 30, 1940, FDR Library, Tugwell Papers, Box 32; and Harold L. Ickes, "Secret Diary," August 4, 1940, Ickes Papers, Box 6, Library of Congress.

26. Ickes promptly waved Tugwell's forthright letter at Roosevelt as a means of protesting that the president was currently shutting him out of Caribbean strategic planning. FDR, with vagueness intended to feed the flames, responded: "I agree with you and Rex that we

ought to start something going." Tugwell, *The Stricken Land*, pp. 7–14, 95–100, 127–128, 137; Tugwell, *The Art of Politics*, pp. 146–150; and Rexford G. Tugwell to Harold L. Ickes, April 10, 1941, Ickes to Franklin D. Roosevelt, April 16, 1941, and Roosevelt to Ickes, April 17, 1941 (all in Ickes Papers, Box 256, Library of Congress).

27. The idea was that, as UPR chancellor on unpaid leave to serve as governor, Tugwell would technically come to La Fortaleza as a Puerto Rican, and leave it at some future time to run the UPR. Rexford G. Tugwell, unpublished diary, December 10, 1940, December 17, 1940, February 15, 1941, February 21, 1941, April 4, 1941, and June 20, 1941, FDR Library, Tugwell Papers, Box 32; Rexford G. Tugwell to Harold L. Ickes, March 20, 1942, and Ickes to Tugwell, March 27, 1942 (both in FDR Library, Tugwell Papers, Box 47); and Franklin D. Roosevelt to Ickes, March 24, 1942, FDR Library, FDR Papers, Official File, Series 400, Puerto Rico file. The UPR deal is well chronicled, but see "Tugwell to Puerto Rico," *Time*, August 4, 1941; "Territories: Luis and Rex," *Time*, August 18, 1941; Tugwell, *The Stricken Land*, pp. 107, 121, 142–145 et seq.; and Muñoz Marín, *Memorias*, pp. 70–72.

28. "Rule or ruin" is Tugwell's characterization of the official Washington line on Muñoz after 1936, as expressed in his *The Stricken Land*. Thomas Mathews quotes educator José Padín's recollection that "President Roosevelt exploded at the mention of Muñoz's name" in a conversation in 1936. Rodríguez Beruff cites Coalición resident commissioner Santiago Iglesias's claim that FDR told him in 1937 that Muñoz was an "educator in the wrong way." That land reform (to include conservation measures) would be Muñoz's central campaign issue in 1940 did not sweeten the atmosphere. There are many sources for this part of the drama. For Tugwell's informed summaries, see his *The Art of Politics*, pp. 146–147, 256–257; Tugwell, *The Stricken Land*, p. 9; Mathews, *Puerto Rican Politics*, p. 307, n. 61; and Rodríguez Beruff, *Strategy as Politics*, p. 186.

29. Ruby Black to Muna Lee and Luis Muñoz Marín, July 13, 1936, Ruby Black Papers, Centro de Investigaciones Históricas, Universidad de Puerto Rico, Recinto de Río Piedras; Mathews, *Puerto Rican Politics*, p. 307, n. 61; and Harold L. Ickes, "Secret Diary," February 6, 1937, Ickes Papers, Box 3, Library of Congress.

30. Eleanor Roosevelt to Ruby Black, February 12, 1937, FDR Library, Eleanor Roosevelt Papers, White House Correspondence, Personal Letters, Series 100, Box 647; Rodríguez Beruff, *Strategy as Politics*, pp. 244, 257, nn. 157, 158; Lieutenant Colonel Thomas Phillips to Military Intelligence Division, War Department chief of staff, November 5, 1940, reprinted in Rodríguez Beruff, *Las memorias de Leahy*, p. 251; Nixon Butt Jr., "Report on Jose Luis Munoz Marin [sic] et al.," April 1, 1943, FBI Files on Puerto Ricans, no. HQ-100-5745, Center for Puerto Rican Studies, Hunter College, City University of New York, NY. Add to the mix the steady flow of US military intelligence reports to the effect that Muñoz was "unreliable" and "erratic" and that the PPD reflected "penetration" by communists and *nacionalistas*. FBI reports were laced with secondhand misinformation and malice; for example, Muñoz was "described by reliable informants to be intellectual with bad case of 'Puerto Rican inferiority complex,' which results in anti-American tendencies.... [He is] known to be personally completely irresponsible."

31. Rodríguez Beruff, *Strategy as Politics*, pp. 374–378; Morales Carrión, *Puerto Rico*, p. 230.

32. Ickes, *Secret Diary*, vol. 3, p. 389; and Ickes, "Secret Diary," August 9, 1941, Ickes Papers, Box 7, Library of Congress. See also Maldonado, *Luis Muñoz Marín*, p. 203. Muñoz's sympathetic biographer A. W. Maldonado, relying on Tugwell, states that Ickes's hostile attitude toward Muñoz was exacerbated by the latter's postelection stance in the winter of 1940–1941, as if he were now in charge of Puerto Rico on a grand scale.

33. Franklin D. Roosevelt to Rexford G. Tugwell, February 3, 1942, FDR Library, Tugwell Papers, Box 23; Tugwell, *The Stricken Land*, p. 137; Maldonado, *Luis Muñoz Marín*, p. 209; and Tugwell, *The Art of Politics*, pp. 256–257.

34. Rexford G. Tugwell to Franklin D. Roosevelt, March 11, 1942, and Roosevelt to Tugwell, March 21, 1942 (both FDR Library, Tugwell Papers, Box 23).

35. Tugwell, *The Art of Politics*.

36. Ibid., pp. 256–257.

37. Luis Muñoz Marín to Franklin D. Roosevelt, December 13, 1941, and Roosevelt to Muñoz Marín, December 15, 1941 (both in FDR Library, FDR Papers, PPF, File 7155).

38. So effective was Black that it's worth noting that her last two significant acts on behalf of Muñoz, as the New Deal took second place to war preparedness, were bull's-eye shots. The first was her strong advisory of December 3, 1940 (addressed to Muñoz and Jesús Piñero), that Washington was still dubious enough about Muñoz to want assurance that he and the PPD were in tight allegiance with the Roosevelt administration on its defense preparedness moves. The second was that it was Black, and Black alone, through Mrs. Roosevelt, who got Muñoz invited to Hyde Park for the president's laying on of hands over Labor Day weekend, 1941. But for reasons too involved to explore here, Black was moving out of the picture by 1941.

39. Ruby Black to Luis Muñoz Marín and Jesús T. Piñero, December 3, 1940, Black to Eleanor Roosevelt, August 14, 1941, and Black to Muñoz Marín, September 19, 1941 (all in Ruby Black Papers, Centro de Investigaciones Históricas, Universidad de Puerto Rico, Recinto de Río Piedras); Ruby Black to Eleanor Roosevelt, August 25, 1941, and Mrs. Roosevelt's secretary (presumably Malvina Thompson) to Luis Muñoz Marín, August 28, 1941 (both in FDR Library, Eleanor Roosevelt Papers, Series 100, Box 734).

40. Sumner Welles to Franklin D. Roosevelt, October 8, 1940, FDR Library, FDR Papers, OF Series 6, Box 4318; Rodríguez Beruff, *Strategy as Politics*, p. 368; Tugwell, *The Stricken Land*, pp. 95–97; Rafael Cox Alomar, *Revisiting the Transatlantic Triangle: The Constitutional Decolonization of the Eastern Caribbean* (Kingston: Ian Randle, 2009), pp. 18–21; and Harold L. Ickes to Roosevelt, April 16, 1941, Ickes to Rexford G. Tugwell, April 16, 1941, and Roosevelt to Ickes, April 30, 1941 (all in Ickes Papers, Box 256, Library of Congress).

41. Charles Taussig to Sumner Welles, March 6, 1941, and Taussig, Memorandum of Conversation with President Roosevelt, September 23, 1941 (both in FDR Library, Taussig Papers, Box 52); Tugwell, *The Stricken Land*, pp. 98–100; and Ickes, *Secret Diary*, vol. 3, pp. 443–444.

42. Rexford G. Tugwell, unpublished diary, February 21, 1941, and February 24, 1941, FDR Library, Tugwell Papers, Box 32; Ickes, "Secret Diary," January 2, 1941, Ickes Papers, Box 7, Library of Congress; Ickes, *Secret Diary*, vol. 3, pp. 505, 513; and Harold L. Ickes to Franklin D. Roosevelt, June 2, 1941, FDR Library, FDR Papers, PSF, Box 65.

43. Rexford G. Tugwell to Charles Taussig, October 2, 1941, enclosing editorial of *El Mundo* of the same date, FDR Library, Taussig Papers, Box 39; Taussig to Tugwell, October 14, 1941, FDR Library, Tugwell Papers, Box 25; Sumner Welles to Franklin D. Roosevelt, October 29, 1941, Welles to Roosevelt, February 4, 1942, and Roosevelt to Welles, February 9, 1942 (all in FDR Library, FDR Papers, OF Box 4630); and Tugwell, *The Stricken Land*, pp. 98–100, 136, 174–175.

44. Rexford G. Tugwell to Franklin D. Roosevelt, November 3, 1941, FDR Library, FDR Papers, PF OF File, Series 400, Box 25; Roosevelt to Tugwell, November 7, 1941, FDR Library, Tugwell Papers, Box 23; and Ickes, *Secret Diary*, vol. 3, p. 513.

45. On one occasion, on word from Tugwell to Ickes that Pagán had a sugar lobby drawing account, FDR authorized an FBI investigation of the matter. Franklin D. Roosevelt to Harold L. Ickes, February 23, 1942, and Ickes to Roosevelt, February 25, 1942 (both in FDR Library, FDR Papers, PSF Confidential File: Puerto Rico, Box 8); and Surendra Bhana, *The United States and the Development of the Puerto Rican Status Question, 1936–1968* (Lawrence: University Press of Kansas, 1975), p. 48.

46. Statement by Harold L. Ickes, February 11, 1942, and Rexford G. Tugwell to Ickes, February 17, 1942 (both in National Archives, Office of Territories, 9-4-82); Ickes to Luis Muñoz Marín, February 17, 1942, Archivo Fundación Luis Muñoz Marín (hereafter AFLMM), Muñoz Marín Papers, Section 4, Series 3, Tugwell File 489; and Rexford G. Tugwell, unpublished diary, March 6, 1942, FDR Library, Tugwell Papers, Box 32.

47. That appropriation stalled, but its need was mooted by the rum tax revenue boom. Nevertheless it showed, as Tugwell noted, that "[t]he President thought of Puerto Rico" when the hour was dark. John Franklin Carter, "Report on Puerto Rico under Governor Tugwell," plus enclosure of unsigned report dated March 5, 1942, FDR Library, FDR Papers, Carter File, PSF, Box 98; Franklin D. Roosevelt to Harold L. Ickes, March 7, 1942, Ickes to Roosevelt, March 9, 1942, and Roosevelt to Ickes, March 1, 1942 (all in Ickes Papers, Box 256, Library of Congress); Rexford G. Tugwell, unpublished diary, June 10, 1940, FDR Library, Tugwell Papers, Box 32; and Tugwell, *The Stricken Land*, p. 209.

48. Rexford G. Tugwell, unpublished diary, June 14, 1942, and June 19, 1942, FDR Library, Tugwell Papers, Box 32; Ickes to Tugwell (undated), Abe Fortas Papers, Box 161, Folder 3, Yale University Library; and Tugwell, *The Stricken Land*, pp. 221–222, 267.

49. In Taussig's and Travieso's minds was the notion that Tugwell would stay in Washington (or return as chancellor of the University of Puerto Rico all over again), and Travieso would be named acting governor, or governor in his own right. Tugwell had in fact authorized Taussig to tell FDR and Ickes that he was prepared to stand aside for the appointment of a Puerto Rican. But Taussig had not revealed to his old friend the full scope of what he was up to. Tugwell concluded that Taussig had been seduced by the "romance" of kingmaking. Rexford G. Tugwell to Charles Taussig, June 22, 1942, and Tugwell to Taussig, June 29, 1942 (both in FDR Library, Taussig Papers, Box 25); Tugwell, unpublished diary, June 28, 1942, June 30, 1942, and July 6, 1942, FDR Library, Tugwell Papers, Box 32; Ickes, "Secret Diary," July 5, 1942, Ickes Papers, Box 9, Library of Congress; and Abe Fortas to Harold L. Ickes, July 23, 1942, enclosing Office of Censorship intercept of report from T. Maldonado to "Pepe," July 3, 1942, and July 5, 1942; and Ickes to Fortas, July 25, 1942, Tugwell to Ickes,

June 25, 1942, and Ickes to Tugwell, July 26, 1942 (all in Ickes Papers, Box 256, Library of Congress).

50. Rexford G. Tugwell, unpublished diary, November 18, 1942, FDR Library, Tugwell Papers, Box 32; Harold L. Ickes to Rexford G. Tugwell, November 25, 1942, FDR Library, Tugwell Papers, Box 47; Ickes to Tugwell, March 6, 1943, Ickes Papers, Box 256, Library of Congress; and Ickes, "Secret Diary," February 27, 1943, Ickes Papers, Box 10, Library of Congress.

51. Rexford G. Tugwell, unpublished diary, July 17, 1943, and July 24, 1943, FDR Library, Tugwell Papers, Box 33.

52. Rexford G. Tugwell, unpublished diary, July 24, 1943, FDR Library, Tugwell Papers, Box 33. For Roosevelt on anticipation that postcolonial insular self-governance would be "bad," see Tugwell, unpublished diary, May 27, 1942, FDR Library, Tugwell Papers, Box 33.

53. Good communication between San Juan and the administration at this time included an order from FDR to the army chief of staff, General George Marshall, "to do the necessary" to "assist the Governor in insuring orderly conduct of the election there this year." The correspondence concerning the opposition's intent to suspend elections is voluminous. See, for example, Rexford G. Tugwell to Harold L. Ickes, February 28, 1944, Ickes to Tugwell, March 10, 1944, and Abe Fortas to Tugwell, March 27, 1944 (all in FDR Library, Tugwell Papers, Box 47); Ickes to Franklin D. Roosevelt, March 10, 1944, FDR Library, FDR Papers, OF 400, Puerto Rico; Tugwell, unpublished diary, March 12, 1944, FDR Library, Tugwell Papers, Box 33; and Roosevelt to General George C. Marshall, September 8, 1944, FDR Library, FDR Papers, PSF Box 48.

54. Rexford G. Tugwell, unpublished diary, July 9, 1944, FDR Library, Tugwell Papers, Box 34; Franklin D. Roosevelt to Bolívar Pagán, October 9, 1944, National Archives, OT 9-8-82; and Tugwell to Luis Muñoz Marín, July 22, 1944, AFLMM, Muñoz Marín Papers, Section 4 (Presidente del Senado), Series 3, Tugwell File.

55. Rexford G. Tugwell, unpublished diary, September 18, 1941, FDR Library, Tugwell Papers, Box 32.

56. That figure, noted Muñoz, was "55% of the total number who voted in the last election, . . . the closest thing to a plebiscite . . . of confidence in [Tugwell's] understanding of our needs and hopes, of our desire to sacrifice for the war effort." Rexford G. Tugwell, unpublished diary, October 22, 1941, July 14, 1942, September 14, 1942, November 3–4, 1942, and March 3–7, 1943, FDR Library, Tugwell Papers, Box 32; Franklin D. Roosevelt to Eleanor Roosevelt, with enclosures, July 4, 1942, FDR Library, Eleanor Roosevelt papers, Series 70, Box 370; and Luis Muñoz Marín and Samuel R. Quiñones to Franklin D. Roosevelt, Harold L. Ickes, et al., September 13, 1942, AFLMM, Muñoz Marín Papers, Section 4 (Presidente del Senado), 1941–1948, Series 1, Gobierno Federal, Folder 4.

57. Rexford G. Tugwell, unpublished diary, May 2, 1943, FDR Library, Tugwell Papers, Box 33.

58. Rexford G. Tugwell, unpublished diary, March 22, 1944, FDR Library, Tugwell Papers, Box 33.

59. In contrast to Ickes and FDR, Fortas rapidly shed himself of the mistrust of Muñoz that had become contagious in Washington. Fortas secured Puerto Rico as one of his first clients when he left the Interior Department and took up his role as a leading Washington "superlawyer" in 1946. The rest is history; which is to say, another big piece of it.

60. Rexford G. Tugwell to Abe Fortas, September 14, 1944, Tugwell to Harold L. Ickes, January 5, 1945, Tugwell to Ickes, April 23, 1945, Ickes to Tugwell, May 5, 1945, and Tugwell to Ickes, May 10, 1945 (all in FDR Library, Tugwell Papers, Box 47); and Tugwell, *The Stricken Land*, p. 594.

61. José Trías Monge, *Puerto Rico: The Trials of the Oldest Colony in the World* (New Haven, CT: Yale University Press, 1997); Bhana, *The United States and the Development of the Puerto Rican Status Question*, pp. 57–65, 102–104; and Rexford G. Tugwell, unpublished diary, May 15, 1942, April 26, 1943, July 1, 1943, July 21, 1943, July 23, 1943, July 24, 1943, July 30, 1943, August 1, 1943, and August 4, 1943, FDR Library, Tugwell Papers, Box 33.

62. Rexford G. Tugwell to Abe Fortas, May 1, 1944, FDR Library, Tugwell Papers, Box 47; Tugwell to Fortas (second letter), May 1, 1941, Tugwell to Fortas (both in Rexford G. Tugwell, unpublished diary, at those dates), FDR Library, Tugwell Papers, Boxes 33–34.

63. In vain, Muñoz tried the gambit of instructing newly elected resident commissioner Jesús Piñero that he "comunícale personalmente a Ickes o a Fortas" that they confide in him, Piñero, as if they were talking to Muñoz himself. Olympian indeed; when Tugwell again suggested that Fortas come to the island, Ickes grumbled that this was "asking the mountain to visit Mohammed." Abe Fortas to Rexford G. Tugwell, December 7, 1944, Tugwell to Fortas, December 11, 1944, Fortas to Tugwell, December 19, 1944, Tugwell to Fortas, December 27, 1944, Tugwell to Harold L. Ickes, January 5, 1945, and Ickes to Tugwell, January 10, 1945 (all in FDR Library, Tugwell Papers, Box 47); Luis Muñoz Marín to Ickes, January 22, 1945, Ickes Papers, Box 256, Library of Congress; Harold L. Ickes, "Secret Diary," May 19, 1945, Ickes Papers, Library of Congress; and Muñoz Marín to Jesús T. Piñero, December 31, 1944, AFLMM, Muñoz Marín Papers, Section 4 (Presidente del Senado), Series 3, Harold Ickes, File 271.

64. See Luis Rosario Albert's chapter, "Geopolitics and Telecommunications Policy in Puerto Rico: ITT and the Porto Rico Telephone Company, 1942–1948," later in this volume.

65. Tugwell, *The Stricken Land*, pp. 458–459, 538–539; and Rexford G. Tugwell, unpublished diary, July 17, 1943, FDR Library, Tugwell Papers, Box 33.

66. Tugwell, *The Stricken Land*, pp. 469–470; Rexford G. Tugwell, unpublished diary, December 26, 1943, FDR Library, Tugwell Papers, Box 33; and Tugwell to Harold L. Ickes, unpublished diary, December 27, 1943, FDR Library, Tugwell Papers, Box 33.

67. Dennis Chávez to Harry S. Truman, December 28, 1945, Robert S. Hannegan to Truman, January 18, 1946, Truman to Chávez, February 15, 1946, Oscar Chapman to Truman, February 22, 1946, Luis Muñoz Marín to Julius Krug, June 19, 1946, Muñoz Marín to Truman, July 15, 1946, and Rexford G. Tugwell to Truman, July 30, 1946, in Héctor Luis Acevedo, ed., *Jesús T. Piñero: el hombre, el político, el gobernador* (San Juan: Inter American University of Puerto Rico, 2005); Bhana, *The United States and the Development of the Puerto Rican Status Question*, pp. 93–108; and Rexford G. Tugwell, unpublished diary, April 7, 1946, FDR Library, Tugwell Papers, Box 34.

The War Economy of Puerto Rico, 1939–1945

José L. Bolívar Fresneda

The Second World War brought about major changes in the Puerto Rican economy, hitherto mainly dependent on sugar exports and federal welfare expenditures. Three income streams provided Puerto Rico, an island with a population of roughly 1.9 million in 1940,[1] with almost $1.2 billion dollars between 1939 and 1947.[2] On a per capita basis, this is a much larger amount than what the United States invested in Europe through the Marshall Plan.[3] The US military invested $709.6 million (see table 2), rum tax receipts returned to the government of Puerto Rico totaled $190.3 million (see table 3), and we estimate that the wage repatriations from Puerto Rican servicemen averaged between $58.5 million and $87.8 million (see tables 5 and 6). Yet, few studies have analyzed the economic history of Puerto Rico from the perspective of the consequences of war, and those that are available provide a general view that glosses over this period and fails to take into account its importance and particularities.[4] A case in point is James L. Dietz's *Economic History of Puerto Rico*, published in 1986, which examines events dating back to 1493. His analysis of the Second World War's impact on Puerto Rican finances suggests that the most relevant factor was the tax revenue returned from sales of Puerto Rican rum to the mainland, particularly from 1942 to 1946.[5] Another well-known study, *Historia económica de Puerto Rico* by Rafael de Jesús Toro, is also a long-term historical approach that only emphasizes the tax revenues of rum sales, disregarding the other major sources of income.[6] The recently published and well-researched book by Francisco A. Catalá Oliveras titled *Promesa rota: una mirada institucionalista a partir de Tugwell* is also a long-term view of the economic history of Puerto Rico, although it concentrates on the institutional developments of the twentieth and twenty-first centuries. As such, the author does not focus his attention on the effect the significant military investments during World War II had in Puerto Rico.[7]

Dry docks at the Roosevelt Roads Naval Base in Ceiba, Puerto Rico, 1943 (Cultural Resources Division, San Juan National Historic Site, National Park Service)

In this chapter, we concentrate on how the war impacted the finances of Puerto Rico in two distinct periods. The first, from 1939 through mid-1943, relates to infrastructure investments. The second, from mid-1943 through 1945 and 1946, has to do mainly with the tax revenue accrued from the rum sales. In addition, the percentage of the salaries that the large numbers of Puerto Rican soldiers repatriated to the island during both periods must be taken into account. This last source of income has largely been overlooked and represents a significant portion of the funds that flowed to Puerto Rican families, if not into the government's coffers.[8]

The fate of Puerto Rico's economy during the Second World War resembled that of a roller coaster: massive military investments, the use of New Deal agencies for war purposes, the sudden closure of the military construction program, and the fluke of the rum bonanza. Prior to the war, Puerto Rico had benefited from some of the programs enacted under Roosevelt's New Deal. The Puerto Rico Reconstruction Administration (PRRA), founded in 1935, was one of these. During the first six years of its existence, its budget of almost $70 million exceeded that of the insular government. However, it was not until the nomination of William D. Leahy to the governorship of

Puerto Rico that the island received a significant boost from the war economy emerging in the United States.[9]

On March 1, 1939, while traveling on board the cruiser USS *Houston*, President Franklin D. Roosevelt told Admiral Leahy, then his chief of naval operations, "that he should prepare himself upon retirement to assume the governorship of Puerto Rico."[10] On September 6, six days after the German invasion of Poland, President Roosevelt officially declared the neutrality of the United States. On September 11, he appointed Leahy as governor of Puerto Rico. Leahy was given the role of "federal coordinator," with practically the entire federal bureaucracy in Puerto Rico under his authority. These resources were much greater than those available to the Puerto Rican government. In 1939, the budget of the Works Progress Administration (WPA) was $2.6 million, that of the PRRA $9.0 million, the Public Works Administration (PWA) $8.4 million, the Civilian Conservation Corps (CCC) $1.0 million, and the US Housing Authority $12.0 million in guaranteed loans. It was an amount of power never enjoyed by any of Leahy's predecessors. As such, Leahy "controlled not only the executive branch of the Puerto Rican government, but also the politically coveted Federal patronage."[11]

During the war, two governors—William D. Leahy and Rexford G. Tugwell (Guy Swope's brief stay was but an interlude)—both personal friends of Roosevelt, both committed to New Deal programs, both supportive of the military buildup, and both interested in maintaining a peaceful environment in Puerto Rico (unlike the previous, tormented rule of Blanton Winship), presided over Puerto Rico's future. The election of November 1940 brought the unexpected electoral victory of the newly formed Popular Democratic Party and its charismatic leader, Luis Muñoz Marín. As president of the Senate and the de facto popularly elected Puerto Rican leader, Muñoz Marín worked alongside Leahy and Tugwell (although not always under harmonious circumstances) in implementing a social and economic partnership.[12]

Preparing for War: The Military Buildup

By early 1939, war loomed both in Europe and in the Pacific. The United States, concerned about the defense of the Panama Canal and the entire Caribbean region, started a program of acquisition and construction of bases in the Panama Canal Zone and throughout the Caribbean. Bases in Cuba, Haiti, the Dominican Republic, and Puerto Rico were either expanded or built from scratch.[13] As Great Britain's ability to pay for supplies was nearing its end, Lord Lothian, the British ambassador to the United States, persuaded a reluctant Winston Churchill to lay the financial facts openly before President Roosevelt. Out of this approach came Roosevelt's call for the Lend-Lease program, which was agreed upon on September 2, 1940.[14] This agreement stipulated that the United States would provide Britain with fifty old destroyers. In exchange, Britain would lease, for a period of ninety-nine years, bases in the Bahamas, Bermuda, Antigua, Jamaica, Saint Lucia, Trinidad, and British Guiana. The United States invested over $180 million in modernizing and upgrading these facilities.[15]

In Puerto Rico, the Isla Grande Naval Base was one of Washington's most expensive construction projects outside the continental United States.[16] However, in spite of the enhanced investment and increased presence, US military forces were not able to overcome the virtual submarine blockade imposed by German U-boats and the terrible toll it took on the island's economy and trade with the Caribbean during 1942 and early 1943. Eighteen months after the United States entered the war—in mid-1943—military construction came to a halt. By that time, it had become clear that the Allies were winning the Battle of the Atlantic, making it possible for the invasion of North Africa, Operation Torch, to proceed successfully.[17] The success of antisubmarine warfare forced the Germans to withdraw their submarines from the Caribbean.

The military buildup in Puerto Rico began in early 1939 with the construction of essential infrastructure projects, accomplished with WPA personnel and financing. On January 14, *El Mundo*, the newspaper with the largest circulation in Puerto Rico, announced the construction of a bridge connecting both sides of the Río Grande de Loíza in Trujillo Alto, a municipality in close proximity to San Juan.[18] The following week, another article noted that eight regional airports would be constructed in various cities around the island.[19] Also, a two-thousand-foot underground tunnel connecting the old Spanish fortification of San Felipe del Morro with forts San Cristóbal and San Jerónimo was to be built. Ironically, the last time these forts were used in battle was against the United States in the Spanish-American War of 1898. As the United States did not want to appear threatening to its colonial neighbors—the French in Martinique, for example—keeping the appearance of neutrality was an important aspect of the Roosevelt administration's foreign as well as domestic policy. As part of this policy, officials of the Department of the Interior would flatly deny that the construction of the regional airports had anything to do with President Roosevelt's defense programs, even though they acknowledged that, in case of war, these airports could play a significant role in the defense of Puerto Rico. The WPA made similar comments regarding the construction of the tunnels below Old San Juan. According to the WPA, these tunnels were of no military value; the fact that they could accommodate a contingent of soldiers and that they were illuminated was just a coincidence.[20]

In addition to the construction of the Isla Grande Naval Base, Leahy oversaw the construction and/or planning phase of a number of military bases, such as Borinquen Air Field in Aguadilla (off the eastern coast of Puerto Rico), a major expansion Fort Buchanan in San Juan, the Salinas Training Center, Fort Bundy in Fajardo, Camp O'Reilly in Caguas, Amelia Farm in Cataño, and others. Some of the construction for these projects would start after Leahy's departure from the island. All told, the armed forces would expropriate 53,484 acres on the island for these projects of which 22,000 acres were expropriated in Vieques alone, covering two-thirds of the island.[21] Other projects included the construction of 450 housing units for army and navy personnel, slated to begin on May 27, while in June another announcement foretold the construction of a base in Ceiba and Vieques at an estimated cost of $42.5 million.[22] On September 19, the army and the National Guard of Puerto Rico announced the construction of a permanent campground in Tortuguero, Vega Baja, at a cost of $2.0 million. On October 26, the construction of an army air force base in Juana Díaz, on the southern portion of the island near Ponce, was begun. It would be named Losey Field.[23] The WPA would engage a significant number of Puerto Rican laborers in this feat.

Another significant infrastructure investment was a modern road originating at Borinquen Air Field in Aguadilla and ending at Fort Buchanan. This road would bypass most urban centers and eliminate many of the curves of the existing roads that dated to Spanish times. It was designed so that the military could transport troops and other equipment quickly and safely between the two most distant bases on the island. All told, this road would cost $5 million, about half the cost of building the Isla Grande Naval Base.[24]

The WPA was also deeply involved in the eradication of malaria. Officially, this was presented as a civilian project designed to improve the health of the local population. While the local population certainly benefited from this effort, the need to eradicate malaria, from the point of view of the military establishment, was critical in reducing the number of sick days and possible deaths of military personnel who would be stationed in Puerto Rico in the event of war.[25] Another aspect of these military preparations was the many safeguards taken by the United States to prevent acts of sabotage. One of these was to use FBI agents in the field to fingerprint all laborers working on federally funded construction projects. Those who refused were fired on the spot.[26] The FBI also kept a close watch over communist and nationalist groups as well as foreign individuals and organizations such as the Spanish Falange.

The Falange, sponsored by the pro-fascist Francisco Franco government in Madrid, had a large following in Puerto Rico.

"Drafting" and Training Military and Civilian Personnel for the War Effort

The dependence of Puerto Rico on federal agencies to employ the masses of unemployed locals posed a striking difference to what was happening in the United States. Once the military draft started its recruiting process, unemployment was no longer a concern for the Roosevelt administration. In fact, the problem was quite the opposite: a lack of employable workers, as most had been drafted by the military. Now, instead of having a large number of unemployed, the United States found itself short of qualified personnel to run its war economy. Given this shortfall, factories turned toward hiring women, and by 1942 more than four million women had been inducted into the workforce. Puerto Rico faced a different reality. The huge number of ships sunk by submarines and the limitations of shipping space due to war requirements created a de facto blockade of all imported goods, which reached crisis proportions in late 1942. This produced a stagnant economy, and unemployment shot up from 11 percent in April 1940 to a high of 37 percent in September 1942. In effect, out of a total labor force of 639,000, the number of unemployed Puerto Ricans was a staggering 237,400. The blockade mostly affected private industry, as agriculture employment increase 7.6 percent between July 1941 and July 1942 and experienced only a slight decrease of 2.1 percent between July 1942 and September 1942, while the armed forces recruited 65,000 Puerto Ricans[27] for the war effort, thus reducing the number of potentially unemployed. In this context, the WPA's role in Puerto Rico became twofold: to develop a military infrastructure and to provide as many jobs as possible to the local population.[28] WPA employment in Puerto Rico increased from 46,000 at the end of 1938 to 37,067 by the end of 1942.[29] On April 27, 1939, President Roosevelt asked Congress to approve $1.477 billion for the WPA and $10 million for the PRRA,[30] the latter headed by Ernest Gruening. By the time of Leahy's governorship, the PRRA was fading, and its responsibilities were taken over by the WPA, probably due to Leahy's preference for the latter.[31]

The role of the federal government in the creation of jobs on the island was of critical importance during the war years. During those times, the economy of Puerto Rico was dependent on sugarcane, as demonstrated by the fact that 229,901 people worked in this industry out of a total labor force of 607,700 (see table 1). This was equivalent to 38 percent of the total labor force. Due to the seasonality of the industry, employment averaged seven months out

Table 5.1: Labor Force Classification, 1940-1942

Month	Year	Agricultural Employees (1, 6)	Federal Employees (2)	Armed Forces (3)	Private Industry (4)	Insular Government (5)	Employed (6)	Unemployed (6)	Total Labor Force (6)	Unemployment Rate
April	1940	229,901	84,316	—	211,289	15,394	540,900	66,800	607,700	11%
July	1941	229,901	82,018	—	196,902	15,579	524,400	99,100	623,500	16%
July	1942	247,373	90,627	47,000	66,192	20,028	471,200	165,600	636,800	26%
September	1942	242,426	90,627	47,000	11,547	10,000	401,600	237,400	639,000	37%

Sources: (1) Eliezer Cuevas Curet, *El Desarrollo Económico de Puerto Rico: 1940 a 1972* (Puerto Rico: Management Aid Center, 1976), Cuadro Número 14, p. 38; (2) Forty-Third Annual Report of the Governor of Puerto Rico, Rexford G. Tugwell, 1943, Table 2; (3) César J. Ayala Casás and José L. Bolívar Fresneda, *Battleship Vieques* (Princeton, NJ: Markus Wiener, 2011), p. 121; (4) Calculations by the author; (5) Forty-Third Annual Report of the Governor of Puerto Rico, Rexford G. Tugwell, 1943, Table 2, p. 77; (6) "The Puerto Rican Economy during the War Year of 1942," June 1943, AFLMM, Section 12, Material de y sobre Luis Muñoz Marín, Proyecto de Recopilación de Documentos, Harry S. Truman Library, p. 18.

of the year with a pay scale of fifteen cents an hour during the 1939–1940 fiscal year, increasing to twenty cents during the 1944–1945 period.[32] Workers would have to get by during the remaining five months with whatever savings they might have garnered or by bartering crops or animals they might own. During the Second World War, the labor situation changed dramatically, as more Puerto Ricans were employed in civil or military endeavors by the federal government than were employed by private industry, while employment in the sugar industry remained basically static.

The skill level required to work in the sugar industry (cutting sugarcane being the most prevalent form of employment) was low, as most of the farm work was performed with simple hand tools. This contrasted to the skill level required in the construction industry. The military, at the time, was involved in the construction of bases, hospitals, housing developments, airports, aircraft hangars, and the entire necessary infrastructure (electricity, water, sanitary facilities) for human habitation. These efforts required a significant number of carpenters, electricians, mechanics, and other technically adept workers who were simply not available on the island. Therefore, a significant amount of technical retraining would be required.[33] In some cases, continental employees were brought to Puerto Rico to train and supervise the construction process.

In addition to the lack of technical skills, the language barrier was another obstacle faced by military contractors. Both private contractors hired to build bases, such as the Arundel Corporation, a Baltimore-based company that was awarded the contract to build bases at Isla Grande, Roosevelt Roads in Ceiba, Mosquito Bay in Vieques, and elsewhere; and federal agencies such as the WPA, employed stateside personnel, most of whom had no working knowledge of Spanish, while most locals had none of English. This situation would result in a number of clashes, misunderstandings, and strikes.[34] Much of the retraining of the Puerto Rican laborers fell on the hands of the insular government, although the funding was provided by the federal government. The island's Department of Education set up vocational training programs and industrial schools adjacent to the construction sites in order to provide hands-on training. By May 1941, approximately nine thousand Puerto Ricans were enrolled in these programs. In July, President Roosevelt authorized $15 million to be allocated for the retraining of laborers in the United States so that they could be of better use to the war industries. Puerto Rico was awarded some of these funds.[35] Unfortunately, this training was not available when the construction of the military programs started in 1939, forcing many stateside contractors to hire mainland personnel as previously mentioned.[36]

As a result of both the language and training difficulties, the military authorities complained frequently about their inability to complete their tasks on time and with the expected level of quality. The military lamented that WPA workers were chosen more for social and economic needs than for the required technical abilities. They also objected to the lack of qualified supervisors, fluent in both Spanish and English. Administrative problems also arose between the WPA and the local government. As an example, the military complained that the Puerto Rican Treasury Department was given authority to purchase supplies and materials for work conducted by the WPA, thereby severely limiting the useful and necessary interaction between the WPA and the suppliers. The military authorities also had conflicts with local suppliers. They claimed that they would bid without having either the means or a definite idea of how to supply materials on time. Even Rafael del Valle Zeno, vice president of the Puerto Rican Technical Committee of the Civil Defense, argued that the inefficiency of the WPA was a well-known fact.[37] All these issues would cause tensions between the military authorities, the local government, and the WPA, resulting in numerous strikes.

Tensions Reach a Boiling Point: Racism and Discrimination

Puerto Ricans complained that the Arundel Corporation exposed them to various forms of discrimination, and when they protested, they were summarily fired. At the time, the US Armed Forces was segregated, and "despite Roosevelt's insistence that it recruit African Americans, [the navy] understood that this would be for kitchen jobs and the like, as it was unthinkable to impose on US white sailors the burden of cohabitation with blacks in ships or submarines."[38] Race and racism affected not only all the branches of the armed forces but also civilian life, especially for the continentals and Puerto Ricans working on US military construction projects.[39] According to 1930, 1935, and 1940 census data, the nonwhite population of Puerto Rico was 25.7 percent, 23.8 percent, and 23.5 percent, respectively.[40]

As César J. Ayala Casás and José L. Bolívar Fresneda point out, the registration of Puerto Ricans for the draft began five weeks later than in the United States, on November 20, 1940.[41] Upon recruitment, the army segregated Puerto Ricans into "white" and "black" units. Quotas were established with a ratio of four whites to one black. Also, a distinction was made between "whites" and "white Puerto Ricans." A white person was described "as light-colored people of Latin origin while blacks were said to be dark skinned and of a different racial origin. According to army records, by the end of 1941, it had become apparent that Puerto Rican men inducted under US standards were drastically inferior to continental troops. They were inferior physically and in other ways."[42] Arundel and other private contractors were certainly influenced by the military's view of Puerto Ricans. During the construction of the naval base in Vieques, for example, Arundel and its subcontractors would not permit Puerto Ricans to drink cold water, as this refreshment was reserved exclusively for continentals. Given that temperatures during the summer months in Puerto Rico can easily reach ninety-five degrees Fahrenheit, this became a significant point of contention among the workers. Another point of discord was the salary differential between locals and continentals. According to a report issued by the insular government's House of Representatives, Puerto Rican workers claimed that continentals were paid $1.57 per hour to drive a truck while they were paid only $0.50 and were obliged to work ten continuous hours a day. The issue of wages became critical, as war shortages had caused food prices to increase dramatically. The report also documented that seating in the buses within the base complex was segregated. If a Puerto Rican sat in a seat designated for continentals, he was made to get off at the next stop and was promptly fired.[43]

Was Puerto Rico any different from the United States in this respect? Was race an issue dividing the continentals from the Puerto Ricans? Scholars debate whether or not race prejudice existed in Puerto Rico. Those who deny its existence point to the extensive "race mixing" among the island's population as evidence of the absence of prejudice. Others insist that Puerto Ricans exhibited their own version of racial prejudice. "Whether race prejudice among Puerto Ricans was refuted or affirmed, early studies all point to the pervasiveness of race-mixing, coupled with a lax definition of whiteness (relative to the United States)."[44] However, racial segregation, as was implemented in Puerto Rico, was truly an American institution. Not surprisingly, this would also be a source of tension between Puerto Ricans and continentals. These problems became so serious that as late as 1948 Governor Jesús T. Piñero (named by presidential decree in 1946 to govern Puerto Rico) complained to the local press that the navy wanted to expropriate additional land (on top of the 53,484 acres that was expropriated during the war) from the Puerto Ricans, but had failed to set up a recruiting station in Puerto Rico during the war. "The complaints of the governor signal one of the most intractable issues in the relations between the Navy and the Puerto Ricans: racism. Racial segregation was part and parcel of military culture during the war."[45] In fact, the armed forces of the United States only began to desegregate after 1947 on the recommendation President Harry Truman's Committee on Civil Rights. This culture permeated the practices of the contractors that the US military brought to Puerto Rico. It was therefore inevitable that conflicts and tensions between the military and civil society would result.[46] The US military promoted racial segregation and discrimination to an extent that had not existed previously on the island.

As noted previously, the wage differential between the continentals and the Puerto Ricans was a significant source of friction. This provoked a major conflict with the Puerto Rican trade unions, some affiliated with their stateside counterparts, making them a formidable force to be reckoned with. By 1940, Puerto Rico's labor movement had undergone a significant transformation ushered in by two labor battles in 1937: the strike of six hundred operatives at the Red Star Manufacturing Company (a button factory) and a strike of the drivers of the White Star Bus Line in San Juan. Four workers were killed during the drivers' strike. Members of the Communist Party of Puerto Rico played a key role in these mobilizations.

A new and forceful trade union was formed in 1939, the Confederación General de Trabajadores (CGT), which was at first allied with the ruling Popular Democratic Party. The CGT grew rapidly. In October 1940, only one year after it was organized, the CGT claimed eighty thousand members in fifty-nine unions.[47] During 1941, with food prices on the rise and unionized workers demanding higher wages, tensions escalated. On January 19, 1942, four thousand unionized CGT workers, supervisors, and skilled laborers working at the Isla Grande Naval Base went on strike.[48]

At first, the incredulous WPA administrators refused to believe that the workers had gone on strike. According to them, the workers had gone to lunch and had decided not to return to work for the afternoon. They were convinced that if any WPA laborer did indeed abandon his work, it was as a result of intimidation on the part of the CGT. In spite of the fact that WPA administrators were claiming that no one in the WPA would participate in a strike, they hardened their position, signaling that any worker who chose to return to work would not be reprimanded. However, those who did not return would be eliminated from the list of eligible candidates that was used to assign available positions.[49]

The Isla Grande strike was settled in a few days, but the wage protests were not yet over. On the day after the end of the strike, CGT representatives met with Governor Tugwell but rejected the wage increases offered by both Arundel and the WPA. They agreed that the workers would return to work with the understanding that their concerns would be evaluated by the Department of Labor in Washington.[50] On February 23, "strikes began in Vieques and Roosevelt Roads. In Vieques, 1,600 workers went on strike, while at the base of Roosevelt Roads in Ceiba, 1,600 workers took part in the strike."[51] On March 8, the Department of Labor issued its opinion, siding with the workers' demands. As a result, salaries were increased between 12 percent and 18 percent, weekly work schedules were limited to forty hours, and any hour worked above the forty-hour limit would be paid at time and a half. There would be no further strikes throughout the remainder of the construction of the bases, which lasted until mid-1943.

The WPA Is Finished, but Puerto Rico Gets a Reprieve

Three developing situations spelled the end of the WPA. First, the war theater in the Atlantic was moving away from the Caribbean. August 1942 marked the start of Operation Torch, the invasion of Morocco and Algeria whose intent was to defeat Erwin Rommel's Afrika Korps.[52] As a result, the importance of the Caribbean to the war effort diminished. In fact, by mid-1943, all military construction was halted. Second, unemployment in the United States—the main reason for the existence of the WPA—was no longer an issue. In fact, the employment picture had reversed; there were more jobs than people available to take them, especially in the war industries. Third, in the 1942 elections, the Democratic Party lost many seats in Congress, and as a result the Roosevelt administration was forced to cut funding to many of the New Deal agencies, including the WPA.

On December 5, 1942, President Roosevelt announced that the WPA was no longer necessary and ordered its liquidation in order to save the significant amounts of funds this agency required to operate. Unfortunately for Puerto Rico, while unemployment in the United States was close to nil, the U-boat blockade was still going strong, further strangling the local economy. In September 1942, unemployment had reached 40 percent. Governor Tugwell and Popular Democratic Party president Luis Muñoz Marín called for continued funding for the WPA in Puerto Rico, as it was imperative to the well-being of the local residents. As of December 19, the WPA was employing 37,067 Puerto Ricans. Unfortunately, Roosevelt's and Tugwell's nemesis, Jasper C. Bell, Democratic representative from Missouri and president of the powerful House Committee on Insular Affairs, recommended cutting the funding for this agency. He also rejected Tugwell's recommendation that the WPA remain in Puerto Rico for two additional years. Upon further lobbing by Muñoz Marín and Governor Tugwell, Bell relented and agreed to fund the WPA in Puerto Rico and the Virgin Islands until November 1943, as opposed to having the funding cut by the summer, as he had originally suggested.[53] Monies from other federal programs, however, continued to be funded for Puerto Rico through 1946. The total investment for these programs between 1939 and 1946 amounted to $709.6 million (see table 2).

Table 5.2: Federal Expenditures in Puerto Rico, 1939–1946 (in millions of dollars)

	1939	1940	1941	1942	1943	1944	1945	1946	Total
War agencies	–	–	–	$60,501	$96,697	$60,934	$74,059	$83,993	$376,184
Credits	11,313	12,342	12,069	10,755	12,733	15,123	22,246	26,654	123,235
Unemployment	18,013	16,502	17,645	17,510	14,156	5,369	23	–	89,218
Veterans' benefits	1,116	1,241	1,287	1,873	2,045	2,551	695	22,016	32,824
War housing	–	–	374	11,115	1,008	4,949	2,711	1,130	21,287
Other expenses	–	–	–	2,335	2,072	3,656	3,876	4,939	16,878
Food relief	1,141	1,450	4,722	–	–	3,279	2,387	3,077	16,056
Social Security payments	–	216	616	2,543	630	1,106	883	1,135	7,129
Soil conservation	103	51	52	750	1,134	1,090	907	945	5,032
Roads and highways	360	874	531	575	1,060	669	608	275	4,952
Health	–	290	727	475	599	585	831	848	4,355
Education	354	326	396	501	499	423	457	516	3,472
Training of defense workers and nurses	–	–	399	844	862	309	341	122	2,877
Agriculture	227	259	295	311	318	424	484	462	2,780
Rivers and harbors	473	1,129	580	–	–	–	–	–	2,182
National Guard	228	401	531	–	–	–	–	–	1,160
Total	$33,328	$35,081	$40,224	$110,088	$133,813	$100,467	$110,508	$146,112	$709,621

Source: Harvey S. Perloff, *Puerto Rico's Economic Future: A Study in Planned Development* (Chicago: University of Chicago Press, 1950), 391–392, Table 99A.

Sales of Puerto Rican Rum to the Mainland

Surprisingly, the closure of the WPA and the suspension of the base construction projects had a smaller impact on the island than expected. This was due to the fact that by mid-1943, the German U-boat menace had mostly subsided, and Puerto Rico was able to sell rum manufactured on the island in the US market. British and North American whiskeys were favored by U.S consumers. However, they became scarce during the war, leaving plenty of room for Puerto Rico to sell its rum. Many English factories had been bombed in the Battle of Britain, and shipping in the Atlantic was disrupted by the submarine war.[54] Also, industrial alcohol was considered a strategic war material, because it was necessary for the elaboration of products such as tires, smokeless gunpowder, and other chemical products, and the US government required that all liquor manufacturers concentrate on the production of industrial alcohol as opposed to consumer-based alcohol.[55]

The increased trade between Puerto Rico and the US mainland from mid-1943 onward was a direct result of the withdrawal of the U-boats from the Caribbean theater. Submarine losses both in this sector and in the Atlantic as a whole had become unaffordable for the Germans. In July alone, four submarines were sunk south of Puerto Rico.[56] As a result of these successes, local rum distilleries, with little or no competition from British- or US-produced whiskey, were able to sell all of their production at a tidy price.[57] Rum consumption in the United States increased 169 percent from 1942 to 1943 and another 24 percent between 1943 and 1944. This increased demand precipitated a fierce competition between Puerto Rican and Cuban rum manufacturers, as well as those of the rest of the Caribbean. In 1943, for example, Puerto Rico represented 40 percent of all rum sales to the United States, while Cuba represented 29 percent and the rest of the Caribbean, which included Jamaica, the French Antilles, and the US Virgin Islands, 31 percent. The following year, Cuban sales increased to 33 percent of the market, Puerto Rico stabilized at 39 percent, and the remainder of the Caribbean lost some market share, dropping to 28 percent in 1944. Even though sales of Cuban and Puerto Rican rum to the United States were similar in volume in the years 1943 and 1944, a broader look at the decade 1937 to 1947 reveals a different picture. During those years, Puerto Rican rum accounted for 47 percent of the US rum market while Cuba's share amounted to 19 percent. In any case, by 1945 the market had shrunk to its prewar size, and with competition from other liquors compounding this situation, both volume of sales and profit margins diminished.[58]

What made this transaction particularly attractive to the Puerto Rican government had to do with a law approved by the US Congress on July 1, 1935,

Rum barrels used in the aging process, circa 1940 (Archivo General de Puerto Rico)

which granted that the excise taxes collected on the sale of rum be returned to the insular government. This provided the government with large, unexpected proceeds that could be used to finance its economic growth programs.[59] The federal government returned to Puerto Rico four dollars per proof gallon sold in the United States.[60] A proof gallon is defined as containing 50 percent alcohol at 60 degrees Fahrenheit.

During the first year of the law's enactment, Puerto Rico received $355,560 from rum tax rebates.[61] By 1944, one year after the end of the construction of the military bases and nine years after the approval of the law, this amount had increased to $65.8 million, a staggering sum representing 65 percent of the government's income. In 1945, even with decreasing sales volumes, tax receipts contributed $37.7 million to the government's coffers. This amount represented 47 percent of the government's income. Unfortunately, this bonanza would be short lived, as the percentage of income received from the rum tax decreased to 42 percent in 1946 and 26 percent in 1947.[62]

Table 3: Revenues of the Government of Puerto Rico, 1941–1947 (in millions of dollars)

Fiscal Year	Government Revenues (1)	Rum Tax Reimbursement (2)	Percentage (3)
1941	$20.7	$4.6	22%
1942	37.7	13.9	37
1943	42.8	13.9	32
1944	104.1	65.8	63
1945	79.6	37.7	47
1946	82.3	34.8	42
1947	76.1	19.6	26
Total	$443.3	$190.3	43%

Sources: (1) Harvey S. Perloff, Puerto Rico's Economic Future (Chicago: University of Chicago Press, 1950), 383. (2) Thomas Hibben and Rafael Picó, Industrial Development of Puerto Rico and the Virgin Islands of the United States (Port of Spain: Caribbean Commission, 1948), p. 208. (3) Author's calculation.

Table 4: Total Rum Consumption in the United States
(In millions of taxable proof gallons), 1939–1947

Year	Puerto Rico	Cuba	Virgin Islands	United States	French Antilles	Jamaica	Other countries	Total
1937	718	304	164	472	10	114	81	1,864
1938	607	193	127	440	10	98	41	1,516
1939	919	176	181	611	10	118	36	2,051
1940	1,445	162	384	647	1	132	31	2,803
1941	2,586	146	642	981	1	144	46	4,545
1942	2,745	165	808	1,304	1	178	28	5,229
1943	5,621	4,116	1,726	1,348	691	442	138	14,082
1944	6,741	5,724	2,661	556	1,177	316	233	17,408
1945	2,909	453	932	527	232	152	136	5,340
1946	4,611	276	689	805	44	176	51	6,652
1947	512	52	205	326	13	71	8	1,186
Total	29,413	11,766	8,518	8,018	2,191	1,941	829	62,676
% Total	47%	19%	14%	13%	3%	3%	1%	100%

Source: "Report on Preliminary Studies of the Market for Rum on the United States Mainland to the Governor's Advisory Committee to the Rum Industry," Arthur D. Little, Chemists-Engineers, Table 8-A. Archivo Fundación Luis Muñoz Marín, Section 4, Presidente del Senado, Cartapacio 237, Documento 3.

Even before Puerto Rico could count on the unusually large income flow resulting from the rum tax receipts, there were controversies in Congress regarding Puerto Rico's implementation of Governor Tugwell's New Deal projects.[63] Given Tugwell's controversial personality, this opposition would not seem unusual. According to historian Michael V. Namorato, Tugwell "was assaulted by opposition from the left and the right. From Mark Sullivan's columns in the *New York Herald Tribune* to the *Saturday Evening Post*, Tugwell was painted as the New Deal subversive revolutionary who secretly planned to destroy American capitalism."[64] As a result of Tugwell's trip to the Soviet Union in 1928 as a member of a trade delegation, his critics, "motivated by their patriotism, tried to convince the public that 'Rex the Red' . . . was 'dangerous.'"[65]

During April and May of 1943, Representative Jasper C. Bell held various meetings in order to discuss Puerto Rico's use of federal funds. Needless to say, the agenda of Bell's House Committee on Insular Affairs was not favorable to the island. The main concern of the committee was that the Puerto Rican government was investing federal monies in the development of state-run enterprises, such as a glass-bottling operation and a corrugated-box manufacturing plant that were meant to service the growing rum industry. The products these factories were to manufacture were already being imported from the United States. According to Bell, these investments would not solve the unusually large unemployment on the island, and, in any case, the money would be better spent supporting private investors. During the summer of 1943, the committee moved its sessions to Puerto Rico, where it interviewed prominent businesspeople and politicians, among them the president of the Senate and founder of the Popular Democratic Party, Luis Muñoz Marín.[66]

As a result of these hearings, on October 22, 1943, New York representative W. Sterling Cole, a member of Bell's committee, presented a blueprint to the committee proposing that the federal government withhold 50 percent of the rum tax receipts, which, under the current law, Puerto Rico was entitled to. In spite of Governor Tugwell's opposition, this proposal was expected to be approved by the committee. If approved, these amendments would reduce the income of the government of Puerto Rico by $25 million, or 24 percent,[67] and adversely affect the planned industrialization initiatives.[68] Fortunately, the proposal was not approved. However, the following month, the rum industry faced another challenge.

In November 1943, a rumor was circulating among the members of the War Production Board in Washington that if the United States did not obtain enough molasses from the Caribbean to produce the required industrial alcohol, it would be necessary to establish import quotas from both Puerto

Transporting Bacardi rum in Puerto Rico, circa 1940 (Archivo General de Puerto Rico)

Rico and Cuba. Luis G. Mendoza, representing one of the larger export consortiums in Havana, reacted sharply to the news. According to Mendoza, all rum and gin exported to the United States was produced with molasses that the federal government would not or could not purchase. Mendoza added that the Cubans had recently incurred hefty expenses by purchasing new distillation equipment in order to meet the current demand for alcoholic beverages. In addition, in order to transport rum and gin to the United States, the Cuban government had organized, at great expense, a small flotilla of noncombatant boats. This effort was required because the Cuban Maritime Commission had earlier assumed ownership and control of all ships whose displacement exceeded five hundred tons. Mendoza, along with many of his counterparts, was extremely concerned that if these measures were implemented, they would have a dire effect on the everyday life of much of the

Cuban population.⁶⁹ Fortunately, by the end of November, the War Production Board had announced that the stateside production of molasses was sufficient to accommodate the required consumption of industrial alcohol, and quotas on the production of Cuban and Puerto Rican molasses would not be necessary.⁷⁰

Two significant events would adversely impact the sale of Puerto Rican rum in the postwar years. First, competition from North American whiskey manufacturers—particularly Seagram's, Schenley, National Distillers, and Hiram Walker—intensified.⁷¹ Given that US consumers largely preferred whiskey to rum, the loss of sales was staggering. However, the Puerto Rican producers lost a valuable opportunity during the years when their competition was limited and they enjoyed strong sales, as they could have positioned rum as a viable competitor to whiskey. Instead, many unscrupulous manufacturers altered the production formulas and shortened the aging process, as a result lowering the quality of the product. Thus, many stateside consumers saw rum as a cheap alternative to whiskey.⁷² Eventually, given the impact that the rum tax receipts had on government income, the administration of Luis Muñoz Marín, by then governor of Puerto Rico, approved on March 14, 1949, a law establishing that the manufacture of rum and its aging process would be supervised by the government, thereby breathing life into this floundering industry.⁷³

Puerto Rican Soldiers Repatriate Their Income

Another source of revenue that the government did not count on was the repatriation of the wages of Puerto Ricans employed oversees by the military authorities. We don't know of any study that has researched this aspect of the war. However, the renowned sociologist Sidney W. Mintz in his now-classic book *Worker in the Cane* stated that when "Pablin" left for Korea in 1954, he would send back sixty-five dollars⁷⁴ a month to his wife so that they could add two additional rooms to their modest home.⁷⁵ Mintz's example is from nearly ten years later, but we believe that, given the economic hardship in Puerto Rico in the mid-1940s, a significant number of the approximately sixty-five thousand Puerto Ricans who served with the US Armed Forces in World War II repatriated some or most of their income.⁷⁶

In order to estimate the amount of money that was repatriated to the island, we first estimated the distribution of military ranks obtained by average Puerto Ricans. We assumed, based on the social and economic factors prevalent at the time, that most recruits would probably not have a high school diploma and would have only a minimal knowledge of English. Consequently,

Table 5: Estimate of Wages Paid to Puerto Rican Soldiers during the Second World War

A. Single Soldiers

Rank	Yearly salary (1)	Estimated expenses (1)	Net salary	% of soldiers holding said rank (2)	Average wage
Private	$540	$180	$360	40%	$144
Private First Class	$598	$180	$418	15%	$63
Corporal	$770	$180	$590	15%	$89
Sergeant	$943	$180	$763	10%	$76
Sergeant Major	$1,202	$180	$1,022	10%	$102
Sergeant First Class	$1,462	$180	$1,282	5%	$64
Master Sergeant	$1,807	$180	$1,627	5%	$81
				100%	**$619**

B. Married Soldiers

Rank	Yearly salary (1)	Estimated expenses (1)	Net salary	% of soldiers holding said rank (2)	Average wage
Private	$1,476	$180	$1,296	40%	$518
Private First Class	$1,534	$180	$354	15%	$53
Corporal	$1,766	$180	$1,586	15%	$238
Sergeant	$1,879	$180	$1,699	10%	$170
Sergeant Major	$2,138	$180	$1,958	10%	$196
Sargent First Class	$2,398	$180	$2,218	5%	$111
Master Sergeant	$2,743	$180	$2,563	5%	$128
				100%	**$1,414**

Average wage (single)	% single (2)	Average wage (married)	% married (2)	Weighted average	
$619	70%	$1,414	30%	$858	

Sources: (1) Malvern Hall Tillit, "Army-Navy Tops Most Civilian's," *Barron's National Business and Financial Weekly*, April 24, 1944, http://www.usmm.org/barrons.html; (2) Author's estimate.

Table 6: Estimate of Wage Repatriation, 1943-1945

% Repatriated	Average wage (1)	Amount repatriated	Num. of soldiers (2)	Annual total	Time served in years	Total repatriated during time served
15%	$858	$129	65,000	$8,385,000	3.5	$29,347,500
30%	$858	$257	65,000	$16,705,000	3.5	$58,467,500
45%	$858	$386	65,000	$25,090,000	3.5	$87,815,000
60%	$858	$515	65,000	$33,475,000	3.5	$117,162,500
75%	$858	$643	65,000	$41,795,000	3.5	$146,282,500

Sources: (1) Table 4; (2) Jorge Rodríguez Beruff, *Política militar de dominación: Puerto Rico en el contexto Latinoamericano* (San Juan: Ediciones Huracán, 1988), p. 154, Table 3.2.

most Puerto Ricans would be enlisted men as opposed to officers. Based on interviews with local military historians, we assumed the following breakdown: 40 percent private, 15 percent private first class, 10 percent sergeant, 10 percent sergeant major, 5 percent sergeant first class, and 5 percent master sergeant. We also estimated that 70 percent of the soldiers were single and 30 percent married. As illustrated in table 5, the weighted average yearly salary of the Puerto Rican soldier would have been $858.00. This compares favorably with $506.33, the average salary paid by the sugar industry on the island, this being the largest employer in Puerto Rico.

Table 6 illustrates various scenarios as to possible percentages of salaries repatriated. We estimated a minimum of 15 percent and a maximum of 75 percent. Based on these assumptions, we calculated that the total amount repatriated during the three and a half years of the conflict to be between a minimum of $29.3 million and a maximum of $146.3 million. Mostly likely, the amount repatriated was in the range of 30 to 45 percent of salary. In that case, the total dollar amount repatriated to the island during the Second World War would be in the range of $58.5 million to $87.8 million. As a means of comparison, and as shown in table 3 above, the rum tax receipts for the years 1941–1947 totaled $190.3 million. As such, the amount we estimate was repatriated to the island was significant when compared to the tax collected by the Puerto Rican government on the sale of locally produced rum.[77]

The Restructuring of Government and Private Institutions

Major institutional changes took place in Puerto Rico during the years of the Second World War. The combination of the significant military investments and the competent political leadership of both Rexford G. Tugwell and Luis Muñoz Marín provided the catalyst for these changes. Although a thorough discussion of this topic is beyond the scope of this chapter, we would like to cover some of what we consider to be the most outstanding and relevant changes that took place during this time. We will therefore review the effects on the private banking sector, and with regard to the public sector we will analyze the Puerto Rico Development Bank (after September 1948 reorganized as the Government Development Bank), the Puerto Rico Industrial Development Company, and the Puerto Rico Water Resources Authority.

During 1942, bank assets in Puerto Rico totaled $137 million, of which National City Bank of New York, by far the largest institution on the island, accounted for $62 million. The three major local banks were Banco Popular with $23 million in assets, Banco Crédito y Ahorro Ponceño with $14 million, and Banco de Ponce with $10 million. All told, the local banks accounted for $47 million in assets, or 34 percent of the total banking industry.[78]

According to the information provided from 1939 through 1942 by Rafael Carrión Pacheco, executive vice president and stockholder of Banco Popular, to his board of directors, the substantial increase in the bank's earnings was due to the enormous military investment on the island. However, from July 1942 onward, with the effective blockade of Puerto Rico by German U-boats, the local economy came to a standstill. Local shipping was significantly reduced, which resulted in a corresponding reduction of commercial imports. As a result, commerce and industry had to liquidate their loans and reduce their inventories. As a consequence, bank portfolios saw a reduction of approximately 30 percent in the amount of loans outstanding and an increase of about 54 percent in commercial deposits.[79] These deposits were invested in war bonds. The difference between the yield of these bonds and the measly interest paid on commercial deposits resulted in enormous increases in the incomes of these institutions.[80] As an example, Banco de Ponce (the only institution for which we were able to obtain a complete set of financial reports from 1939 to 1948) reported income of $118,000 in 1939 and $560,000 in 1945. The end of the blockade did not materially alter the bank's portfolio. It was only after the war that the income of these institutions started to decline.[81]

The Puerto Rico Development Bank, founded in 1942, was initially capitalized with $500,000. It would become an instrument of government policy, and it was hoped, at least by Governor Tugwell, that the bank would provide loans that were "risky" and therefore loans that commercial banks might not approve.[82] Unfortunately, the loan policy of this bank was quite conservative, in step with that of the commercial banks. However, the great contribution of this institution was its ability to package and sell the bonds of Puerto Rican public corporations, such as those of the Puerto Rico Water Resources Authority.[83]

The Water Resources Authority, founded in 1941 and still operating today under a different name,[84] was able to sell a bond emission of $50 million in 1947 with the financial assistance of the Development Bank. The proceeds of these bond sales were used to pay off the previous bond emission and to complete the electrification projects stared during the first years of operation of this public corporation.[85] On the same day that the Development Bank was incorporated, May 11, 1942, a sister public corporation, the Puerto Rico Industrial Development Company, was also incorporated; the latter organization, still in operation today, was given the task of formulating and implementing an industrial plan for Puerto Rico.[86] Although its initial investments in publicly run corporations were sold to a wealthy and influential Puerto Rican family, the Ferrés, as the losses of these enterprises were unsustainable, later efforts to attract stateside investors proved successful.[87]

Conclusion

Federal expenditures had a lasting effect on Puerto Rico. The island completed an impressive array of infrastructure projects such as roads, hospitals, telecommunications projects, regional airports, and port facilities, among others. It provided vocational training to thousands of Puerto Ricans in the arts of carpentry, electricity, plumbing, and similar skills. These would prove useful in the postwar industrial period, when economic growth was explosive.

Just as the federal initiatives provided much-needed infrastructure and jobs, a significant portion of the rum tax receipts was invested by the government of Puerto Rico to create a more efficient and modern government structure. Among the many efforts of the period, we can point to the creation of the Puerto Rico Industrial Development Company and its program to industrialize the island by either acquiring or building state-run companies; the creation of the Development Bank, which funded many infrastructure programs; and the creation of the Water Resources Authority, whose mission was to provide electricity and water services, among other services. Some of these efforts ended in success, others in failure. However, without the income streams identified in this chapter, many of these projects could not have been accomplished.

Finally, the wage repatriation of Puerto Rican servicemen has been an unexamined topic in the literature about Puerto Rico. Our calculations demonstrate that these repatriations had a greater impact on the island than many other programs. It is most likely that this income was used for consumption rather than investment and thus would have fulfilled short-term needs, as opposed to local and federal investments, which had a longer-term impact on the economy.

Puerto Rican historiography has not fully analyzed the nature and specific sources of income during this period, particularly through the institutional changes that we briefly touched upon in this chapter. It is our hope that this study motivates other historians and social scientists to further review this period so that a more complete picture of the financial structure of the military investments in both Puerto Rico and the Caribbean can be obtained.

Notes

1. Eliezer Cuevas Curet, *El desarrollo económico de Puerto Rico: 1940 a 1972* (San Juan: Management Aid Center, 1976), p. 11.

2. The Marshall Plan for the reconstruction of Europe represented an investment of $13 billion. José L. Bolívar Fresneda, *Guerra, banca y desarrollo: el Banco de Fomento y la industrialización de Puerto Rico* (San Juan: Fundación Luis Muñoz Marín; Instituto de Cultura Puertorriqueña, 2011), p. 7.

3. Ibid., p. 7.

4. The most recently published book on this topic is Bolívar Fresneda, *Guerra, banca y desarrollo*.

5. James L. Dietz, *Economic History of Puerto Rico: Institutional Change and Capitalist Development* (Princeton, NJ: Princeton University Press, 1986), p. 206.

6. Rafael de Jesús Toro, *Historia económica de Puerto Rico* (Cincinnati: South-Western, 1982), pp. 175–198.

7. For additional information, see Francisco A. Catalá Oliveras, *Promesa rota: una mirada institucionalista a partir de Tugwell* (San Juan: Ediciones Callejón, 2013).

8. José L. Bolívar Fresneda, "Las inversiones y los programas militares: construyendo la infraestructura y los recursos humanos de la posguerra," in *Puerto Rico en la Segunda Guerra Mundial: baluarte del Caribe*, ed. Jorge Rodríguez Beruff and José L. Bolívar Fresneda (San Juan: Ediciones Callejón, 2012), pp. 137–171.

9. Archivo Fundación Luis Muñoz Marín (hereafter AFLMM), *Final Report on the WPA Program* (Washington, DC: Work Projects Administration, 1943), pp.110–113.

10. Jorge Rodríguez Beruff, *Strategy as Politics: Puerto Rico on the Eve of the Second World War* (Río Piedras: University of Puerto Rico Press, 2007), p.63.

11. Ibid., p.237.

12. Bolívar Fresneda, *Guerra, banca y desarrollo*, pp. 49–54.

13. César J. Ayala Casás and José L. Bolívar Fresneda, *Battleship Vieques: Puerto Rico from World War II to the Korean War* (Princeton, NJ: Markus Wiener, 2011), p. 21.

14. Gerhard L. Weinberg, *A World at Arms: A Global History of World War II* (Cambridge: Cambridge University Press, 1994), p.241.

15. Humberto García Muñiz, *La estrategia de Estados Unidos y la militarización del Caribe* (Río Piedras, PR: Instituto de Estudios del Caribe, University of Puerto Rico, 1988), pp. 50, 53.

16. "Sgt. Claude A. Swanson, Departamento de la Marina al Secretario de lo Interior," December 29, 1934, Archivo General de Puerto Rico (hereafter AGPR), Fondo: Obras Públicas, Ser. Asuntos Varios, Leg. no. 398, Caja no. 240; and "Armando Morales Caños, Jefe de la División de Terrenos Públicos al Comisionado Interino," January 8, 1941, AGPR, Fondo: Obras Públicas, Ser. Asuntos Varios, Leg. no. 98, Caja no. 241.

17. For additional information on Operation Torch, see Rick Atkinson, *An Army at Dawn: The War in North Africa, 1942-1943* (New York: Henry Holt, 2002).

18. "Interior sacó ayer a subasta varias obras importantes," *El Mundo* (San Juan), January 14, 1939, p. 1.

19. "Interior proyecta construir ocho modernos aeropuertos," *El Mundo* (San Juan), January 21, 1939, p. 1.

20. "Se realizan obras en los túneles," *El Mundo* (San Juan), March 23, 1939, p. 1.

21. Bolívar Fresneda, *Guerra, banca y desarrollo*, pp. 36-38. See the chapter entitled "Vieques: The Impact of the Second World War" for additional details regarding the expropriations in Vieques.

22. Minutes of the Board of Directors of the Arundel Corporation, private library of José L. Bolívar Fresneda, March 17, 1941.

23. "Comenzara pronto construcción base Juana Díaz," *El Mundo* (San Juan), October 26, 1940, p. 1.

24. "Comenzó trazado de la nueva carretera," *El Mundo* (San Juan), October 19, 1940, p. 1.

25. "Obras de ingeniería de la 'PRRA,'" *El Mundo* (San Juan), November 14, 1939, p. 6.

26. Samuel E. Badillo, "Toman las huellas digitales a miles de empleados: en las obras que se realizan en Isla Grande y Punta Santiago, a solicitud de la FBI," *El Mundo* (San Juan), December 2, 1939, p. 1.

27. Jorge Rodríguez Beruff, *Política militar y dominación: Puerto Rico en el contexto Latinoamericano* (San Juan: Ediciones Huracán, 1988), p. 154, table 3.2.

28. "The Puerto Rican Economy during the War Year of 1942," June 1943, AFLMM, Section 12, Material de y sobre Luis Muñoz Marín, Proyecto de Recopilación de Documentos, Harry S. Truman Library, p. 18.

29. AFLMM, *Final Report on the WPA Program*, pp. 110-113.

30. "Roosevelt pide diez millones para Puerto Rico," *El Mundo* (San Juan), April 28, 1939, pp. 1, 24.

31. Jorge Rodríguez Beruff, ed., *Las memorias de Leahy: los relatos del almirante William D. Leahy sobre su gobernación de Puerto Rico, 1939-1940* (San Juan: Fundación Luis Muñoz Marín, 2002), pp. 205, 209.

32. Harvey S. Perloff, *Puerto Rico's Economic Future: A Study in Planned Development* (Chicago: University of Chicago Press, 1950), p. 154.

33. "Obreros para la construcción de obras militares," *El Mundo* (San Juan), May 31, 1940, p. 1.

34. "Jefe de la WPA comenta el paro de Isla Grande," *El Mundo* (San Juan), January 16, 1942, p. 1; and "Seguía ayer el paro de obreros de Isla Grande," *El Mundo* (San Juan), January 20, 1942, p. 6.

35. "Más asignaciones especiales para la Isla," *El Mundo* (San Juan), June 6, 1941, p. 1.

36. "Base de Vieques será levantada por obreros portorriqueños," *El Mundo* (San Juan), February 27, 1941, p. 8; "Progresan rápidamente el entrenamiento de obreros," *El Mundo* (San Juan), April 13, 1941, p. 1; and "Se espera otra asignación destinada a Puerto Rico," *El Mundo* (San Juan), May 24, 1941, p. 1.

37. "De: Rafael del Valle Zeno; A: Sergio Cuevas," March 14, 1942, AGPR, Fondo: Obras Públicas, Ser. Asuntos Varios, Leg. no. 253A, Carta. no. 197, pp. 1-2.

38. Ayala Casás and Bolívar Fresneda, *Battleship Vieques*, p. 107.

39. Ibid., p. 108.

40. Mara Loveman and Jeronimo Muñiz, "How Puerto Rico Became White: Boundary Dynamics and Intercensus Racial Reclassification," *American Sociological Review* 72, no. 6 (December 2007): 915-939.

41. Ayala Casás and Bolívar Fresneda, *Battleship Vieques*, p. 117.

42. Ibid.

43. "Arundel no permite que los puertorriqueños tomen agua fría; es para los continentales," *El Imparcial* (San Juan), April 14, 1943, p. 5.

44. Loveman and Muñiz, "How Puerto Rico Became White," pp. 915-939.

45. Ayala Casás and Bolívar Fresneda, *Battleship Vieques*, p. 107.

46. Ibid.

47. César J. Ayala and Rafael Bernabe, *Puerto Rico in the American Century: A History since 1898* (Chapel Hill: University of North Carolina Press, 2007), pp. 136-145.

48. Ayala Casás and Bolívar Fresneda, *Battleship Vieques*, p. 115.

49. "Jefe de la WPA comenta el paro de Isla Grande," *El Mundo* (San Juan), January 16, 1942, p. 1; "Seguía ayer el paro de obreros de Isla Grande," *El Mundo* (San Juan), January 20, 1942, p. 6; and "Aceptan las demandas de los obreros de las bases," *El Mundo* (San Juan), March 8, 1942, p. 1.

50. "Jefe de la WPA comenta el paro de Isla Grande," *El Mundo* (San Juan), January 16, 1942, p. 1; "Seguía ayer el paro de obreros de Isla Grande," *El Mundo* (San Juan), January 20, 1942, p. 6; and "Aceptan las demandas de los obreros de las bases," *El Mundo* (San Juan), March 8, 1942, p. 1.

51. Ayala Casás and Bolívar Fresneda, *Battleship Vieques*, p. 115.

52. C. L. Sulzberger, *The American Heritage Picture History of World War II* (New York: American Heritage Publishing, 1966), p. 220.

53. "The Puerto Rican Economy during the War Year of 1942," June 1943, AFLMM, Section 12, Material de y sobre Luis Muñoz Marín, Proyecto de Recopilación de Documentos, Harry S. Truman Library, p. 18; and Bolívar Fresneda, *Guerra, banca y desarrollo*, pp. 28-31.

54. Bolívar Fresneda, *Guerra, banca y desarrollo*, pp. 39-46.

55. United Press, "Se admite que quizás se limiten las importaciones," *El Mundo* (San Juan), November 17, 1943, p. 1.

56. See http://www.uboat.net/fates/losses/1943.htm, accessed April 26, 2013.

57. Memo written by Teodoro Moscoso, president of the Puerto Rican Development Company, to representatives of local rum manufactures, February 8, 1943, AFLMM, Section 4 (Presidente del Senado), Series 2 Gobierno Insular, Folder no. 382, Document no. 25.

58. "Report on the Preliminary Studies of the Market for Rum on the United States to the Governor's Advisory Committee on the Rum Industry," Arthur D. Little, Inc., Chemist-Engineers, Table 2, AFLMM, Section 4 (Presidente del Senado), Folder no. 237, Document no. 3.

59. Guy J. Swope, *Forty-First Annual Report of the Governor of Puerto Rico*, 1941, p. 9.

60. "Report on the Preliminary Studies of the Market for Rum on the United States to the Governor's Advisory Committee on the Rum Industry," Arthur D. Little, Inc., Chemist-Engineers, Table 2, AFLMM, Section 4 (Presidente del Senado), Folder no. 237, Document no. 3.

61. Guy J. Swope, *Forty-First Annual Report of the Governor of Puerto Rico*, 1941, p. 9.

62. Thomas Hibben and Rafael Picó, *Industrial Development of Puerto Rico and the Virgin Islands of the United States: Report of the United States Section, Caribbean Commission* (Port of Spain: Caribbean Commission, 1948), pp. 208–209.

63. Ayala and Bernabe, *Puerto Rico in the American Century*, p. 145.

64. Michael V. Namorato, *Rexford G. Tugwell: A Biography* (New York: Praeger, 1988), p. 1.

65. Ibid., pp. 2, 38.

66. Otto Janssen, "El Comité Bell desilusionado con Compañía de Fomento; se espera que recomendará cambio de política de manera que la entidad sea de mayor beneficio contra desempleo," *El Mundo* (San Juan), July 19, 1944, pp. 1, 14.

67. Hearings before the Subcommittee of the Committee on Insular Affairs, House of Representatives, 78th Cong., 1st Sess., Pursuant to H.R. 159, 1943 (Washington, DC: Government Printing Office).

68. "Ya funciona nuevo Banco de Fomento de Puerto Rico: cerró operación que envuelve un millón de dólares," *El Mundo* (Santa Fe), October 22, 1943, p. 1.

69. Otto Janssen, "Plan para imponer cuota a ron de Cuba y Puerto Rico," *El Mundo* (San Juan), November 8, 1943, pp. 1, 12.

70. United Press, "Se admite que quizás se limiten las importaciones," *El Mundo* (San Juan), November 17, 1943, p. 1; and Bolívar Fresneda, *Guerra, banca y desarrollo*, pp. 41–42.

71. Peter Foster, *Family Spirits: The Bacardi Saga; Rum, Riches and Revolution* (Toronto: Macfarlane Walter and Ross, 1990), p. 71.

72. José A. Bolívar, interview by the author, Guaynabo, Puerto Rico, February 2008. Bolívar, an engineer by profession, is a retired vice president of the Bacardi Corporation who worked at Bacardi from 1949 to 1993 at Santiago de Cuba; San Juan; Recife, Brazil; and Jacksonville, Florida.

73. Laws of Puerto Rico, no. 354, May 14, 1949, Tomo 13, Artículo 1679, 867–868.

74. In order to contextualize the amount received by Pablin's family, we obtained a listing of the average salaries the US Navy paid its enlisted personnel between 1949 and 1951. These salaries ranged from a low of $80.00 per month for those having less than two years' experience to a high of $198.45. Therefore, $65.00 per month is likely to be a significant share of the salary paid to ordinary servicemen. See http://www.navycs.com/charts/1949-military-pay-chart.html, accessed April 29, 2013.

75. Sidney W. Mintz, *Taso, trabajador de la caña* (San Juan: Ediciones Huracán, 1988), p. 90.

76. Jorge Rodríguez Beruff, *Política militar y dominación: Puerto Rico en el contexto Latinoamericano* (San Juan: Ediciones Huracán, 1988), p. 154, table 3.2.

77. For additional information, see Bolívar Fresneda, "Las inversiones y los programas militares," pp. 137–171.

78. Biagio di Venuti, *Banking Growth in Puerto Rico* (Baltimore: Waverly Press, 1950), p. 32; Archivo Histórico Banco Popular de Puerto Rico (hereafter AHBPPR), Banco Popular de Puerto Rico, *Informe Anual*, 1942, pp. 6, 7; AHBPPR, Banco de Ponce, *Memoria*, 1942, p. 9; and Laws of Puerto Rico, no. 252, May 13, 1942, 1445–1447.

79. AHBPPR, Banco Popular de Puerto Rico, *Informe Anual*, June 30, 1941, p. 1; AHBPPR, Banco de Ponce, *Memoria*, 1942, p. 5.

80. AHBPPR, Banco de Ponce, *Memoria*, 1942, pp. 5–7.

81. AHBPPR, Banco de Ponce, *Informes Anuales*, 1939, 1940, 1942–1945, 1947, 1948.

82. An Act to Provide for the Establishment of a Bank, March 16, 1942, AFLMM, Section 4 (Presidente del Senado), Folder no. 152, Document no. 40.

83. AGPR, Fondo: Oficina del Gobernador, Tarea 96-20, Caja 831, Banco de Fomento de Puerto Rico, *Informes Anuales*, Fiscal Year 1947–1948, pp. 7, 9.

84. Eugenio Látimer Torres, *Historia de la Autoridad de Energía Eléctrica* (San Juan: S.E., 1997), pp. 369, 371.

85. Archivo Histórico Banco Gubernamental de Fomento (hereafter AHBGF), Banco de Fomento de Puerto Rico, *Minutas de la junta de directores*, Libro de Actas II, February 4, 1947, p. 151.

86. A. W. Maldonado, *Teodoro Moscoso and Puerto Rico's Operation Bootstrap* (Gainesville: University Press of Florida, 1997), pp. 25–30.

87. "Problema de la industrialización: alegan mala administración causa el fracaso de Fomento," *El Mundo* (San Juan), June 27, 1948, pp. 1, 10.

The German Blockade of the Caribbean in 1942 and Its Effects in Puerto Rico

Ligia T. Domenech

The United States officially became involved in World War II on the side of the Allies on December 7, 1941. This decision was a result of the devastating Japanese attack on the naval base at Pearl Harbor, Hawaii. Although the Americans were aware of them, German submarines were not a major worry in the United States or in the Caribbean because, at that time, the common belief was that they couldn't operate so far away from the French coast without refueling or recharging batteries, in a land whose possession the Germans still had not secured.[1] The most expected method of attack was aerial or naval. According to historian Gaddis Smith, the condition of US defenses was "disastrous" and consisted of a "crippled" navy, an unprofessional, inexperienced, and poorly equipped army, and a still incipient war industry.[2]

As early as December 29, 1941, British intelligence analysts detected five German submarines moving toward the US Atlantic coast. They were part of Operation Paukenschlag,[3] which marked the beginning of German U-boat activity in America in mid-January 1942. The objective of this military operation was to attack shipping along the East Coast of the United States. The general idea of the tactical possibilities of the German U-boats was about to change, and Winston Churchill recognized this in his memoirs: "The only thing that ever really frightened me during the war was the U-boat peril."[4]

German Submarines or U-boats

The operations of the German U-boats were directed from Germany by Grand Admiral Karl Dönitz as commander of the submarine fleet (Führer der

German U-boat 534 (Australian War Museum)

Unterseeboote). The commander's confidence in the capacity of the U-boat fleet to bring about a German triumph was unshakeable. In his diary, Dönitz wrote: "I am going to show that the U-boats by themselves can win the war.... There is nothing impossible to us!"[5]

Soon before the U-boat attacks in the Caribbean, Dönitz asked for twenty-five U-boats of the 1,200 ton Model IX-C.[6] But Hitler, in a decision later questioned, denied this request and kept a reserve of twenty U-boats in Europe in case the British attacked Norway.[7] For that reason, only five submarines crossed the Atlantic to begin Operation Paukenschlag. Later, other submarines would join the Caribbean patrol.

Submarine warfare has been compared to guerrilla war because both rely on the surprise attack, and in both of them a small force penetrates enemy territory without being detected. This strategy can enable the attacking units to inflict serious damage on the enemy's forces and communication capabilities. Afterward, submarines, like guerrilla units, often escape unharmed, provoking frustration on the enemy's side.[8] In the narrow sea routes of the Caribbean, U-boats generally attacked independently.

U-boats never went hunting at random; they were controlled from a command center in Germany to which they had to report regularly. From February 1942 on, the Germans performed their communications with a new coding machine called Enigma, which the British initially couldn't decode. But on October 30, 1942, the British, through a secret cryptanalysis procedure called Ultra, succeeded in deciphering the German Enigma code after successfully seizing the codes from the U-559 just before its sinking. This important advantage resulted in significant Allied naval victories by December 1942; the Germans, for the rest of the war, never suspected that their valuable secret code had been compromised.

The Principal Targets of the German U-boats in the Caribbean

German submarine activities were concentrated at the mouth of the Mississippi River and in three primary areas of the Caribbean in which merchant ships had to pass through "asphyxia points": the Windward passage, the Curaçao-Aruba passage, and the Trinidad area.

The general German objective was to block the flux of all war-related supplies that were essential to the Allies such as refractory chromium supplied by Cuba exclusively to the United States, along with nickel and tungsten; bauxite from British Guiana and Dutch Guiana, needed for the production of aluminum and, therefore, for the manufacture of airplanes;[9] long-thread cotton used to make parachutes and barrier balloons; and copper as well as some gold and silver, all produced in the Caribbean and all of vital strategic importance in wartime.[10] As stated by Dönitz, the Germans' aim during this period was "to sink as much enemy shipping as quickly as we could."[11]

The Impact of Operation Neuland in the Caribbean

Germany began Operation Neuland on February 16, 1942, as an offensive separate from Operation Paukenschlag, and the U-boats that performed in it were in addition to those already operating on the East Coast of the United States. Operation Neuland began with the attack of the U-156 against the port and refinery of Aruba.[12]

The U-boat captains who participated in Neuland were surprised when they noticed that the Caribbean coasts and the merchant ships navigating in the Caribbean were completely lit up and carried out their communications without codes. In February 1942 alone, U-boats sank forty-five ships, many of them large tankers, and no U-boat was lost. Tanker crews, feeling a general sense of fear, mutinied and refused to embark unless escorted by naval forces. Frequently, the attacks were so quick and so fierce that the attacked ships didn't even have time to send out an SOS message and disappeared without leaving any trace of their cargo or crew. Stories about the German attacks, some true and some fabricated, kept both the merchant sailors and the civil population on the islands in a permanent state of tension.[13]

Operation Neuland lasted twenty-eight days, during which the five U-boats remained undamaged as they destroyed forty-one ships, eighteen of which were tankers. The sunken tonnage amounted to 222,651 tons of freight. The success of Operation Neuland then developed into the Germans' Caribbean Campaign.

The commander of the Caribbean Sea Frontier based in San Juan, Vice Admiral John H. Hoover, was defenseless against the massive German attack. His forces consisted of "some British corvette vessels, 2 hulls from the Dutch Navy and ... some units from the Brazilian Navy."[14] Additionally, the United States was not yet implementing convoys or coastal blackouts and continued to use wireless communications with peacetime procedures, all of which were deadly in time of war.

The most analyzed and criticized failure in the US High Command at this juncture was its reluctance to adopt the convoy system that had proven successful for the British during World War I and again in the North Atlantic in the early stages of World War II. The US navy commander, Admiral Ernest J. King, declined to implement a convoy system, stating that it was preferable not to organize a convoy rather than to organize a poorly escorted convoy.[15] His obstinate attitude lasted for months and led to the loss of thousands of lives as well as tonnage vital for the Allied regiments and for the now isolated civilian population in the conflict areas, which is what the Caribbean now was. Only the direct and forceful intervention of President Roosevelt got King to modify his negative attitude.[16]

Meanwhile, Dönitz calculated that if his U-boats were able to sink seventy thousand tons of freight per month, Germany would be able to win the Battle of the Atlantic. For him, this was a tonnage war. For the Americans, on the contrary, it was an economic battle of production, and the strategy was to build more merchant ships than the submarines could sink.[17] The American strategy, of course, ignored the loss of lives. In May and June 1942, the Germans sank ships in the Caribbean at a rate that was double that at which they were built in the United States. Faced with this grim reality, the United States finally decided to establish the Caribbean convoy system.

Life in Puerto Rico during the German U-Boat Blockade

On February 25, 1939, well before the war, 175 airplanes flew over San Juan in a bombing simulation exercise preparing the island's defenses for a possible aerial attack designed to seize Puerto Rico. Soon after, the construction of military roads and aerial and naval bases began. These measures were led and carefully planned by Puerto Rico's governor, Admiral William D. Leahy (1939–1941), the retired chief of naval operations and a close friend of President Roosevelt.

In Puerto Rico, politics were to interfere with plans and policies during this emergency. Critics of the colonial government's actions were constant: mistakes were exaggerated and good ideas were disregarded. Leahy's successor as governor, Rexford Guy Tugwell (1941–1946), commented in his personal diary:

> [E]ven the leading Socialista and Republicano politicos felt impelled to suggest a truce in their war on me.... I soon found, however, that their notion of co-operation was peculiarly one-sided and wholly political. They thought their local party committees should be given the responsibility for civil defense.[18]

Because of the German blockade emergency, Governor Tugwell considered it necessary, at least during the war, to exempt Puerto Rico from the dispositions of the Coastal Trading Act, which since 1917 had required that all goods transported by water between US ports be carried in US-flagged ships built in the United States, owned by US citizens, and crewed by US citizens or US permanent residents.[19] This way, friendly foreign ships would be able to provide Puerto Rico with some of its needs and to take with them some of the island's exports. The United States was extremely reluctant to give up this exclusive right over Puerto Rican imports and exports, but the emergency and the scarcity of American vessels forced them to finally authorize the use of foreign merchant vessels in Puerto Rican trade operations.[20]

The scarcity of equipment and supplies combined to increase the helplessness of the Puerto Ricans. In contrast to the lack of foresight of the US military, and as early as December 1941, Tugwell was concerned that the island had no radar or other means of identifying submarines that could attack by surprise.[21] In the event of an attack, there were no airplanes, antiaircraft weapons, artillery, patrols, or the like. He was concerned that, given its size and its proximity to the Panama Canal, Puerto Rico might be an important target for the enemy. But his greater worries were the facts that Puerto Rico was an island, and that the geographical position of the city of San Juan, with its seventy thousand inhabitants, was exposed: it was on a vulnerable coastline, instead of being protected in the central zone, and it was vulnerable to being isolated by the mere destruction of the bridges that connected the islet of San Juan to the rest of the island. According to Tugwell, "It asked to be attacked."[22]

In December 1941, for security reasons, an order was given to evacuate from the island all family members of US-born soldiers. The measure implied that Puerto Rico was not a safe place for them. US citizens are routinely evacuated from hostile places in time of war, but Puerto Rico was a US territory and the people who allegedly remained in danger on the island were as much American citizens as the families of soldiers whom the federal government sought to evacuate. This posed a serious problem for Governor Tugwell, who had to maintain the confidence of the Puerto Ricans. So Tugwell sent a series of messages to Washington to emphasize his position. These messages were ignored without explanation for a long time, but his approach is interesting:

> Someone had forgot, I said, that Puerto Rico was American territory and that families were as precious as those of army and navy men. If there were to be evacuation because of the risk of attack, we should be accused of discrimination and of saving Continentals first.[23]

In his diary, as he had done in the newspapers and on the radio, Tugwell listed the security measures that were expected from the civilian population: to stay in their homes at night, to cover or seal windows with cardboard, to provide shelters, and to protect public water supplies and electricity. For its part, and with the aid of volunteers, the government would maintain miniclinics with stretchers, ambulances, and other equipment and develop a fire service to respond in rescue and demolition missions. About the outcome of these efforts, Tugwell said: "In some of this we did well; in some of it, we did badly."[24]

While the military and other authorities did the best they could with the scarce materials, equipment, and personnel available, the population lived in an atmosphere of unending fear. In May 1942, Tugwell was aboard an amphibious plane traveling between Cuba and Jamaica and, after spotting a German submarine, the pilot made a fast dive. After that, Tugwell tried to drop a bomb on the U-boat with his bare hands while leaning through the window.[25]

Citizens from enemy nations—namely Germans, Italians, and Japanese—residing in Puerto Rico were treated as belligerents and suspected of aiding the Axis powers. In October 1942 the Board of Hearings for Foreign Enemies, aided by the FBI, the Immigration and Naturalization Department, the Insular Police, federal prosecutors, and the US Armed Forces, investigated all German citizens living in Puerto Rico. A total of 167 cases of Germans were analyzed and registered, and all those over fourteen years of age had to carry an ID booklet at all times. The United States also forbade any foreign enemy aliens in its territory to possess shortwave radios, radio transmitters, or receivers.[26]

Throughout 1942, the military preparations continued: radar and modern communications equipment were set up in the mountains and on islets, civilians were put through mobilization practices, antiaircraft artillery installations were mounted on the coasts, and soldiers were recruited. The government of the island established in every town first aid corps, rescue units, police services, civil defense operations, auxiliary fire brigades, and antiaircraft alarm personnel. As part of the campaign for the prevention and control of fires, 125 water pumps and 38,000 firefighting kits, including fire hoses, fire extinguishers, fireproof capes, and hardhats, were distributed in several towns.[27]

Tugwell discerned himself from those believing that the war was lost in feeling that the United States would come through. In the spring of 1942 he commented on the mood that pervaded over the island:

> [I]t was difficult to maintain confidence in Puerto Rico in the spring of '42, with ships sinking all around and their survivors landing in hundreds, with food, medical and industrial supplies becoming scarce, with no knowledge of actual corrective measures reaching us from any source, and with no obvious reason for trusting that the problems were being solved.[28]

Young people were often encouraged to participate in the war effort. In the summer of 1942, the US Department of Agriculture coordinated the establishment of "Victory Gardens" along with the collection of metals (aluminum, lead, steel, iron, tin, and silver) and rubber tires by working through local high schools.[29] Also, in carpentry classes children began to make model airplanes to be used in military instruction.[30] 4-H Club members in rural areas were organized in the "Victory Program," in which they helped in the production and conservation of essential foodstuffs; learned how to avoid wastefulness; promoted the collection of old metal scraps, used paper, rubber tires, and other items; and served as volunteers in the Civil Defense.[31] The Boy Scouts went house to house collecting recyclable metal materials such as knives, dishes, pots, pans, and aluminum toys to be sent to the United States.[32]

Women also contributed to the war effort.[33] For example, they made caps for soldiers, invited some of them to their homes for dinner for special occasions, and volunteered for the Red Cross. Some volunteered in the Civil Defense and, under the direction of Grace Tugwell, the governor's wife, assisted in providing first aid to the sick and wounded making thousands of gauzes and bandages, sewing clothes and bed linens for soldiers, preparing first aid kits, and organizing first aid rooms. Additionally, they were expected to help by being more efficient with their housekeeping tasks; for example, by reducing the amount of food discarded unnecessarily and buying fewer consumer goods.

The War Activities Program coordinated the sales of war bonds and stamps, and raised $1,037,619.[34] The Puerto Rican Chapter of the American Red Cross organized lots of activities to raise funds to be used in case of disasters or emergencies related to the war, and between 1940 and 1945 it surpassed its assigned goals by collecting over half a million dollars. In addition, through the efforts of Senator Luis Muñoz Marín, a "Victory Tax" was introduced to increase the amount of public funding so much needed to cover the costs of local services.[35] The Victory Tax was imposed at a rate of 5 percent on the earnings of Puerto Rican workers.

Other activities in support of the war were organized. The National War Fund Campaign for Victory exceeded its goals and ended up contributing over two hundred thousand dollars. Other efforts included the First Dollar Committee and the Library Committees. The Optimistic Club, presided over by Lieutenant Thomas P. Lynch (from San Juan's naval station), directed an island-wide campaign to squelch war rumors, and the Rumors Clinic also worked toward this goal through a Rumors Column published in all newspapers every Monday.[36]

Local national defense committees were organized by the American Legion. These groups organized meetings in public squares, schools, and social centers to promote patriotism among civilians and to explain rationing policies along with the importance of avoiding waste. "Liberty speakers" were also organized throughout the island: these were civic leaders who volunteered to make short speeches in cinemas on war themes such as democracy, collective safety, and war events.[37]

There was much propaganda in support of the war effort in the press and on the radio, along with many war-related advertisements. For example, ads for Chesterfield cigarettes showed two soldiers embracing a woman. Bubble gum companies no longer included the traditional cards featuring big-league ballplayers; instead, they substituted them with cards depicting warships, aircraft, soldiers, cannons, and marines.[38] Another popular item was a set of three ashtrays with the faces of Adolf Hitler, Benito Mussolini, and Emperor Hirohito. Creative slogans encouraged civilians to support the war effort by eating less (to ensure more food for soldiers): "With mouth munitions we'll win the war"; or to avoid revealing where family members were stationed to prevent the bombing of that place by the enemy: "Loose lips might sink ships."

The war changed Puerto Ricans' daily habits in many other ways. For example, beginning on February 16, 1942, the civil service changed its daily schedule so that not all workers would have the same hours. Some agencies began at 7:45, some at 8:00, some at 8:15, and some at 8:30, and then they punched out at the same intervals. This way, less fuel was lost in traffic jams.[39] The lunch hour was reduced by the government from one and a half to one hour, and then to half an hour so that civil workers would no longer go home for lunch, which had been a general custom. This measure reduced the need for public transportation, which was so precious at that time. Finally, working half days on Saturday was suspended, and all civil employees instead had to work an additional hour from Monday to Friday, thus working seven and a half hours a day.[40] Later, the Puerto Rican government, as did Cuba, advanced the clocks one hour to save electricity.[41] Also, Governor Tugwell declared all Fridays "Creole Cookery Day," so that on those days homes and restaurants would cook exclusively with locally grown products.[42]

Measures to deal with the war situation that were issued in Washington often did not reflect the reality on the ground in Puerto Rico, and Tugwell was constantly complaining about them. For example, the colonial government struggled to avoid the enforcement of an executive order banning the use of molasses to produce any distilled spirits such as rum. The measure was related to an American war need. Because the rubber that was needed so much for tires had been replaced by products made from alcohol, the US government wanted to allocate all of its alcohol resources to that chemical process.[43] For Puerto Rico, the issue was completely different. On the island, molasses had no use other than in the production of rum; if it could not be used for that purpose, it would be discarded, and no alcohol would be produced. Also, the production of rum from molasses generated much-needed jobs locally; moreover, it was a booming business that generated substantial tax revenue for Puerto Rico.[44] Finally, on February 3, 1942, the War Production Board (WPB) exempted both Puerto Rico and the US Virgin Islands from this executive order.[45]

Soon after, new problems hindered the export rum industry. One of them was the scarcity of glass bottles. Prewar federal legislation banned the shipping of bottles from the United States to Puerto Rico, and this was not repealed until December 1942. This meant that the rum distilleries were only able to use their bottles in the local market, where they were retrievable and reusable. The bottles sent to the continental United States, however, remained there. Many distilleries had to keep their rum in pipes, aging and waiting for unavailable bottles. The Puerto Rico Industrial Development Company (PRIDCO) finally established the Puerto Rico Glass Corporation, a bottle factory, to overcome this difficulty.[46]

The lack of seagoing vessels to carry the rum for export also affected the local liquor industry. Although they had orders from US importers in excess of $10 million, local distillers had to stop packaging rum for export for lack of enough storage facilities for the crates of rum that were constantly accumulating while waiting for cargo space to be sent to the United States.[47] In April, distillers exported around 183,000 crates of rum; in May, 150,000; in June, just 25,000; and in July, fewer than 20,000 crates. To get around this difficulty, some rum distilleries, knowing that the War Production Board had no jurisdiction over ships of less than one thousand tons, bought some for transporting their product to the United States. Later, the government of the island considered buying more such boats directly, but the insurance costs were "prohibitive," so they joined the distillers in forming a corporation and provided 65 percent of the $1.2 million needed to acquire second-hand schooners for rum transport to the United States.[48]

The garment industry was also affected by the German blockade, and garment factories closed because they could not get access to the imported raw materials needed for the production of nets, socks, underwear, lace, handkerchiefs, and the like.[49] The industry finally had a breakthrough after long negotiations in Washington when the US Army and the US Navy decided to have some of their uniforms made in Puerto Rico.[50] However, only after the end of the submarine blockade in mid-1943 would this industry have some impact, minor as it may have been, on the employment situation on the island.[51]

Unemployment on the island continued to rise as the various industries ran out of raw materials and the federal government showed little interest in addressing the issue. In 1942, the unemployment rate was around 12 percent (or 225,000 people out of work), while price data showed an increase of 6 points per month, generating huge inflation.[52] At the same time, salaries were completely inadequate to cope with rising prices, and the purchasing power of Puerto Rican workers was in constant decline, thus affecting the quality of their diet.[53] From November 1941 to November 1942, prices in Puerto Rico increased 53 percent, compared to 16 percent in the United States. This was largely attributable to higher freight charges due to the war risk insurance that was required in every import transaction.[54]

Trying to curtail the unemployment crisis, Puerto Rico's Department of the Interior initiated in 1942 a municipal roads construction project employing three thousand workers in twenty-four municipalities. Later, the War Production Board authorized a public works program that included the construction and repair of roads, buildings, schools, and hospitals as well as specific projects such as a water supply system for San Juan, the completion of the Capitol building, a parking garage for government workers, and a containment wall for the Jayuya River.[55] At the end of 1942, the island's legislature assigned $10 million to provide jobs in agricultural projects to increase the production of subsistence foodstuffs, fish, hens and eggs, rabbits, pigs, and fruit trees.[56]

Torpedoed tanker in the Caribbean, 1942 (Library of Congress)

Unlike the strategy in most other Caribbean islands, in Puerto Rico there was less emphasis on the development of new local enterprises to produce what was no longer available by import. The main reason, according to Governor Tugwell, was that the island had "a population long divorced from the production arts."⁵⁷ This island had no fewer resources than the others, but it had far more dependency on US imports. During the blockade, Puerto Rican leaders spent more of their energies asking Washington for more tonnage than promoting import substitution or encouraging changes in eating habits throughout the island. Only the Agricultural Extension Service (AES) responded to this goal.⁵⁸ According to an article in the *New York Herald Tribune*:

> In San Juan nobody dies of inanition but in all the streets you can see examples of acute malnutrition. Two thirds of all school kids are undernourished. . . . If any difficulties come about in Puerto Rico, it will be due to the misery of the empty stomachs.⁵⁹

The Scarcity Problem

As early as December 1941, just two days after the attack on Pearl Harbor, Governor Tugwell sent a cable and a letter to President Roosevelt and Secretary of the Interior Harold Ickes expressing concern about the possibility of a naval blockade, in which he requested badly needed stocks of food, building materials, and medicines for the island.⁶⁰ Specifically, he requested that $15 million be allocated to acquiring supplies sufficient for three months of consumption. This request was repeated throughout the following year but remained unfilled by the Washington bureaucracy until 1944.[61] Part of the delay in the approval of this aid was the result of political struggles on the island that were largely incited by the resident commissioner, Bolívar Pagán, who belonged to the Coalition Party, which fiercely opposed Tugwell. Pagán showed himself to be out of touch with the seriousness of the war situation and of the U-boat blockade when he requested the US Congress to end Tugwell's plan for making Puerto Rico self-sufficient in terms of foodstuffs. He argued that the island's economy had historically depended on its exports and that there was no other way of properly supporting it.[62]

Each month, Puerto Rico regularly received about one hundred thousand tons of food, medicines, and other products. In the first six months of 1942, German military actions had already decreased these imports to some ten thousand to twenty thousand tons per month, and in September 1942 only seven thousand tons were received. From September to October 1942, only one ship arrived. In December, the situation had become so desperate that hundreds of needy people would go to the San Juan Crematorium every day looking for scrap food in the garbage.[63]

Puerto Rico was very densely populated compared to other Caribbean islands.[64] This, coupled with the fact that the economy of Puerto Rico by then was focused on the monoculture of sugar for export and on the import of subsistence products, quickly led to a crisis situation, described by Tugwell as follows:

> We sat helpless on our island while ship after ship coming to us with food, medicines, fire equipment, munitions, and all the other necessities was sunk. Our losses gradually came to exceed survivals. Our hospitals were filled with rescued passengers and seamen; our warehouses were gradually emptied of food ... chlorine for the water-supply system; insulin and sulfa drugs; [and] repair parts for some essential machines. But food was the worst of the worries.[65]

Tugwell's government decidedly promoted the production of food crops by the so-called Plan de Siembras (Planting Plan) or Plan López Domínguez through its Department of Agriculture and Commerce, but results were not as expected. Although by July 1942 the efforts of the Agricultural Extension Service had increased food crops by 30 percent from their 1940 level, the AES was still only utilizing 21 percent of available farmland. The amount of foodstuffs produced was far from enough to supply the needs of Puerto Ricans.[66] The sugar estates were needed for food crop production.

Tugwell stressed that, because of the blockade, sugar growers weren't in any way able to export their total output of sugar. Therefore, to use these productive lands to plant sugarcane was "a tragic waste" in such an emergency. Furthermore, the US government continually resisted purchasing the entire Puerto Rican sugar production, as it was supplementing its needs with Cuban sugar.[67] In April 1942, the decision by the United States to buy 200,000 tons of sugar from Martinique and Guadeloupe after sealing an agreement with the Vichy government further demonstrated that the United States, even while rationing sugar, was not interested in buying all of Puerto Rico's output.[68] Martinique and Guadeloupe were almost a thousand miles farther than Puerto Rico from most US ports, and they were considered unfriendly to the United States and its allies given that they were administered by the Vichy government.

Even in a war emergency, most sugar farmers put their personal interests ahead of the common good. Sugarcane farmers who were organized as the Farmers Association of Puerto Rico joined forces with the American Federation of Labor (AFL) of Puerto Rico, resident commissioner Bolívar Pagán, and the local press. They even took their case before the US Congress, where they accused Tugwell of being a "fascist" and "socialist" and called for his removal from the governorship of the island; Pagán said: "Tugwell is a Quisling, betraying Puerto Rico."[69] The opposition of the sugar lobby was eventually overcome only through government subsidies that equated the gains from the production of food crops with those of producing sugar. To force the sugar producers to use a part of their lands for the production of the needed foodstuffs, the Agricultural Adjustment Agency (AAA) in San Juan established a new requirement to get access to the subsidies: to be eligible for these funds, sugar producers would have to devote at least 7 percent of their lands to the production of leguminous food crops.[70]

The War Production Board paid a number of workers to produce fruits and vegetables to be distributed to school canteens and various charitable institutions. These institutions, as well as poorer families, also received surplus food from the United States, such as apples, beans, cornmeal, lard, evaporated milk, plums, canned tomatoes, and wheat flour.[71] The Agricultural Marketing Association (AMA) of Puerto Rico was the agency in charge of the procurement and distribution of foodstuffs, and it also facilitated the production and acquisition of more foodstuffs.

Although now and then people became hysterical about the possibility of a military attack on the island, such outbursts were not constant, and most of the time Puerto Ricans were only worried about their access to food, transportation, and services. Again and again, different civil officers stated that Puerto Ricans acted as if they were unaware of the severity of the blockade. They protested because of the effects of the blockade but tended to put the blame on their governor or on federal agencies, and they resisted changing their daily habits.[72] On this, C. S. Jamison, director of the War Production Board, said before San Juan's Lions Club: "Puerto Rico hadn't still noticed the seriousness of the situation it faces."[73]

Many federal and local agencies dealt with the scarcity problem. The director of the War Board of the US Department of Agriculture, J. Bernard Frisbie, insisted that Puerto Rico would have to accept the food shortage "without protest" and emphasized that consumers "must eat substitute foodstuffs even if they didn't like them as much."[74] There was also the Food Storage Program for Puerto Rico, the US Virgin Islands, and Alaska, organized by the Department of the Interior and directed by Paul Gordon. This agency understood that it was essential to substitute for scarce products like rice and lard, a policy that would radically change the Puerto Rican diet. The Food Storage Program was also preoccupied with the lack of appropriate refrigeration facilities on the island and of ships that might transport foodstuffs to Puerto Rico in order to sustain its population.[75] Large quantities of food remained in US ports for months waiting for cargo space in ships servicing the island. In some cases, the waiting was so long that the food spoiled before arriving at its destination.

Therefore, out of pure necessity, at least some eating habits had to change. Rice, beans, codfish, meat, and flour had to be replaced by malangas, yucca, yautias, breadfruit, and plantains, which, although more expensive, were at least available. Many other products were substituted for or modified, including coffee, which was mixed with soybeans, chickpeas, and other cereals to make it last longer, although altering its flavor. The rice from the traditional plate of rice and beans was frequently substituted with *funche* or *marota* made of corn flour, creating a new plate called *el segundo frente* (the second front).[76] Also, when filling in the traditional black pudding sausages (*morcillas*), rice was substituted with bread.

When the Agricultural Marketing Association of Puerto Rico received and distributed bad cattle feed that sickened the cows, killing many of them, there was a serious reduction in local milk production to about one third the normal level. The situation was aggravated by two factors: Puerto Rican milk was primarily used to supply the needs of the soldiers garrisoned on the island, and there was a serious shortage of milk bottles and milk bottle caps.[77] By September 1942, production was not enough for the local market, and priority was given to covering the army's needs; the remaining available milk had to be mixed with water to make it last longer. Eventually the civil defense established around three hundred "milk stations" where toddlers and children up to seven years old were provided with evaporated milk donated by the AMA.[78]

When laundry soap became scarce, as happened on other islands in the Caribbean, some people began to make laundry soap from beef fat.[79] Lard was very scarce and was replaced by vegetable oil; however, when this oil also became scarce, some merchants mixed it with mineral oil, with bad results because the latter caused oil stains in pants and skirts. To substitute for not-easily-available Three Stars–brand matches, some people improvised a small box with two parallel wires and a cotton ball soaked in alcohol, producing a spark that lit the cotton; this device served as a cigarette lighter.[80] These were sold for three or four dollars.

To make car tires last longer, Puerto Ricans repaired them by coating them with a good chunk of some other rubber that was held in place with screws. Also related to tire conservation, civilians volunteered to pick up from streets and roads any sharp objects that might damage tires, such as broken bottles, cans, wires, and nails. Furthermore, the federal authorities recommended that cane growers use steel wheels for their carts and trucks, avoid overloading them, and reduce speeds to a minimum.[81] For the general population, the tire companies placed advertisements advising consumers how to lengthen the life of their tires.

The Office of Price Administration (OPA), in charge of rationing and price fixing and the enforcement thereof, was highly respected. Rationing was implemented for the use and consumption of the most important products. Many luxury products such as silk and nylon stockings were no longer available, because their raw materials were now being used for military purposes.[82]

Some people took advantage of the rationing system, for instance with gasoline. For a while, taxi and other commercial vehicle drivers got coupons from the government enabling them to buy five gallons of gasoline per week, and four tires every six months. Some of these drivers, because the fares they could charge were too low to cover their costs, sold many of their coupons.[83] Eventually, during the summer of 1942, the situation got so serious that for some periods no gasoline was sold to private car owners or for tourism transportation, and the San Juan government had to suspend its cleaning services because maids and janitors couldn't get to work.[84] In June, a new system of rationing was established, and private cars were allowed to buy gasoline from Monday to Thursday as determined by the order of the numbers on their license plates. That system was soon modified again and made stricter by requiring a special gasoline coupon that was to be distributed.[85]

One of the most pressing concerns was the need for chlorine for treating drinking water. Without this chemical, people's lives were endangered because of the epidemics that unchlorinated water could trigger.[86] In the worst months of 1942, Governor Tugwell had to ask for an emergency airlift via a navy aircraft to bring in a ton of the substance. Less serious because impacting a smaller part of the population was a scarcity of iron and steel, which led to many items disappearing from stores (cars, refrigerators, bicycles, typewriters, many hardware items, construction materials, air conditioners, water coolers, agricultural machinery, camera film, etc.).[87]

Other products whose scarcity was cause for alarm were gas specifically for public transportation vehicles and diesel fuel for the operation of sugar mills, rum distilleries, and the electrical power stations that supplied military installations, hospitals, and refrigerators in private homes and food storage facilities. The government responded to this situation by closing some factories, cutting off electricity for several hours each day, and restricting public transportation to a few buses. The courts were instructed to limit the suspension of hearings in order to prevent litigants and witnesses from having to make multiple visits during the transportation emergency. The island government even requested that families limit any gatherings that might necessitate traveling.[88] Governor Tugwell also urged people to use fuel reserves responsibly:

> In these days and months ... gasoline and fuel oil are sailors' blood. We ought not to use them for frivolous purposes.... [W]e must not use our automobiles unnecessarily; we must not use electric light whenever we can get along without it. We must learn again the pleasures of staying at home.[89]

Alternatives to gasoline were considered, including a substitute fuel composed of molasses alcohol mixed with gasoline, locally known as "alcolina." A committee was appointed by Governor Tugwell to analyze the feasibility of alcolina, and it was estimated that Puerto Rico would need at least forty thousand gallons of the fuel per day.[90] Consideration was given to mixing gasoline and alcohol in a proportion of seventy-five to twenty-five units; for this process, the island would still need to import thirty thousand gallons of gasoline and five thousand gallons of fuel oil each day. Furthermore, to produce the other ten thousand gallons of alcolina, the island would need thirty thousand gallons of molasses. Because the benefits would be so limited, and the required imported products would occupy almost the same cargo space as the gasoline itself, the project was considered unfeasible.[91]

To counter speculation on meat prices, the island's Food Commission fixed the price at eight cents a pound. However, many cattle suppliers rejected that price and decided not to butcher any animals until it was raised or removed, thus causing a meat shortage that lasted several days.[92] Some dealers sold meat at their own rates and simply ignored the official list of prices. The local

Department of Agriculture and Commerce, following a practice common in the United States, eventually decided for a while to authorize the sale of meat from tuberculosis-infected cows, under the supervision of veterinarians who had to certify that the tuberculosis was focalized and not active and that only healthy parts of the cows were used.[93] Many meat sellers refused to sell that meat because they knew that their customers would not accept it. Soon the government, in response to public protests, banned the slaughtering of diseased cows. By December 1942, the only fresh meat available was pig tail and ear.[94]

Even if they had the money to buy things, people weren't able to find what they needed. The colonial government established the rationing of foodstuffs such as rice, lard, butter, meat, and coffee through a system of coupon books consisting of differently colored stamps.[95] These books were distributed each month, and people had to present the corresponding stamp to buy the specified amount of a given product.[96]

Like in the rest of the Caribbean islands, and in response to the scarcity of many foodstuffs, a black market developed in Puerto Rico. There, a pound of rice normally worth three cents sold for a dollar fifty, but one was additionally able to get anything from laundry soap to chocolates. Another illegal practice was that some wholesalers charged retailers according to the maximum prices fixed by the government, and simultaneously required them to pay additional money in cash without showing it on the bill, before they would close sales. Others simply sold their products above the legal rates, confident that people would pay without reporting them. However, if such transactions were reported, the wholesalers had to pay fifty dollars to the retailer in addition to a fine determined by the court.[97]

Governor Tugwell's requests to Washington for funds and assistance were continuous, but communication was sporadic, and the federal government's lack of organization was an open secret. Unexpected situations that arose from bureaucratic complexities were a constant headache for the Puerto Rican government. The most arbitrary and irresponsible wartime decision made in Washington with respect to Puerto Rico was that of August 1942 allocating the inadequate amount of a mere thirty thousand tons of monthly shipping to the island (less than one-third of its peacetime needs).[98] Puerto Rican government authorities claimed that, because the island imported 55 percent of its foodstuffs, it needed at least 56,500 tons per month; this reality was constantly stressed to Washington by Governor Tugwell, Resident Commissioner Pagán, and Chamber of Commerce president Filipo de Hostos, to no avail. According to a column in the *Washington Post*, the United States failed to comply with its obligations toward Puerto Rico while it provided foreign nations with food:

> There is a small island in the Caribbean Sea attacked by poverty, which this country has overlooked in its program of global salvation. It is rare to forget this place, because it belongs to the U.S. It is a kind of stepchild adopted against its wishes, and which we have never really liked a lot....
>
> We promised to love, honor and care [for] our new possession. We also vowed ... to offer its people more education, good health and eternal happiness in a democratic manner.... None of these promises has been met successfully. Not even in peacetime....
>
> Some friends of PR have given me information about the miserable conditions prevailing there. Reserves usually remain depleted.... There are no fresh vegetables. There is no meat.... Forty percent of all employable people are jobless.... 200,000 of the 350,000 public school students suffer from malnutrition....
>
> The U.S. warships daily send food convoys to remote countries that have nothing to do with the United States. Certainly we should not forget our stepson. We cannot allow it to starve in front of our own doors.[99]

Political intrigues persisted in the middle of the worst part of the blockade of 1942. Even after the approval of the allocation of $15 million requested by Governor Tugwell to "encourage sugar planters and other producers to grow more food," it took years to move forward due to the excessive bureaucracy in Washington's Division of Territories and to the political intrigues working against him.[100] In June 1942, the War Board of the US Department of Agriculture in Puerto Rico sent a letter to Secretary of Agriculture Claude A. Wickard declaring Governor Tugwell persona non grata and recommending a state of martial law rather than his government on the island.[101]

Certainly, Tugwell's administration made several mistakes managing the island in wartime and in the middle of a blockade, but the local opposition to the Tugwell administration was mostly instigated by business leaders who felt that his emphasis on the general interest rather than on promoting purely capitalistic interests harmed them.[102] It is interesting to note that the problem of insufficient food for the inhabitants of Caribbean territories was approached by the United States from a political-military point of view, as evidenced by this communication from Secretary of State Sumner Welles to President Roosevelt dated June 12, 1942, concerning the supply of food in the Caribbean:

> It is clear that this Government must act immediately to alleviate a situation that threatens the military and political position of the United States in the Caribbean.[103]

Fortunately, after December 1942, when the convoy system began to bear fruit, the situation of the flow of food and other necessities began to stabilize.[104] Puerto Rican tables again started to see rice and beans, and prices began to be controlled. Islanders had overcome the worst.

Boat Sinkings and Puerto Rico[105]

Some Puerto Ricans ended up waiting to be rescued from Caribbean waters after their vessels were torpedoed by German U-boats. These attacks were not necessarily close to Puerto Rico, but Puerto Ricans were among their victims. A few specific cases of Puerto Rican victims of U-boat attacks were reported. The most interesting one was the case of Frank Nuñez, twenty-nine years old, who had been a crew member on five different torpedoed ships.[106]

According to a US Coast Guard report submitted to the Tenth Naval District, the British ship *Jumna*, carrying sacks for the Puerto Rican sugar industry, had a close encounter with a submarine near the city of Isabela, located on the northern coast of Puerto Rico and close to the Mona passage.[107] But the first ship sunk in the vicinity of Puerto Rico was the 5,127-ton American merchantman *Delplata* on February 20, 1942. When the ship sent out its SSS (sinking ship signal) after coming under attack from the U-156, its message was received in Puerto Rico, and the admiral in charge of the Caribbean Sea Frontier thus learned that submarines were attacking in its three Caribbean sectors.[108] All thirty-nine crew members from the *Delplata* were rescued by a US Army ship and taken to hotels in Puerto Rico.[109]

Captain Werner Hartenstein's U-156 was very active in the waters surrounding Puerto Rico and is credited with having bombarded Mona Island's emergency landing strip and its Civil Conservation Corps camp.[110] On February 25, 1942, Captain Hartenstein attacked the 5,685-ton British tanker *La Carriere* south of the Mona passage, where it took a whole day to sink deep into the Paseo de los Muertos. Out of its crew of forty-two men, twenty-nine were rescued from the sea and taken to Puerto Rico's Guánica Sugar Company complex, where they received medical care and were then repatriated.[111]

The Puerto Rico Sector of the Caribbean Sea Frontier was the obligatory route for ships coming from the Gulf of Mexico. During May, for example, four submarines operated exclusively in the Windward passage and the Puerto Rico Sector: the U-107, U-108, U-172, and U-558. Together they sank fifty-three merchant ships, mostly small vessels but with a total shipping weight of 246,063 tons. As a result of these sinkings, and as also happened

Destroyer entering San Juan Bay, 1945 (Archivo Fundación Luis Muñoz Marín)

frequently in neighboring Caribbean islands, Puerto Rico had to accommodate the survivors, and by April 1, 1942, "over 300 Norwegian, Swedish, Dutch, Irish and Canadian sailors" were reportedly being given care on the island.[112]

The last sinking in waters near Puerto Rico happened on June 5, 1944, when the U-539 sank the 1,517-ton Panamanian merchant ship *Pillory* a few miles away from the Mona passage. A short time later, the U-529 itself was attacked by a VP 204 aircraft and retired from combat after being damaged.[113] In any event, the last recorded U-boat operating in the Caribbean was the U-530, commanded by Kurt Lange, in July 1944.

The End of the War

After January 1943, the German U-boats "were never again a menace in the Caribbean, only a nuisance."[114] Allied losses in 1943 were less than one-third those of 1942. By the end of the war, the final German tally for the Caribbean was an impressive four hundred merchant ships sunk, while they only lost seventeen of their own U-boats. It is becoming clear that the Caribbean military campaign was Germany's most cost-efficient campaign of the entire war.[115]

The dissatisfaction with the way in which the United States managed the war emergency was evident in Puerto Rico, where Governor Tugwell at some point feared the worst:

Puerto Ricans had begun to think, *not* that the great nation to which they were attached was *unable* to reach them with supplies, but that it *did not want to*—at least not badly enough to risk the necessary ships. From my point of view this was worse.... They were much inclined to indignation at our neglect.[116]

The significant changes in the lifestyles of Caribbean people because of the German siege led them to seriously question their condition of colonial subjection. The adoption of the Atlantic Charter by Roosevelt and Churchill after the Pearl Harbor attack, particularly its Article III, introduced among Caribbean intellectuals inspiring concepts such as "the right of every nation to select the form of government under which [it] will live." The path was thus ready and fertile for a succession of nationalist and independence movements that would culminate in the decolonization of most of the Caribbean over the next few decades. Governor Tugwell had foreseen this in his diary with this annotation dated March 10, 1942:

We are in for it now; and we run the risk of all colonial occupations. I should think that after the war the old colonialism will be dead. What has apparently beaten the British and the Dutch in the East ... has been betrayal by the "natives."[117]

The Caribbean experience also forced the United States to reevaluate the region and to get acquainted with its inhabitants a little bit more; it had to, in order to deal with the evolving problems that the United States faced in that region. Washington's new focus on the Caribbean, along with its significant military presence there, especially its naval bases centered around the main operational base on Puerto Rico, helped to strengthen US influence in the area.

For the inhabitants of the Caribbean, the war changed their vision of themselves and of their place in the world. The German blockade crisis forced the Caribbean peoples to communicate with each other in spite of their language barriers and to deal with their common threats and necessities. Self-determination for the Caribbean nations would still be years away, but at least the process toward independence had begun.

Notes

1. Actually, the U-boats were able to stay in the Caribbean for up to three weeks while carrying nineteen torpedoes.
2. Gaddis Smith, *American Diplomacy during the Second World War, 1941–1945* (New York: John Wiley and Sons, 1967), p. 3.
3. Translated in English as "roll of the drums."
4. Winston S. Churchill, *Memoirs of the Second World War* (Boston: Houghton Mifflin, 1987), p. 410.
5. Homer H. Hickam Jr., *Torpedo Junction: U-Boat War off America's East Coast, 1942* (New York: Dell Publishing, 1989), p. x.
6. César de Windt Lavandier, *La Segunda Guerra Mundial y los submarinos alemanes en el Caribe* (Santo Domingo: Editora Amigo del Hogar, 1997), p. 71.
7. G. H. Bennett and Roy Bennett, *Hitler's Admirals* (Annapolis, MD: Naval Institute Press, 2004), pp. 139–140.
8. Juan R. Torruella, "Why Did Germany Turn to Submarine Warfare as Its Principal Naval Strategy of World War I?," *Boletín de la Academia Puertorriqueña de la Historia* 20–21, nos. 59–62 (January 2000–July 2001): 114.
9. To protect their access to the vital bauxite, and with the consent of the queen of the Netherlands, in September 1941 a thousand US soldiers and a bomber and artillery squadron occupied Dutch Guiana. See Humberto García Muñiz, *La estrategia de Estados Unidos y la militarización del Caribe* (Río Piedras, PR: Instituto de Estudios del Caribe, University of Puerto Rico, 1988), p. 62.
10. Anglo-American Caribbean Commission, *The Caribbean Islands and the War: A Record of Progress in Facing Stern Realities* (Washington, DC: Government Printing Office, 1943), p. 11.
11. Karl Dönitz, *Memoirs: A Documentary of the Nazi Twilight* (New York: Belmont Books, 1961), p. 29.
12. Ibid., p. 57. See also Rexford Guy Tugwell, *The Stricken Land: The Story of Puerto Rico* (Garden City, NY: Doubleday, 1946), p. 240, on the impact of this attack on Puerto Rico.
13. Gaylord T. M. Kelshall, *The U-Boat War in the Caribbean* (Annapolis, MD: Naval Institute Press, 1994), p. 43.
14. De Windt Lavandier, *La Segunda Guerra Mundial*, p. 227.
15. Kelshall, *The U-Boat War*, p. 16.
16. Roosevelt's action was influenced by a private group of oil men, the Petroleum Industry War Council Committee, who informed him that, if the sinking of tankers continued at the rates of January and March, there wouldn't be enough oil for sustaining the war after 1942. About this, see Hickam, *Torpedo Junction*, p. 166.
17. Kelshall, *The U-Boat War*, p. 16.
18. Tugwell, *The Stricken Land*, p. 191.
19. The Coastal Trading Act, also called the Cabotage Act, was in Section 9 of the Foraker Act (Organic Act of 1900, Pub. L. no. 56-191, 31 Stat. 77), initially proposed by Senator Joseph B. Foraker. Its purpose was to sustain the US Merchant Marine, and it is still in force.

20. *El Mundo* (San Juan), September 25, 1942, p. 1. The disposition was made by the US Treasury Department in response to a petition by Secretary of the Interior Harold I. Ickes.

21. Tugwell, *The Stricken Land*, pp. 196–197.

22. Ibid., p. 195.

23. Ibid., pp. 224–225. The order was meant to be applied in Hawaii. Eventually, the federal government exempted Puerto Rico from the order's mandate.

24. Ibid., p. 194.

25. Rexford Guy Tugwell, *La tierra azotada: memorias del último gobernador estadounidense de Puerto Rico*, ed. Jorge Rodríguez Beruff (San Juan: Fundación Luis Muñoz Marín, 2009), pp. 285–286.

26. Ché Paralitici, *No quiero mi cuerpo pa' tambor: el servicio militar obligatorio en Puerto Rico* (San Juan, Ediciones Puerto, 1998), pp. 311, 312.

27. Gerardo M. Piñero Cádiz, *Puerto Rico: el Gibraltar del Caribe* (San Juan: Editorial Isla Negra, 2008), p. 144.

28. Tugwell, *The Stricken Land*, p. 240.

29. In response to the scarcity of copper and nickel, after 1943 the US penny was no longer made of 95 percent copper and 5 percent tin and zinc but of 100 percent steel or brass. US five-cent coins, known as "nickels" but made of 25 percent nickel and 75 percent copper, were then made of silver, copper, and manganese. This lasted until 1946. See Francisco M. Rivera Lizardi, *La Segunda Guerra Mundial en Caguas* (Caguas, PR: Ediciones Situm, 2003), p. 182; and *El Mundo* (San Juan), August 13, 1942, p. 6. Silver was also used to substitute for tin in welds and copper in electric energy conductors; *El Mundo* (San Juan), April 9, 1942, p. 3. The collected metals were classified and compacted by the Civil Defense in San Juan and sent to the United States. The money earned would pay for defense needs; *El Mundo* (San Juan), February 27, 1942, p. 1. A total of 7,224,270 pounds of old iron was collected in Puerto Rico; *El Mundo* (San Juan), December 12, 1942, p. 7.

30. Rivera Lizardi, *La Segunda Guerra Mundial en Caguas*, pp. 110, 136.

31. *El Mundo* (San Juan), February 4, 1942, p. 6.

32. They collected even small fragments of metal such as wires, kitchenware, utensils, empty tubes of creams and ointments, batteries, etc.; *El Mundo* (San Juan), May 5, 1942, p. 1.

33. *El Mundo* (San Juan), February 28, 1942, p. 8.

34. José Collazo, *Guerra y educación: la militarización y americanización del pueblo puertorriqueño durante la Segunda Guerra Mundial, 1939–1945* (Santo Domingo: Editora Centenario, 1998), pp. 192–197.

35. Rivera Lizardi, *La Segunda Guerra Mundial en Caguas*, p. 141; and *El Mundo* (San Juan), June 30, 1942, p. 8.

36. Paralitici, *No quiero mi cuerpo pa' tambor*, pp. 237–238. The Rumors Clinic was a committee composed of federal judge Jorge Luis Córdova Díaz; the insular police chief, Colonel Luis Ramírez Brau; and a US attorney, Phillip F. Eric. They analyzed rumors about food supplies, racial prejudice, the army's moral, and other concerns and determined their veracity; *El Mundo* (San Juan), November 15, 1942, p. 8. Some of the rumors discussed in the column were that no more rice would be imported to Puerto Rico during the war, and that no more

American cigarettes would be imported during the war. They challenged both. *El Mundo* (San Juan), November 23, 1942, p. 10.

37. Rivera Lizardi, *La Segunda Guerra Mundial en Caguas*, pp. 96, 105.

38. Ibid., p. 154.

39. *El Mundo* (San Juan), February 11, 1942, p. 6. A curious project developed to alleviate traffic congestion in San Juan consisted of digging tunnels to connect the Julián Blanco School with Plaza de Colón, and the Central High School with Ponce de León Avenue, both school zones. These tunnels were also meant to be used as shelters in case of bombings; *El Mundo* (San Juan), May 26, 1942, p. 1.

40. Barbara Tasch Ezratty, *Puerto Rico: Changing Flags; An Oral History, 1898–1950* (Baltimore: Omni Arts, 1986), p. 205; *El Mundo* (San Juan), April 1, 1942, p. 1; and *El Mundo* (San Juan), May 8, 1942, p. 1.

41. *El Mundo* (San Juan), April 4, 1942, p. 3; May 2, 1942, p. 1; and September 1, 1942, p. 1.

42. Rivera Lizardi, *La Segunda Guerra Mundial en Caguas*, p. 98.

43. Luis Muñoz Marín, *Memorias, 1940–1952* (San Juan: Fundación Luis Muñoz Marín, 2003), p. 164. By November 1942, the United States had ceased the manufacture of whiskey, gin, and all other liquors, because all alcohol from the country's 124 distilleries was to be used in synthetic rubber production and to produce smokeless gunpowder. *El Mundo* (San Juan), September 1, 1942, p. 1.

44. The US Congress had decreed that the Puerto Rican government would receive back 70 percent of all the taxes on rum, money that would allow the Popular Democratic Party, which controlled the Puerto Rican Senate, to set in motion its project of land redistribution and industrialization. See Ronald Fernández, *The Disenchanted Island: Puerto Rico and the United States in the Twentieth Century* (New York: Praeger, 1992), pp. 145–146. The shortage of distilled beverages in the United States gave impetus to the Puerto Rican rum industry and produced huge amounts of federal excise taxes for the local government. In 1937–1939, the government's average income from the rum tax was $1.4 million annually, but in 1944 it soared to $65.9 million. This money helped the island pay her debts and build reserves. See Ena L. Farley, "Puerto Rico: Ordeals of an American Dependency during World War II," *Revista/Review Interamericana* 6, no. 2 (Summer 1976): 204.

45. *El Mundo* (San Juan), February 3, 1942, p. 1; and September 2, 1942, p. 4.

46. Rexford G. Tugwell, *Changing the Colonial Climate: The Story, from His Official Messages, of Governor Rexford Guy Tugwell's Efforts to Bring Democracy to an Island Possession Which Serves the United Nations as a Warbase* (San Juan: Bureau of Supplies, Printing, and Transportation, 1942), p. 157.

47. *El Mundo* (San Juan), May 16, 1942, p. 1; and July 1942, p. 1.

48. All ships of over one thousand tons were authorized to sail exclusively for war purposes. These smaller vessels had been used before as recreational yachts but now were easily converted into small cargo vessels capable of carrying about three hundred to five hundred tons. Their purchase cost ranged between $25,000 and $50,000. *El Mundo* (San Juan), August 7, 1942, p. 4; August 23, 1942, p. 1; August 27, 1942, p. 3; October 8, 1942, p. 4; and October 30, 1942, p. 5.

49. Claus Füllberg-Stolberg, "The Caribbean in the Second World War," in *General History of the Caribbean*, vol. 5, *The Caribbean in the Twentieth Century*, ed. Bridget Brereton (London: Macmillan; UNESCO Publishing, 2004), p. 109; and *El Mundo* (San Juan), August 29, 1942, p. 1.

50. The Puerto Rican garment entrepreneurs were asked to make khaki shirts and pants for the troops stationed in Puerto Rico. *El Mundo* (San Juan), June 17, 1942, p. 1; July 1, 1942, p. 8; and September 23, 1942, p. 1.

51. *El Mundo* (San Juan), May 23, 1942, p. 7; and May 29, 1942, p. 3.

52. Füllberg-Stolberg, "The Caribbean in the Second World War," p. 115; and *El Mundo* (San Juan), April 30, 1942, p. 1, and November 7, 1942, p. 5.

53. According to estimates by the University of Puerto Rico, in 1939 the Puerto Rican worker needed $1.32 a day to get an adequate diet. In 1942, he was earning an average of $0.41 a day. See Farley, "Puerto Rico: Ordeals of an American Dependency," p. 206. In 1942, it was reported that the hospital diet (for patients as well as workers) suffered when milk and eggs were no longer provided and the food consisted mainly of bread, vegetables, and root tubers. *El Mundo* (San Juan), October 21, 1942, p. 4.

54. *El Mundo* (San Juan), May 19, 1942, p. 1.

55. *El Mundo* (San Juan), November 3, 1942, p. 5; and November 20, 1942, p. 2.

56. *El Mundo* (San Juan), November 1942, p. 4.

57. Tugwell, *Changing the Colonial Climate*, p. 239.

58. The AES established thirty-six nutrition centers in rural areas of the island to offer a balanced nutrition to three thousand undernourished children from preschool age to sixteen years old. The idea was to change their eating habits by familiarizing them with foods that they usually considered undesirable. The food was cooked by volunteer women and 4-H members, who tried to get the children to eat all the food they were served. *El Mundo* (San Juan), August 2, 1942, p. 1.

59. Translation by the author. The article was written by Homer Bigart, after a short stay on the island. It put the blame for the food crisis squarely on Governor Tugwell, for not having a war reserve and for lacking a plan to prioritize cargo, and on local politics. *El Mundo* (San Juan), November 18, 1942, pp. 2, 11.

60. Tugwell, *The Stricken Land*, pp. 208–209.

61. Although the $15 million was not assigned until 1944, the storage of foodstuffs supplies sufficient for three months began in March 1942 on a smaller scale through the Storage Coordination Committee (made up of fifty local importers and supplies wholesalers) organized by Governor Tugwell. They stored twenty-three articles considered of vital need: beans, canned fruits and vegetables, canned soups, canned tomato sauce, oatmeal, cheese, foods for dairy cows and poultry, dried fish, flour, matches, rice, canned meats, fresh and smoked meats, evaporated and powdered milk, butter and its substitutes, salted pigs' feet, sausage (salted, canned, and smoked), smoked pork, and laundry soap. *El Mundo* (San Juan), February 27, 1942, p. 1.

62. *El Mundo* (San Juan), July 12, 1942, p. 11.

63. Some even fought among themselves for access to the discarded and rotting food. The group of around three hundred people included old people, women, men, and children,

and they particularly looked for the garbage from the US military bases. The crematorium guards were unable to control the situation. *El Mundo* (San Juan), December 31, 1942, p. 13.

64. According to the 1940 census, Puerto Rico had a population of 1,869,255 in 3,423 square miles of territory and a population density of 546.1 inhabitants per square mile. See Dr. Leon E. Truesdell, *Population, First Series, Number of Inhabitants, Puerto Rico* (Washington, DC: Government Printing Office, 1942), pp. 5, 7.

65. Tugwell, *The Stricken Land*, p. 212.

66. Of the 283 million pounds of rice needed, only 11 million pounds were expected; beans and legumes were expected to be 48 million pounds short; only root tubers such as plantains and yams were expected in sufficient quantities, in excess of 107 million pounds. The expected net deficit was 470,000 calories. *El Mundo* (San Juan), July 1, 1942, p. 13. To promote agricultural jobs, every person employed in agricultural enterprises was deferred from the Selective Service. *El Mundo* (San Juan), November 27, 1942, p. 4.

67. Beginning in 1937, Governor Tugwell had asked the US government to buy all the Puerto Rican sugar crop, but Washington wouldn't do it even though they bought the entire Cuban sugar crop. Great Britain bought all the sugar production of its West Indies colonies and that of the Dominican Republic. See Tugwell, *Changing the Colonial Climate*, p. 229. The sugar freight charges were the same for Puerto Rico as they were for Cuba, even though Puerto Rico was a domestic zone. But Puerto Rican sugar was at a disadvantage because it had to travel a longer distance to US ports and couldn't use the kind of tramp vessels that Cubans used to sail to the Florida Keys. Puerto Rican sugar exporters had to pay war risk insurance of seven cents for every one hundred pounds of sugar. *El Mundo* (San Juan), May 17, 1942, p. 1.

68. *El Mundo* (San Juan), April 4, 1942, p. 3. Even the *Philadelphia Record* criticized this US action: "We can't find boats to Puerto Rico but we find them to bring sugar from Martinique. The distance from Philadelphia to Martinique is 2,248 miles; from Philadelphia to Puerto Rico is 1,606 miles.... We don't hesitate to qualify Martinique as an enemy country. Martinique is Vichy; Vichy is Hitler." *El Mundo* (San Juan), April 16, 1942, p. 5; translation by the author.

69. Tugwell, *The Stricken Land*, p. 216; Muñoz Marín, *Memorias*, p. 94; and *El Mundo* (San Juan), May 25, 1942, p. 1. Since *El Mundo* was overtly against Tugwell's administration, its editors depicted Tugwell's opposition as "massive" even though only a few sectors of sugar industrialists and merchants supported this opposition: "The cry of that class echoes the words and feelings of Puerto Rico." *El Mundo* accused Tugwell of "engaging in changing [Puerto Rico's] economy ... promot[ing] serious divisions in our island ... almost doubl[ing] the budget of the Executive Mansion, [and] creating the largest bureaucracy in our history." *El Mundo* (San Juan), May 26, 1942, p. 8. Other groups who protested against Tugwell and asked for his recall were the War Board of the US Department of Agriculture in Puerto Rico and Puerto Rico's Chamber of Commerce. *El Mundo* (San Juan), June 1, 1942, pp. 1, 8.

70. Leguminous food crops were recommended because they enriched the soil with nitrogen, which, during the war emergency, was difficult to get as chemical fertilizer. They were also recommended as a substitute for dairy cattle feed. *El Mundo* (San Juan), June 30,

1942, p. 5; September 5, 1942, p. 4; and October 24, 1942, p. 7. Of the 7 percent of their arable land dedicated to leguminous crops, sugar producers would have to dedicate 80 percent to edible legumes such as any kind of beans, and the other 20 percent might be dedicated to yams, corn, rice, ñames, sweet potatoes, apios, or cassava. *El Mundo* (San Juan), December 28, 1942, p. 2.

71. *El Mundo* (San Juan), May 5, 1942, p. 5. The number of families receiving government aid was reduced in 1942 from 185,000 to 107,000 after an investigation showed that many were physically and mentally able to work. *El Mundo* (San Juan), May 6, 1942, p. 1.

72. The *New York Herald Tribune* said that in San Juan, US visitors and the native elite were still buying canned goods paying three times the US price and that "on Saturday nights the regulars at the Normandie, Condado, Escambrón, Jack's, and the Morocco were as happy and noisy as in tourism days." Translation by the author from *El Mundo* (San Juan), November 18, 1942, pp. 2, 11.

73. *El Mundo* (San Juan), March 5, 1942, p. 1. The interior commissioner of Puerto Rico also commented: "Most people in Puerto Rico haven't realized that we are engaged in a war of gigantic proportions that directly and significantly affects all the activities of our people." *El Mundo* (San Juan), June 25, 1942, p. 4; translation by the author.

74. *El Mundo* (San Juan), March 4, 1942, p. 9; translation by the author.

75. *El Mundo* (San Juan), February 13, 1942, p. 4. As an example, on one occasion the AMA bought 2.5 million pounds of bacon that turned rancid and yellowish because it was packed with less salt than required to be preserved for the long time it spent in port; in another incident, the AMA bought 5,235 bags of corn that became spoiled after waiting too long in a Gulf port and had to be auctioned in Puerto Rico, but only as animal feed. *El Mundo* (San Juan), August 11, 1942, p. 1; and August 21, 1942, p. 1.

76. Rivera Lizardi, *La Segunda Guerra Mundial en Caguas*, p. 156. The name made reference to the "second front" that Joseph Stalin asked for in order to distract the Germans, who were attacking the Soviet Union with their full force, and that finally was established when the Allies disembarked in French Morocco and Algeria.

77. *El Mundo* (San Juan), September 30, 1942, p. 5; and November 18, 1942, p. 4.

78. The service was offered for free to all children aged two to seven, every day from 9:00 a.m. to 12:00 noon to guarantee their nutritional needs during the emergency. The program served canned evaporated and powdered milk, because there were not enough refrigeration devices to hold fresh milk in the countryside. Each station was able to feed two hundred children a day, providing three glasses of milk a day for each participant. Some stations also provided the children with soda crackers. *El Mundo* (San Juan), October 16, 1942, p. 5; October 28, 1942, p. 4; and November 20, 1942, p. 6.

79. Carlos Hernández Hernández, "Historia y memoria: representaciones de la Segunda Guerra Mundial en la ciudad señorial de Ponce" (Ph.D. diss., University of Puerto Rico, Río Piedras, January 2005), pp. 159, 171.

80. Rivera Lizardi, *La Segunda Guerra Mundial en Caguas*, pp. 198, 206, 223.

81. *El Mundo* (San Juan), May 1, 1942, p. 5.

82. Silk and nylon stockings were recycled for making parachute cords and gunpowder bags, which had earlier been made from materials imported from Asia that were no longer

available. Clean, used stockings were collected at shops, federal and local government agencies, clubs, and other places. *El Mundo* (San Juan), December 10, 1942, p. 10; and December 29, 1942, p. 4.

83. Hernández Hernández, "Historia y memoria," p. 160. Puerto Rico had four gasoline providers: Shell, West India Oil, Texaco, and Pyramid Oil. *El Mundo* (San Juan), September 1, 1942, p. 1.

84. Available gasoline was then sold only to the army, the navy, public transportation vehicles, private cars owned by doctors and nurses, ambulances, fire trucks, milk transportation vehicles, and government vehicles. *El Mundo* (San Juan), June 4, 1942, p. 1; and June 5, 1942, p. 5. Later, a fine was imposed on all public carriers benefiting from special concessions of fuel that, having seats available, ignored the stop calls of potential passengers, refusing to carry them. The penalty imposed was between five and fifty dollars. *El Mundo* (San Juan), August 12, 1942, p. 5. Another gasoline crisis came in September, when private cars were banned from using gas, and the only services provided with gasoline by the government were the "essential ones." *El Mundo* (San Juan), September 25, 1942, p. 1.

85. *El Mundo* (San Juan), June 12, 1942, p. 8; June 15, 1942, p. 4; and July 17, 1942, p. 5. The island had 30,304 vehicles, of which 16,717 were private cars and 5,740 were public carriers. In comparison, the US Virgin Islands only had 1,400 vehicles. *El Mundo* (San Juan), July 14, 1942, p. 5; and August 23, 1942, p. 1.

86. *El Mundo* (San Juan), April 6, 1942, p. 8; and May 6, 1942, p. 5.

87. *El Mundo* (San Juan), April 8, 1942, p. 2; April 14, 1942, pp. 1, 14; May 19, 1942, p. 1; July 5, 1942, p. 6; July 7, 1942, p. 7; October 1, 1942, p. 9; and December 22, 1942, p. 7.

88. *El Mundo* (San Juan), December 10, 1942, p. 2; and December 17, 1942, p. 6.

89. Tugwell, *Changing the Colonial Climate*, pp. 182–183. For a while, and to save oil, the government suspended public lighting after 11:00 p.m., and the Porto Rico Railway Light and Power Company suspended electric tram services after 11:15 p.m. *El Mundo* (San Juan), April 28, 1942, p. 1; and May 3, 1942, p. 1.

90. *El Mundo* (San Juan), July 3, 1942, p. 5; July 7, 1942, p. 6; and July 8, 1942, p. 5. Other countries were substituting gasoline. Brazil and Canada used charcoal; Denmark used flax waste. *El Mundo* (San Juan), July 19, 1942, p. 1. An expert from the tenant company of the Petroleum Monopoly of Spain (CAMPSA) offered a conference at the Ateneo Puertorriqueño to discuss the substitution of gasoline in Spain and France with gaseous fuels such as alcohol and benzene, produced by the distillation of wood and charcoal. The recommended mixture was seventy parts gasoline, twenty parts alcohol, and ten parts benzene. The problem was that, although the island had an excess of alcohol, it only had limited amounts of benzene. *El Mundo* (San Juan), July 19, 1942, pp. 5, 15.

91. *El Mundo* (San Juan), August 19, 1942, p. 4.

92. Rivera Lizardi, *La Segunda Guerra Mundial en Caguas*, p. 107; and *El Mundo* (San Juan), August 19, 1942, p. 5.

93. Some people doubted whether the proper supervision of the process was possible, given that there were only twenty-two professional veterinarians on Puerto Rico, among whom only seven had expertise in tuberculosis, while the island had seventy-five

slaughterhouses. *El Mundo* (San Juan), October 21, 1942, p. 1; October 22, 1942, pp. 3, 5; October 23, 1942, pp. 1, 9; and October 24, 1942, p. 1.

94. Farley, "Puerto Rico: Ordeals of an American Dependency," p. 209; according to Bolívar Pagán's testimony.

95. Juan M. García Passalacqua, *Casa sin hogar: memoria de mis tiempos, Puerto Rico, 1937–1987* (Río Piedras, PR: Editorial Edil, 1990), pp. 27–28.

96. Amy Bentley, *Eating for Victory: Food Rationing and the Politics of Domesticity* (Champaign: University of Illinois Press, 1998), p. 16.

97. For example, a pound of rice with a fixed price of eleven cents could be sold for twelve cents or even sixteen cents. *El Mundo* (San Juan), June 1, 1942, p. 4; October 22, 1942, p. 2; and December 16, 1942, p. 5. Other used the "convoy system," asking the client to buy putrid beans in order to buy a pound of rice for twelve cents. *El Mundo* (San Juan), November 14, 1942.

98. According to Lieutenant Commander Thomas C. Hennings, Governor Tugwell's naval assistant, in 1941 Puerto Rico received 2,330,000 tons of shipping, of which 1,721,000 covered the civil population's needs and 609,000 covered military needs. Therefore, he insisted that Puerto Rico needed at least 750,000 tons annually to cover its civil needs. He visited Admiral Emory S. Land, president of the National Maritime Commission, to present Puerto Rico's particular situation, but he got no results. *El Mundo* (San Juan), April 1, 1942, p. 6; and December 20, 1942, p. 1.

99. *El Mundo* (San Juan), December 16, 1942, p. 7; translation by the author.

100. The House Agriculture Committee stipulated that none of the money could be spent while Tugwell was governor. Nevertheless, President Roosevelt reiterated his support to Tugwell. Farley, "Puerto Rico: Ordeals of an American Dependency," p. 207; and *El Mundo* (San Juan), October 21, 1942, p. 8, and November 18, 1942, pp. 1, 11. Even when another $15 million was to be assigned by Congress to induce sugar producers to plant some cane fields, Pagán opposed it and convinced a number of senators that Tugwell wanted the money to spend it on anti-American politicking. The project was aborted. Muñoz Marín, *Memorias*, pp. 98–99, 109.

101. The board consisted of representatives from the Agricultural Adjustment Administration, the Farm Security Administration, the Soil Conservation Service, the Agricultural Credit Administration, the Farm Purchasing Administration, the Forestry Service, the Agricultural Extension Service, the Biological and Entomological Quarantine Service, the Bureau of Animal Industries, and the Agricultural Experimental Station. The letter was significant because Tugwell was a former US secretary of agriculture. *El Mundo* (San Juan), June 1, 1942, pp. 1, 8.

102. Some of the Tugwell administration's mistakes are discussed by Ena L. Farley as presented by Puerto Rican senator Lino Padrón in a US congressional hearing held in December 1942, and most have been discussed here earlier: spending $75,000 to buy ripe pineapples that had to be discarded; buying 2.5 million pounds of rancid and yellowish bacon worth $25,000 (it was packed with less salt than required to be preserved); buying the wrong kind of flour; and buying cases of what was presumed to be stewing meat but what

turned to be cattle fat. Farley, "Puerto Rico: Ordeals of an American Dependency," 207; and *El Mundo* (San Juan), April 11, 1942, p. 5, and August 11, 1942, p. 1.

103. Anglo-American Caribbean Commission, *The Caribbean Islands and the War*, p.19.

104. *El Mundo* (San Juan), December 12, 1942, p. 7; December 14, 1942, pp. 1, 9; and December 18, 1942, p. 2.

105. For further details on Caribbean sinkings from February to August 1942, see De Windt Lavandier, *La Segunda Guerra Mundial*, pp. 361–383.

106. *El Mundo* (San Juan), May 5, 1942, p. 1. In another article, a twenty-nine-year-old Frank Muñiz is mentioned as a Puerto Rican who has been survivor of four U-boat attacks. He was probably the same person, a married father of five, resident at El Fanguito in Santurce, who said that he was willing to sail back. *El Mundo* (San Juan), December 22, 1942, p. 5.

107. Piñero Cádiz, *Puerto Rico: el Gibraltar del Caribe*, p. 146.

108. In reference to the Panama Sector, the Trinidad Sector, and the Puerto Rico Sector, as defined by the Allies.

109. *El Mundo* (San Juan), February 23, 1942, p. 1.

110. This attack was reported two miles south of Mona Island. Thirty charges were made with no harm to 170 youths working there for the National Youth Administration. Mona Island is forty-five miles west of Puerto Rico, and is seven miles by two miles in size. *El Mundo* (San Juan), March 4, 1942, p. 1.

111. *El Mundo* (San Juan), February 26, 1942, p. 9. Another castaway from the *La Carriere* was rescued from his lifeboat on February 27 after one and a half days adrift. He was two miles east of Caja de Muertos island. *El Mundo* (San Juan), February 28, 1942, p. 1. Another survivor was rescued by the coast guard vessel *Unalga* clinging to a wooden contraption six miles from the spot where the ship sank. *El Mundo* (San Juan), March 1, 1942, p. 5. Finally, the *La Carriere*'s captain, sixty-one-year-old R. H. Cairns, on his last voyage after forty-two years at sea, was rescued by a navy ship a few miles off the coast of Ponce after drifting for eighty hours on a piece of debris, using his arms as oars. Only fourteen crew members remained missing and were presumed lost. *El Mundo* (San Juan), March 2, 1942, pp. 1, 16.

112. De Windt Lavandier, *La Segunda Guerra Mundial*, p. 61.

113. Ibid., p. 312.

114. Stetson Conn, Rose C. Engelman, and Byron Fairchild, *Guarding the United States and Its Outposts* (Washington, DC: US Army Center of Military History, 2000), p. 436.

115. Ibid., p. 312; Kelshall, *The U-Boat War*, pp. 446–449.

116. Tugwell, *The Stricken Land*, p. 288. Italics in the original.

117. Ibid., p. 269.

Vieques: The Impact of the Second World War

César J. Ayala Casás
José L. Bolívar Fresneda

The historical development of the island of Vieques was different from that of the main island of Puerto Rico. Whereas Puerto Rico was first settled by the Spanish in 1508, the island of Vieques was not permanently settled until the 1830s. When it was settled, it was French sugar planters who took on the task, bringing with them their slave populations and establishing a pure plantation economy along the lines of the French sugar islands. Thus, in spite of being connected historically to Puerto Rico, Vieques maintained its own sui generis history and social structure. Its inhabitants had a sense of belonging to a small but very unique society. The impact of World War II on Vieques accentuated the divergence between its historical path of development and that of the island of Puerto Rico.

During the Second World War, the armed forces of the United States acquired 53,484 acres of land in Puerto Rico, some through expropriations and some ceded or transferred by the insular government. Of these land acquisitions, 41 percent was expropriated on the island of Vieques.[1] Practically two-thirds of the island was transferred to the US Navy during the Second World War.[2] However, this does not mean that two-thirds of the residents of Vieques left the island. On the contrary, 90 percent of the population remained, concentrated in the central portion of the island, while the eastern and western sections were transferred from civilian hands to the US Navy. In terms of their most important economic resource, land, the inhabitants' assets per capita were reduced to one-third of what they had been before the expropriations. No other municipality in Puerto Rico experienced expropriations of such magnitude (two-thirds of the land) or of such destructive consequences. The residents of the two other municipalities that experienced significant expropriations, Ceiba and Aguadilla, could move to adjacent locations. The

Sugarcane workers in Vieques go on strike demanding the return of Central Playa Grande's cane fields expropriated by the navy, 1943. (Colección *El Mundo*, University of Puerto Rico)

residents of Vieques did not have that option. They stayed on the island, concentrated in the central portion, waiting for a time when the US Navy would return the land that had been expropriated from them. The impact of the expropriations on Vieques was therefore unique and much more destructive than what was experienced by other municipalities in Puerto Rico.

The war, federal expenditures as a result of the military buildup, and revenue derived from rum exports under exceptionally favorable wartime conditions had a long-term positive impact on the Puerto Rican economy.[3] During the 1940s, the federal government spent the spectacular sum of $1.2 billion in Puerto Rico. One can appreciate the significant economic impact of this federal expenditure by recalling, for example, that the Marshall Plan for European reconstruction entailed an expenditure of $13 billion for all of Europe.[4] During this period, the population of Puerto Rico was under two million inhabitants. In other words, the per capita expenditure of federal funds was much greater in Puerto Rico than it was in Europe. In addition to this wartime boom, due to German U-boat attacks in the Atlantic, the bombings of London, and shifting war priorities, British whiskey was no longer available to the American consumer, and this was precisely the most popular alcoholic beverage in the United States. This conjuncture opened for Puerto Rican rum manufactures an unexpected opportunity. They could sell all of their production at an attractive price without fear of competition from Great Britain. The federal government returned to the insular government all of the excise tax collected as a result of purchases by US consumers. This resulted in a significant increase in local government revenues. Rum tax receipts increased from

$53 million in 1941 to $141 million in 1947.[5] These added revenues facilitated the agricultural reform and other development projects that were driven by Governor Rexford G. Tugwell's administration and the Partido Popular Democrático (PPD).

During the war years, economic growth was achieved through the construction of roads, the electrification of the island facilitated by the new capability of public corporations to emit bonds after 1938, the creation of the Puerto Rico Development Bank in 1942, and an agrarian reform driven by the PPD to promote self-reliance in food production. The PPD confronted Puerto Rico's traditional reliance on the sugarcane industry, which it blamed for many of the island's problems, by enforcing the 500 Acre Law. This law, enacted in 1900 by the US Congress in response to demands for protection by continental sugar beet growers, limited land ownership in Puerto Rico to five hundred acres at a time when most of the large *centrales* had considerably more land. It went unenforced for decades. Once the PPD achieved victory in the US Supreme Court over the implementation of the 500 Acre Law in 1941,[6] the stage was set for the Tugwell administration to begin to carry out the agrarian reform.[7]

The sugar mill owners fought back, lobbying Congress to cut funding derived from the rum excise tax.[8] The insular government staunchly defended the agrarian reform project, arguing that it was absolutely necessary in order to avoid catastrophic food shortages looming as a result of the possibility of a naval blockade of the island by German submarines. Such a blockade did in fact occur in 1942, causing food shortages and riots. In response, the Tugwell administration and the PPD boosted their economic reform program, which initiated the replacement of the sugar plantation economy with an industrial one. This clearly was realized by the 1950s. The war, therefore, had a positive long-term effect on the economy of Puerto Rico as a whole, insofar as it strengthened the hand of those forces within Puerto Rico seeking agrarian reform while also helping to steer the island away from its extreme dependence on sugar exports and toward an industrial economy.

Vieques, on the other hand, did not benefit from any of the positive changes produced in Puerto Rico by the conjuncture of World War II. The sugarcane industry disappeared, but the island did not benefit from industrialization. The lands acquired by the navy were not returned to the residents once the war was over but remained under military control. This made agricultural development impossible, while limitations on civilian maritime transportation to the island hampered the development of industry on Vieques. The navy impeded the expansion of maritime and air transportation between Puerto Rico and Vieques by rerouting maritime transportation to a longer route and by restricting the expansion of the small airport in Isabel Segunda, causing the island's economy to stagnate for decades. Vieques suffered all the negative effects of the war without experiencing any of its benefits. As a result of economic stagnation, and the fact that the island was used as a target range after 1948, the population of Vieques declined steadily from this period onward, reaching its lowest recorded point in 1970.

The unique impact of the expropriations in Vieques cannot be attributed solely to land acquisitions by the navy. The expropriations were particularly catastrophic because of the island's preexisting social structure. Since the nineteenth century, Vieques had depended on sugar production. The industry relied on wage workers in the twentieth century, but in its early years in the 1830s it had depended on slave labor. Between 1800 and 1850, as a response to the vacuum in the international sugar market produced by the Haitian revolution of 1791–1804, cane plantations spread throughout the coastal plains of Puerto Rico, especially in the municipalities of Ponce, Mayagüez, and Arecibo, major centers of slave sugar production. The initial expansion of sugar production to Vieques was part of this same historical cycle generated by the Haitian revolution. Indeed, Vieques was initially colonized by planters from the French Caribbean. The entire landowning structure of Vieques was formed, from the beginning, in the context of a slave-based sugar plantation economy. Until then, the island had been depopulated. During the eighteenth century, the Spanish government had sent regular expeditions to expel English colonists who tried to settle in Vieques with their slaves. Geopolitically, Vieques was too close to Puerto Rico to allow these settlements.[9] However, the Spanish Crown did not populate the island until the nineteenth century, and when it did, it allowed French planters to start the enterprise.

The fact that Vieques transitioned from being a depopulated island to being an island settled by slave-owning sugar planters produced a social structure in Vieques that was different from that of the main island of Puerto Rico. Vieques lacked the independent peasantry that had existed in Puerto Rico from the sixteenth century until the sugar boom of 1800–1850. In Puerto Rico, that sugar boom prompted the relocation of the peasantry from the best coastal lands to the central highlands, and the peasantry survived the transition. Small farmers continued to be a factor in the economy, especially in the highlands. Vieques, by contrast, was characterized by the absence of that independent peasantry. As a result, all available agricultural land was taken over by the sugar *ingenios* of the nineteenth century and subsequently, in the twentieth century, by large *centrales*. The fact that Vieques was a pure plantation economy and not a mixed economy like Puerto Rico meant that land ownership was much more concentrated than in Puerto Rico, where the

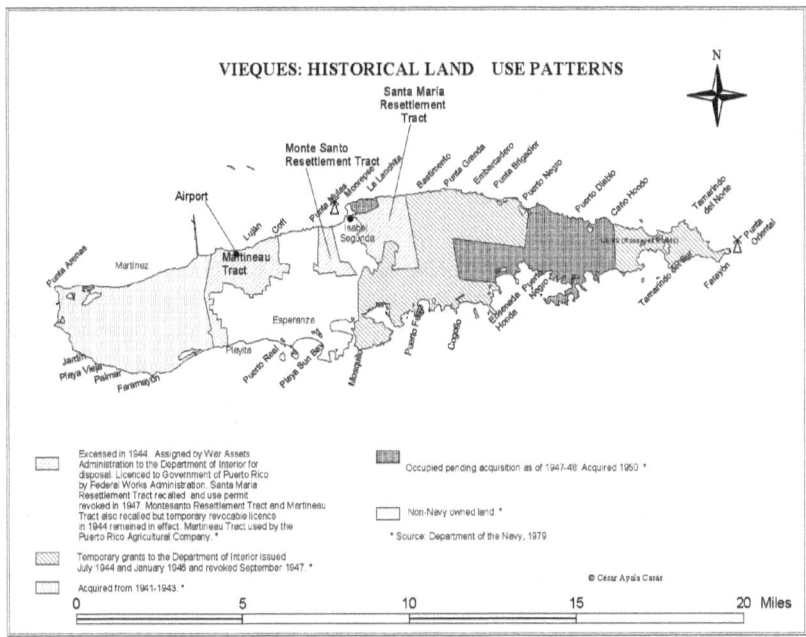

US Navy historical land tenure patterns on Vieques (personal archives of César J. Ayala Casas)

centrales coexisted with the independent peasantry. In Vieques, the *centrales* were always dominant. This social structure resembled the pure plantation economies typical of the English and French sugar islands more than the Hispanic Caribbean societies, in which peasants were never entirely displaced by the sugar mills. In this regard, the historical social structure of Vieques is closer to that of the Lesser Antilles than to that of Puerto Rico.[10]

The Expropriations

Before the arrival of the US Navy, the majority of the rural population of Vieques were *agregados*, agricultural workers who worked small tracts of land in usufruct but did not own them. The traditional arrangement between landowners and agricultural workers known as *agrego* dates from the early nineteenth century. Initially, *agrego* spread in a context in which owners had to compete for laborers during the coffee and sugar harvests.[11] In order to secure a labor force, landowners offered parcels of land in usufruct to workers, who then worked for wages during the harvest. In Vieques, the *centrales*, who in essence were the large landowners, had workers who lived on the farms as *agregados*. *Agrego* contracts were typically oral contracts between landowners and agricultural workers. They were recognized universally as a valid contractual relation, and the obligation to work on the land of the landowner was reciprocal to the assignment of land in usufruct to the *agregados*. Landowners who purchased land typically inherited from the previous landowner all the obligations and privileges entailed by the existing *agrego* contracts of those settled on the land. However, *agregados* had no title to the land they lived on, and they could not sell it. The majority of the population relocated as a result of the navy expropriations were thus *agregados*, who had traditional contracts with the landowners but who had no title to the land. The navy paid the large landowners for the titles to the land but it refused to recognize any liability toward the *agregados*, who in the past had enjoyed continuity in their *agrego* contracts when land they lived on was sold to a new landowner. However, those *agregados* who were relocated to navy lands were now required to work on navy construction projects. Thus, the navy invoked the obligation of the *agregado* to work for the landowner or face expulsion from the land,[12] but it did not recognize any of the obligations toward the *agregados* that the established local social norms required.

The acquisition of land by the navy in 1941 was brought about through a handful of transactions, as there were but few owners of large tracks of land on Vieques. To give an idea of the level of concentration of land ownership on Vieques, two owners, Central Playa Grande and the Eastern Sugar Associates, had title to 78 percent of the island's surface area.[13] The majority of the rural population were *agregados*, that is, they had usufruct rights but not title to the property under *agrego* contracts as described above. This land concentration was devastating among those who suffered the effects of the expropriation. When the large landowners sold their property, the *agregados* lost, in a single act, their jobs, their homes and belongings, and their subsistence crops and animals. In contrast to urban workers, plantation workers lived in a "total" environment in which workplace and residential space were intertwined. During the times that the sugar industry was not active, laborers lived on subsistence activities from the land that they used, but did not own, according to the established *agrego* arrangement. The impact of the expropriation was such that it destroyed (1) their source of income during the sugar harvest (their wages); (2) their subsistence plots, where they grew food crops and raised animals, an important source of income during the off-season; and (3) their place of residence, all in the same blow.

The first expropriations led to the expulsion of seven hundred families who lived on the eight thousand expropriated acres belonging to the Central Playa Grande.[14] The navy relocated half of these families to the Santa María resettlement tract, which became a slum, each family receiving a lot measuring fifty feet by forty feet. The first wave of expropriations greatly reduced the income of the municipality of Vieques, most of which was in the form of property taxes. Accordingly, the municipality was left virtually bankrupt. As a result of the decline in property tax revenues, the island's budget shrunk by a whopping 38.5 percent, from $52,903 to $32,557. Mayor Leoncio T. Davis, who was also the only medical doctor on the island, complained that the municipality could no longer count on revenues from the land on which sugarcane was cultivated. The expropriations destroyed the sole industry of the island—sugarcane—and severely depleted the coffers of the municipality.[15]

Expropriations began in late 1941, prior to the United States entering the war. The main landowner, Juan Angel Tió, lost his land on November 12, 1941, just three weeks before the attack on Pearl Harbor. Approximately eight thousand acres belonging to the Eastern Sugar Associates were also expropriated in 1941. In 1942, the Benítez-Rieckehoff family suffered the next round of expropriations, as the navy acquired one thousand acres that had belonged to them. Other families lost two thousand acres in the same year. All told, the navy expropriated twenty-two thousand acres.[16]

Rise and Decline of the Military Economy

The devastating impact of the expropriations was not felt in full until June 1943. Immediately after the expropriations of 1941, the economy of Vieques entered a boom period, which the island's chronicler, Justo Pastor Ruiz, referred to as an exuberant surge of cash that drowned the logical realization that the boom would not last forever.[17] The construction of a breakwater on the northern coast of Vieques employed most of the available local laborers. In fact, some had to be imported from Puerto Rico, increasing for the first time in decades the island's population. Naval construction generated jobs that paid $2.25 per day, approximately 50 percent more than the daily wages paid by the sugarcane industry. In addition, and in contrast to the sugar industry, military construction contracts offered employment without the disruptions of the downtime months or *tiempo muerto* typical of the sugar industry. Working eleven months instead of seven, with a daily wage 50 percent higher than that of the sugar industry, the average worker made more than twice the amount paid by the sugar industry over a twelve-month period. Initially, therefore, the rise in employment buffered the negative impacts of the naval expropriations.[18]

This situation ended in June 1943. By then, the attacks on commercial shipping by German submarines had subsided;[19] six months earlier, the war had moved to North Africa and then to Europe.[20] As a result, the United States froze all construction of bases in Puerto Rico, and many of the military personnel stationed on the island were relocated. The insular government of Puerto Rico was notified around March 1943 that construction of the naval base on Vieques would cease by the summer of that year. Luis Muñoz Marín, president of the Senate of Puerto Rico, commissioned Dr. Rafael Picó, who ran the Planning Board on the island, to undertake a study of the situation on Vieques, with particular attention to how the closure of the base and the halting of all military construction on the island would affect employment. By the end of the summer of 1943, as base construction came to an end, the plentiful cash that it generated as well as the unprecedented wages the laborers of Vieques derived from their work came to an abrupt halt. There was nothing to take its place, as the only other livelihood afforded to the residents of Vieques, working for the Central Playa Grande, was no longer an option. The workers had already been deprived (since 1941) of the subsistence plots they had historically received under the *agrego* arrangement, which had sustained them when wages were not available. The expropriations had completely destroyed the sugar industry. Demonstrations ensued, and workers waived black flags clamoring for work and a return to the "old ways."[21] The director of the Federal Works Agency for Puerto Rico and the Virgin Islands described the situation to Muñoz Marín in July 1943 as follows:

> In my opinion, conditions are really worse over there than they were at that time [March 1943]. This is occasioned primarily because the then private contract work being done for the Navy has all ceased, and nothing new has been opened to take its place. With that condition, and with the sugar cane industry being so handicapped through the purchase of lands formerly planted in cane, the outlook is indeed very dismal.... Of course, we could not take care of all of the unemployed, but we could put some people to work on fixing the main streets and maybe some road work and particularly malaria control.[22]

Picó agreed with this assessment. He stated in a somewhat frustrated tone in July 1943 that "undoubtedly, the problem that we anticipated in our report of March is already a reality in Vieques."[23] This situation was referred to by Vieques mayor Antonio Ávila Camacho in 1947 as one in which the people of Vieques were in a "pre-agonizing state."[24] Certainly, after the summer of 1943, the residents of Vieques felt the impact of the expropriations. There was no employment, the population was concentrated in slums in the central part of the island, and they lacked access to subsistence crops and domestic animals, which they previously could rely on as *agregados*. They could neither bathe on most of the beaches of the coastline, nor fish in the island's surrounding waters, nor seek sustenance in the mangrove forests, as most of the coastline was now located within the areas controlled by the military. The sugar latifundia had at least guaranteed free access across the island to subsistence crops, to fishing and crabbing in the mangroves, and to grazing land for domestic animals. None of this was now available to them.

The Insular Government's Intervention

Abandoned by the military and with no hope of finding work, the residents of Vieques aimed their hopes toward Luis Muñoz Marín and the PPD. One alternative was for Vieques to industrialize; another to install a new Central Playa Grande. Since its creation in 1942, the Puerto Rico Industrial Development Company, headed by Teodoro Moscoso, had attempted to industrialize Puerto Rico with a view toward reducing unemployment and poverty on the island. In 1944, it began operating the Puerto Rico Glass Corporation to produce bottles for the rum industry. The following year it opened the Puerto Rico Pulp and Paper Corporation to supply Porto Rico Container, a producer of cartons for the rum and milk industries, with corrugated cardboard. The residents of Vieques had hoped that some of these initiatives would benefit them. However, Moscoso showed no interest in either establishing manufacturing operations run by the Development Company on Vieques or reverting to the reviled sugar industry, considered by many a villain and the cause of Puerto Rico's poverty and misery. From the point of view of development, a transition from a sugar plantation economy toward an industrial economy could have improved the situation on Vieques, as it did elsewhere in Puerto Rico. However, the residents of the small island experienced the dismantling of the plantation economy but not the subsequent establishment of industrial plants. The dismantling of agriculture was not coupled with the development of industry. As much as the residents of Vieques reviled the miserly wages and terrible working conditions of the sugar plantation economy, at least there was work and workers were paid. After the navy expropriations, the residents began to retrospectively long for the return of the sugar industry, because it had at least provided employment to the local population.

Two years elapsed before the government of Puerto Rico took any decisive action to assist the people of Vieques.[25] Military construction ceased during the summer of 1943. It was not until March 24, 1945, with the creation of the Puerto Rico Agricultural Company (PRACO), that the insular government took the plight of the residents of Vieques seriously.[26] PRACO was capitalized with an initial investment of $12.2 million. As a point of comparison, the Puerto Rico Development Bank was capitalized with only $500,000 in 1942. PRACO was created to expand agricultural and fishing activities and to develop distribution channels so that these products would become available to the Puerto Rican consumer at competitive prices. In fact, its purpose was twofold. PRACO was meant to support the economy of Vieques as well as to compete with the large food importers, whom Muñoz Marín accused of excessive profiteering and monopolistic practices.

In order for PRACO to start functioning, an agreement had to be reached with the military authorities so that land could be made available to the organization. This leasing arrangement with the military would later emerge as the principal cause of the demise of the Puerto Rico Agricultural Company. The military authorities made thirteen thousand acres available to PRACO, but the title to the land remained with the federal government. It was agreed (although the insular government had little say in the matter) that if and when the military authorities needed those thirteen thousand acres or any portion of them, the military could notify PRACO and the insular government with only a few months' notice. The federal government finally agreed to transfer the land in January 1946. The title was transferred to the Department of the Interior, which authorized its use to the government of Puerto Rico, which in turn handed it over to PRACO. The title thus remained with the US government, which eventually returned the land to the navy in 1948.[27]

Between 1946 and 1948, PRACO was the main source of employment in Vieques. It started buying additional land that Thomas Fennell, the company's general manager, believed would be necessary to achieve the company's farming and animal husbandry goals. PRACO purchased parcels from private owners at prices higher than what the navy had paid in the expropriations of 1941–1942, and well above the land's appraised value. As an example, it purchased land belonging to Tomás González for $159 an acre, although the land's assessed value was only $59 an acre.[28] It also purchased 1,373 acres from the Eastern Sugar Associates at $282 an acre, 47 percent above the valuation prepared by the Puerto Rican Land Authority in 1944.[29] When questioned, Fennell responded that the PRACO program had to be implemented as soon as possible regardless of cost.

The company's finances suffered. PRACO recorded losses of $250,000 in 1946 and $2.4 million in 1950, its last year of operation. The accumulated losses from 1946 to 1950 amounted to $6.3 million.[30] This financial performance reflected the obvious fact the PRACO was a company created in the spirit of the New Deal, whose main purpose was to generate jobs and not necessarily income. Its existence demonstrated that the PPD not only paid attention to the plight of the residents of Vieques but also was willing to provide massive subsidies to the economy of this small island. Even so, what exactly was the impact of PRACO on the employment situation on Vieques and what caused the company to fail?

The workforce on Vieques averaged 2,794 persons from 1941 to 1948. During the years it operated, PRACO employed 1,113 people, or 40 percent of the available workforce, at an average salary of $2.00 per day.[31] This compared favorably with the typical wages paid by the sugar industry, which averaged $1.50 per day, and almost equaled the $2.25 per day paid by federal contractors during the construction of the military base on the island.[32]

The distressing losses incurred by PRACO led *El Mundo*, the newspaper with the highest circulation in Puerto Rico, to accuse Fennell of embezzlement. What the significant losses demonstrated, however, was that the insular government was serious about subsidizing the economy of Vieques. The company sank not because of poor management but as a result of the decisions made in Washington concerning the future of the navy. According to Washington, the navy needed additional land in order to prepare for the Cold War. In January 1948, the navy reacquired the thirteen thousand acres previously leased to PRACO, thereby sealing the fate both of the company and of Vieques. PRACO attempted to dispose of the additional properties it had purchased, but the price it obtained under these circumstances was much lower than what it had paid twenty-four months earlier. The government of Puerto Rico disbanded PRACO, and its remaining assets were incorporated into the Land Authority on July 1, 1950. This ended the insular government's attempt to solve the employment problems on Vieques.[33] After 1948, the situation in Vieques remained precarious. During the 1950s, while Puerto Rico was transitioning from a sugar plantation economy to an industrial one with new factories opening weekly under the PPD's Operation Bootstrap program, Vieques experienced very little development.

Long-Term Effects

The economy of Vieques, contrary to that of the rest of Puerto Rico, experienced a prolonged economic downturn as a result of the land expropriations that started during the Second World War. Once PRACO closed, the possibility of an economic recovery faded. The island lost population. Many of its inhabitants migrated to neighboring Saint Croix in the US Virgin Islands, Puerto Rico, or the continental United States. The population of Vieques had peaked in 1920, when the census counted 11,651 persons living on the island.

Table 1: Population Grown in Vieques and Puerto Rico, 1800–2000

Year	Vieques Population	Puerto Rico Population
1899	5,927	953,000
1910	10,425	1,118,000
1920	11,651	1,299,800
1930	10,582	1,543,900
1940	10,362	1,869,300
1950	9,228	2,210,700
1960	7,210	2,349,500
1970	7,767	2,712,000
1980	7,662	3,196,500
1990	8,602	3,522,000
2000	9,106	3,808,600

Source: US Census Bureau

During World War I, the price of sugar had soared to unprecedented levels, and it remained high until it dropped precipitously in October 1920, ending the famous "Dance of the Millions" that made the sugar mill owners of the Caribbean fabulously wealthy. During this sugar boom, the population of Vieques increased, but with the drop in the price of sugar in the 1920s some locally owned sugar mills in Puerto Rico (and in Vieques) began to experience difficulties. The population of Vieques remained stable at around 10,000 people for the next twenty years. The precise figures are 10,582 persons in 1930, 10,037 in 1935, and 10,362 in 1940. Even before the expropriations, Vieques could not support an increasing population, and each year a number of Viequenses emigrated, some to Puerto Rico and others to Saint Croix.

The expropriations of the 1940s impacted an economy that was already in decline as a result of the Great Depression. Between 1930 and 1940, 26 percent of the population of Vieques emigrated (2,749 persons), most of them to Saint Croix. In 1947, there were more than three thousand Puerto Ricans living on Saint Croix, most of them from Vieques. Despite the fact that Saint Croix had been experiencing a protracted economic contraction and long-term population decline, from 26,681 persons in 1835 to 11,413 in 1930, the residents of Vieques migrated there because the employment situation on Vieques was even more dismal in the 1930s. A study published in 1947 pointed out that migrating to an island such as Saint Croix seemed like "jumping out of the frying pan into the fire."[34] Nevertheless, the residents of Vieques moved there due to lack of employment in the sugar industry on their home island. Thus, the land expropriations further affected an island that was already unable to support the

Table 2: Vieques and Puerto Rico, Internal Income Per Capita (Current $) and Yearly Growth Rates

Region	Years		Yearly growth rate
	1950	1960	1950 to 1960
Puerto Rico	$270	$574	7.8%
San Juan Region	$286	$644	8.5%
Fajardo Sub Region	$304	$435	3.6%
Vieques	$271	$291	0.7%

Source: Oficina de Servicios Legislativos. *Estudio sobre condiciones socio-económicas del municipio de Vieques* (San Juan: Estado Libre Asociado de Puerto Rico, Oficina de Servicios Legislativos, 1970), p. 10.

population level it had reached in 1920. Table 1 shows the population growth trends for Puerto Rico and Vieques since 1899. As can be seen, there was practically no population growth in Vieques after 1950.

During the expropriations, residents of Vieques had to sell their livestock at ridiculously low prices due to the lack of rangelands. For some time, some growers were able to continue farming cane. They would then ship the cane to Humacao on the eastern cost of Puerto Rico, where it was processed in the Pasto Viejo sugar mill. However, from 1953 onward the federal government restricted the daily shipments of sugarcane to eight hours instead of the usual twenty-four hours during the harvest season. This greatly hampered the operations of the growers. The municipal government of Vieques suspected that the federal government was attempting to suffocate the island economically in an effort to depopulate it.[35] Why would sugarcane coming from Vieques be required to pass US customs in Humacao, six miles away, when both Vieques and Humacao were part of Puerto Rico and therefore within the US customs wall? Mayor Antonio Rivera of Vieques complained that "as far as we know, Vieques continues to be part of the Commonwealth of Puerto Rico."[36] The blockage of commercial life and the difficulties in marine and air transport that the navy forced on Vieques created a generalized sense that the US government intended to completely remove the civilian population from the island. In fact, in 1964 the navy tried unsuccessfully to evict the remaining residents of Vieques in what became known locally as *Plan Drácula*, as the eviction included disinterring and relocating human remains buried in the cemeteries.[37]

Unlike the rest of Puerto Rico, none of the positive changes that came about as a result of massive military investment during the Second World War had a lasting effect on Vieques. The explosive economic growth of the postwar years catapulted development on the large island but, unfortunately, largely bypassed Vieques, leaving it decades behind Puerto Rico, the United

States, and, ironically, both West Germany and Japan, America's former foes, who benefited from generous reconstruction aid.

During the explosive decade of the 1950s, when industrial plants were being established in Puerto Rico sometimes at the rate of one a week, the economy of Puerto Rico experienced growth at the rate of 7.8 percent annually. Vieques, lacking any such investment in industrial plants, experienced by contrast growth rates of 0.7 percent annually. Because this is below the inflation rate, the real income of the residents of Vieques actually shrank during the 1950s.

The sugar industry finally collapsed in the 1950s, forcing many workers to take up fishing as a survival activity. The economy of Vieques became dependent on the purchasing power of the thousands of troops who periodically descended on the island for maneuvers. Some of the commercial establishments in Isabel Segunda survived and began catering to the troops. There was a proliferation of bars and restaurants, reflected in the tax records of the municipality of Vieques.[38] A report by the Puerto Rico Planning Board stated in 1955 that the proliferation of bars and restaurants in Vieques was probably a response to the periodic concentration of military personnel on the island for military maneuvers.[39] The service economy also featured the spread of prostitution, as is usual in the vicinity of military bases, and periodic conflicts between civilians and military personnel in public places in Isabel Segunda. This new service economy, however, provided employment only when military maneuvers were taking place in Vieques. This was probably two months out of twelve in an average year, leading to stagnation the rest of the year. The navy never stationed large numbers of personnel permanently in Vieques, but instead used the island periodically for maneuvers. Thus, contrary to the situation in the United States, where military bases are a source of good jobs for surrounding populations, the facilities in Vieques never provided adequate employment to the local population. This situation remained unchanged for the next fifty years. In 1999, Puerto Rico's resident commissioner in Washington complained that, in contrast to the situation in the continental United States, the navy presence in Vieques did not generate prosperity: "If Vieques is indeed safe, why hasn't the Navy headquartered troops to live there? Why hasn't the Navy made it a home port with the economic prosperity and commitment that such an action would entail?"[40]

The long-term stagnation suffered by the economy of Vieques can be seen in the figures for household income compared to those of Puerto Rico's other *municipios*. During the heyday of the sugar industry, Vieques had been an average *municipio* in terms of wealth, enjoying incomes in the middle of the distribution of Puerto Rico's municipalities. In 1960 it ranked forty-third

The Seabees pontoon causeway becomes an all-purpose pier as equipment and supplies are uploaded onto it on Vieques Island during the navy's 1949 winter maneuvers in the Caribbean, 1949. (CEC/Seabee Archives, CEC/Seabee Museum)

in income out of a total of seventy-five *municipios*; in 1970 it ranked forty-sixth; but in 1980 it ranked seventy-sixth out of seventy-eight, positioning the island as the third-poorest *municipio* in Puerto Rico. In 1990 and 2000, it ranked seventy-seventh out of seventy-eight, the second-poorest *municipio*. Whereas median household income on Vieques was 73 percent of the average in Puerto Rico in 1960, by 2000 median household income on Vieques had descended to 65 percent of the average. The figures are even more dismal if we compare Vieques to some municipalities in Puerto Rico that experienced the highest growth rates. Whereas Vieques had a median household income of 50 percent of Puerto Rico's richest *municipio*, Guaynabo, in 1960, by 2000 it was lagging at 36 percent of Guaynabo's income. Table 2 shows the median household income of Vieques relative to Puerto Rico, San Juan, and Guaynabo, and also its income rank relative to Puerto Rico's other *municipios*. Clearly, these figures show consistent stagnation relative to the rest of Puerto Rico. The long-term effects of the land expropriations of World War II were to create inferior and increasingly divergent economic conditions in Vieques relative to other *municipios*. It should be noted, however, that since the navy left

Vieques in the early 2000s, median household income has improved relative to Puerto Rico, San Juan, and Guaynabo, and the income rank of Vieques in relation to other *municipios* has improved from second poorest to the middle of the pack (thirty-seventh out of seventy-eight), returning therefore to the rank the island held before the expropriations took place.

Notes

For a more detailed analysis of the transformations that occurred on Vieques during the 1940s, see César J. Ayala Casás and José L. Bolívar Fresneda, *Battleship Vieques: Puerto Rico from World War II to the Korean War* (Princeton, NJ: Markus Wiener, 2011).

1. The term "expropriation" does not imply lack of compensation. It refers to the compulsory nature of the transfer of land to the state. The navy has on some occasions argued that there were no expropriations because the landowners were compensated. See, for example, James D. Hessman, "Opposed Landings: Vieques, the Navy Comes under 'Constant Bombardment,'" *Sea Power Magazine* (March 1979): 12–16. However, the fact is that without the state exercising its right of eminent domain, the landowners would not have sold their lands. The Superior Court of Puerto Rico has a *Sala de Expropiaciones* to deal with private owners who seek further compensation when the government uses its right of eminent domain. We thank Professor Juan A. Giusti of the University of Puerto Rico for this information.

2. José L. Bolívar Fresneda, *Guerra, banca y desarrollo: el Banco de Fomento y la industrialización de Puerto Rico* (San Juan: Fundación Luis Muñoz Marín; Instituto de Cultura Puertorriqueña, 2011), pp. 36–38.

3. See José L. Bolívar Fresneda's essay titled "The War Economy of Puerto Rico, 1939–1945" in this volume.

4. Bolívar Fresneda, *Guerra, banca y desarrollo*, p. 7.

5. Ayala Casás and Bolívar Fresneda, *Battleship Vieques*, p. 168.

6. People of Puerto Rico v. Rubert Hermanos, Inc., 309 US 543 (1940).

7. See César J. Ayala and Rafael Bernabe, *Puerto Rico in the American Century: A History since 1898* (Chapel Hill: University of North Carolina Press, 2007), pp. 50–51, 184–187.

8. Hearing before the Subcommittee on Insular Affairs, 78th Cong., Pursuant to H.R. 159 (Washington, DC: Government Printing Office, 1943); "Investigation of Political, Economic and Social Conditions in Puerto Rico," Hearings before the Committee on Insular Affairs, 78th Cong., Pursuant to H.R. 159 (Washington, DC: Government Printing Office, 1943); and *Report of the Committee on Insular Affairs*, 79th Cong., Pursuant to H.R. 159 and H.R. 99 (Washington, DC: Government Printing Office, 1945).

9. Bibiano Torres, "La isla de Vieques," *Anuario de estudios americanos* (Seville) 12 (1955): 449–466.

10. The best succinct statement on plantation economies in the Caribbean is Lloyd Best, "The Mechanism of Plantation Type Societies: Outlines of a Model of Pure Plantation Economy," *Social and Economic Studies* 17, no. 3 (1968): 283–326.

11. Laird Bergad, *Coffee and the Growth of Agrarian Capitalism in Nineteenth-Century Puerto Rico* (Princeton, NJ: Princeton University Press, 1983).

12. Ayala Casás and Bolívar Fresneda, *Battleship Vieques*, p. 57.

13. Ibid., pp. 170–172. We examined data of the properties in Vieques for the fiscal years 1940, 1945, and 1950. Property ownership provides a basis to compare the socioeconomic conditions of Vieques before and after the expropriations. The information provides quantitative data on who suffered from the expropriations, how much land was expropriated from each resident, and where each plot of land was located. The appraised value of these expropriated plots can be found in the Archivo General de Puerto Rico. The data is organized by municipality, in volumes measuring fifteen inches by twenty-one inches. All the information is handwritten and organized as follows: (1) the name of the property owner (from this we can usually determine gender); (2) the type of property (for example, rustic farmland, municipal plot, personal property); (3) the location of the property (barrio in cases of farms; street and number in cases of urban lots); (4) the size of the lot measured in acres; (5) the appraised value of the land; (6) the type of any upgrades made to the property; (7) the appraised value of the upgrades; (8) a description of any personal property (for example, truck, car, cattle); and (9) the appraised value of the personal property. We photocopied all the data available in the archives and created a database, which we then analyzed using the statistical programs SPSS and STATA. For further details, see the tables in the appendix of Ayala Casás and Bolívar Fresneda, *Battleship Vieques*.

14. According to the 1940 census, the average family residing on Vieques consisted of 4.5 individuals, as compared to 5.3 in Puerto Rico. The seven hundred families expelled by the navy therefore consisted of 3,150 men, women, and children. The population of Vieques, also according to the 1940 census, was 10,362. Thirty percent of these people were affected by the expropriations.

15. Dr. Leoncio T. Davis, mayor of Vieques, to Vicente Géigel Polanco, president of the Municipal Legislative Reforms Committee, December 22, 1941, Archivo Fundación Luis Muñoz Marín (hereafter AFLMM), Section 4, Presidente del Senado, Series 7, Folder 2669.

16. Luis Muñoz Marín, AFLMM, Section 4, Presidente del Senado, Series 7, Folder 2669; in Ayala Casás and Bolívar Fresneda, *Battleship Vieques*, p. 177. Ayala Casás and Bolívar Fresneda provide seven different estimates of the total acreage expropriated during the first round of expropriations.

17. Justo Pastor Ruiz, *Vieques antiguo y moderno, 1493–1946* (Yauco, PR: Tipografía Rodríguez Lugo, 1947), p. 206.

18. Rafael Picó, *Committee for the Investigation of Conditions in the Island of Vieques* (Santurce, PR: n.p., 1943), p. 1.

19. Ayala Casás and Bolívar Fresneda, *Battleship Vieques*, pp. 11–28.

20. See Ligia T. Domenech's essay titled "The German Blockade of the Caribbean in 1942 and Its Effects in Puerto Rico" in this volume.

21. Pastor Ruiz, *Vieques antiguo y moderno*, p. 205.

22. Roy Schroder, director of the Federal Works Agency, Puerto Rico and Virgin Islands Headquarters, to Luis Muñoz Marín, July 5, 1943, AFLMM, Section 4, Gobierno Insular, Subsection 1, Datos y estadísticas, Folder 286, Vieques 1943, Document 15.

23. AFLMM, Section 4, Gobierno Insular, Subsection 1, Datos y estadísticas, Folder 286, Vieques 1943, Document 16.

24. Ángel Cruz Cruz, "Una comisión de Vieques irá donde Barbey: pedirá explicación en cuanto a cómo afectará nueva base la economía; se celebró debate Rieckehoff Avila; al final se decidió el envío de la comisión Mítines celebrados," *El Mundo* (San Juan), October 28, 1947.

25. Bolívar Fresneda, *Guerra, banca y desarrollo*, p. 38.

26. Laws of Puerto Rico, no. 31, April 24, 1945.

27. Although PRACO was intended to operate throughout Puerto Rico, in reality most of the operations undertaken by this public corporation were centered on the island of Vieques. Bolívar Fresneda, *Guerra, banca y desarrollo*, pp. 35–75.

28. Picó, *Committee for the Investigation of Conditions*.

29. César J. Ayala Casás and José L. Bolívar Fresneda, "The Cold War and the Second Expropriations of the U.S. Navy in Vieques, Puerto Rico, 1946–1948," *Centro: Journal of the Center for Puerto Rican Studies* 18, no. 1 (2006): 11–35; Rafael Picó, *The Geographic Regions of Puerto Rico* (Río Piedras: University of Puerto Rico Press, 1950), pp. 210–213; and Archivo Histórico de Vieques, *El Eco de Vieques*, April 1947.

30. César J. Ayala Casás and José L. Bolívar Fresneda, "Entre dos aguas: economía, sociedad e intervención estatal en Vieques, 1942–1948," *Revista de Ciencias Sociales* 13 (2004): 52–79.

31. AFLMM, Section 4, Presidente del Senado, Series 2, Folder 55; and Archivo General de Puerto Rico, Oficina del Gobernador, Tarea 96-20, Box 838. We found and analyzed audited financial statements for 1946, 1947, 1949, and 1950.

32. AFLMM, Section 4, Presidente del Senado, Series 2, Subsection, Datos y Estadísticas, Folder 55.

33. Ayala Casás and Bolívar Fresneda, "Entre dos aguas."

34. Clarence Senior writes: "Puerto Rican migration to an island in such a depressed condition would seem like 'jumping out of the frying pan into the fire.' The answer lies partly in the fact that sugar cane continues to be the main crop of the island, and that cane needs seasonal labor. The Danes formerly brought in workers for the cutting season from the nearby British islands. This practice continued until 1927. The immigration laws of the United States were applied to the Virgin Islands in that year and the cane growers had to look elsewhere for their labor. They found a situation made-to-order for them in the depressed conditions of the sugar industry on the island of Vieques. Sugar acreage and yield on that island of 51 square miles had been decreasing steadily since 1910 and people were looking for a chance to make a living elsewhere. Agents for the growers recruited sizable groups for transportation to St. Croix. Some of those who went on temporary jobs stayed. The tendency of Puerto Rican migration to St. Croix has been upward since that time." Clarence Senior, *The Puerto Rican Migrant in St. Croix* (Río Piedras: University of Puerto Rico Social Science Research Center, 1947), pp. 1–2.

35. In fact, the suspicions of the residents of Vieques were well founded, as demonstrated by this memo from the Department of the Interior: "My proposal is that the present population of Vieques be transferred and resettled in St. Croix. As you know, St. Croix is entirely

agricultural and very sparsely inhabited. The island could support not only the 15,000 persons now living on Vieques, but substantially many more from the main island of Puerto Rico." Department of the Interior, Office of the Secretary, Division of Territories and Island Possessions, Irving W. Silverman, acting director, to Undersecretary Chapman, Subject: Vieques Island, Puerto Rico, August 8, 1947. Archivo Histórico de Vieques, Expropiaciones.

36. Juan Luis Márquez, "Alcalde acusa grave situación en Isla Vieques," *El Mundo* (San Juan), March 15, 1953, p. 12.

37. Evelyn Vélez Rodríguez, *Proyecto V-C: negociaciones secretas entre Luis Muñoz Marín y la marina; Plan Drácula* (Río Piedras, PR: Editorial Edil, 2002).

38. Ayala Casás and Bolívar Fresneda, *Battleship Vieques*, p. 154.

39. Puerto Rico Planning Board, *Plan de desarrollo, 1955* (San Juan: Puerto Rico Planning Board, 1955), p. 14.

40. Carlos Romero Barceló, "Testimony before the Committee on Armed Services, U.S. Senate," October 19, 1999, at http://www.armed-services.senate.gov/statemnt/1999/991019cr.pdf, accessed June 6, 2014.

The Anglo-American Caribbean Commission: A Socioeconomic Strategy Designed for Military Security, 1942–1946

Mayra Rosario Urrutia

During the tumultuous decade of the 1930s, colonial possessions in the Caribbean posed political, economic, and military demands on the United States and Great Britain. The responses formulated by both metropolitan governments regarding these needs were shaped by their colonial policies, the effects of the Great Depression, the newly configured strategic and military importance of the Caribbean during the Second World War, and the grievances voiced throughout the islands in the form of uprisings and public protests.

One of the steps the United States and Great Britain took to attend to the situation was the creation, in 1942, of the first formal regional cooperation initiative, namely the Anglo-American Caribbean Commission. The purpose of the commission was framed as follows: "For ... encouraging and strengthening social and economic cooperation between the United States of America and its possessions and bases in the area known geographically and politically as the Caribbean, and the United Kingdom and the British Colonies in the same area."[1]

The purpose of this essay is to analyze the framing and implementation of this socioeconomic strategy—devised for the purposes of military security and coordinated by both world powers at the beginning of the 1940s—in light of the distinct historical circumstances surrounding its creation. Particularly, this chapter will explore the US position on the measures adopted for the formation of the Anglo-American Caribbean Commission, with special emphasis on Puerto Rico's initial reaction and participation in the project. At the time, Puerto Rico, as a colonial territory with a newly formed legislature dominated by the Partido Popular Democrático (PPD), held a key role in

Advertisements for the purchase of war bonds in Ponce (Archivo Fundación Luis Muñoz Marín)

the exchange of information and technical assistance among its Caribbean neighbors.[2] Puerto Rico actively collaborated in projects aimed at remedying the socioeconomic deficiencies in the region within the framework of US foreign policy. By analyzing the configuration of the commission, its main goal, and the construction of a strategy, the complex colonial structure dominated by the United States and Great Britain can be understood, along with the ways in which the colonial powers sought to ensure their legitimate dominance, or hegemony, through regional cooperation in times of socioeconomic crisis.[3]

The proposed argument is that, in spite of having been put forth as a strategy for improving the failing economies of the Caribbean, the Anglo-American Caribbean Commission was in fact created to satisfy the need for civil stabilization at the juncture of war. In order for the United States and Great Britain to maintain regional hegemony, the causes for distress had to be placated and military personnel had to be effectively integrated into civilian communities. These objectives would be expedited through the creation of economic opportunities and the illusion of public participation that the commission offered.

After examining the regional crisis of the 1930s, the discussion then focuses on the time period between 1940 and 1946. Agreements pertaining to the creation of the commission were reached between 1940 and 1942, and from 1942 to 1946 the commission remained active until it was replaced by the Caribbean Commission. Unlike its predecessor, the Caribbean Commission included the participation of the Netherlands and France, widening the sphere of international cooperation.

The Composition of the "Caribbean"

By the time of the Second World War, the Caribbean region comprised fifteen colonial territories that were held by four imperial powers: the United States, Great Britain, France, and the Netherlands. The eight British colonies were Jamaica, Trinidad, British Guiana, the Bahamas, the Leeward Islands, the Windward Islands, Barbados, and British Honduras. The United States politically dominated the Virgin Islands and Puerto Rico.[4] The significance of territories held by other metropolitan countries and of independent countries in the region—namely Cuba, Haiti, and the Dominican Republic—cannot be ignored because they also directly influenced the development of a military strategy.

The commission geopolitically defined and demarcated the region as follows:

> The term "Caribbean area" has been taken to include the United States territories in the Caribbean; the European possessions (British, Netherlands, and French) which are considered politically or geographically part of the West Indies; and the independent island republics (Cuba, the Dominican Republic, and Haiti). The three Guianas on the South American mainland (British Guiana, French Guiana, and Netherlands Guiana, which is known as Surinam) and British Honduras, are commonly regarded as part of the Caribbean.... The Bahamas are included although they do not lie within the Caribbean Sea.[5]

The series of previous agreements between the United States and Great Britain can be placed within the sequence of military security plans that both powers had outlined since the beginning of the twentieth century in order to thwart a possible German advance in the region:

> Military expansion developed within the framework of an informal agreement with Great Britain, the main European power in the region, which ensured the

United States continued political control over its colonies in America and its economic interests, in exchange for recognizing the regional preeminence of the United States and collaborating in a sort of "Anglo-Saxon" pact, primarily designed to oppose Germany.[6]

By 1939, the population of the region had reached 13,941,000, the majority of whom were dependent on food imports for subsistence. In 1942, aware of the "Achilles' heel" that this region posed for the United States and Great Britain, German forces intensified attacks on ships carrying provisions destined for the Caribbean territories, as well as those leaving the ports of the territories carrying crucial raw materials such as bauxite and oil intended for US defense needs.[7]

Hunger, overpopulation, and economic hardship were common tribulations shared by the Caribbean colonial possessions. These, however, were not the only reasons for popular discontent. The political restrictions to which these Caribbean countries were subjected were also cause for tension. In the 1930s, many Caribbean nations questioned the colonial regimes that had guided their political and socioeconomic destinies thus far. A series of disturbances that began in Saint Kitts in 1935 spread to other dependent territories in the region, including Barbados, Trinidad, Jamaica, and British Guiana.[8] Between 1937 and 1938, the disturbances took a more dramatic turn. There were also upheavals in Puerto Rico, where people had rallied against the colonial model imposed by the United States at the beginning of the twentieth century. The crisis in Puerto Rican society is evinced in the following statement:

> The thirties were a turning point for Puerto Rico, and not only because of the open and often brutal form that resistance to continued U.S. domination took. Struggles by workers, nationalists, and students emerged when they did because the colonial model of development itself was in severe crisis.[9]

Although worldwide depression influenced the expression of resistance during this decade in Puerto Rico, the crisis of the monoculture model for economic development had been fermenting since the invasion by the United States. The state of affairs in Trinidad was another case following this pattern. In 1937, a series of labor strikes revealed the prevalent disgust of the black working class, who demanded a better standard of living from the hegemonic white capitalist class.[10] The struggle between social classes had produced an acute state of conflict in the region. The nature of the disturbances in the Caribbean was not homogeneous, because each county's individual reality influenced its reason for unrest. However, a constant that did influence regional heterogeneity was the racial composition of the population. For example, in the British islands, the majority of the population was black workers, but they were dominated by an elite white minority that held political power. The economies of the Caribbean also suffered the consequences of fluctuations in world trade. Although economic hardship and political restrictions existed long before the 1930s, it was during this period that these problems intensified, as a result of the Great Depression and the global capitalist crisis.

Driven by the forecast of scarcity and instability, Charles Taussig, the principal shareholder of the American Molasses Company, which had economic interests in the Caribbean islands, toured the region in 1937 together with Rexford Tugwell (who would become governor of Puerto Rico in 1941) to study up close the grave situation in the British islands, whose economies were controlled by monopolies.[11] Taussig knew the islands very well as a result of the constant trips he took to secure the interests of his companies. Although at the time the Caribbean was not the first line of defense for the United States, Tugwell and Taussig reported alarmingly on the neglected state of affairs in the Caribbean to President Roosevelt.

Instability created a serious concern for Great Britain and the United States. For this reason, both countries sent commissions to study the region. In 1938, the West Indian Royal Commission, headed by Lord Moyne, was designated by Great Britain to investigate the situation. The study was completed the following year, confirming Taussig's and Tugwell's preliminary observations in more detailed fashion. The Moyne Report identified problems, including monoculture, low wages, unemployment, lack of job security, malnutrition, inefficiency, and lack of housing.[12] In spite of the urgency of these problems, the British government decided to keep the report strictly confidential for five years. The reason for this was fear that German propagandists would use it against Great Britain, pointing to the country's maltreatment of its possessions as the cause for the disturbances.[13]

During the 1930s, the Caribbean began to figure among the major strategic points identified by the US Navy. Until this time, the need to safeguard military bases was mainly limited to the Pacific, which was vulnerable to Japanese expansionism.[14] It was precisely in 1938 when hemispheric defense became a major concern for the United States, particularly on the subject of its weak system of defense in the Caribbean. Since the beginning of the twentieth century, the main concern of the United States both in the Caribbean and in the Western Hemisphere was the defense of the Panama Canal and its bases in Florida, Cuba, Puerto Rico, Culebra, and the Virgin Islands. This system protected access to the Gulf of Mexico and the Caribbean Sea from the north, but it left the southwest Caribbean, which was replete with interisland travel, exposed.[15]

In June 1938, William Leahy, chief of naval operations of the United States who would serve as governor of Puerto Rico in 1939–1940, spoke about the importance of increasing defense funding before the Congressional Committee on Naval Affairs of the House of Representatives. More than just obtaining additional staff and naval equipment, the request specified a need to build bases in "strategic positions."[16] President Roosevelt assigned this task to the navy and the army, because new technological developments in aviation and navigation allowed for the possibility of an attack on the United States from any hostile point in the Western Hemisphere.[17]

In 1939, the Joint Planning Committee of the army and navy carried out an investigation of possible US war strategies. One of the priorities became the military protection of the Panama Canal, a key piece in naval strategy in both the Atlantic and Pacific Oceans.[18] The Caribbean was crucial in the defense of the canal. To that end, the army devised five war plans called "Rainbow," addressing different strategies for hemispheric defense. Rainbow 1 placed importance on the acquisition and building of new bases. At that time, bases in the Caribbean were showing signs of deterioration—considerable in some British colonies—and were becoming a source of vulnerability.[19]

Meanwhile, the Nazi threat to France, the Netherlands, and Great Britain was becoming a matter of concern for the US government, because it represented a possible transfer of power within the Caribbean region. This is why on July 17, 1940, the United States issued a communiqué to the German government reaffirming the Monroe Doctrine, which stated:

> In accordance with its traditional policy relating to the Western Hemisphere, the United States would not recognize any transfer, and would not acquiesce in any attempt to transfer, any geographic region of the Western hemisphere from one non-American power to another non-American power.[20]

The US position was ratified at the Convention on the Provisional Administration of European Colonies and Possessions in America during the Second Meeting of Consultation, which the various foreign ministers of Western Hemisphere nations attended. The meeting was held in Havana in June 1940. The United States was thereby authorized to "intervene in the colonies of any country conquered by Germany, thus protecting the Western Hemisphere."[21]

This agreement was never carried out. Nevertheless, it became the antecedent of the Anglo-American Commission given that it gave notice to the world that the fate of the colonies was a matter of international concern. The commission may very well be considered an international measure circuitously designed to defend the Western Hemisphere.

The Caribbean lay vulnerable and defenseless for three main reasons. First, the advance of German power in Europe, following the military intervention in France and the Netherlands in September 1940, heightened the awareness of a possible German threat lurking in the Caribbean. Both invaded countries held colonial possessions in the area, a fact that amplified US and British fears of losing control of the region. In addition, the United States anticipated that Great Britain would suffer the same fate as France and the Netherlands, leading to a complete German victory in Europe. As a result, their Caribbean colonies might be occupied by the German advance. Second, conditions became more difficult because of political and socioeconomic instability in the region, where colonial power had been openly questioned since the 1930s. Finally, the system established to secure and defend the Western Hemisphere was in a precarious state. Shortages of food supplies, which were already widespread throughout the islands, would become more severe in 1942 due to a German U-boat blockade of ships carrying provisions to Caribbean ports.

Throughout the process of formulating a political-military strategy for hemispheric defense, both the United States and Great Britain looked toward the Caribbean, concerned with strengthening British naval power in case of a German invasion.[22] The efforts by both metropolitan governments to secure a strategic position, and their simultaneous confrontations with socioeconomic crises in their respective possessions, intensified. To defend their position, the United States and Great Britain signed an agreement to establish American military bases in British territories. The need to appease those on the islands who were creating conflict and supply the region with provisions was fundamental to incorporating military base personnel into British colonial communities.

On September 2, 1940, the Marquis de Lothian, British ambassador to the United States, discussed the matter with the US secretary of state, Cordell Hull, through an exchange of notes. He made known his government's acquiescence to lease naval and air bases to the United States for a period of ninety-nine years with the purpose of safeguarding the Western Hemisphere.[23] The final agreement between the two world powers was signed on March 27, 1941; the leases were obtained in exchange for fifty obsolete naval destroyers that Great Britain would receive from the United States. The American bases would be located in Newfoundland, Bermuda, Jamaica, Saint Lucia, Antigua, Trinidad, British Guiana, and the Bahamas.[24] In addition, the government of the Netherlands invited the United States to establish military, naval, and air bases in Curaçao, Aruba, and Dutch Guiana.²⁵ At the same time that the initial exchange of notes occurred and the resulting agreement for the establishment of bases took shape, the United States sent a commission, officially headed by Taussig, Lieutenant Colonel A. F. Kibler, and Lieutenant Commander W. S. Campbell, to study the economic and military situation of the British islands, Puerto Rico, and the Virgin Islands.

> The Commission was immediately concerned with such matters as *the attitude of the people of the West Indies toward the establishment of bases in particular and toward the United States in general.* But the Commission also gave consideration, so far as time permitted, to the fundamentals of the Caribbean problem.²⁶

This official statement reveals the purpose of the commission, which featured the participation of representatives of the US Army and Navy. As a result, the pressing Caribbean problem was deferred in light of US strategic needs. Tugwell, in *The Stricken Land*, also pointed out the danger of antagonistic relations between island populations and military bases:

> If we had bases in the Caribbean, and especially air bases, had we not a real and immediate interest in the tranquility, even the loyalty of its people? How could we build a chain of fortresses on thickly settled islands which were hostile?²⁷

The Taussig Report was submitted in January 1941, acknowledging the contributions of the Moyne Report. It also pointed to the derivative advantages of having colonial possessions in the Caribbean working as a unit in response to the immediacy of war, carrying out long-term plans to develop agriculture, labor, and social services.²⁸ Taussig suggested that the joint committee include representatives from the US Navy and the Departments of State and War, as well as delegates from Puerto Rico and the Virgin Islands. He also recommended the creation of an advisory committee consisting of six members, three from each government:

> This committee might be assigned non-military duties especially in respect to problems arising from the construction and operation of American military bases in the Caribbean.²⁹

The foundations for the creation of the Anglo-American Caribbean Commission had already been set. Its aim consisted of satisfying the strategic needs of war and effectively improving conditions in the possessions and colonies in harmony with metropolitan interests. The strategic importance of the Caribbean would continue to develop and strengthen once the war began:

> The Caribbean islands form an ideal barrier against any encroachment from the east, with its air and naval bases judiciously placed along the string of islands, which makes it possible to keep any enemy a distance of 2,000 miles from Panama.[30]

In the spring of 1942, the Allied cause was facing grave difficulties in North Africa, Russia, and the East. The same year the commission was established, German U-boats had become a major concern for countries in the Caribbean. The Puerto Rican press described the situation as follows:

> New malignant acts by German submarines against navigation in the Western Hemisphere ... are indicative of a campaign that began [in] mid-January [and that] continues to develop with greater intensity.[31]

Aside from cutting off the food supply, submarine attacks on ships carrying oil and bauxite from British Guiana, Trinidad, Venezuela, and the Netherlands Antilles were an additional threat. News of the first sinkings in the Caribbean coincided with the creation of the Anglo-American Caribbean Commission.

Cordell Hull, secretary of state and US strategist during the Second World War, underscored the importance of the Western Hemisphere in military defense plans:

> In many ways we are trying to make the Western Hemisphere into a *solid barrier against the forces of aggression* and a region where liberal governments and free institutions can continue to exist.[32]

Consequently, the Caribbean became one of the most important strategic points during the war. However, in order to carry out defense strategies, it was of the essence to assuage troubles in the region, secure provisions, and facilitate the incorporation of military base personnel into British colonial communities. The Anglo-American Caribbean Commission would assume this task.

> Dependence upon imported food has been accentuated by the construction of the United States bases in the Caribbean area. This development meant more mouths to feed; it has brought a diversion of labor from agriculture to

Rexford G. Tugwell, governor of Puerto Rico, 1941–1946 (Archivo Fundación Luis Muñoz Marín)

construction; and the accompanying increase in purchasing-power resulted in greater demand for food.[33]

Although the effects of economic unrest in the islands were known to both metropolitan powers, the creation of the commission was a reaction to circumstances surrounding the Allied military crisis of 1942. A regional alternative to address the economic crisis in the Caribbean was ignored for a long time.[34] Only when security and hegemony were at stake did this first regional cooperation effort emerge.

Devising the Strategy

The main events that influenced the configuration of a socioeconomic strategy for regional cooperation in the Caribbean have now been described. US colonial policy and the increased strategic importance of the Caribbean would continue to drive measures that were supported by various officials close to President Roosevelt within an atmosphere of economic restrictions, a corollary to the Great Depression.

It is fitting to ask why the United States decided not to use military intervention as a response to uprisings in British possessions, where military bases had been established since 1940. Direct military intervention to suppress the situation was an option. However, the United States had been developing a noninterventionist policy since the end of the Herbert Hoover administration and the beginning of Roosevelt's presidency.

Jorge Rodríguez Beruff calls attention to the fact that the Great Depression brought a redefinition of US military policy and an "abandonment of the policy of direct intervention." Rodríguez Beruff ascribes this strategic shift to two factors: first, cuts in military funding, and second, the "rise in anti-imperialist agitation in every country in the region."[35] Furthermore, military intervention would produce negative repercussions throughout Latin America. Roosevelt's "Good Neighbor" policy entailed an agreement on hemispheric solidarity that sought political backing from Latin American and Caribbean countries in exchange for economic, military, and technical assistance.

Nevertheless, in the case of US possessions, a more careful study of the impact of this policy is necessary. In fact, in the 1930s, Puerto Rico suffered one of its greatest manifestations of oppression as a colonial state. The nationalist movement that openly denounced US imperialism drove the metropolis to appoint government officials with a strong military background, such as Governor Blanton Winship, who, with the aid of the Federal District Court, made sure for over a decade that the movement, spearheaded by Pedro Albizu Campos, was squashed. The planned political concessions to US territories remained to be seen, given that the noninterventionist policy included neither negotiating US strategic-military positions nor tolerating, by any means, public opposition that would jeopardize their stability.

> This policy of partial concessions and military withdrawal, nevertheless, attempted to secure control over traditional military enclaves in the Panama Canal, Guantanamo Bay, and Puerto Rico, considered non-negotiable and crucial to the strategic interests of the United States.[36]

Roosevelt considered the indefinite existence of colonial empires to be a possible cause for war. For this reason, he favored a gradual move of territories toward independence after a period of tutelage under the metropolis. The protectorate system, the "antithesis of 'imperialism,'" sought to promote political concessions and address the principal economic problems in the territories. Some authors argue that Roosevelt's anticolonial attitude spurred the eventual decolonization of the European empires.[37]

In light of political and economic pressures, Taussig, who had a great deal of influence over the president, advised him on the negative repercussions that would arise should the military resources of an interventionist policy be used, both in British and US colonies, in the event of confrontation. Economic underdevelopment was considered the root of all evil. Thus, if not solved, there would always exist the possibility of popular revolt in the colonies. Taussig urged the consideration of an agreement with Great Britain to address the economic crisis, promoting long-term stability.[38]

Secretary of State Cordell Hull held a similar position. Hull proposed concrete steps to achieve self-governance in dependent territories, while more developed countries would achieve independence after a certain period of time.[39] In order to reach these goals, it was of the utmost importance that colonies achieve economic equality. Hence, Hull's position was in line with the socioeconomic strategy that would later be realized. Sumner Welles, also a State Department official, was in charge of discussing the possibilities of an agreement on Anglo-American cooperation in the Caribbean with the British ambassador to Washington, Lord Halifax. Welles supported the regional approach to the socioeconomic problems in the region. His vision was akin to the British approach to addressing colonial problems.[40]

British Prime Minister Winston Churchill did not share President Roosevelt's opinion. He believed that the future of world order lay in the power, prosperity, and prestige of the British Empire at the height of the nineteenth century.[41] Churchill's imperialist attitude contrasted with Roosevelt's more liberal position. However, the US stance toward colonial protectorates was considered an excuse for its concealed expansionism.

> This is understood to mean establishing greater military security, making a greater effort to include the interests of the colonial peoples in the system of economic exploitations—in short, adjusting the colonial system to the new world basis on which international security and economic well-being must clearly rest.[42]

In order to dispel any suspicions, in 1940 Roosevelt stated that he was not interested in possessing British colonies, since that would represent a "headache" for the United States.[43] In 1941, Churchill and Roosevelt issued a joint statement supporting the self-determination of the peoples and the concessions that would follow:

> [Churchill and Roosevelt] respect the right of all peoples to choose the form of government under which they will live; and they wish to see sovereign rights and self-government restored to those who have been forcefully deprived of them.[44]

The change in US policy can be analyzed in the context of a new power structure designed by the state. Emilio Pantojas-García offers an explanation regarding the role of the state in this new regional cooperation strategy, basing his argument on Antonio Gramsci's definition of hegemony and "its ability to guide, together with its ability to oppress."[45] Even though Pantojas-García formulates his theory to explain the new relations that emerged from the Caribbean Basin Initiative (launched in the 1980s), his argument is equally applicable to the situation described during the 1940s, in that military intervention becomes invisible, giving way to apparent economy-stabilizing priorities. He argues that hegemony entails rearticulating a system of relations that coherently unites the process of accumulation, legitimacy, and oppression on a regional scale under the leadership of the state and US capital.[46] It is along these lines—noting the exception that during the Second World War the distribution of power in the Caribbean was in jeopardy—that plans that were then in development can be better understood. The United States clearly wanted to consolidate hegemony by defending its strategic position.

In May 1941, Lord Halifax informed Welles of Great Britain's willingness to jointly address the Caribbean predicament. In October of the same year, the Caribbean Office was created within the State Department as a prelude to the Anglo-American Commission, for the purpose of considering "problems relating to labor, agriculture, housing, health, education, finance, trade relations, and tariffs," in addition to other types of aid.[47] The diplomat Coert DuBois was assigned to take charge of this office.

The creation of other organizations strengthened the implementation of the plan. One of these organizations was the American Advisory Board, designated by Roosevelt in October 1941 to advise the commission on socioeconomic issues affecting both British and US possessions. Its members included Taussig; Tugwell; Puerto Rico Supreme Court Justice Martín Travieso; Judge William H. Hastie, a civilian aide to the secretary of war; and Carl Robbins, chairman of the board of a tobacco company.[48] The appointment of Travieso indicated the first step toward direct participation of a Puerto Rican government official in the plan. This appointment, among other things, was intended to placate Puerto Ricans, who were generally not in favor of the plan; most Puerto Ricans trusted Travieso. When the commission was established, its members became part of the Caribbean Advisory Committee, appointed by the president to carry out the same functions.

In October, the Presidential Advisory Committee was selected. Tugwell, Taussig, and DuBois, the three American members of the future Anglo-American Caribbean Commission, were appointed members. Their main charge consisted in finding ways to keep the region supplied with provisions.[49] Without a doubt, Tugwell's presence in the whole process was a source of mistrust among some Puerto Ricans. Since Tugwell was the governor of Puerto Rico, there was speculation over a connection between the plan and Puerto Rico's economic and political future.

These two bodies—the Caribbean Advisory Committee and the Presidential Advisory Committee—had no authority other than to "formulate recommendations" for the governments of the United States and Great Britain, as well as for Roosevelt, who would have the power to make the final decision.[50]

On March 9, 1942, the plans elaborated by the United States and Great Britain came to fruition. The communiqué that announced the creation and purpose of the Anglo-American Caribbean Commission indicated the following:

> Members of the Commission will concern themselves primarily with matters pertaining to labour, agriculture, housing, health, education, social welfare, finance, economics and related subjects in the territories under British and United States flags within this territory and on those matters will advise their respective governments.[51]

The communiqué ratified the commission's advisory capacity, underscoring its main purpose. This statement made clear that the commission could not meddle directly in issues pertaining to the possessions, but rather could present recommendations for the consideration of both governments. The Anglo-American Caribbean Commission basically managed two types of projects. One was a long-term operation, aimed at improving the region's socioeconomic conditions. Its purpose was to strengthen the region in order to prevent totalitarian regimes from threatening colonial power. The fruits of this plan would lead to hegemonic control through the growth of Caribbean economies. Thus, the state and US capital were to be seen in the eyes of the subordinated as beneficial influences offering them security.

The second project was a short-term operation, addressing the immediate needs and demands of war. In addition to being chairman of the Presidential Advisory Committee, Charles Taussig would be cochairman of the commission, along with British representative Sir Frank Stockdale. Initially, the commission was formed of six members, three from each government.

The functions of the commission were similar to those of the Caribbean Office; the relationship between the organizations was clarified by the State Department. For the purposes of administrative convenience, the US section of the commission would become an integral unit within the State Department. The Caribbean Office would serve as an "Executive Agency for the US section of the Anglo-American Commission"[52] and would have the following responsibilities in relation to the commission:

(1) Furnish technical assistance on plans or projects worked up by the Commission;

Caribbean officers alongside a Spitfire (602 Squadron Museum)

(2) Maintain liaison jointly in behalf of the Department and the Commission with other offices of the Department and other departments and agencies; and,
(3) Keep the Commission appropriately apprised of all developments in its field of activity, as well as of plans, projects or procedures developed on its own initiative and of common interest.[53]

Despite the fact that the commission was formed under the influence of war and the strategic needs of the colonial powers, it was expected to last beyond the state of emergency. The following section provides an analysis of how different sectors in Puerto Rico reacted to the news about the formulation of a Caribbean plan and how they were integrated into some of the commission's more important work.[54]

The Reaction of Sectors in Puerto Rico

In some British colonies, animosity emerged in reaction to the establishment of a regional cooperation plan. The US position could not hide its imperialist agenda. In addition, historical ties linked the British islands to Europe more than to the United States. Many Caribbean leaders considered the strategy as collective colonialism with goals that opposed their own respective political aspirations.[55] This position grew from fears that the commission would formulate decisions at odds with their collective will. Puerto Rico would play a fundamental role in regional opposition by uncovering the first steps taken by the United States and Great Britain.

The reception by different groups within Puerto Rico—the Coalición Republicano-Socialista, the Partido Nacionalista, the PPD, and the Federación Libre de Trabajadores, among others—to the plan for the Anglo-American Caribbean Commission revealed great controversy on the island.[56] The atmosphere was plagued with uncertainty and sharp criticism—as will be illustrated shortly—born from speculation concerning the political and economic consequences of Puerto Rico's inclusion in an external regional coordination effort. Suspicions in Puerto Rico began seeping in through the press. *Newsweek* published an article that, according to the Puerto Rican newspaper *El Mundo*, would contribute to inciting debate among the various groups in Puerto Rico over the Caribbean plan.[57] The article, published on July 28, 1941, predicted the creation of the Anglo-American Caribbean Commission and pointed to the possible reorientation from a single-crop economy based on sugar to an economy based on agricultural diversification. The federal government supposedly had plans to immediately implement the project in Puerto Rico.

In spite of the fact that the Senate majority leader at the time, Luis Muñoz Marín, declared that he knew nothing of the plan, the first concrete signs of its existence became known to the public after a series of conferences between Muñoz and officials from the US Department of Agriculture, in which the production of hemp, using jute harvested on other Caribbean islands, was suggested for Puerto Rico. These discussions increased suspicion of a regional cooperation strategy.[58] Although conversations between Muñoz and the Department of Agriculture have not been corroborated, in 1941 one measure established by the Land Authority was the promotion of an individual farms program to stimulate agricultural diversification.

> Formally, agrarian reform put forward diversification in agriculture and a break with the monoculture enclave and its exploitative dominance over field workers.[59]

In October of the same year, *El Mundo*, unrelenting in its opposition to the Tugwell-Muñoz administration, accused the senate majority leader of being an alleged supporter of the plan that was being developed in the United States to economically control the Caribbean. The Coalición Republicano-Socialista flatly rejected the inclusion of Puerto Rico in a strategy that intended to fix problems together with "Jamaica, Trinidad, and other wretched colonies" of Great Britain. Muñoz's support of the Taussig plan was considered a betrayal, because the person behind it, as previously stated, was the chairman of industries competing with Puerto Rican sugarcane interests.[60]

While in Puerto Rico speculation over the actual phasing in of the plan arose, the first step toward implementing the plan—the creation of the

Caribbean Office within the State Department—was already underway. This step did not enjoy popular consensus on account of the possibility that the Department of the Interior's jurisdiction over Puerto Rico would pass to the State Department.[61] It was argued that this apprehension was due to the fact that the State Department "never even had a compassionate thought of relief for Puerto Rico." Among other arguments, upon negotiating a reciprocal treaty with Switzerland, the State Department had allegedly destroyed Puerto Rico's garment industry in the process.[62]

Resident Commissioner Bolívar Pagán, member of the Coalición Republicano-Socialista, addressed Secretary of State Hull and voiced his warning:

> Grave unrest and anguish can be felt in Puerto Rico as a result of the alleged plan because the news indicates that the plan is to deprive us of our political and economic conditions without considering public opinion in the island.[63]

Pagán expressed fear over the economic and political consequences Puerto Rico might suffer on account of the agreement. He refused to accept the plan because it considered Puerto Rico to be a "nation or a foreign country." In addition, he rejected "Puerto Rico's projected company with Caribbean colonies of inferior civilization, lower standards of living, different traditions and civic experiences, and different political and social aspirations compared to Puerto Rico."[64] Pagán described the future as "grim, miserable, and desperate" because, at the time, he harbored no doubts that the plan would benefit big business and powerful foreign interests. Everything pointed to the fact that Taussig's presence inspired mistrust in many Puerto Ricans. According to Pagán, the Caribbean islands, especially Puerto Rico, could not build an economy based on the exchange of a diversity of products.[65] In spite of all this, the State Department merely stated that the plan was designed to benefit its participants. The Coalición Republicano-Socialista was not unaware of the Anglo-American Caribbean Commission's military interests:

> Negotiations are being held to include Puerto Rico in the effects of a plan that basically has no other purpose than to ameliorate the economic situation of British colonial possessions in order to strengthen public support for the newly established US military bases in these islands.[66]

Opposition by the PPD was more moderate. On October 28, 1941, PPD legislators, through Senate Resolution no. 1, set fifteen points of strict cooperation that should prevail between the people of Puerto Rico and the Roosevelt administration regarding economic coordination among the Caribbean peoples. Among other things, the resolution stated the following:

> It is our duty to represent the strongest point of opposition to any plan, measure or purpose that may lower the standard of living of our people. It is equally our clearest duty to cooperate in the realization of any plan, measure or purpose that, in our judgment, will better the standard of living of our people and bring it closer to the aspirations of economic justice and social security.[67]

It was believed that the program would be completely blocked if opposition further progressed. Tugwell, who was active in the formulation of the plan from its beginning, allegedly drafted a petition to President Roosevelt to leave Puerto Rico's inclusion in the plan in the hands of the insular legislature.[68]

Puerto Rican opposition had its impact on Washington. The program was postponed for almost a year due to the opposition of leaders who accused it of being an attempt to alter Puerto Rico's political status.[69] Conferences and investigations continued, and Coert DuBois, future member of the commission and director of the Caribbean Office, was assigned the task of dealing with Puerto Rican protests. DuBois tried to mitigate Pagán's opposition by stating that Puerto Rico would suffer no harm under the Caribbean program, which was then being studied.[70]

After the official announcements on the creation of the Anglo-American Caribbean Commission, the Puerto Rican legislature, through the Senate, expressed its satisfaction with the subject in light of the commission's aim of socioeconomic advancement. Appreciation was also given for the commission's having recognized Puerto Rico and ensuring its right to "intervene in the orientation, approval, and carrying out of whatever plans [affect] our economic relations and the social advancement of our people."

The new resolution ratified the main points of the 1941 resolution, stating that the organization should have "no political powers whatsoever" and that its powers should solely be those of investigation, orientation, and recommendation.[71] Members of the PPD were making sure that the economic aims of the plan would not result in the degradation of the standard of living in Puerto Rico but would rather seek to use its power wisely. They also requested that sugar production not be decreased if its substitution by other products would increase poverty and compromise social security on the island. Furthermore, they requested initiating agricultural diversification, facilitating the implementation of the Land Law of 1941, and stimulating industrialization in order to reduce unemployment.[72]

Statements by legislators on the protection of Puerto Rico's "best interests" are telling. While they made their voices heard by demanding the protection of their particular interests, legislators promised not to hinder US national defense needs. They concurred

> that these purposes be in form and substance entirely consistent with the highest level of efficiency for US national defense in the civilian sphere, to which it is the opinion of this Senate that Puerto Rico has a profound personal interest, in addition to interest and loyalty towards US democracy.[73]

Taussig also made statements regarding Puerto Rico's role in the Caribbean. He assured Puerto Ricans that the island's situation would be addressed based on its own interests and pointed out as "obvious" that Puerto Rico was very important in any US program concerning the Caribbean.[74] Although he admitted that the commission was not primarily interested in Puerto Rico, it would take the situation on the island into account, considering that Puerto Rico was the largest US territory in the Caribbean. He reiterated that the commission's functions were purely advisory. The convenience of promoting greater trade between the United States and the Caribbean islands was the foundation, but not the principal function, of the commission:

> The primary task is to reach a solution to the problems of civil economy brought on by war throughout the whole Caribbean area.[75]

Tugwell also approved of a proposal that would allow Puerto Rico to play a unique role in the Caribbean plan. He suggested the possibility that the island should become a center of operations for the research the commission would carry out. He expressed confidence that the situation allowing for Puerto Rico to become the project's administrative center "cannot be improved upon."[76] One of factors behind Tugwell's concurrence was Puerto Rico's strategic position in relation to the Panama Canal. Another was that the Spanish language and the mix of Hispanic and American cultures would serve the purpose of positioning the island as a mediator and ambassador of the plan for hemispheric solidarity.[77] The relationship between Tugwell and the University of Puerto Rico must also be mentioned, because he was concurrently the dean of the university during his first years as governor. During the 1950s, the University of Puerto Rico would play a dominant role in training Caribbean and Latin American students in various academic fields. Plans forged in the 1940s to make Puerto Rico a "bridge between the two cultures" and a "window to democracy" would come to fruition in the 1950s. In contrast, Bolívar Pagán commented bitterly on Tugwell's appointment to the commission. He attributed it to Tugwell's role as governor of Puerto Rico, not to his questionable ability to make sensible suggestions on such an important issue.[78]

The final agreement for the creation of the commission was cloaked within another agenda. The shift was attributed to protests in Puerto Rico, which had contributed to halting the commission's implementation and "scaring its authors away." Some sectors were still offended by the idea that plans for the Caribbean involved Puerto Rico within the terms of a colonial agreement:

> In order to serve the needs and conveniences of Defense in this area, in this continent, and in the whole world, Puerto Rico never once needed nor should have needed now the constraints of a colonial agreement pairing us with Jamaica, Trinidad, and Guiana.[79]

Despite protests, a vast number of Puerto Ricans would participate in the research commissions into which the Anglo-American Caribbean Commission was divided and would contribute their knowledge to the socioeconomic improvement plans for their Caribbean neighbors. Without a doubt, what Luis A. Passalacqua called "the first step towards a relationship" between Puerto Rican government leaders and other Caribbean governments during the time of US domination was no easy task, nor was it characterized by mere acceptance.[80] Mistrust surrounded the Caribbean plan, and its authors were considered conspirators against the people:

> The men who tried to hide the situation from Puerto Rico, the men who made themselves accomplices of this attack, the men who irresponsibly handed over the country's fate, will have their day in History.[81]

Initial protests would end in accommodations. Puerto Rico would actively collaborate in the new colonial scheme by channeling the government program all through the commission, and the United States would manage to mollify Puerto Rico's animosity. The commission would recommend adopting the Elective Governor Act, because the act "ought to command the support of most elements in the Puerto Rican population" and "would clearly show that the United States has no ambitions to be a colonial power."[82]

During its existence, the Anglo-American Caribbean Commission held seven official meetings and two conferences, during which its projects and socioeconomic and military strategies were elucidated.[83] In addition, the commission appointed two official bodies for investigation and technical assistance to address the Caribbean's socioeconomic problems from a regional standpoint. The regional focus was the most novel aspect of the strategy, because both Washington and London had previously relied on bureaucracies, legislation, and other interagency resources designed to manage the situations in their respective colonies. The United States and Great Britain attempted to maintain regional hegemony by way of this mechanism, which France and the Netherlands would later join.

In the following section, the commission's most significant projects will be analyzed, specifically that of synchronizing US military and economic interests with the islands' problems. The emphasis on long-term projects had to be modified in light of the immediate demands of war when the United States entered World War II in December 1941.[84] The need for food and goods was entering a crucial stage, and one of the commission's priorities would be to secure food supplies and maintain dietary levels in the region in order to curb local hostilities and protests threatening military security. Improving relations between local populations and military base personnel was essential, given that at the start relations were antagonistic and charged with resentment.[85] By no means do I intend to belittle the importance this mechanism placed on promoting health centers and agricultural, educational, and research programs in general. In fact, prior to the establishment of the commission, there was no mechanism for the exchange of information among the governments of the dependencies to discuss their needs.[86] Nonetheless, war and its demands shaped such a strategy.

Meetings of the Commission

The first meeting of the commission was held in Trinidad between March 26 and March 31, 1942. The main task was to address the dearth of provisions in the midst of the first sinkings by German U-boats. For this reason, the first meeting took the shape of a "war council." Some of the islands were visited, Puerto Rico among them, in order to explore the situation up close.[87] The following describes the shortages Puerto Ricans were experiencing:

> At Ponce early yesterday morning long files of people lined up at the entrances of the stores facing the public square to buy 1 pound of rice each; and they did not disperse until it was proven to them that the rice had not yet been distributed. There was considerable fighting, and shoving, and police intervention was necessary.[88]

A conference was immediately held in Jamaica with officials who had expertise in supplies to devise a plan. The main goal was to establish the "Schooner Pool," a flotilla of ships to coordinate trade in the eastern area of the British islands "from the Leeward Islands in the north to British Guiana in the south." This mechanism centralized control over navigation among the islands to give priority to the most urgent services.[89] Its counterpart was the "Land-Water Highway," a route specifically designed to evade German submarines.

> The first section of the Highway was a shuttle service between Florida and Gulf ports and Habana, Cuba. The other links in the system were a railroad from Habana to Santiago de Cuba, on the eastern end of the island; small boat service across the narrow straights separating Santiago de Cuba and Port-au-Prince, Haiti; a truck service from Port-au-Prince across the island [to] Santo Domingo [and] San Pedro de Macorís, Dominican Republic; and another small boat service from San Pedro de Macorís to Mayagüez, Puerto Rico.[90]

Although seemingly complicated, this route reduced eight hundred miles of exposure to German submarine threats. Three independent republics were involved in the agreement. Bernard Poole indicates that, in exchange for cooperation, these countries reaped benefits. For example, Haitian and Dominican truck owners who lent their services on the emergency route received a guaranteed supply of tires and equipment for heavy machinery. In Cuba, improvements were made to railroad tracks.[91]

Another of the commission's urgent tasks was minimizing the psychological impact of Nazi propaganda on Caribbean populations. The Germans had broadcast the region's critical position through the media. For this reason, the commission launched a radio program, the "*West Indian Radio Newspaper*, to counteract the effects of German propaganda.[92] Among other programs carried out by the commission, it is worth mentioning the recruitment of Caribbean agricultural laborers for work in the United States to contribute to alleviating unemployment throughout the islands, as well as the prevention and cure of venereal disease and the development of local food production through fisheries.[93]

The Caribbean Research Council and the West Indian Conference were the two auxiliary bodies of the commission. The first came into effect during the fourth meeting of the commission in August 1943. Its objectives were to explore the needs of the territories; to determine additional studies to be carried out in certain areas; to plan the exchange of technical and scientific information; and to recommend necessary investigation and cooperation.[94] Its principal areas of work were nutrition, agriculture, fisheries, and forestry. By this time, the Netherlands Antilles had also joined its membership.

At the sixth meeting of the commission held in March 1945, the Caribbean Research Council was established as a permanent body. Carlos E. Chardón, Pablo Morales Otero, Teodoro Moscoso, and Rafael Picó were all invited to become members. They all were Puerto Rican professionals and members of the PPD.[95] Morales Otero, director of the School of Tropical Medicine, led the first year of works for the council.[96] Puerto Rican participation in the council's research committees was noticeable. Among the fourteen members who were active in the areas of agriculture, nutrition, fisheries, and forestry, five were Puerto Rican. In health, out of ten members, three represented Puerto Rico. In the area of industrial technology, there were two Puerto Ricans out of a total membership of eight. In the area of social sciences, out of twenty-three members, ten were from Puerto Rico. In engineering technology, of twelve members, five represented Puerto Rico.[97] The incorporation of the PPD elite into the process was unmistakable, given that they were well positioned in administrative and professional centers. And so the role that Tugwell had assigned to Puerto Rico, a training center conforming to metropolitan interests, was shaped.

The first West Indian Conference, held in Barbados in March 1944, was the most far-reaching of its period. This instrument widened participation in the shared problems of the Caribbean through two local colonial representatives. The Puerto Rican representatives who signed the report for the Conference were Rafael Picó and Antonio Fernós Isern. The nature of the West Indian Conference, as with the commission in general, was advisory and aimed to widen the base of democratic participation. The agenda for the first conference included discussions on nutrition, public works, housing, education, agriculture, health, industries, and the reintegration of war personnel into civilian life.[98] By June 30, 1945, the governments of the United States and Great Britain decided to increase representation for each country from three persons to four. The additional member for the United States was Rafael Picó, chairman of the Puerto Rico Planning Board.

This was the beginning of a US strategic military policy in which the necessities of war accelerated plans for socioeconomic advancement in the colonial territories. The Anglo-American Caribbean Commission would change its name to the Caribbean Commission once the war was over and would increase participation in the region, while at the same time being recognized on an international level.[99] Rafael Picó and former governor Jesús T. Piñero would be the US representatives in the commission. The Caribbean Commission would now have to deal with another problem: implementing the political strategy of the Cold War. This problem, however, is the subject of another investigation.

Reflections

The socioeconomic deterioration of the Caribbean islands by the 1930s and subsequent protests that went so far as to threaten national security pressed the colonial powers to take immediate action. Although interagency organizations gradually took remedial action, this was not enough to solve the multiple problems ailing the region, especially the shortage of food. In addition, the region lacked representation in international forums and effective political participation at the local level. Anti-imperialist movements, the growing strategic-military importance of the Caribbean region, and economic adjustments caused by the Great Depression stimulated a search on behalf of the United States and Great Britain for new ways of addressing the islands' problems.

Plans for regional cooperation in the Caribbean were churning even before the United States entered the Second World War, and the pressures of war led to measures for socioeconomic advancement throughout the US and British possessions. Both metropolitan countries were aware of the situation, yet the decision to address the crisis was put aside until the Caribbean ultimately was incorporated into a strategy for hemispheric defense. The strategic importance of the region guided decisions toward economic strengthening. This strategic military link was a result of the belief that countries with solid economic bases could better repel totalitarian threats, in this case, German expansionism.

The Anglo-American Caribbean Commission was a new model for regional cooperation intended to address the problems shared by colonial governments in agreement with metropolitan interests. Although a study of the impact of the commission's socioeconomic measures is not the aim of this chapter, I have illustrated the fundamental problems in the Caribbean region such as food, education, housing, health, and administration, among others, co-opting groups that sooner or later were accommodated into the strategy. Colonial representatives could make their voices heard through participative mechanisms created for that purpose, and, through these channels, they presented recommendations to address specific problems. Nonetheless, the commission's nature as an advisory body ensured that metropolitan countries would retain power, and only those decisions that did not contradict their interests could be adopted. In this sense, the Anglo-American Caribbean Commission contributed to the consolidation of US and British hegemony in the Caribbean.

In spite of the fact that the commission was created as a long-term agency designed to attend to problems during a period of peace, the needs of war established an infrastructure designed to secure regional support that would safeguard military power and protect military personnel. Long-term projects suddenly became short-term projects, with the aim of preserving regional hegemony.

During this stage, colonial powers changed their strategy of dominance; even though they kept and expanded their military installations, colonial control was now disguised through socioeconomic reform. The plan formulated had to be in agreement with the needs of war and national security. Thus, the state created new forms of subordination and acquiescence by way of partial concessions and the rearticulation of political-economic and military interests. But the accommodation for rearticulating metropolitan interests with the colonies was not unilateral. Colonial pressures modified the strategy and returned it "cloaked" in their own objectives. A new, economically powerful elite was establishing itself in Puerto Rico, intertwined with the PPD. Able to press its political and economic agendas, it would eventually displace the coalitionist group associated with the prewar sugar monoculture. The fate of the territories was subject to the shifting priorities of military security. Consequently, colonial possessions became reactionary entities, despite the fact that they could initiate policy on their own.

The Anglo-American Caribbean Commission cannot be understood as a mere mechanism for stimulating economic development, nor can it be seen as an isolated entity supporting the military plans for the region. The commission's strategic aspects gave structure to both the purpose and significance of broader public policies with multiple interests. In addition, the commission set the foundations for Puerto Rico's role in the 1950s as a "window to democracy." Its role in facilitating technical assistance to developing countries through President Harry Truman's Point Four Program was essential in the internationalization of Operation Bootstrap, which became the development model for dependent territories, and the promotion of the autonomic formula of the free associated state.

Notes

This chapter was originally published in *Avance de Investigación*, no. 11, Centro de Investigaciones Académicas, Universidad del Sagrado Corazón, Puerto Rico (1991). This version maintains the original argument, and only a few changes have been made. I would like to thank Dr. Jorge Rodríguez Beruff for offering to include my article in this publication. Also, I want to thank Melanie Kinch Pérez from the Translation and Research Center of the Graduate Program in Translation, University of Puerto Rico, for translating this article from the Spanish.

1. "Joint Communiqué of the United States and British Governments on Cooperation with Regard to the Caribbean," in *Documents on International Relations in the Caribbean*, ed. Roy Preiswerk (Río Piedras: Instituto de Estudios del Caribe, University of Puerto Rico, 1970), p. 36.

2. Technical assistance was supported by the development theory that gained popularity after the Second World War. This mechanism has commonly been used by developed

countries as a form of domination and of political and economic penetration in developing countries. The needs of the receiving nation are frequently subordinate to the interests of the source, perpetuating asymmetrical relations of power. Puerto Rico consolidated its role as a provider of technical assistance under President Harry S. Truman's Point Four Program in the context of the Cold War and in accordance with the PPD. See Mayra Rosario Urrutia, "Detrás de 'La vitrina': expectativas del Partido Popular Democrático y política exterior norteamericana, 1942–1954," in *Del Nacionalismo al populismo: cultura y política en Puerto Rico*, ed. Silvia Álvarez Curbelo and María Elena Rodríguez Castro (Río Piedras, PR: Ediciones Huracán; Decanato de Estudios Graduados, University of Puerto Rico, 1993), pp. 147–177.

3. Quite useful was the first chapter of the book by Emilio Pantojas-García, *Development Strategies as Ideology: Puerto Rico's Export-Led Industrialization Experience* (Río Piedras: University of Puerto Rico Press, 1990), in which the author analyzes the concept of hegemony in his study on Puerto Rico's development strategy. For an explanation of the concept of hegemony, see Antonio Gramsci, *Selections from the Prison Notebooks* (London: Lawrence and Wishart, 1971).

4. Bernard Poole, *The Caribbean Commission: Background of Cooperation in the West Indies* (Columbia: University of South Carolina Press, 1951), p. xiii.

5. Ibid., pp. xiv, xv.

6. Jorge Rodríguez Beruff, *Política militar y dominación: Puerto Rico en el contexto latinoamericano* (Río Piedras, PR: Ediciones Huracán, 1988), p. 22.

7. *The Caribbean Islands and the War: A Record of Progress in Facing Stern Realities*, Department of State Publication 2023 (Washington, DC: Government Printing Office, 1943), p. 4.

8. Charles W. Taussig, "A Four Power Program in the Caribbean," *Foreign Affairs*, July 1946, p. 699.

9. James L. Dietz, *Economic History of Puerto Rico: Institutional Change and Capitalist Development* (Princeton, NJ: Princeton University Press, 1986), p. 136.

10. For an analytical account of the protests in Trinidad of 1937, see W. Richard Jacobs, "The Politics of Protest in Trinidad: The Strikes and Disturbances of 1937," *Caribbean Studies* 17, no. 1 (1977): 5–54.

11. Rexford Guy Tugwell, *The Stricken Land: The Story of Puerto Rico* (Garden City, NY: Doubleday, 1946), pp. 64–65. According to Tugwell, in the Caribbean Taussig worked for the president through voluntary public service and held no formal position in the government.

12. Taussig, "A Four Power Program," p. 700.

13. Ibid.

14. Humberto García Muñiz, "El Caribe durante la Segunda Guerra Mundial: el Mediterráneo Americano," in *Puerto Rico y el Caribe hoy*, ed. Carmen Gautier Mayoral et al. (Buenos Aires: Clacso-Cerep, 1987), p. 139.

15. For a detailed discussion on the immediate precursor of the lease agreement of bases between the United States and Great Britain and the state of defense of the region, see Fitzroy André Baptiste, "The British Grant of Air and Naval Facilities to the United States in Trinidad, St. Lucia and Bermuda in 1939 (June–December)," *Caribbean Studies* 16, no. 2 (1976): 9.

16. Annette C. Palmer, "The United States and the Commonwealth Caribbean: 1940–1945" (Ph.D. diss., Fordham University, 1979), p. 30. This dissertation was later published as *World War II in the Caribbean: A Study of Anglo-American Partnership and Rivalry* (Baltimore: Black Academy Press, 1998).

17. García Muñiz, "El Caribe durante la Segunda Guerra Mundial," p. 139.

18. Palmer, "The United States and the Commonwealth Caribbean," p. 30.

19. Ibid.

20. See quotation in Herbert Corkran, *Patterns of International Cooperation in the Caribbean, 1942–1969* (Dallas: Southern Methodist University Press, 1970), p. 22.

21. Ibid.; and Luis A. Passalacqua, "Puerto Rico y el Caribe: cinco etapas en una relación," in *Problemas del Caribe contemporáneo*, ed. Ángel Calderón Cruz (Río Piedras: Instituto de Estudios del Caribe, University of Puerto Rico, 1979), p. 64.

22. García Muñiz, "El Caribe durante la Segunda Guerra Mundial," p. 141.

23. Cephil Alric Percy St. Hill, Appendix 1, "Exchange of Notes Regarding United States Destroyers and Naval Air Facilities for the United States in British Transatlantic Territories," in "The Chaguaramas Question: The Origins and Consequences of the United States–United Kingdom Leased Bases Agreement, 1941; A Trinidad and Tobago Viewpoint" (Master's thesis, University of the West Indies, 1967).

24. See the final contents of said agreement in Preiswerk, *Documents on International Relations*, pp. 596–607.

25. Corkran, *Patterns of International Cooperation*, p. 25.

26. *The Caribbean Islands and the War*, p. 14 (emphasis added).

27. Tugwell, *The Stricken Land*, p. 69.

28. *The Caribbean Islands and the War*, p. 14.

29. Poole, *The Caribbean Commission*, p. 184.

30. "Desde Londres explican las implicaciones del Plan Caribe; dicen afiliaciones políticas perjudican estrategia," *El Mundo* (San Juan), March 12, 1942, pp. 5, 14.

31. "Arrecia la campaña submarina alemana," *El Mundo* (San Juan), February 24, 1942, p. 3.

32. "Cordell Hull destaca importancia de la nueva Oficina del Caribe," *El Mundo* (San Juan), February 17, 1942, p. 1 (emphasis added).

33. *The Caribbean Islands and the War*, p. 4.

34. In Puerto Rico, for example, in the 1930s, President Roosevelt's New Deal programs were implemented through the Puerto Rico Reconstruction Administration (PRRA) and the Puerto Rico Emergency Relief Administration (PRERA) in an effort to counteract the economic crisis. These rehabilitation attempts did not produce the desired effect, because Puerto Rico's economy required further transformations.

35. Rodríguez Beruff, *Política militar y dominación*, p. 31.

36. Ibid.

37. William Roger Louis, *Imperialism at Bay: The United States and the Decolonization of the British Empire, 1941–1945* (New York: Oxford University Press, 1978), p. 3.

38. Howard Johnson, "The United States and the Establishment of the Anglo-American Caribbean Commission," *Journal of Caribbean History* 19, no. 1 (1984): 28.

39. Louis, *Imperialism at Bay*, p. 176.
40. Ibid., p. 177.
41. Ibid., p. 5.
42. "What Will Happen to Colonies? Caribbean Offers One Answer," *Newsweek*, January 3, 1944, p. 70.
43. Johnson, "The United States and the Establishment," p. 40.
44. Héctor Álvarez Silva, *Documentos básicos de la historia de los Estados Unidos de América* (Río Piedras, PR: A. Álvarez, 1967), pp. 368–369; see also "Atlantic Charter," Lillian Goldman Law Library, at http://avalon.law.yale.edu/wwii/atlantic.asp, accessed April 30, 2012.
45. Emilio Pantojas-García, "Hacia la restauración de la hegemonía: la complementariedad entre los niveles militar, económico y político del proyecto norteamericano para la Cuenca del Caribe," in *Puerto Rico en el Caribe hoy*, ed. Carmen Gautier Mayoral et al. (Buenos Aires: Clasco-Cerep, 1987), p. 223.
46. Ibid.
47. Poole, *The Caribbean Commission*, p. 185.
48. Ibid.
49. Ibid., p. 186.
50. Ibid., p. 188.
51. Clovis Beauregard, "Pan American Cooperation," in *Documents on International Relations in the Caribbean*, ed. Roy Preiswerk (Río Piedras: Instituto de Estudios del Caribe, University of Puerto Rico, 1970), p. 228.
52. Caribbean Commission Correspondence, Departamento de Estado, Comunicado no. 59, December 19, 1942, Archivo General de Puerto Rico, Tarea 78-11, Caja 1.
53. Ibid.
54. Charlie Whitham, *Bitter Rehearsal: British and American Planning for a Post-War West Indies* (Westport, CT: Praeger, 2002). See also Tony Martin, "Eric Williams and the Anglo-American Caribbean Commission: Trinidad's Future Nationalist Leader as Aspiring Imperial Bureaucrat, 1942–1944," *Journal of African American History* 88, no. 3 (Summer 2003): 274–290.
55. For a discussion on the standpoint of British possessions at the time, see Palmer, "The United States and the Commonwealth Caribbean," pp. 150–163.
56. For background on the controversy surrounding the Caribbean plan, see articles printed in *El Mundo* in October 1941. In addition to news about the project, which appeared almost on a daily basis, the power of the editorials opposing the plan is worth mentioning.
57. "Headache in Sugar, U.S. Acts to Veer Puerto Rico from Its Single Crop Economy," *Newsweek*, July 28, 1941.
58. "Una maniobra desgraciada," *El Mundo* (San Juan), October 4, 1941, p. 10.
59. Emilio Pantojas-García, "Desarrollismo y lucha de clases: los límites del proyecto populista en PR durante la década de 1940," *Revista de Ciencias Sociales* 19, nos. 3–4 (1985): 382.
60. "Con Puerto Rico o con el Plan Taussig," *El Mundo* (San Juan), October 2, 1941, p. 8. The Coalición Republicano-Socialista, advocate for Puerto Rico sugarcane interests, became the strongest resister of socioeconomic reform, which the PPD supported.

61. "¿Hasta cuándo, Puerto Rico?," *El Mundo* (San Juan), October 7, 1942, p. 8.
62. Ibid.
63. "Departamento de Estado se sorprende ante protesta en la isla: fuentes informadas dicen se había consultado a líderes," *El Mundo* (San Juan), October 14, 1941, p. 1.
64. "Del plan del Caribe hablan en Washington hace meses," *El Mundo* (San Juan), October 7, 1941, p. 16.
65. Ibid.
66. "¿Hasta cuándo, Puerto Rico?," p. 8.
67. See the full text in Spanish in "Resolución," *El Mundo* (San Juan), October 29, 1941, p. 5.
68. Tugwell, *The Stricken Land*, p. 185.
69. "Nombran comisiones encauzan Plan del Caribe," *El Mundo* (San Juan), March 10, 1942, pp. 1, 8. One of the many questions posed by the opposition on the island was to what degree the British islands joined and collaborated in delaying the formation of the commission.
70. Ibid.
71. See the complete resolution of March 1942 in "Plan del Caribe y commission, Speaker ante Senado," *El Mundo* (San Juan), March 10, 1942, pp. 1, 15.
72. Ibid.
73. Ibid.
74. "Taussig señala alimentos como objetivo inmediato Plan Caribe: dice habrá de enfocar situación a base de la Isla," *El Mundo* (San Juan), March 11, 1942, p. 4.
75. Ibid.
76. Ibid., p. 8.
77. Tugwell, *The Stricken Land*, pp. 111, 123, 130–131, 134.
78. "Taussig señala alimentos," *El Mundo*, p. 4.
79. "¡El Plan del Caribe era una mentira!," *El Mundo* (San Juan), editorial, March 11, 1942, p. 8.
80. Passalacqua, "Puerto Rico y el Caribe," pp. 61–81.
81. "¡El Plan del Caribe era una mentira!," *El Mundo*, p. 8.
82. Tugwell, *The Stricken Land*, p. 328.
83. Poole, *The Caribbean Commission*, p. 192.
84. Johnson, "United States and the Establishment," p. 42.
85. For a discussion of protests and struggles in Trinidad and Tobago regarding the establishment of the Chaguaramas base, see Percy St. Hill, "The Chaguaramas Question."
86. Corkran, *Patterns of International Cooperation*, p. 37.
87. Anglo-American Caribbean Commission, *The Caribbean Islands and the War*, p. 18.
88. Ibid., p. 5.
89. Corkran, *Patterns of International Cooperation*, p. 59.
90. Ibid., p. 57.
91. Poole, *The Caribbean Commission*, p. 200.
92. Ibid., p. 63.
93. Beauregard, "Pan American Cooperation," p. 228.

94. Anglo-American Caribbean Association, *Report of the AACC to the Government of the United States and Great Britain for the Year 1944* (Washington, DC: Anglo-American Caribbean Association), p. 11.

95. Charles Taussig to Rafael Picó, April 3, 1945, Archivo General de Puerto Rico, Tarea 78-11, Caja 1.

96. "Conclusions with Respect to the Caribbean Research Council," March 20–23, 1945, Archivo General de Puerto Rico, Tarea 78-11, Caja 1.

97. Ibid.

98. Anglo-American Caribbean Association, *Report of the West Indian Conference Held in Barbados* (Washington, DC: Anglo-American Caribbean Association, 1944), pp. 1–5.

99. James A. Bough, "The Caribbean Commission," *International Organization* 3, no. 4 (November 1949): 643–655; and Frank Stockdale, "The Work of the Caribbean Commission," *International Affairs* 23, no. 2 (April 1947): 213–220.

Geopolitics and Telecommunications Policy in Puerto Rico: ITT and the Porto Rico Telephone Company, 1942–1948

Luis Rosario Albert

In 1945, during the final months of the Second World War, Paul Porter, chairman of the Federal Communications Commission, expressed that during the first decades of the twentieth century the US communications industry had experienced accelerated development all over the world.

According to Porter:

> [O]ur present situation [is such that] the managements of international communications companies are in a position to shape our international communications policy through their ability to negotiate and make arrangements with the representatives of foreign governments. Indeed, management of communications companies may at times be in the position of serving interests other than their own national interest.[1]

During the latter part of the nineteenth century and until the First World War, the telegraph was a symbol of Great Britain's domination in Europe. Later, during the first fifty years of the twentieth century, the telephone became the symbol of US expansion and power.[2] Aside from the Radio Corporation of America (RCA), the strength of US radio and telephone companies abroad was mostly associated with the business activities of International Telephone and Telegraph (ITT). Its president and founder, Colonel Sosthenes Behn, who at the time was considered the "Prince of Telephones,"[3] had developed ITT's corporate vision as "a peace keeping influence."[4] Between 1920 and 1945, ITT not only was a new form of diplomacy, it had also become a listening post for American military intelligence activities during World War II.[5]

Geopolitics and Telecommunications Policy

Printed news of the Second World War was provided on an almost daily basis by *El Mundo*, the most widely circulated newspaper on the island. (Archivo General de Puerto Rico)

This chapter analyzes a component of the public telecommunications modernization plan in Puerto Rico, a colonial territory of the United States, between 1942 and 1948: a project aimed at nationalizing the Porto Rico Telephone Company (PRTC), an ITT subsidiary. This analysis is focused on two areas: (1) the United States' geopolitical vision during World War II; and (2) the upgrading of government communications in Puerto Rico, an initiative of appointed governor Rexford G. Tugwell and Senate president Luis Muñoz Marín.

The United States developed economic and military plans, through the Hemisphere Communications Committee, to place telecommunications companies operating in the Western Hemisphere in the hands of US interests. Despite limited historiographical research about communications in Puerto Rico at that time, we argue that the project to nationalize the Porto Rico Telephone Company contradicted President Franklin D. Roosevelt's executive order conditioning the sale of the PRTC.

As we will show, the controversy over this transaction attracted the attention of one of the most powerful persons in the world, the president of the

United States, commander in chief of a nation fighting in the most destructive armed conflict of the twentieth century.

During Tugwell's tenure as governor, an extensive project was begun to modernize Puerto Rico's government and the economy. In Tugwell's first years in office, the colonial government backed agrarian reform, minimum wage laws, and the protection of labor, as well as the acquisition of American and foreign companies to provide basic needs such as electricity, water, and telephone service. Once nationalized, the Puerto Rico Railroad and Light Company and the San Juan Aqueduct became among the first companies to operate as government monopolies, which, aside from providing improved basic services to the people, promoted a "production battle" and helped overcome "social injustice, extreme poverty [and] the overwhelming despair that prevailed."[6] A component of this modernization was the development of public communications in Puerto Rico, with the creation of the Puerto Rico Communications Authority (ACPR by its Spanish abbreviation) in 1942 as a starting point.

Between 1942 and 1948, the attempt to nationalize the PRTC was basically an initiative of Governor Tugwell's economic plan. Although the Popular Democratic Party government had already promoted agrarian reform with the 500 Acre Law, the conversion of sugar mills into public corporations, the distribution of lots to workers, the promotion of labor unions, and upgrades to the island's infrastructure, the acquisition of the Porto Rico Telephone Company was one project that was specifically promoted by Governor Tugwell.[7]

The Origins of ITT: From Sugar Cane to Communications

During the first four decades of the twentieth century, the Caribbean was characterized by an enormous concentration of large estates and landlords as a result of US capital investment in the sugar industry, particularly in Cuba and Puerto Rico.[8] Until then, the results of colonialism in Puerto Rico had been extreme poverty, inadequate housing, serious public health problems, illiteracy, and unemployment, among others. Sosthenes Behn, ITT's president to be, was born on Saint Thomas in the Virgin Islands, then a Danish colony, on January 30, 1882. His father, of Dutch origin, was France's consul in the Danish Virgin Islands, and his mother was French-Italian. Together with his brother Hernand, later also his business partner, he studied in Corsica and Paris.

In Puerto Rico, the Behn brothers were of the social elite and were influential in the world of politics, the Republican Party, and the emerging radio and telephone industry on the island and throughout the Caribbean.⁹ In 1906, they appeared as corporate officials of the Porto Rico General Telephone Company, which had coverage in the northern part of the island, and in 1912 they acquired the South Puerto Rico Telephone Company, which managed a telephone system in the southern and eastern parts of the island.¹⁰ In 1922, ITT founded the first commercial radio station in Puerto Rico, WKAQ Radio, located in the PRTC Building.

Sosthenes Behn served in the US Signal Corps and as cabinet head for General George Russell during the First World War. While there, he learned about military communications systems. After the war, Behn retired as a colonel in the US Army and was decorated by the French government with the Légion d'honneur. He returned to the United States to work at American Telephone and Telegraph (AT&T), founded by Alexander Graham Bell, inventor of the telephone.

In 1914, at the beginning of World War I, Puerto Rico's Executive Council granted Hernand Behn the Porto Rico Telephone Company franchise, incorporated in Delaware, which was a result of the merging of the Porto Rico General Telephone Company and the South Puerto Rico Telephone Company. Franchise no. 322, dated 1914, created the Porto Rico Telephone Company by authorizing the installation and operation of telephone service in a good number of the island's towns, except those adjacent to Caguas and the islands of Vieques and Culebra, which remained under the control of Puerto Rico's commissioner of the interior.

The franchise was granted for twenty years, at the end of which Puerto Rico's insular government could acquire it at the appraised value. Should the insular government decide against the acquisition, the PRTC could renew the franchise automatically for a period of ten additional years. From then on, the Porto Rico Telephone Company became the first subsidiary of what would be International Telephone and Telegraph, founded six years later in 1920.¹¹

From 1920 to 1948, ITT developed as one of the first conglomerates in telecommunications with subsidiaries engaged in the operation of telephones in Spain, Britain, France, Germany, Italy, the Netherlands, Denmark, Hungary, Austria, Belgium, Czechoslovakia, Romania, Norway, Portugal, Switzerland, and Sweden. In Asia, operations were concentrated in Shanghai (China) and Japan. In Latin America, ITT had subsidiaries in Puerto Rico, Cuba, Mexico, Argentina, Brazil, Peru, Paraguay, Chile, Uruguay, Ecuador, and Bolivia.¹² By 1948, ITT had become an impressive international conglomerate with more than seventy companies engaged in manufacturing; research and development; and sales and management of telephone, radio, wireless, and cable systems in the United States, Europe, Asia, and South America.¹³

The Caribbean Battle

With the onset of World War II, the Western Hemisphere once again became the scene of hostilities among European powers. Control of telecommunications—telegraph, telephone, and radio services—was added to achieving supremacy in naval and land power in American geopolitical formulations. In 1938, as a result of political instability in Europe, the US Army designated the Panama Canal Zone as a strategic territory needed to effectively defend the Western Hemisphere. At that time, the armed forces were prepared only to defend the continental United States, the Panama Canal Zone, and, to a certain extent, the Hawaiian archipelago. In November 1938, President Roosevelt decided to make preparations to resist an attack in the Western Hemisphere, issuing an executive order aimed at the armed forces. According to historian Humberto García Muñiz:

> During 1938 and 1939, the role of Puerto Rico is evaluated and it is determined that new developments in aviation and the new role of the Panama Canal make it imperative to establish an Army base in Puerto Rico whose purpose would be: to defend Puerto Rico and the Virgin Islands against attacks by land, sea and air, ... to install and operate an Army base; [support] naval forces in control of the Caribbean Sea and adjacent waters; and support operations against ground targets.[14]

In 1941, the Caribbean Defense Command was created, divided into three geographical sectors: Puerto Rico, Panama, and Trinidad. Each sector was responsible for a specific territory, and their overall mission was to protect the entire Caribbean, including the Panama Canal Zone and the coast of Venezuela. While the Caribbean had acquired a new role in US geopolitical formulations, namely to serve as a bulwark to defend the Western Hemisphere, President Roosevelt based his decision on the economic importance of Latin America and the Caribbean. The production, refining, and transportation of raw materials such as petroleum (Curaçao, Aruba, Venezuela), bauxite (Dutch Guiana) and more than thirty other products considered essential for the war effort created attractive targets for German submarines, resulting in the destruction of 336 ships in the Caribbean along with 1,559,422 tons of cargo.[15]

The Fraternity was the name coined by Charles Higham in 1983 to identify a group of major US corporations during World War II that conducted financial transactions and trade with the Axis, through special permission of the Department of State. The General License under Section 3(a) of the Trading with the Enemy Act was authorized by President Roosevelt on December 7, 1941. These companies did not consider that the Second World War in Europe should in any way affect the business activities that propelled the economies of the countries in conflict: "[W]ithin the ideology of business as usual, bound by identical reactionary ideas, the members sought a common future in fascist domination, regardless of which world leader might further that ambition."[16]

According to Higham, these companies advocated a business philosophy that at the very least was considered unpatriotic in some circles. In 1940, the investment of companies in the Fraternity in Nazi Germany was estimated at $475 million, distributed as follows: Standard Oil of New Jersey, $120 million; General Motors, $35 million; Ford Motor Company, $17.5 million; and ITT, $30 million.[17]

After the attack on Pearl Harbor in 1941, ITT operations in the Axis countries were centralized and coordinated between offices in Spain and Switzerland. In Germany, Sosthenes Behn had become an important ally of Hermann Göring. As a token of appreciation, Göring managed to sell Baron von Schroder and Sosthenes Behn 28 percent of the shares of Focke-Wulf, a company engaged in the manufacture of the same German bombers that later attacked London and squadrons of Allied ships.

According to Higham, the partnership of ITT and Nazi Germany was so close that some leaders of the Nazi military intelligence establishment were among the company's shareholders. Higham says on this subject:

> Indeed, in the case of ITT, perhaps the most flagrant of the corporations in its outright dealings with the enemy, Hitler and his postmaster general, the venerable Wilhelm Ohnesorge, strove to impound the German end of the business. But even they were powerless in such a situation: the Gestapo leader of counterintelligence, Walter Schellenberg, was a prominent director and shareholder of ITT by arrangement with New York—and even Hitler dare not to cross the Gestapo.[18]

Between 1941 and 1945, ITT received US government approval to continue its business relationships with subsidiaries in Germany and Japan. During this same time period, various US government agencies conducted espionage activities against ITT in Latin America, intercepting calls and telegrams addressed to officers and friends of the company. However, ITT also worked with US intelligence, facilitating the infiltration of agents in its subsidiaries in Bolivia, Paraguay, and Argentina. Higham and Anthony Sampson contend that, from 1941 to 1945, ITT was considered a formal instrument of US intelligence and a "listening post" for communications between the Axis powers and the countries of Latin America and the Caribbean.[19] It is in this sense that Higham established the profile of ITT and Sosthenes Behn in different circles of power within the US establishment:

> In Washington, there were differing views of [Behn's] loyalties; the State Department had great doubts and watched him closely, the FCC thoroughly distrusted his foreign connections and stockholders, and the Justice Department was preparing anti-trust action to break up the company. Among many politicians and journalists, the unreliability of ITT was well known.[20]

ITT's activities in the context of war, and the intentions of the governor of Puerto Rico to nationalize the PRTC, were issues that Harold Ickes and Abe Fortas, secretary and assistant secretary, respectively, of the Department of the Interior, examined and discussed with Governor Tugwell and President Roosevelt. These officials, members of Roosevelt's "Brain Trust," were faced with the dilemma of buying a subsidiary of ITT in Puerto Rico, a move that conflicted with Sosthenes Behn's efforts to defeat or delay the proposed consolidation of the two telephone systems then in existence on the island.

In 1942, the same year the Puerto Rico Communications Authority was founded, the process to nationalize the Porto Rico Telephone Company began. President Roosevelt charged Nelson A. Rockefeller with the preparation of a study on communications systems in Latin America as part of his responsibilities as coordinator of Inter-American Affairs. Some time later, Roosevelt designated the issue of telecommunications as a priority in US geopolitical planning. On this, Higham states:

> On May 4, 1942, the President had sent a memorandum to Henry Wallace in his role as chairman of the Board of Economic Warfare, ordering him to ensure disconnection of all enemy nationals in the radio, telephone and telegraph fields. He had urged Wallace to eliminate all Axis control and influence in telecommunications in Latin America, acquire hemisphere interests of all Axis companies, insure loyalty in employees, and disrupt direct lines to the enemy. He had asked for a corporation to be set up to handle the financial aspects of the program with the assistance and advice of an advisory committee.[21]

President Roosevelt's executive order of 1942 that gave rise to the Hemisphere Communications Committee established as public policy the protection of the commercial hegemony of US interests in communication systems in the Western Hemisphere during the war. The directive took both a governmental and a corporate form. At the time of the Hemisphere Communications

Committee's creation, the US Commercial Company, the committee's commercial branch, was also founded. Meanwhile, Robert A. Gantt, ITT's vice president, was second in command at the US Commercial Company.[22] In 1943, a secret report prepared by the FCC for the Hemisphere Communications Committee identified subsidiaries of ITT in Mexico, Argentina, Uruguay, Chile, Colombia, Cuba, Ecuador, and Bolivia as well as in Puerto Rico. The report also confirmed economic activities and collaboration with the enemy through the operations of ITT in Latin America.

The Sale of the Porto Rico Telephone Company

With the appointment of Rexford Tugwell as governor of Puerto Rico in 1941, Puerto Rico's modernization project, begun in 1940 with the victory of the Popular Democratic Party, acquired a valuable ally. Tugwell entered public service with a background in economics from the Wharton School of Business at the University of Pennsylvania. During the early years of the New Deal, from 1933 to 1935, Tugwell was assistant secretary and undersecretary of the US Department of Agriculture. During this period, he was involved in drafting the Agricultural Economic Act and the National Industrial Recovery Act. He headed the Resettlement Administration and the legendary Farm Security Administration, and intervened in the Greenbelt Communities, a pilot project for the development of sustainable communities. He also directed the Planning Board of the State of New York, a position he held from 1938 to 1940.

In his memoirs, Luis Muñoz Marín described Tugwell's personality and political profile:

> He was an American radical ... in the sense of the person who delves into the roots of the specific and general problems he faces. This had nothing to do with Marxist radicalism. Certainly, as a professional economist, he had read and examined the works of Marx with intellectual honesty rather than dogmatism.... Tugwell had high quality administrative experience in one of the world's most complex governments.[23]

In Puerto Rico, Tugwell's and the Popular Democratic Party's economic planning for the island was focused on overcoming extreme poverty, landlordism, and high mortality rates among other ills associated with a form of capitalism that Tugwell had already faced during the New Deal. In his inaugural speech as governor, he expressed: "The time has passed in which absentee capitalists can extract outrageous percentages of income, using the needs of the people and their own power and their own monopolistic ways to force the acceptance of usurers' conditions."[24] Tugwell's ideas were based on a liberal political vision and represented a concerted attack on the oligopoly of the sugar industry and "special interests" in Puerto Rico.

Between 1914 and 1942, the telephony market in Puerto Rico was controlled by the Porto Rico Telephone Company and the island's government. Since 1914, the PRTC had had the island's only franchise for the commercial exploitation of the telephone. In 1942, the PRTC had approximately 1,800 customers.[25] Its only competitor was the insular government, which operated the telegraph system, already established under Spanish sovereignty in the late nineteenth century, and geographically limited phone service that used the telegraph infrastructure.

By 1942, the PRTC managed 90 percent of the telephone lines on the island. The remaining 10 percent were held by a public corporation, the newly created Puerto Rico Communications Authority (ACPR). Puerto Rico lagged considerably behind other nations in its telephone infrastructure. For example, in 1946, the thirty-six US states with a similar population density averaged two hundred telephones per thousand inhabitants. Puerto Rico, on the other hand, had ten telephones per thousand inhabitants. In a memorandum send to Julius Krug, then secretary of the Department of the Interior (the federal agency in charge of Puerto Rican affairs), ACPR general manager Rafael Delgado Márquez stated that ITT's service in Puerto Rico did not meet US standards of service for the 1940s. The memorandum titled *The Modernization of the Telephone System of Puerto Rico* states:

> The amount of telephone service in Puerto Rico compares unfavorably with every progressive country in the world. Thus, Puerto Rico has fewer telephones, on the average than Cuba, Argentina, Chile, Uruguay, Belgium, Hungary, Italy, Portugal, Spain or Japan. It has a mere fraction of the average number in such comparatively progressive countries as Denmark, France, Germany, Great Britain, Netherlands, Norway, Sweden, Switzerland and New Zealand. It has less than half of the world average. Perhaps Puerto Rico is so poor that it should be compared with places like Greece, Hungary and Rumania than with Massachusetts, New York or even Mississippi or France.[26]

From the standpoint of public services, government, and industry, ITT's major difficulty was that it had become an obstacle to the modernization of government communications. The company had outdated telephone equipment made in Belgium, and its telephone service was notoriously poor.[27]

The Puerto Rico Communications Authority was created by Act no. 212 (the ACPR Act) of May 12, 1942, as a public corporation responsible for the management of existing communication services in Puerto Rico. The law was an effort to organize, regulate, and promote government efficiency in the field of communications. The law states that the new organization was to

> develop and improve, own, operate, and manage any and all types of communications to and from the people of Puerto Rico and provide, as economically as possible, the increase of benefits and, in so doing, improve general welfare, trade and prosperity.[28]

The ACPR Act called for the relocation of the telegraph system, which until then had been in the Office of the Commissioner of the Interior, to the ACPR. One of the main objectives of the legislation was the modernization of the telephone service by consolidating the Porto Rico Telephone Company into the new authority. Among the provisions of the act was the nationalization of the Porto Rico Telephone Company by acquiring it legally through negotiation or expropriation. Pursuant to Section 20 of the franchise granted to the PRTC in 1914, as described above, the people of Puerto Rico, over the first twenty years of the franchise, could exercise their right to purchase and operate the assets of the franchise. In 1934, the island's government did not claim its right to purchase the PRTC, and the franchise was automatically renewed for ten additional years, so the next opportunity would be in 1944. If the right to purchase the franchise was not claimed, the people of Puerto Rico would have to wait until 1954.

The ACPR was established on August 21, 1942, and members of its first board of directors were Benjamín Ortiz, Rafael R. Ramírez, Manuel Seoane, Joseph R. Quiñones, and Gaspar Fernández. On September 4, the board was constituted and a general manager, a controller, and a secretary-general counsel were appointed. Rafael Delgado Márquez, an engineer, was appointed the ACPR's first general manager.

In October 1942, the government of Puerto Rico notified the PRTC of its interest in acquiring the properties of the telephone company. The ACPR established an Appraisal Board. It was composed of a representative of the insular government appointed by the governor, a PRTC representative, and a third member appointed by the representatives of the insular government and the PRTC. In April 1944, the Board of Appraisal submitted a report. The board determined that the PRTC's value was $6,288,206. The government had nine months to complete the transaction, which required the approval

Telephone operator, circa 1940 (private collection of Luis Rosario Albert)

of a law and allocation of funds by both the legislature and the governor of Puerto Rico.

Following the disclosure of the report by the Board of Appraisals, public controversy began. The appraisal was criticized in the press for overpricing the PRTC's assets. While the transaction was approved by the Senate, then presided over by Luis Muñoz Marín, the House of Representatives did not consider it and instead approved a bill postponing the acquisition of the PRTC in order to further investigate the appraisal. The House created a special commission to carry out this investigation. However, this did not produce any results, and the board of directors then authorized the general manager of the ACPR to hire one or more lawyers to assist in the legal proceedings related to the purchase of the PRTC.[29]

Negotiations between ITT and Puerto Rico's insular government continued from 1942 to 1948. This negotiation period was divided into two stages. The first took place between 1942 and 1945, and the second between 1946 and 1948. During the first stage, the ACPR was represented by Rafael Delgado Márquez, Benjamin Ortiz (the ACPR's chairman of the board), and American lawyer James E. Curry, the ACPR's counsel. ITT was represented by Sosthenes Behn, José D. Domínguez (vice president of operations of the PRTC), and Robert A. Gantt (vice president of ITT and director of the US Commercial Company).

To Muñoz Marín and Tugwell, the Puerto Rico Communications Authority was in a better position than the PRTC to modernize the island's telephone service.[30] Since its inception, the ACPR had shown the will to complete this task. The administrative and technological achievements of the ACPR are described as:

> publishing a telephone directory, creating an "information service," conducting a study on the automation of telephone centers, forming a "special information service" for elections in Puerto Rico, installing long-distance phone service between San Juan and Ponce, and implementing the executive order of January 1, 1944, in which the governor, Rexford Tugwell, entrusted the Puerto Rico Communications Authority to take over the telephone service of all government agencies and departments of the insular government that were under the Porto Rico Telephone Company. By March of that same year, the ACPR had taken over the administration of the government lines, which represented annual savings of about $10,000 in the government's telephone costs.[31]

However, this collaboration also showed the beginnings of a serious conflict regarding the best and most effective use of public funds in order to modernize the telephone service. Muñoz Marín considered that the problems caused by the German submarine blockade in the Caribbean, poverty, the unequal distribution of wealth on the island, and other matters of a socioeconomic nature warranted that the public funds being considered for the purchase of the PRTC be used for these other purposes.

According to documentation, beginning in April 1943 Sosthenes Behn attempted to derail the process to nationalize the PRTC[32] by lobbying directly to President Roosevelt, Governor Tugwell, and Muñoz Marín. With these actions, Behn was trying to prevent the purchase of the PRTC or, at best, to postpone it until after the end of the war. The main arguments outlined by Behn were as follows:

(1) The purchase of the PRTC would stimulate the nationalization of ITT's subsidiaries in Latin America.
(2) The nationalization of telephone companies would weaken trade ties with the United States, and, as a result, Latin American countries would increase their reliance on European countries.
(3) The purchase would delay the integration of the telephone system developed by ITT in Latin America.
(4) While World War II was continuing, the purchase of the PRTC would adversely affect the efficiency and security of telephone communications in a strategic area.

The first conversation between Behn and Tugwell on the purchase of the PRTC occurred during a telephone call initiated by Behn on July 6, 1943. By then, the Public Service Commission of Puerto Rico had authorized the insular government to establish a Board of Appraisal, and the first administrative steps had been taken toward the purchase of the PRTC. Behn's phone call was the first obstacle to the transaction. In his diary, Tugwell described Behn as a "high powered smoothie." In that conversation, Behn informed Tugwell that the navy and the US military in general did not favor the sale of a subsidiary of ITT. Also, he reported on a three-hour meeting between Muñoz Marín and himself in which the former had spoken out against the purchase of the PRTC. According to Behn, Muñoz Marín acknowledged that it would be very difficult to convince Governor Tugwell to change his policy on the PRTC.[33] On an earlier occasion, Behn also told Muñoz Marín of his intention to participate in an important commission created by President Roosevelt, made up of Puerto Ricans and Americans, to revise the Organic Act of Puerto Rico. This commission was the result of investigations by the Bell Committee, a committee chaired by US representative Jasper C. Bell that was critical of Tugwell's role as governor of Puerto Rico. At the time, Muñoz Marín was trying to secure an allocation of $300 million as part of a rehabilitation plan for Puerto Rico. According to Tugwell, Muñoz Marín thought that Behn's presence would be beneficial. If not successful, he would accuse the political opposition and the federal government of not supporting the development of Puerto Rico. Tugwell understood that an agreement was brewing between Muñoz Marín and Behn.

Four days later, Tugwell and Muñoz Marín discussed Behn's inclusion in the PRTC negotiations. Tugwell and Benjamín Ortiz, chairman of the board of the ACPR, interpreted the agreement between Behn and Muñoz Marín as, at the least, showing a lack of loyalty to the governor. Tugwell said:

> We both pointed out, also, the impossibility of explaining to the public a reversal of policy. Muñoz admitted that he had, in effect, proposed a deal to Behn—that he should support a rehabilitation plan for Puerto Rico in return for keeping the phone company. I denounced such a deal in plain language. I warned Muñoz that it was impossible to get anything that way, that Behn had no influence worth any such sacrifice, that it would be found that the interests of the public had been sold out for nothing. He said he would deal with the devil for the good of the people and that the President had lost his leadership and deals would not have to be made with the enemy. I said that such a Jesuitical procedure was an outrageous betrayal of me, of the President and of all those who had worked so hard to improve the Puerto Rican situation, and that I would not only not be party to

it but that if he persisted I would denounce him publicly. That might not do any good but would keep him from betraying all of his followers. He agreed from the beginning that the processes should go on.³⁴

Tugwell left for Washington after the meeting. At the time, Harold Ickes and Abe Fortas knew of Sosthenes Behn's efforts to stop the sale of the PRTC and the differences that existed between Tugwell and Muñoz Marín. As Tugwell suspected, Sosthenes Behn had notified Ickes and Fortas that Tugwell would make compromising expressions upon his arrival in Washington. On this, Tugwell says:

Someone had called him to warn him that I was about to make "a damaging statement which ought to be stopped." That looked as though Muñoz had gone to Behn again and told him of my threat to make their deal "public." And Behn was now working around Washington.³⁵

According to Tugwell, the agreement was the result of the political pressure exerted on Muñoz Marín by the Bell Committee. On this, Tugwell says:

So I told him [Ickes] the whole story, as I had told Fortas. He, and the others who hear it, register amazement at the lack of agreement, on an important issue, between Muñoz Marín and me; but they get the point when I explain it was the result of a shrewd political mind, of the Bell Committee carryings on. If the administration has too little control, Muñoz Marín must argue, he must have other means of support. It is natural that he should turn to people like Behn and his kind who have always been in American Life.³⁶

After the briefing, Ickes decided to inform President Roosevelt about what was happening between Behn and Muñoz Marín and the possible political consequences of the Bell Committee. One result of this effort was the vote of confidence that President Roosevelt gave Tugwell. According to Tugwell's diary, that night he dined with Paul Porter, who presided over the FCC. Despite Sosthenes Behn's failure in his efforts to stop the sale of PRTC, he had chosen to bring the matter directly to President Roosevelt's attention. However, through the intervention of Ickes, Tugwell had already informed him.

During our research at Puerto Rico's General Archives, we discovered revealing correspondence between President Roosevelt and Governor Tugwell. It confirmed Behn's intention to stop the process of nationalizing the PRTC through a petition to the US executive branch. On February 11, 1944, Edwin M. Watson, an assistant to President Roosevelt, addressed a memorandum to the president reminding him that in July 1943, Colonel Behn had met with President Roosevelt in order to discuss government plans to acquire the Porto Rico Telephone Company.

In a conversation with Roosevelt's assistant, Sosthenes Behn said: "The President indicated that he would speak to Governor Tugwell and to Marin."[37] However, Behn learned from Muñoz Marín that he had had no communication with the president about plans to nationalize the PRTC. Given the priority of war-related issues, Roosevelt's lack of interest in this topic might be understandable. According to Behn, Muñoz Marín had indicated

> that if such indication was forthcoming, the project of law to take over the system which is likely to pass in April, could be avoided. An indication to Governor Tugwell to delay action for at least the duration should not cause any political difficulty in Puerto Rica [sic], and I believe that the precedent should be avoided because of the consequence to American communication systems in South America.[38]

The memo confirmed Sosthenes Behn's plan to have Roosevelt himself apply his executive intervention to halt the plans to acquire a subsidiary of ITT in Puerto Rico, or, at best, to postpone them until after the war. In the words of Sosthenes Behn:

> My fear [was] that it would establish a precedent as a result of which I expected Cuba, as well as Argentina and other South American Republics would want to acquire a telephone system. If those governments did acquire these systems now operated by Americans, there is the likelihood of German, Swedish and other infiltration, both from the point of view of the adoption of their technique and use of their equipment, but also the employment of aliens in the communication system.[39]

On February 14, 1944, President Roosevelt wrote a note to Governor Tugwell asking for his opinion as to Sosthenes Behn's allegations contained in Watson's memorandum. In his statement, Roosevelt said: "Dear Rex: I know nothing about this except what Colonel Behn told me. What is your slant? With all good wishes, as ever yours. FDR."[40] On March 2, Governor Tugwell replied to President Roosevelt, informing him of what he hoped to achieve with the purchase of the PRTC and of the political and economic interests of Behn. The latter went against the welfare of the people of Puerto Rico. From the below statement by Tugwell, Behn was obstructing the purchase of the PRTC, although offering other motives for doing so:

The decision to exercise the option was prompted, I believe, by the very unsatisfactory nature of the present telephone service. I do not see why the mere fact of our acquisition should encourage other Governments to do likewise unless they have reasons of their own for doing so, if they have such reasons they would not, it seems to me, need the Puerto Rican precedent.... I should like to suggest that the fears voiced by Col. Behn are in reality camouflage for his real concern which is to postpone the acquisition in the hope of a change in insular government administration and a concomitant reversal of policy with regard to the acquisition.[41]

According to Behn, by 1944, the attempt to nationalize the PRTC did not serve US geopolitical interests; instead, it would facilitate the infiltration of the "enemy" in those other countries that followed suit in nationalizing their telecommunications industries. The impact of the purchase of the Porto Rico Telephone Company was a threat to the commercial hegemony of ITT in Latin America and the Caribbean. Also, Sosthenes Behn and ITT were facing another powerful force in international politics: nationalism. The ITT empire faced major economic threats from regimes politically linked to Colonel Behn and ITT. General Juan Perón in Argentina and Francisco Franco in Spain intended to nationalize the phone companies in their countries.[42]

In Puerto Rico's political scenario, this first stage of negotiations to nationalize the PRTC did not achieve the desired results. Between mid-1945 and 1948, under Act no. 301 of 1945, the legislature of Puerto Rico approved legislation to continue the modernization of public telecommunications. The act authorized and in fact ordered the ACPR and the commissioner of the interior to begin negotiations, contracts, or agreements with the Porto Rico Telephone Company, to take any other action believed necessary for the use of the lines of the Porto Rico Telephone Company, and to make all other interconnections with the Puerto Rico Communications Authority telephone system, under the provisions of the original franchise of 1914.

The negotiations were in the hands of Rafael Delgado Márquez and the ACPR's legal counsel, James Curry, in a scenario of power tempered by public controversy, a vigorous legislation that saw a forced expropriation of the PRTC, an aggressive expansion plan on the part of the ACPR, and the filing of a lawsuit by the PRTC in the District Court of the United States.

Faced with the delay in its purchase of the PRTC, the island's government reaffirmed its strategy—its willingness to acquire the company's assets and property by means of negotiation or expropriation.[43] The government focused its attention on an issue of vital importance to ITT: the profits of the PRTC. Act no. 301 conferred on the ACPR the power to impose a 2 percent tax on telegraph or telephone posts generated by the PRTC. The lawsuit against the ACPR and the island's government was a reaction to progress in the modernization of Puerto Rico's telephone infrastructure, the expansion of the ACPR's San Juan–Ponce line, and the new 2 percent tax levied on the PRTC.

In his last message to the Puerto Rican legislature in 1946 and after unsuccessful attempts to acquire the Porto Rico Telephone Company, Governor Tugwell said:

> According to the policy laid down by the Legislature and supported by the people in the last election, we continue our efforts to acquire the properties of the Telephone Company. They should be acquired at a reasonable price, by means of negotiation or expropriation if necessary. If negotiations fail, we should at least make possible our pattern of public ownership.[44]

Although the island government had agreed to fund the purchase of the PRTC through a bond issue of $5 million, there was still a deficit that Governor Tugwell tried to resolve through an additional allocation of public funds. According to Muñoz Marín, the allocation of public funds would be the main point of difference between the two men. Muñoz Marín agreed with the bond financing but did not support the use of public funds to complete the transaction. Tugwell conditioned the signing of several bills on the legislature's approval of the million and a half dollars that were needed for the purchase of the PRTC.[45] This agreement did not materialize due to differences between Tugwell and the Puerto Rican legislature.

The Sale of the Puerto Rico Communications Authority

The death of President Roosevelt on April 12, 1945, Harry Truman's inauguration as US president, the end of the Second World War, and the Popular Democratic Party's claim for a greater degree of self-government in Puerto Rico precipitated a series of changes in the political relationship between the United States and Puerto Rico, still a colonial territory. One was the appointment on July 26, 1946, of Jesús T. Piñero, then resident commissioner of Puerto Rico in the US Congress, as governor. Piñero was the island's last governor by presidential appointment. Governor Piñero, landowner, forerunner of the radio in Puerto Rico, and friend of Muñoz Marín, did not support the stance of his predecessor regarding the purchase of ITT.

It should be mentioned that on February 16, 1946, Major General Harry C. Ingles, chief of the US Signal Corps, representing President Truman, gave

Sosthenes Behn the Medal of Merit for services rendered during World War II.[46] However, a Puerto Rico Communications Authority memorandum dated June 28, 1946, referred to Sosthenes Behn and the activities of ITT as a matter of concern for the US government. The report states:

> The International Telephone & Telegraph Corporation is incorporated in New Jersey. Sosthenes Behn, its President, is, we presume, an American citizen. The Corporation is *legally* an American concern. But in spirit and in fact it is foreign. Its telephone systems are located in places where American standards are little known by those in control. Its operations in Puerto Rico are not, in our opinion, conducted by American standards.[47]

After Piñero's swearing in in September 1946, a dialogue began between the PRTC and the island's government in order to sell the assets of the Puerto Rico Communications Authority to the Porto Rico Telephone Company. One of the earliest references to this transaction was dated October 31, 1946. In it, José D. Domínguez, vice president of operations for the PRTC (and one of the negotiators for ITT during the first stage of talks to nationalize the PRTC), told Governor Piñero the disposition of the PRTC to acquire the ACPR telephone system, pending a change in government policy. Domínguez said:

> Similarly, we confirm our willingness to purchase the telephone system operated by the Puerto Rico Communications Authority as a part of the Porto Rico Telephone Company system in the event that the policy of the Government should not be to acquire the properties of the Porto Rico Telephone Company.[48]

The change in government policy was a controversial issue. The island's government was proposing to sell the authority's telephone system to the same company that it had been trying to acquire since 1942. To the surprise of many, including Rexford Tugwell and Harold Ickes, there had been a "suspect" public policy shift in the insular government of Puerto Rico. This new situation explains what cannot be interpreted as a coincidence: the February 1947 publication in *Harper's*, a magazine with national circulation in the United States, of an article titled "Puerto Rico's Bootstraps" signed by Rexford G. and Grace F. Tugwell.

In it, Tugwell discusses several topics based on his experiences as an administrator in Puerto Rico, including the country's main problems, the contributions of a group of relatives and friends, and the political future of the island. At that time, Tugwell was aware of the change in the government's policy that now favored the sale of the ACPR to ITT, and he was trying to stop it. He used the article in *Harper's* to pressure Muñoz Marín to desist from these initiatives. The article revealed the agreement between Behn and Muñoz Marín in 1943 describing the proposed sale of the ACPR to the PRTC, which surely infuriated Muñoz Marín. In the article, Tugwell affirmed the following:

> In the telephone matter there occurred another kind of misfortune. Just as matters were coming to a head in 1944, Munoz conceived the idea that Mr. Dewey was going to become President, and that if he did Puerto Rico had better have some friends among the inner circle of business men who controlled the Republican Party. Mr. Sosthenes Behn could be thought to be influential in this group. And it was in pursuit of some such alliance that Muñoz altered his own view of the expediency of the expropriation.... Mr. Dewey might win over Roosevelt and so they went ahead, but in rather crippled fashion, for when Munoz changes his mind it appears that Puerto Rico had adopted a new policy. His hold on his people's mind is that strong.[49]

The compromising announcement that Harold Ickes and Abe Fortas thought Tugwell would make in the summer of 1943 did not occur until February 1947. On February 4, 1947, *El Mundo*, a general circulation newspaper in Puerto Rico, published a translation of the *Harper's* article on its front page. The sale of the ACPR was becoming a politically sensitive issue for Governor Piñero and Luis Muñoz Marín.

On March 21, 1947, a little over a year into Piñero's administration, Samuel R. Quiñones, vice president of the Senate, introduced legislation to authorize the governor of Puerto Rico to sell all assets of the Puerto Rico Communications Authority to the Porto Rico Telephone Company. The proceeds of the sale would be used to pay the outstanding debts and obligations related to the transaction, and the surplus, after payment of any debt, would be at the discretion of Governor Piñero "to be spent on slum clearing projects."[50] Telegraph service was transferred to the island's Department of the Interior. This action would "dissolve and liquidate the Puerto Rico Communications Authority."[51]

This legislation caused another public controversy and was rejected by the Communications Workers Union of Puerto Rico, the Puerto Rican Independence Party, and a while later by Luis Muñoz Marín, then candidate for governor. Once negotiations began between Governor Piñero, Sosthenes Behn, and Roberto Sánchez Vilella, special assistant to the president of the Senate, Behn wrote to Piñero on February 26, 1947, expressing that the PRTC should be able to acquire all the properties of the ACPR, including the telegraph. Sánchez Vilella stated that the latest plan "submitted by the Telephone Company is, overall, a substantial improvement over the Five Year program of August 6, 1946, and October 17, 1946, filed by the Company."52 Sánchez Vilella expressed Muñoz Marín's position regarding the controversy surrounding the possible sale of ACPR assets to the PRTC.53

After the Tugwells' article was published in *El Mundo* and once legislation was filed in the Senate for the sale of the ACPR's telephone system to the PRTC, the Communications Workers Union of Puerto Rico, chaired by Antonio Quiñones Bird, began a campaign against the liquidation of the ACPR. In a letter addressed to the new secretary of the interior on March 27, 1947, the union president wrote:

> One of our dailies says the Governor's message is the result of negotiations with the directors of ITT that began after the Republican victory this past fall. The project would cost the government more than $200,000 a year in lost revenue, and we estimate it would cost phone subscribers about $800,000 a year to pay higher rates.[54]

That same day, Luis Muñoz Marín admitted in a radio message the important role that Tugwell played in the purchase of the PRTC. In a "settling of scores" on Tugwell's governorship, Muñoz Marín said:

> The initiative for the purchase of the Telephone Company was Governor Tugwell's and the case was presented to the Legislature in a manner that indicated that these public service properties could be acquired by the Communications Authority without disbursement from the Treasury, based on the issuance of bonds secured by the operation of the property itself.[55]

In his message, Muñoz Marín defended the use of available public funds for the country's other needs. He argued that, because the PRTC did not agree on a government investment plan and improvements to the telephone service, the government should retain the right to the phone company's properties.[56] Governor Piñero, who did not share Tugwell's view on the need to nationalize the PRTC, had reached an agreement with Muñoz Marín. According to the press release:

> We agreed ... that the money allocated—a million and a half dollars—could play a much more effective and creative role in our production problems, dedicated to the work of other public corporations, such as the Housing Authority, the Industrial and Agricultural Development Bank, the Aqueducts Service or education, health and roads.[57]

President Roosevelt calls Luis Muñoz Marín the "Prime Minister of Puerto Rico" during a celebration in Hyde Park, August 1941. (Archivo Fundación Luis Muñoz Marín)

Muñoz Marín's statements regarding the sale of the ACPR endorsed the efforts of Governor Piñero's administration, which continued negotiations with Sosthenes Behn and ITT's vice president, Wolcott Pitkin.[58] On January 29, 1948, Pitkin wrote a memorandum to Governor Piñero incorporating modifications to the agreement already reached between ITT and the island government. The document proposed eliminating the 2 percent tax of 1945, establishing a charge on the proceeds of the PRTC, and empowering the legislature to determine rates to subscribers. In exchange, ITT was to establish a factory for manufacturing telephones in Puerto Rico.[59]

On April 28, 1948, the ACPR, through legal counsel James Curry, reaffirmed its interest in acquiring the PRTC from ITT.[60] This offer did not get the expected result. As for the process of nationalizing the PRTC, between 1946 and 1948, political pressure from ACPR union workers and pressure brought to bear by Tugwell through the publication of his article in *El Mundo* formed a negative public opinion of the legislation intended to abolish the ACPR.[61] Given the pressures in the political and labor environments, Governor Piñero's administration decided against selling the ACPR and returned to the original plan of acquiring the PRTC. *El Mundo* reviewed the news, stating the terms of the proposal submitted by Rafael Delgado Márquez and expressions of support from workers at Ponce's telegraph office:

> The ACPR's president, John Gesualdo, and his secretary, Mrs. Josephine Q. Ducos, held a meeting as soon as they were informed on this subject, and unanimously agreed to request of the President of the Senate, Luis Muñoz Marín, the prompt acquisition of the Porto Rico Telephone Company's properties. They claim that "this acquisition would greatly benefit the people of Puerto Rico, and help justify the purpose for which the Communications Authority was created."[62]

The offer did not prosper. From then, and up to Luis Muñoz Marín's swearing in in January 1949 as the first governor elected by Puerto Ricans, the original project to nationalize the Porto Rico Telephone Company was halted. Despite the difficulties and the outcome of the process, ITT continued its technological development and geographic expansion.

On September 22, 1948, Governor Piñero and the Cuban president, Dr. Ramón Grau San Martín, inaugurated direct radiotelephone service between Puerto Rico and Cuba, operated by the Radio Corporation of Porto Rico, the Radio Corporation of Cuba, and the Cuban Telephone Company. The three companies were ITT subsidiaries.

Conclusions

The Porto Rico Telephone Company was the first subsidiary of International Telephone and Telegraph, a powerful communications conglomerate. The field of public communications, which included the telegraph, telephone, and radio, played an important role during the Second World War as a means of security in the region and was a vehicle for modernizing a miserably poor Puerto Rico. The creation of the Puerto Rico Communications Authority in 1942 and the proposal to nationalize the PRTC were part of a project that attempted to reform the colonial status and modernize the economy of Puerto Rico during World War II. The acquisition of the PRTC was meant to reject the business model represented by the PRTC's experience since 1914; instead, the consolidation of the PRTC with the young Puerto Rico Communications Authority would result in a state monopoly market structure. The Porto Rico Telephone Company in the end managed to stay in business in Puerto Rico, and the Puerto Rico Communications Authority continued to pursue its development plan to modernize and expand its telephone system, and launched Puerto Rico's first public radio station, WIPR Radio, in 1949.

President Roosevelt's geopolitical considerations during the Second World War; the economic interests and hegemony of ITT in international markets in Europe, Asia, and Latin America; and the political and managerial differences between Rexford G. Tugwell, Luis Muñoz Marín, and Jesús T. Piñero regarding how best to integrate the phone system, managed to derail an important component of the modernization of public communications in Puerto Rico. It wasn't until 1974, when the Porto Rico Telephone Company, known then as the Puerto Rico Telephone Company, was finally acquired by the government of the Commonwealth of Puerto Rico, only to be later privatized in 1998.

Notes

I want to express my gratitude to Teresita Santini for translating the original version. While researching this paper I had the opportunity to discuss several of my findings with Dr. Jorge Rodríguez Beruff, who was kindly available for multiple queries and encouraged me to continue with the investigation. José Roberto Martínez, Esq., and Julio Quirós, director and head of archives, respectively, at the Luis Muñoz Marín Foundation, provided access to documents and people who turned out to be key during the investigation. Also, Ángel Martín, Esq., a former aide to Governor Rexford G. Tugwell, shared his comments after reading a preliminary draft. All of them helped clarify a topic that had barely been investigated in the framework of media policies in Puerto Rico with interesting ramifications in social, economic, and political life.

1. Anthony Sampson, *The Sovereign State of ITT* (New York: Stein and Day, 1973), p. 21.

2. Luis Enrique Otero Carvajal, "El teléfono, el nacimiento de un nuevo medio de comunicación 1877–1936," in *Las comunicaciones en la construcción del estado contemporáneo en España, 1700–1936*, ed. Ángel Bahamonde Magro, Gaspar Martínez Lorente, and Luis Enrique Otero Carvajal (Madrid: Ministry of Public Works, Transportation, and Environment, 1993).

3. According to Sampson, the abbreviation for International Telephone and Telegraph was IT&T until the 1950s, when the ampersand was removed. Sampson, *The Sovereign State of ITT*, p. 21.

4. Ibid.

5. Charles Higham, *Trading with the Enemy: The Nazi-American Money Plot, 1933–1949* (New York: Barnes and Noble, 1995), p. xvi.

6. Luis Muñoz Marín, "Discurso en el banquete en que Puerto Rico le rindió un homenaje," Archivo Fundación Luis Muñoz Marín (hereafter AFLMM), March 23, 1968, p. 10.

7. Luis Muñoz Marín, "La compra de la Compañía Telefónica de Puerto Rico," Luis Muñoz Marín Collection, AFLMM, radio message, March 27, 1947, Series 15, Box 1, Folder 2.

8. Eric Williams, *From Columbus to Castro: The History of the Caribbean, 1492–1969* (New York: Vintage Books, 1970), p. 430.

9. For example, in 1906, the Behn brothers promoted the construction of the Condado, a residential area for wealthy families, and the Dos Hermanos Bridge. See also Sampson, *The Sovereign State of ITT*, pp. 22–23; and Higham, *Trading with the Enemy*, pp. 93–94.

10. "Memorandum: Execution of an Option to Buy the Business and Properties of the Puerto Rico Telephone Company," Fund: Office of the Governor, Rexford G. Tugwell's period, vol. 1: boxes 426, 464; vol. 2: boxes 2039, 2049, Archivo General de Puerto Rico (hereafter AGPR), San Juan, March 26, 1943, pp. 1–6. In 1912, Sosthenes Behn served as a delegate from Puerto Rico at the Republican National Convention in the United States. Lawrence Kestenbaum, "The Political Graveyard," at www.politicalgraveyard.com, accessed February 2, 2007. In 1908, the Behn brothers expanded to Cuba with the establishment of the Cuban Telephone Company (CTC), presided over by Hernand Behn. Carmen Cabrera, "La Cuban Telephone Company: viejos métodos para una nueva era," Sixth International Conference of the Association of Iberian and Latin American Studies of Australasia (AILASA), Flinders University, Adelaide, 2004.

11. Ismael Rodríguez Bou, *Caminos del Aire* (San Juan: Higher Education Council, University of Puerto Rico, 1951), p. 31.

12. Compiled by the author. See Sampson, *The Sovereign State of ITT*, pp. 33–39; Higham, *Trading with the Enemy*, pp. 99, 103–104; and *International Review of the International Telephone & Telegraph Corporation* 4, no. 1 (1948).

13. According to Sampson, ITT was "one of the first multinational corporations, in the modern sense, establishing factories and management all over the world. But from its foundation in 1920, it was a maverick company." Sampson, *The Sovereign State of ITT*, p. 22.

14. Humberto García Muñiz, *La estrategia de Estados Unidos y la militarización del Caribe* (Río Piedras, PR: Instituto de Estudios del Caribe, University of Puerto Rico, 1988), p. 46.

15. As part of the implementation of the new US defense plans, construction began in Puerto Rico of Borinquen (Ramey) Air Field and the naval base in Ceiba (Roosevelt Roads), two important components for the defense of the Panama Canal Zone and the east coast of the United States. Garcia Muñiz, *La estrategia de Estados Unidos*, pp. 46–65.

16. Higham, *Trading with the Enemy*, p. xiv.

17. Ibid., p. xvi.

18. After the outbreak of hostilities in Europe, Germany's minister of finance and the German National Bank promised executives in US companies that, after Hitler's victory, their properties would not be affected or expropriated. Ibid., pp. xiv–xvi.

19. Sampson, *The Sovereign State of ITT*, pp. 34–42.

20. Ibid., p. 39.

21. Higham, *Trading with the Enemy*, p. 101.

22. Ibid.

23. Luis Muñoz Marín, *Memorias, 1940–1952* (San Juan: Fundación Luis Muñoz Marín, 2003), p. 77.

24. Rexford G. Tugwell, "Message to the Legislature of Puerto Rico," September 21, 1941, AFLMM, p. 15.

25. Ramón Morales Cortés, "Telecommunications in Puerto Rico," at http://www.vii.org/papers/puer.htm, accessed February 12, 2007.

26. Rafael Delgado Márquez, "The Modernization of the Telephone System of Puerto Rico," Fund: Office of the Governor, Rexford G. Tugwell's period, AGPR, San Juan, June 28, 1946, pp.1–20. See also James E. Curry Collection, Box 16, pp. 1–20. This collection was examined in May 2014.

27. Ibid., pp. 1–5.

28. Laws of Puerto Rico Annotated, Puerto Rico Communications Authority Act, AFLMM, p. 117.

29. The ACPR also appointed a new committee to reassess the first appraisal recommended by the Board of Appraisal. By the end of December 1944, this committee presented its recommendations.

30. Within the framework of the economic regime imposed on Puerto Rico during the Second World War, and months after founding the ACPR, Tugwell considered abolishing the institution. Tugwell said: "However, after further consideration, I decided to recommend, for my part, that the Authority be abolished and its powers and duties be transferred to the Water Resources Authority. This is based on administrative economies that should be made. The Water Resources Authority has the personnel to meet the maintenance and repair of transmission lines, has an organization to keep in touch with consumers; it has, in fact, a communications system of its own. It seems economical to make this change immediately. If we choose the option of the telephone there will be no break in service." Rexford G. Tugwell, "Message to the Legislature of Puerto Rico," October 27, 1942, AFLMM, p. 28.

31. Luis Rosario Albert, "Telecomunicaciones con un propósito," *Centro Journal* (Hunter College) 18, no. 2 (2006): 190–213.

32. Rexford G. Tugwell, unpublished diary, July 6–10, 1943, FDR Library, Tugwell Papers.

33. Ibid.

34. Ibid.

35. Ibid.

36. Ibid.

37. Edwin M. Watson, "Memorandum for the President," White House Correspondence, Fund: Office of the Governor, Rexford G. Tugwell's period, AGPR, San Juan, February 11, 1944, p. 1.

38. Ibid.

39. Ibid.

40. Franklin Delano Roosevelt, "Letter to Governor Rexford G. Tugwell," Fund: Office of the Governor, Rexford G. Tugwell's period, AGPR, San Juan, February 14, 1944, p. 1.

41. Ibid.

42. In Spain, after Franco's military victory, Sosthenes Behn managed to negotiate ITT's continued administration of the country's telephone company until 1945. Luis Enrique Otero Carvajal, "Las telecomunicaciones en la España contemporánea, 1855–2000," *Cuadernos de Historia Contemporánea* 29 (2007): 128–133. In 1946 in Argentina, Perón's government nationalized the telephone system. Sampson, *The Sovereign State of ITT*, p. 49. This argument would later be invoked by Behn during the Puerto Rico insular government's attempt to nationalize the Puerto Rico Telephone Company from 1942 to 1945.

43. For example, Delgado Márquez put it this way in 1945: "The insistence of the Communications Authority to acquire the [Porto Rico] Telephone Company and Puerto Rico's government policy of centralizing, in the hands of the state, the telecommunications services, places Puerto Rico within the general tendency of the civilized world today, to put in the hands of state or government, the control, operation, and maintenance of all telecommunications services of the nation." Rosario Albert, "Telecomunicaciones con un propósito," p. 195.

44. Rexford G. Tugwell, "Message to the Legislature of Puerto Rico, Governor of Puerto Rico," AFLMM, February 12, 1946, p. 103.

45. Luis Muñoz Marín, "La compra de la Compañía Telefónica de Puerto Rico," AFLMM, March 27, 1947, Series 15, Box 1, Folder 2.

46. Higham, *Trading with the Enemy*, p. 115.

47. Rafael Delgado Márquez, "The Modernization of the Telephone System of Puerto Rico", pp. 3–10.

48. In the same communication, Domínguez also proposed the sale of the PRTC to the insular government for $6,288,206, the value agreed to in 1943 by the first Board of Appraisals. José D. Domínguez, "Letter to Hon. Jesús T. Piñero," Fund: Office of the Governor, Jesús T. Piñero's period, vol. 1, boxes 426, 464, 829, 855; vol. 2, boxes 2039, 2049, AGPR, San Juan, October 31, 1946.

49. Rexford G. Tugwell and Grace F. Tugwell, "Puerto Rico's Bootstraps," *Harper's*, February 1947, pp. 160–169. Colección *El Mundo*, University of Puerto Rico, San Juan, February 4, 1947.

50. Rosario Albert, "Telecomunicaciones con un propósito," p. 200.

51. Ibid.

52. Roberto Sánchez Vilella, "Carta al Hon. Jesús T. Piñero," Fund: Office of the Governor, Jesús T. Piñero's period, AGPR, San Juan, February 26, 1947, p. 1.

53. It is noteworthy that Sánchez Vilella proposed to Governor Piñero not only hiring specialized lawyers and technicians for the structuring of the sale of the ACPR but also drafting a new franchise in favor of the PRTC. Sánchez Vilella said: "You could consider using the services of Mr. Fortas in this respect." Sánchez Vilella, "Carta al Hon. Jesús T. Piñero," p. 2.

54. The negotiation referred to by the union is the 1943 agreement between Muñoz Marín and Behn that Tugwell revealed in his *Harper's* article. See Communications Workers Union of Puerto Rico, "Carta al Honorable Secretario del Interior," Fund: Office of the Governor, Jesús T. Piñero's period, AGPR, San Juan, March 27, 1947, pp. 1–3.

55. Muñoz Marín, "La compra de la Compañía Telefónica de Puerto Rico," p. 335.

56. Sánchez Vilella, "Carta al Hon. Jesús T. Piñero," p. 1.

57. Muñoz Marín, "La compra de la Compañía Telefónica de Puerto Rico."

58. Sosthenes Behn, "Letter to Hon. Jesús T. Piñero, Governor of Puerto Rico," Fund: Office of the Governor, Jesús T. Piñero's period, AGPR, San Juan, April 9, 1947.

59. Wolcott Pitkin, "Letter to Hon. Jesús T. Piñero, Governor of Puerto Rico," Fund: Office of the Governor, Jesús T. Piñero's period, AGPR, San Juan, January 29, 1948, pp. 1–2.

60. James E. Curry, "Carta a la International Telephone and Telegraph Corporation," Puerto Rico Communications Authority Fund, Fund: Office of the Governor, Jesús T. Piñero Series, AGPR, San Juan, April 28, 1948, pp. 1–2.

61. Communications Workers Union of Puerto Rico, "Carta al Honorable Secretario del Interior," pp. 1–3; Communications Workers Union of Puerto Rico, "Mensaje especial a los miembros de la legislatura," March 29, 1947, pp. 1–2; Communications Workers Union of Puerto Rico, "Mensaje especial a los legisladores," James E. Curry Collection, AGPR, San Juan, March 31, 1947, Box 16, 17, pp. 1–2.

62. Carlos Nieves Rivera, "La AC reitera su oferta por la Telefónica," Colección *El Mundo*, University of Puerto Rico, San Juan, April 29, 1948.

What Did You Do in the War, Daddy? A Story of a Puerto Rican in the Second World War and Korea: Captain Harry Chabrán Acevedo, 1925–1986

Rafael Chabrán

For

Rafael Chabrán Rodríguez (1900–1994)
Captain Harry Chabrán Acevedo (1925–1986)
Rafael Luis Chabrán (1979–2002)
Raphael Chabrán Méndez (1966–2010)

In memoriam

Boys, we will sail
To distant lands to fight
Through the paths of law and goodness
Marching with the Regiment of my Borinquen[1]

"The Warrior's knowledge as expressed in memories, novels, poems and plays by soldiers, together with reports by oral historians and essay journalists posits a lifetime about war that contradicts the war-monger at virtually every level."[2] The contradictions and the questions have always been there. The earliest memories I have of him are those of him in his uniform: a young, sharp second lieutenant. I knew all of his friends since my childhood. They were all Puerto Ricans in California, far from the island. They were part of the Puerto Rican diaspora.[3] And yet, they all looked so strange to me in their US Army uniforms, with emblems, ribbons, stripes, and medals.[4] They looked so strange to be in their uniforms, speaking in Spanish, as they always did.

He never spoke about the war, or wars, and I never asked. "No le gusta hablar de esas cosas" (he does not like to talk about those things), my mother

US Selective Service Board in Puerto Rico, 1940 (Archivo Fundación Luis Muñoz Marín)

warned me many times as I was about to ask or had asked without thinking. She would frequently repeat, "Never ask him, ever." All I had and still have are those pictures in family albums that I loved to look at when I was a child. Many times, frequently and even today, I spend hours looking at those rich visual texts, especially the color slides of the war that he and his war buddies took. Those photographs are profoundly evocative and full of history.[5] Finally the time came, when we still lived in Seaside and Monterey, California, I met some of the men in the pictures. I remember their names: Félix Oramás, William la Luz. They were my father's friends and close family friends. They were all Puerto Ricans in the US Army.

Nevertheless, the moment of truth finally arrived. As an adult and with youthful boldness and spirit, I found the courage to ask: "Papí, ¿qué hiciste durante la Guerra?" (Daddy, what did you do during the war?). The historical context for my inquiry was of the utmost importance. It was during the time of the Vietnam War, and my question was tied to my application for conscientious objector status, which many of my generation were seeking. My father's response was similar to a line of dialogue from the dramatic work *Soldado Razo* by the Chicano dramatist Luis Valdéz and his Teatro Campesino: "esas gentes eran iguales que nosotros y nosotros teníamos que matarlos" (those people were just like us and we had to kill them).[6] As George Mariscal, professor of literature at the University of California, San Diego, has indicated, creative literature (novels, poems, and plays) can help us understand our father's and mother's, brother's and sister's feelings and attitudes toward wars.[7]

The present essay is a narrative of the life of Captain Harry Chabrán Acevedo (1925–1986).[8] As such, it documents his military experiences in the US Army during Second World War and the Korean War, the latter sometimes called "the Forgotten War."[9] Our essay narrates Chabrán's life from the time he joined the service until he retired from the Army Reserves in 1960. Captain Chabrán's life history in the military will be contextualized within the background of Puerto Rican participation in Second World War and Korea, especially with respect to "All Puerto Rican" units.[10] In this essay, I have followed the model of ethnobiography as described in the work of Carlos Vélez-Ibáñez,[11] who, in his study *Borders Visions* (1996), writes:

> I chose to interpret this case from a bioethnographic viewpoint in order to "reconstruct a literate" text, if not a literal text, while admitting that my view of experience is not only colored, but that I participated in its creations."[12]

This essay is also informed by Vélez-Ibáñez's concept of the "distribution of sadness," in which the author chronicles the sadness Latinos face because of the effects of miseducation, poverty, physical and mental illness, crime, drugs, and, what is more important to us here today: their participation in wars.[13] In addition, in the section of his book called "Trading Souls," Vélez-Ibáñez also details how Mexicans and Puerto Ricans participated disproportionately in combat units (and suffered casualties) during the Second World War.[14]

Puerto Rico on the Eve of the War: The Militarization of the Island

Perhaps we should begin our military biography when Harry Chabrán was fifteen years old. Surely our young Puerto Rican teenager from Arecibo quickly became aware that his island was "becoming a beehive preparing for war."[15] The year was 1940, and the Puerto Rican people were very much aware of all the new military construction throughout the island. Among this construction was the expansion of Fort Buchanan, El Moro in San Juan, and Borinquen Field in the city of Aguadilla.[16] As Jorge Rodríguez Beruff has observed in his excellent study, *Strategy as Politics*, Puerto Rico on the eve of the Second World War cannot be understood outside of a consideration of the international crises of the 1930s and early 1940s and the preparations for war, as well as the military strategies that formed the political realities of the island and the Caribbean in general.[17] As a young teenager, Chabrán had plenty of opportunity to go to the movies and watch films such as *Men with Wings* and *Vámonos con la Marina* (Join the Marines). In his classes, as in all public schools on the island, he would also be taught to celebrate Veterans Day and support the US National Guard.[18]

It is important to recall that the Second World War affected Puerto Rico in many ways. More than seventy-six thousand people (the majority of them men, but also many women) served in the US Armed Forces.[19] However, we must remember that that those who remained on the island also suffered from the consequences of the war. More than ever, the experiences of the Second World War highlighted the total dependence of the island on the United States—as always is the case for colonies. The island was totally dependent on the US mainland for all its material and economic needs.[20] The young Chabrán, like many of those of his generation on the island, soon found himself sailing off to foreign lands to complete his military training. At that time, the island found itself more isolated than ever from the rest of the world with a very high rate of unemployment and serious economic problems, much like today. Many things have not changed.

A Military Biography and Its Historical Context

We will begin our chronicle in 1944, when our young Puerto Rican enlisted in the US Army. He, along with many of his compatriots, joined with a strong desire to seek his fortune and find adventures off the island. At this time the war was in full force. The American Fifth Army had launched an attack on Monte Cassino in Italy. At the same time, Allied forces landed at Nettuno and Anzio south of Rome as part of Operation Shingle. The historic monastery of Monte Cassino was bombed in one of the hardest battles of the war.

On the other side of the globe, in the Pacific, US troops were completing the conquest of the Solomon and Marshall Islands. By June 1944, Monte Cassino and Rome were in Allied hands. The Normandy landings and the battles of Orvieto (Italy) and Cherbourg (France) would soon follow.[21] During these fateful times, a nineteen-year-old Chabrán joined the US Army along with many young men from the rural areas of his native Arecibo. First,

Lieutenant Harry Chabrán (private collection of Rafael Chabrán)

he was sent to Panama and Cuba.[22] From there, he was posted to Fort Bliss, Texas, near the border town of El Paso.

What made this young man leave his native Borinquen and join the army? His family? His friends? The only thing we know is that he had dropped out of high school before completing his senior year, much to the dismay of his father, who was a rural schoolteacher. Like many men, he was bored and felted confined on the island. He was young, rebellious, and impulsive and wanted to get off Puerto Rico, get away from his parents' home in Arecibo and see the world, search for his identity, and follow the paths he set for himself like so many young men of his age. So, he joined the army. He was not particularly patriotic. Nor did he know much about Anglo-American culture, nor did he speak English very well.[23] Many years later, when he had already returned from Korea and left the service and was working at the Bank of America in Monterey, California, he would be forced to pay for special speech lessons to help him "get rid of his accent." He was never totally successful. He would carry his accent with him until the end of his life.

But before we continue with the chronicle of this Puerto Rican's life in the military, a word or two must be said about Puerto Rico's considerable military history. Much has been written about this topic, and all we can do here is give a very brief sketch of this complicated history. Puerto Rico has a rich and considerable military history[24] spanning four centuries under Spanish rule and a century under US control, which began with the Spanish-American War of 1898 and the military invasion of the island. If we limit ourselves to the US period, a considerable number of Puerto Ricans served in the First World War, the Second World War, Korea, Vietnam, the first Gulf War (Desert Shield and Desert Storm), and the more recent incursions in Iraq and Afghanistan.[25] Within the chapters of this complicated overview, we find the history of the noted Sixty-Fifth Infantry Regiment of the US Army.[26] According to some accounts, more than sixty-five thousand Puerto Ricans served in the US Army during the Second World War. During this conflict, the Sixty-Fifth Infantry Regiment trained at and guarded the Panama Canal, as well as participating in combat on the Italian-French border in the winter of 1944. In addition, at the beginning of the Korean War, the Sixty-Fifth was ordered to Korea and was assigned to the army's Third Infantry Division, where Puerto Ricans earned many citations and commendations for bravery and heroic service.[27] In 1956, the Sixty-Fifth was inactivated because the army no longer wanted any units composed exclusively of a single ethnic group. That same year, the Sixty-Fifth became part of the Puerto Rican National Guard (Guardia Nacional de Puerto Rico).[28]

From Fort Bliss to Fort Ord

Returning to our military biography of Harry Chabrán, in 1944, after spending some time in Panama, the young Puerto Rican was sent to Fort Bliss, Texas, near El Paso and the Mexican border town of Ciudad Juárez. As we will see, this posting will mark a significant milestone in Chabrán's life. Fort Bliss was established in 1848 at the end of the Mexican-American War.[29] The primary purpose of the base was to establish and reinforce the US presence on the Mexican border and to protect Texas settlers against Indians and bandits. Fort Bliss was originally founded as an infantry and cavalry base on the shores of the Rio Grande along the border. As such, this base was one of the oldest military installations in the southwestern United States. In the course of its long history, many infantry and cavalry units passed through its gates. However, today as in the 1940s, primary purpose of this base is air defense artillery.

In December 1944, Chabrán found himself a member of the 891st Anti-Aircraft Artillery Battery at Fort Bliss.[30] By this time, he had earned some stripes and was already a sergeant. During this same year, at Fort Bliss, Chabrán met his first wife, Angelina González, a young Mexican American woman from El Paso known as Angie. She was the daughter of Cruz González and Isabel Quesada, natives of the Mexican state of Chihuahua and political exiles from the Mexican revolution. In the winter of 1944, Sergeant Chabrán married Angie González in El Paso's Guardian Angel Church (Iglesia del Santo Angel). Like many young men of the time, in his wedding photo Chabrán proudly wore his military uniform.

The Second World War ended in Europe in 1945, and Japan surrendered on September 2 of that same year. And so, our young Puerto Rican soldier, far from his island, surrounded by other Puerto Ricans, Mexicans, and Chicanos in Texas, never got the opportunity to fight in the war. However, he would

Company in which Lieutenant Chabrán served, December 31, 1944 (private collection of Rafael Chabrán)

soon have the opportunity to know firsthand the pains and passion of war. Very soon after his wedding he was posted to Fort Ord near Monterey, California, one of California's early capitals.

Fort Ord was founded in 1917 on Monterey Bay near Seaside, California. For many years it was the home of the Sixth Infantry Division of the US Army. As such, it was an important point of departure and return for army troops during the Korean War. In 1994, the facility ceased to be a military installation, and today it is home to California State University, Monterey Bay. In February 1947, Chabrán's first son, Rafael Chabrán, was born at Monterey County Hospital. The child was taken to his first home at Ord Village, a residence for married soldiers at Fort Ord.

Even though the Chabrán family would move to many other cities (Monterey, Seaside, and El Paso), California would be their more or less permanent home until the 1950s. Two of their children would be born in Monterey and the other two in El Paso. They were all "Chicano-Riqueños in Aztlán." Three of the four would become university professors specializing in Latino studies.[31]

But we must continue with the story of our Puerto Rican soldier. In 1948, Chabrán returned to El Paso, but not for long. He was quickly posted to White Sands Missile Range in White Sands, New Mexico, one of the largest military installations of its type in the United States. However, very soon afterward he was selected to attend Officer Candidate School (OCS) in San Antonio, where his leadership skills soon became evident.

In 1950 we find Chabrán, now an officer, stationed at Fort Ord, but only for a very short time. Soon he was sent to the Presidio in San Francisco.[32]

But before the year was over, Chabrán would be on the road again. This time he was off to Fort Benning, Georgia. Fort Benning serves as the home of the US Army Infantry School, inaugurated in 1918 and one of the most important infantry schools in the country. During the 1940s, Fort Benning was well known for its Airborne Training School as well as for its noted Rangers School, in addition to its Officer Candidate School. After finishing his training in advanced infantry—the most advanced of the time—Lieutenant Chabrán again returned to California. Soon he would be given the opportunity to put into practice the infantry skills he had just learned.

However, lest we give an incomplete picture of historical events, we must note that not all Puerto Ricans were in favor of the Korean War. Earlier, the Puerto Rican Nationalist Party (Partido Nacionalista de Puerto Rico), established in 1922, had not supported the US role in World War II, especially the obligatory draft of Puerto Ricans.[33] Members of the Nationalist Party were repressed and attacked by US government measures as well as by authorities of the insular government. Among the measures taken was the Puerto Rican Gag Law (Law 53). Many Nationalists also received harsh and long prison terms for their political activities.

In October 1950, when many Puerto Ricans were dying in the battlefields of Korea, others were proclaiming the Grito de Jayuya (the Jayuya Uprising) and organizing nationalist uprisings in Ponce, Mayagüez, Naranjito, San Juan, and Arecibo, Chabrán's hometown. Shortly afterward, in November 1950, several Puerto Rican nationalists attacked Blair House in Washington, DC, in an attempted assassination of President Harry S. Truman.[34]

Returning to our chronology of the war, in June 1950, North Korean forces invaded South Korea and captured Seoul. These events set off a military conflict between North and South Korea that lasted until an armistice was signed on July 27, 1953. During this famous "state of emergency," Chinese forces crossed into Korea in large numbers and fought on the North Korean side. Meanwhile, Lieutenant Chabrán, like many of his Puerto Rican compatriots, found himself sailing to far-off lands to carry out his military service. At that time, his island home was more isolated than ever before with high rates of unemployment and serious economic problems.

Puerto Ricans In Korea

Finally with their feet on Korean soil, our Puerto Rican soldiers encountered landscapes and a climate that were totally different from anything they had previously encountered on their own island or on the US mainland.[35] The summers were very hot and the winters were extremely cold—icy cold. Many of these soldiers, if not the majority of them, had never seen snow before. It has been suggested that many Puerto Ricans did not have the proper clothing and uniforms for this type of weather and combat. Chabrán would never forget the cold that he suffered in Korea. That experience remained with him throughout his entire life. Many years later, when his children begged him to take them out in the snow, he would respond with great emotion: "I hate the snow."[36] Lieutenant Chabrán and the men he commanded fought in some of the fiercest battles of the Korean conflict. As part of the Third Division, the Sixty-Fifth Regiment participated in the famous End Run campaign on the eastern coast of Korea. In June 1951, Chabrán and his men crossed the Hantan River and in July of the same year they captured the city of Chorwon.

However, as in all wars, not everything involved fighting. During his free moments, Chabrán would relax, drink a beer, and write letters to his family. Some soldiers, at the behest of Chabrán, set up an impromptu radio station, where they transmitted Puerto Rican music. The music was of course *bien jíbara* (real Puerto Rican music from the country), like the music that Chabrán always loved, especially the songs of Don Rafael Hernández (1892–1965) and Don Pedro Flores (1894–1979). Who could forget such songs as "Sin Bandera" (Without a flag), "Amor Perdido" (Lost love), or "Despedida" (Farewell)?[37] This unforgettable music had a special place in Chabrán's life and in that of his family. Many years later, his oldest son would attempt to re-create a discography of his father's Puerto Rican war songs.

The End of the War: Return to California

As with all wars, the end had to come. Our young Puerto Rican soldier had the good fortune to return to his family and children, safe and in good health. By this time, all his family was in California, including his father, Rafael Chabrán Rodríguez, and his mother, María Acevedo Chabrán. They had followed their son from Puerto Rico to California. However, our young soldier would never be able to forget the memories and trauma of his war experience. Those memories, even though they remained silent, as with most veterans, always remained with him. Perhaps now and then he would share them with his Puerto Rican war buddies. His army friends remained his friends long after the war. They were his friends for life. But our young soldier would never be able to share his memories with his family or children.

When Chabrán returned to the United States, things were different, very different. Nothing was the same, as all veterans experience to some degree.

Chabrán suffered from post-traumatic stress disorder, which is common among war veterans. This battle fatigue was accompanied by strong bouts of depression. His family, his wife and children, remembered how he would wake up in the middle of the night with terrible nightmares in which he could hear the sounds of machine gun fire. The family would refer to these episodes as *ataques* (attacks) or *nervios* (nerves). A more thorough discussion of what became known as "Puerto Rican Syndrome" is beyond the scope of this essay.[38]

When all was said and done, Chabrán could no longer continue with his military career. However, as was often the case, he joined the US Army Reserves after he left the active service. He wanted a way out, a better future, and started looking for a job as a civilian while still retaining his status in the military. By 1959 he had reached the rank of first lieutenant in the reserves, where he stayed until 1960, retiring with the rank of captain. During his time in the service, he had taken courses in accounting and business administration but had no formal training in these areas.

In the summer of 1956, Chabrán secured a position at the main branch of the Bank of America in Los Angeles. This job relocation meant a radical move for the Chabrán family from northern California to southern California. During the summer of 1956, all of the family—parents, grandparents, and children—moved to southern California. With this move came a search for a new house, and so the family began house hunting. During this time, Chabrán was still in the reserves. Each time he was called for duty or training, his commitment to the reserves, especially in the summers, became more and more difficult for him. His activities with the reserves took place at Fort MacArthur in San Pedro, California.[39]

These were good times for our young veteran. With help from a Veterans Administration loan and a new job at the Bank of America, Chabrán began to search for the house of his dreams. He set off looking in the recently constructed tract homes of the San Gabriel Valley and soon found what he was looking for in a new subdivision in West Covina. Proudly, he took his family to see the new home that he had found. The house had recently been constructed; it was "brand spanking new." It even smelled new. It was just what the family wanted, just like the new homes they had seen on television.

However, something went unexpectedly wrong, very wrong. That house would never be "the house." The children did not understand why they didn't get their dream house. Much later, it was explained to them that the people selling the house "did not sell to Mexicans." The oldest child was perplexed and in his young innocence asked: "But aren't we Puerto Ricans, and didn't Daddy fight in the war?" With the passage of time, the family found another house, in the city of La Puente in another part of the San Gabriel Valley in a neighborhood with a large number of Mexican American veterans who had also fought in World War II and Korea.

As the years passed, Chabrán returned to his beloved island and took part in what has been called the process of "reverse/circular migration."[40] He returned to his Puerto Rican roots, this time with a new family. The children of his second marriage, even those who had been born in California, considered themselves to be profoundly Puerto Rican. Chabrán and his new family found a new home in Vega Baja and a new job at the Daniel International Construction Company (of the Fluor Group). Sadly, however, with the passing of time Chabrán developed cancer, and in 1984 he decided to move to Orlando, Florida, for the better medical care than he could find in Puerto Rico and a calmer life. In the end, our veteran lost his fight with cancer, and he was buried in the Veterans Cemetery near Saint Petersburg under a tree surrounded by other veterans who had also fought overseas.[41]

Conclusion

In this essay, we have attempted to sketch the biography of a Puerto Rican veteran during the time of World War II and the Korean War. The number of living Puerto Rican veterans who fought in World War II or Korea is unfortunately dwindling, as are opportunities to obtain oral histories and narratives of their war experiences. Some service records still survive, as well as collections of photographs, newspaper articles, and personal correspondence ("Korean Love Letters"),[42] which can provide the anxious researcher with primary sources that can paint a more comprehensive picture of the social, political, and cultural realities of Puerto Ricans during these war years.

Notes

The present essay is a version of a paper first presented in 2000 at the US Latinos and Latinas, World War II Conference, Department of Journalism, University of Texas at Austin. The current essay is a English translation of an expanded Spanish version, "Papí, ¿qué hiciste durante la guerra? la historia de un Boricua en la Segunda Guerra Mundial y Corea" (2011). Acknowledgments are due to Mrs. Angie Chabrán, Professor Richard Chabrán (the University of Arizona), Ken Butler (US Marine Corps, retired), and Captain Fred Bergerson (US Army, retired), Department of Political Science, Whittier College.

1. Alexis Brau, "El himno del Regimiento 65 de Infantería," *El Boricua*, at http://www.elboricua.com/Borinqueneers.html:

Arriba muchachos vamos a zarpar
A lejanas tierras vamos a pelear
Por los caminos de la ley y el bien.

This translation, as well as all others in this chapter, is ours. Chabrán was a proud member of the Sixty-Fifth Regiment and always honored and respected its members. Throughout his life he kept and treasured the insignias of this noted regiment.

2. James W. Gibson, *The Perfect War: Technowar in Vietnam* (Boston: Atlantic Monthly Press, 1986), cited in George Mariscal, ed., *Aztlán and Viet Nam: Chicano and Chicana Experiences of the War*, American Crossroads 4 (Berkeley: University of California Press, 1999), p. 3.

3. On the Puerto Rican diaspora, see Carmen Teresa Whalen and Víctor Vázquez-Hernández, eds., *The Puerto Rican Diaspora: Historical Perspectives* (Philadelphia: Temple University Press, 2005).

4. Among Chabrán's military awards, medals, and distinctions, he earned the Combat Infantryman Badge, Jungle Expert distinction, the Jungle Operations Training Center (Panama) Badge, the Bronze Star Medal, the Purple Heart Medal, the Army Good Conduct Medal, the American Defense Service Medal, the WWII American Campaign Medal, the WWII Asiatic Pacific Campaign Medal, the WWII Victory Medal, the Korean Service Medal, and the United Nations Service Medal.

5. Special thanks to my mother, Mrs. Angie Chabrán, and my brother, Richard Chabrán, for the use of their personal family albums in the preparation of this essay. Another valuable collection of stories about Puerto Rican soldiers of this time can be found in "Special Announcements: The 65th Regiment," at http://www.valerosos.com/anouncements.html.

6. Luis Valdez, *Soldado Razo*, in *Early Works: Actos, Bernabé, and Pensamiento Serpentino* (Houston: Arte Público Press, 1990), pp. 121–133.

7. Mariscal, *Aztlán and Viet Nam*, pp. 1–45. The translation is ours. See also Cristina Alsina Rodríguez, "La literatura testimonial de la Guerra de Vietnam: algunas consideraciones sobre los problemas formales planteados por la representación del dolor," in *Visiones contemporáneas de la cultura y literatura norteamericana en los sesenta*, ed. Pilar Martín Madrazo (Seville: University of Seville, 2002), pp. 49–59; and Bridget A. Kevane, *Latino Literature in America*, Literature as Windows to World Cultures (Westport, CT: Greenwood Press, 2003), digital version.

8. For some unexplained reason, which subsequently caused great confusion for his children, the spelling of Chabrán's surname was changed in his military records to "Chabram." After he left the service, Chabrán continued to use his true family name.

9. Notably, Clay Blair, *The Forgotten War: America in Korea, 1950–1953* (New York: Times Books, 1987).

10. See Gilberto N. Villahermosa, *Honor and Fidelity: The 65th Infantry in Korea, 1950–1953* (Washington, DC: US Army, Center of Military History, 2009); W. W. Harris, *Puerto Rico's Fighting 65th U.S. Infantry: From San Juan to Chorwan* (San Rafael, CA: Presidio Press, 1980); José Norat Martínez, ed., *Historia del Regimiento 65 de Infantería, 1899–1960* (San Juan: La Milagrosa, 1960); Jorge Rodríguez Beruff, "Puerto Rican Units," in *The Oxford Companion to American Military History*, ed. John Whiteclay Chambers II (New York: Oxford

University Press, 1999), p. 580; and Jorge Rodríguez Beruff, *Strategy as Politics: Puerto Rico on the Eve of the Second World War* (Río Piedras: University of Puerto Rico Press, 2007).

11. Carlos G. Vélez-Ibáñez, *Border Visions: Mexican Cultures of the Southwest United States* (Tucson: University of Arizona Press, 1996). We have also used the Spanish version of this work for our study: Carlos G. Vélez-Ibáñez, Carlos Monsiváis, and Katia Rheault, *Visiones de frontera: las culturas mexicanas del suroeste de Estados Unidos* (Mexico City: Miguel Angel Porrúa, 1999).

12. Vélez-Ibáñez, *Border Visions*, p. 131.

13. Ibid., pp. 182–206.

14. Ibid., pp. 200–204.

15. Rodríguez Beruff, *Strategy as Politics*, p. ix.

16. Ibid., p. xi.

17. Ibid.

18. Ibid., pp. 111–113.

19. History Task Force, Centro de Estudios Puertorriqueños, *Labor Migration under Capitalism: The Puerto Rican Experience* (New York: Monthly Review Press, 1979), p. 124.

20. Ibid.

21. "Puerto Ricans in World War II," Wikipedia (English), at http://en.wikipedia.org/wiki/Puerto_Ricans_in_World_War_II; and "Puertorriqueños en la Segunda Guerra Mundial," Wikipedia (Spanish), at http://es.wikipedia.org/wiki/Puertorrique%C3%B1os_en_la_Segunda_Guerra_Mundial.

22. Chabrán's military records indicate that he had been in Cuba before going to Panama. We understand that he was at Batista Army Air Field not far from Havana. We have information about other Puerto Rican soldiers in Cuba; see the interview with Angel Antonio Velásquez in Maggie Rivas-Rodríguez, et al., *A Legacy Greater than Words: Stories of U.S. Latinos and Latinas of the WW II Generation* (Austin: University of Texas Press, 2006), p. 154. While we have no exact information, it seems that he was part of Company C (Juncos), 295th Infantry Regiment, Third Battalion, in Panama. The Chabrán family also has several photographs of Chabrán in Panama. For more information on Puerto Ricans and the Sixty-Fifth Regiment in Panama, see Stetson Conn, Rose C. Engelman, and Byron Fairchild, *Guarding the United States and Its Outposts* (Washington, DC: US Army Center of Military History, 1964); Rivas-Rodríguez, *A Legacy Greater than Words*; and Gilberto N. Villahermosa, "America's Hispanics in America's Wars," *Army Magazine*, September 2002, p. 8. On the strategic military importance of Panama and the Panama Canal for the United States, see Rodríguez Beruff, *Strategy as Politics*, chapter 3.

23. On the use of Spanish by Puerto Ricans in the US Army, there is much to say. See, for example, on "the near-universal use of Spanish by members of the 65th Infantry Regiment," Thomas E. Hanson, review of Gilberto N. Villahermosa, *Honor and Fidelity: The 65th Infantry in Korea, 1950–1953*, H-War, H-Net Reviews, December 2010, at https://www.h-net.org/reviews/showrev.php?id=29512.

24. M. A. Warren, "Military Participation in WWII," in *The Latino Encyclopedia*, vol. 4, ed. Richard Chabrán and Rafael Chabrán (New York: Marshall Cavendish, 1996), pp. 1029–1030; and Ernest Acosta, *The Puerto Rican U.S. Army 65th Infantry Regiment* (n.p.: US Army 65th

Infantry Regiment Recognition Committee, 1996). See also "65th Infantry: Selected Readings," at http://www.history.army.mil/html/topics/hispam/65th-bib.html; Rodríguez Beruff, *Strategy as Politics*; and Villahermosa, *Honor and Fidelity*.

25. More studies and oral histories are needed on the participation of Puerto Ricans in the military conflicts in Iraq and Afghanistan.

26. In many of Chabrán's military photographs, the insignias of the Sixty-Fifth Regiment are clearly present.

27. Villahermosa, "America's Hispanics in America's Wars."

28. On the history of the Puerto Rican National Guard, see José Norat Martínez, *Historia del Regimiento 65 de Infantería, 1899–1960* (San Juan: La Milagrosa, 1960).

29. Leon C. Metz, Millard G. McKinney, Frederick T. Carter, and Placido Cano, *Fort Bliss: An Illustrated History* (El Paso: Mangan Books, 1981); *Desert Army: Fort Bliss on the Texas Border* (El Paso: Mangan Books, 1988); and *El Paso: Guided through Time* (El Paso: Mangan Books, 1999).

30. The 891st was earlier based in Panama. See US War Department, *History of the 891st Antiaircraft Artillery Gun Battalion*, September 1942–February 1945.

31. Rafael Chabrán is professor emeritus at Whittier College, Whittier, California. Richard Chabrán taught at the University of California, Riverside, and is currently associate professor at the University of Arizona in Tucson. Angie Chabrán is professor of Chicano studies at the University of California, Davis.

32. The Presidio in San Francisco is one of the oldest military installations in the United States. It dates from the Spanish period, having been founded in 1776. In 1822 it passed to Mexican control, and finally to US control in 1850. In 1994 the Presidio ceased to be the home of the US Sixth Army and was transferred to the Golden Gate National Recreation Area.

33. Richard Dello Buono, "Puerto Rican Nationalism," in *The Latino Encyclopedia*, vol. 6, ed. Richard Chabrán and Rafael Chabrán (New York: Marshall Cavendish,1996), p.1316; and José Bolívar, "Puerto Ricans: White, Black, or Hispanic?," *Puerto Rico Daily Sun*, June 8, 2010, at http://www.prdailysun.com/index.php?page=perspectives.article&id=1276026249. See also "Puerto Ricans in World War I," Wikipedia, at http://en.wikipedia.org/wiki/Puerto_Ricans_in_World_War_I.

34. On the Puerto Rican Nationalist Party, see Dello Buono, "Puerto Rican Nationalism," pp. 1316–1318.

35. On the differences in landscapes and climate between Puerto Rico and Korea, see Villahermosa, "America's Hispanics in America's Wars," p. 16.

36. See David Halberstam, *The Coldest Winter: America and the Korean War* (New York: Hyperion, 2007).

37. Ruth Glasser, *My Music Is My Flag: Puerto Rican Musicians and Their New York Communities, 1917–1940* (Berkeley: University of California Press, 1995); and Josean Ramos, "La Guerra en el cancionero boricua," at http://www.herencialatina.com/La_guerra_en_el_cancionero/La_Guerra_en_el_Cancionero.htm.

38. Patricia Gherovici, *The Puerto Rican Syndrome* (New York: Other Press, 2003). See also Janet Thormann, review of Patricia Gherovici, *The Puerto Rican Sindrome* [sic],

Psychomedia: Journal of European Psychoanalysis 23, no. 2 (2006), at http://www.psychomedia.it/jep/number23/gherovici.htm; and Geneva Reynaga-Abiko, review of Patricia Gherovici, *The Puerto Rican Syndrome*, American Psychological Association, Division 39, at http://www.division39.org/pub_reviews_detail.php?book_id=240.

39. Fort MacArthur dates from 1914. For many years it served as home to the California National Guard and the US Army Reserves. Between 1950 and 1974, it was part of the Nike Missile Command. It ceased to be a military instillation in 1982.

40. See Abigail S. McNamee, *Belonging to Puerto Rico and America: New York Puerto Rican Children's Developing Conceptualization of Their Own Cultural Group* (New York: Nova Science Publishers, 2009).

41. Captain Chabrán is buried at Bay Pines National Cemetery, Bay Pines, Florida.

42. We have information on the existence of a collection of personal correspondence between Chabrán and his first wife, Angie Chabrán but have been unable to examine it. Many more collections of this type must exist. See "From Korea: Love Letters Home," in *Modern America: A Documentary History of the Nation Since 1945*, ed. Gary Donaldson (Armonk, NY: M. E. Sharpe, 2007), pp. 18–20.

Contributors

César J. Ayala Casás, Ph.D., is a professor in the Department of Sociology at the University of California, Los Angeles. His publications include, with Rafael Bernabe, *Puerto Rico en el siglo americano: su historia desde 1898* (San Juan: Ediciones Callejón, 2011); with José L. Bolívar Fresneda, *Battleship Vieques: Puerto Rico from World War II to the Korean War* (Princeton, NJ: Markus Wiener, 2011); with Rafael Bernabe, *Puerto Rico in the American Century: A History since 1898* (Chapel Hill: University of North Carolina Press, 2007); and *American Sugar Kingdom: The Plantation Economy of the Spanish Caribbean, 1898-1934* (Chapel Hill: University of North Carolina Press, 1999).

Fitzroy André Baptiste, Ph.D., a distinguished Grenadian scholar and senior lecturer at the University of the West Indies, died on July 7, 2007. He is the author of the classic study on the Caribbean during the Second World War, *War, Cooperation, and Conflict: The European Possessions in the Caribbean, 1939-1945* (Westport, CT: Greenwood Press, 1988), for which he was awarded the Outstanding Academic Book prize. In addition to his writings on the war, he made important contributions in the field of African history and African studies. He wrote the essay in this volume, published here for the first time, on occasion of a visit to the University of Puerto Rico, where he had been invited by Jorge Rodríguez Beruff to give a seminar. The text is dated November 17, 1999. We are glad to include it in this volume with the approval of his family and have made only minor corrections. For further information about this distinguished scholar, see Claudius Fergus, "In Memoriam: Dr. Fitzroy André Baptiste," *Caribbean Studies* 35, no. 2 (July-December, 2007): 176-179.

José L. Bolívar Fresneda, Ph.D., is an engineer and independent researcher. He published *Guerra, banca y desarrollo: el Banco de Fomento y la industrialización de Puerto Rico, 1942-1948* (San Juan: Fundación Luis Muñoz Marín; Instituto de Cultura Puertorriqueña, 2011). He coauthored with César J. Ayala

Casás *Battleship Vieques: Puerto Rico from World War II to the Korean War* (Princeton, NJ: Marcus Wiener, 2011), selected by *Choice* as a Distinguished Title for 2011; is coeditor and author with Jorge Rodríguez Beruff of *Puerto Rico en la Segunda Guerra Mundial: baluarte del Caribe* (San Juan: Ediciones Callejón, 2012); and is a contributor to *Contra viento y marea hacia el futuro: historia de la Asociación de Industriales de Puerto Rico, 1928-2013* (San Juan: Asociación de Industriales de Puerto Rico, 2014). He is a frequent columnist for the Puerto Rican newspaper *El Nuevo Dia*. Bolívar Fresneda and Rodríguez Beruff are currently working on publishing the second volume of *Puerto Rico en la Segunda Guerra Mundial*.

Rafael Chabrán, Ph.D., is professor emeritus in the Department of Modern Languages and Literatures at Whittier College, Whittier, California. His essay in this volume was first presented at the US Latinos and Latinas, World War II Conference hosted by the Department of Journalism at the University of Texas at Austin in 2000. He is coeditor with Richard Chabrán of *The Latino Encyclopedia* (New York: Marshall Cavendish, 1996), a six-volume study designed for high school and university students.

Ligia T. Domenech, Ph.D., is assistant professor at Northern Essex Community College in Haverhill, Massachusetts. She authored *¡Que el pueblo decida! La gobernación de Roberto Sánchez Vilella, 1964-1968* (San Juan: EMS Editores, 2007), and is currently working on a book titled *Imprisoned in the Caribbean: The 1942 German U-Boat Blockade*.

Michael Janeway, professor emeritus in the Department of Journalism at Columbia University, died on April 27, 2014. He was the editor of the *Boston Globe* and executive editor of the *Atlantic Monthly*. He joined the *Globe* in 1978 as the Sunday magazine editor and worked his way up the ranks. When the influential and much-loved editor Thomas Winship retired in 1985, Janeway was named to succeed Winship. He left the *Globe* in 1986. In 1989, he was named dean of the Medill School of Journalism at Northwestern University in Evanston, Illinois, a post he held until 1996, when he was named head of the arts journalism program at Columbia University's Graduate School of Journalism, at which time he began writing books. His first, titled *Republic of Denial: Press, Politics, and Public Life* (New Haven, CT: Yale University Press, 1999), was a dark vision of the near future describing how both journalists and politicians have lost touch of their essential roles. His second book, *The Fall of the House of Roosevelt: Brokers of Ideas and Power from FDR to LBJ* (New York: Columbia University Press, 2004), focused on

President Franklin D. Roosevelt's inner circle of advisers, a group known as the Brain Trust, which included his father, Eliot Janeway, and future governor of Puerto Rico Rexford G. Tugwell. His father's connections probably led young Michael to become enchanted with Puerto Rico and encouraged him to visit the island and write about its relationship with the Roosevelt era decades later. His father later became an adviser to President Lyndon Johnson, which is why his book covers that period as well. Michael Janeway believed that the New Deal had its beginning and its end with these two presidents, hence the reason for including them both in his book. He contributed an essay on Tugwell and his relationship to Puerto Rico in *Puerto Rico en la Segunda Guerra Mundial: baluarte del Caribe*, ed. José L. Bolívar Fresneda and Jorge Rodríguez Beruff (San Juan: Ediciones Callejón, 2012). For additional information on Michael Janeway, see http://www.nytimes.com/2014/04/19/business/media/michael-janeway-former-editor-of-the-boston-globe-dies-at-73.html.

Jorge Rodríguez Beruff, Ph.D., is a full professor in the Department of Social Science, the University of Puerto Rico. His publications include *Los militares y el poder* (Lima: Mosca Azul, 1983); *Política militar y dominación: Puerto Rico en el contexto latinoamericano* (Río Piedras, PR: Ediciones Huracán, 1988); coeditor of *Conflict, Peace, and Development in the Caribbean* (London: Macmillan, 1989); *Security Problems and Policies in the Post–Cold War Caribbean* (London: Macmillan, 1996); editor of *Cuba en crisis: perspectivas económicas y políticas* (Río Piedras: University of Puerto Rico Press, 1995); editor of *Fronteras en conflicto* (San Juan: Red de Geopolítica, 1999); and *Las memorias de Leahy: los relatos del almirante William D. Leahy sobre su gobernación de Puerto Rico, 1939–1940* (San Juan: Fundación Luis Muñoz Marín, 2002). His most recent publications are *Strategy as Politics: Puerto Rico on the Eve of the Second World War* (Río Piedras: University of Puerto Rico Press, 2007); and coeditor with José L. Bolívar Fresneda of *Puerto Rico en la Segunda Guerra Mundial: baluarte del Caribe* (San Juan: Ediciones Callejón, 2012). Bolívar Fresneda and Rodríguez Beruff are currently working on publishing the second volume of *Puerto Rico en la Segunda Guerra Mundial*.

Luis Rosario Albert, Ph.D., is assistant professor in the Department of Communications at the University of Turabo in Puerto Rico. He is currently working on a book about the history of telecommunications in Puerto Rico. His latest publication is "Geopolítica y política de medios de comunicación en Puerto Rico: el caso de la IT&T y la Porto Rico Telephone Company (1942–1948)," in *Puerto en la Segunda Guerra Mundial: baluarte del Caribe*, ed. José L. Bolívar Fresneda and Jorge Rodríguez Beruff (San Juan: Ediciones Callejón, 2012).

Mayra Rosario Urrutia, Ph.D., is a full professor in the Department of History at the University of Puerto Rico. Her primary publications are related to crime and transgressions in Puerto Rico, alcohol prohibition, the party politics of Puerto Rico in the twentieth century, and US–Puerto Rico relations during the Second World War and the postwar period. She is the coauthor of *Senderos para un sueño: geografía e historia de Estados Unidos de América* (San Juan: Editorial la Biblioteca, 2000); and *Relaciones internacionales de los Estados Unidos de América* (San Juan: Editorial la Biblioteca, 2000). She also coauthored three other text books. She has participated in academic forums in Puerto Rico, Spain, the Caribbean, and the United States; in diverse workshops for teachers of the educational system; and on boards for academic journals. She has also provided other professional services to academic institutions.

Index

Abbazia, Patrick, 22, 27, 28
ABC-1, plan and talks, 44–47, 50, 52, 53
Acevedo, Héctor Luis, 110
Aegean Sea, 31
Africa, 7, 13, 19, 30, 31, 32, 37, 45, 50, 114, 135, 176
African Americans, 119
Afrika Corps, 122
Agricultural Adjustment Agency (AAA), 151, 167
Agricultural Credit Administration, 167
Agricultural Development Bank, 237
Agricultural Economic Act, 225
Agricultural Extension Service (AES), 149–50
Agricultural Marketing Association, 152
Aguadilla, Puerto Rico, 9, 115, 169, 248
Alaska, 17, 21, 30, 38–40, 70, 86, 152
Albizu Campos, Pedro, 12, 64, 198
Alessandri, Arturo, 19
Aleutian Islands, 38
Algeria, 122, 165
Almirante Bay (Panama), 58
American Civil Liberties Union (ACLU), 20, 64, 75
American Molasses Company, 93, 192
Andrews, Adolphus, 18, 20
Anegada Passage, 6, 7
Anglo American Caribbean Commission (AACC), 93, 94, 188–97, 200–17, 249
Antigua, 19, 48, 114, 194

Antilles, 6, 11, 19, 26, 34, 54, 78, 124, 126, 173, 196, 209
Antongiorgi, Ángel Esteban, 65
Anzio, Italy, 248
Aqueduct, San Juan, 220
Arenas Bank, 36
Argentina, 18, 27, 221, 223, 225, 226, 232, 233, 242
Army, United States, 10, 14, 17, 22, 45, 46, 47, 50, 96, 115, 119, 144, 148, 152, 157, 193, 195, 221, 222, 245–54; Air Corps, 18; bases, 9, 17, 222; intelligence, 70
Aruba, 48, 52, 95, 141, 195, 222
Arundel Corporation, 118–20, 135–36
Asia, 4, 31, 165, 221, 240
Atlantic Charter, 92, 159, 215
Australia, 31, 58, 140
Ávila Camacho, Antonio, 176
Azores, 29, 32, 46

Bacardi Rum, 128, 137
Badger, Charles J., 34, 56, 57
Bahamas, 8, 19, 47, 48, 51, 114, 190, 194
Bailey, Sidney, 44
Bailey Committee Report, 44
Baker, Virgil, 33
Balboa (Panama), 39
Baltimore, Maryland, 55, 105, 138, 162, 214
Barceló, Antonio R., 62, 73
Banco de Fomento, 27, 134, 137, 138, 184, 261
Banco Popular, 132, 138

Bank of America, 249, 254
Bank of France, 48
Barbados, 6, 7, 55, 190, 191, 210, 217
Batista, Fulgencio, 22, 257
Bauxite, 32, 47, 48, 56, 59, 141, 160, 191, 196, 222
Beals, Carleton, 11, 25, 80
Béarn (French carrier), 48
Bell, Alexander Graham, 221
Bermuda, 10, 29, 47, 48, 50, 51, 114, 194, 213
Beverley, James, 63
Bloch, Claude C., 20
Bolivia, 221, 223, 225
Boutiny, Vaisseau P. de, 54
Brazil, 6, 13, 18, 19, 27, 30, 31, 46, 48, 137, 166, 221
Bureau of Aeronautics, 42, 43

Campos del Toro, Enrique, 71
Canada, 27, 31, 32, 46, 55, 158, 166
Caperton, William B., 66
Caracas, Venezuela, 10, 30
Cárdenas, Lázaro, 22
Caribbean, 3–69, 86, 89, 93–95, 103–14, 122, 124, 126, 127, 134, 137, 139–53, 155, 156–63, 165, 167, 168, 180, 184, 185, 188–217, 220, 222, 224, 229, 233, 240, 248, 261, 264; as "American Lake," 10, 24, 33, 34, 38, 47
Caribbean Office, Department of State, 200, 201, 204, 205
Caribbean Sea Frontier (CSF), 43, 44, 51–55, 60
Cartagena, Colombia, 8
Casablanca, 8
Ceiba, Puerto Rico, 112, 115, 118, 121, 169, 241
Chaguaramas, Trinidad-Tobago, 214, 216
Chapman, Oscar, 90, 110, 187
Chardón, Carlos E., 64, 209
Charlotte Amalie, St. Thomas, 4, 6, 11, 34, 80
Chicanos/Chicanas, 247, 250, 256, 258
Chile, 19, 221, 225, 226
China, 35, 221, 252

Churchill, Winston, 92, 93, 94, 114, 139, 159, 160, 199
Cienfuegos, Cuba, 52
Citadelle, Haiti, 8
Civilian Conservation Corps (CCC), 113
Claiborne, Robert W., 75, 81
Clark, Frank S., 13
Colombia, 33, 34, 48, 52, 58, 225
Colonialism, 91, 159, 202, 220
Communists, 106, 115, 121
Confederación General de Trabjadores (CGT), 121
Convention for the Provisional Administration of European Colonies and Possessions, 193
Coolidge, Calvin, 15, 63
Crockett, Cary I., 9, 24
Crowder, Enoch, 63
Cuba, 4, 18, 19, 22, 26, 30, 33, 34, 38, 39, 51, 52, 54, 55, 58, 61, 63, 66, 83, 113, 124, 126, 128, 137, 141, 144, 147, 164, 190, 192, 209, 220, 221, 225, 226, 232, 239, 241, 249, 257, 263
Culebra, Puerto Rico, 4, 6, 7, 19, 20, 34, 35, 36, 38, 42, 50, 51, 55, 58, 192, 221
Cummins, USS, 19
Curacao, 6, 33, 47, 48, 52, 195, 222
Czechoslovakia, 5, 221

Daladier, Edouard, 5
Daley, Edmund, 11, 21
Daniels, Josephus, 56, 58
Davis, Leoncio T., 175
Decolonization, 54, 107, 159, 198, 214
Delgado Márquez, Rafael, 226, 227, 228, 233, 239, 242, 243
Del Valle, Pedro, 102
Denmark, 32, 33, 34, 47, 166, 221, 226
Destroyers for Bases Agreement, 22, 48, 53, 93, 114
Domínguez, José D., 228, 235, 243
Dominican Republic, 19, 20, 22, 54, 55, 57, 58, 66, 113, 164, 190, 209
Donitz, Karl, 139, 140, 141, 149, 160

Dutch East Indies, 31, 32
Dutch Guiana, 47, 48, 51, 141, 160, 195, 222

Earle, Edward Mead, 8
Ecuador, 221, 225
Eliot, George Fielding, 5, 6, 7, 23, 26, 263
Expansionism, 3, 5, 7, 192, 199, 211

Fajardo, Puerto Rico, 37, 115, 181
Falange Española, 115, 116
Fanguito, El, 168
Farm Purchasing Administration, 167
Farm Security Administration (FSA), 166, 225
Fascism, 11, 13, 18, 19, 22, 24, 70, 78, 84, 151, 223
Federal Bureau of Investigation (FBI), 106, 108, 115, 135, 144
Federal Communications Commission (FCC), 224, 225, 231
Fennel, Thomas, 178, 179
Fernández García, Benigno, 67, 71, 79
Fernós Isern, Antonio, 210
Filardi, Carmelo, 30
Fiske, Bradley A., 42
Fiz Jiménez, Epifanio, 71, 72, 79
Florida, 16, 30, 38, 40, 43, 51, 54, 55, 61, 62, 103, 137, 164, 192, 209, 255, 259
Folliard, Edward T., 11, 25
Fortas, Abe, 95, 96, 100, 108–10, 224, 231, 236, 243
Fortaleza (Govenor's residence), 21, 66, 76, 79, 95, 106
Franco, Francisco, 116, 233, 242

Galapagos Islands, Ecuador, 58
García Méndez, Miguel Ángel, 68, 71, 72, 77, 245
Geiger, Roy S., 20
General Board of the Navy, 34, 47, 53
German National Bank, 241
Ghormley, Harold Rainsford, 44
Góes Monteiro, Pedro Aurélio de, 19

Gore, Robert H., 61, 77
Goring, Hermann, 223
Grau San Martín, Ramón, 239
Great Britain, 4, 14, 15, 22, 26, 31, 32, 35, 45–48, 50, 54, 86, 88, 113, 114, 124, 164, 170, 188, 189–94, 199, 200, 201, 202, 203, 208, 211, 213, 217, 218, 221, 226
Greece, 226
Greenland, 29, 31
Greenslade, John W., 28, 52, 53
Gruening, Ernest, 64, 70, 78, 79, 85, 86, 87, 89, 90, 104, 116
Guadeloupe, 11, 19, 47, 48, 52, 54, 60, 151
Guam, 13, 16, 17, 20, 38, 39, 40, 76
Guánica Sugar Company, 157
Guantánamo, Cuba, 4, 6, 7, 16, 19, 33, 34, 38, 39, 42, 43, 47, 48, 50, 51, 58, 198
Guayanilla, Puerto Rico, 19

Haglund, David, 22, 27
Haiti, 4, 8, 18, 33, 54, 55, 66, 113, 190, 209
Halifax, Lord (E. F. L. Wood), 199, 200
Harding, Warren, 15
Harry S. Truman Library, 117
Hartenstein, Werner, 157
Havana, Cuba, 55, 61, 128, 193, 209, 257
Hawaii, 9, 10, 20, 21, 38, 39, 139, 161
Hepburn, Arthur J., 26, 38
Hepburn Board Report, 8, 14, 15, 22, 26, 28, 38, 42, 53
Hispaniola, 4, 50, 55
Hitler, Adolf, 4, 5, 18, 89, 146, 160, 164, 223, 241
Honduras, 190
Hoover, John H., 52, 142
Houston, USS, 20, 21, 28, 65, 69, 113
Hull, Cordell, 194, 196, 199, 214
Humacao, Puerto Rico, 181

Iceland, 31, 45
Ickes, Harold, 12, 18, 64, 65, 67, 70, 71, 72, 76, 78, 82, 83, 85, 87–91, 93–110, 149, 161, 224, 231, 235, 236

Iglesias, Santiago, 68, 72, 73, 75, 78, 79, 80, 81, 106
Imperialism, 7, 12, 26, 86, 198, 199, 202, 214, 215
Intelligence community, 5, 19, 24, 56, 63, 70, 79, 106, 139, 218, 233
Ireland, 45, 76, 158
Iron, 38, 145, 154, 161
Isabela, Puerto Rico, 50, 157
Isla Grande Naval Base, 2, 16, 17, 39, 42, 114
Italy, 7, 13, 15, 23, 26, 27, 31, 50, 221, 226, 248

Jamaica, 6, 47, 48, 55, 60, 114, 124, 126, 144, 190, 191, 194, 203, 207, 208
James, Earle K., 11
Japan, 2, 7, 12, 13, 15, 23, 26, 32, 43, 45, 182, 221, 223, 226, 250
Jíbaros (peasants), 9, 73, 253
Johnston Island, 17, 38, 39, 40, 58

Kalbfus, Edward C., 18, 20
Kaneohe Bay, 17, 38, 40
Kerensky, Alexander, 83
Key West, Florida, 16, 57
Kibler, A. F., 195
King, Ernest J., 52, 142
Kodiak, Alaska, 17, 38, 39, 40
Korea, 129, 245, 247, 249, 250, 252, 253, 255, 256, 257, 258, 259
Krug, Julius, 102, 110, 226

La Guardia, Fiorello, 86, 93, 100, 104, 250
Land, Emory S., 167
Lange, Kurt, 158
Las Grazas Hydroelectric Project, 68, 70, 71
Latin America, 4, 11, 13, 19, 22, 24, 25, 26, 27, 28, 31, 44, 47, 48, 57, 69, 92, 101, 119, 206, 221, 222, 223, 224, 225, 229, 233, 240, 241
Leahy, William D., 6, 7, 15, 65–70, 73–75, 103, 113, 143, 193, 263
Lend-Lease program, 114
Long, E. John, 10, 25

Losey Field, 115
Lothian, Lord (Philip Kerr), 113, 194

Macarthur, Fort, 254, 259
Machado, Gerardo, 3, 61
Magoon, Charles, 63
Mahan, Alfred Thayer, 6, 10, 22, 23, 43
Malaria, 115, 176
Marquart, E. J., 26
Marshall, George, 21, 109, 111, 134, 170
Marshall Islands, 58, 248
Martínez Nadal, Rafael, 68, 69, 70, 71, 73, 76, 78, 79, 80, 240, 256, 258
Martinique, 11, 25, 47, 48, 52, 54, 114, 151, 164
Massachusetts, 36, 226, 262
Mayagüez, Puerto Rico, 172, 209, 252
McLean, Ephraim, 10, 24
Mediterranean, 31, 32, 45
Mendoza, Luis G., 128
Mexican American War, 250
Mexico, 4, 10, 13, 25, 27, 30, 33, 38, 51, 58, 63, 157, 193, 221, 225, 251, 257
Miami, Florida, 10, 81
Mississippi, 141, 226
Mississippi, USS, 43
Mitchell, William, 43, 63
Mona Island and Passage, 6, 19, 50, 54, 59, 60, 157, 158, 168
Monserrat Island, 19
Morocco, 53, 122, 165
Moscoso, Teodoro, 137, 138, 177, 209
Moyne Report, 192, 195
Muñoz Marín, Luis, 31, 32, 62–65, 72–77, 80–113, 122, 127, 129, 132, 146, 177, 178, 203, 219, 225, 228, 229, 230, 231, 232, 236, 237, 238, 239, 240
Mussolini, Benito, 5, 146

Namorato, Michael V., 103, 127, 137
Nanking, China, 3
Natal, Brazil, 19, 48
National Guard (California), 259

Index

National Guard (Puerto Rico), 65, 115, 123, 250
National Guard (US), 248
National Youth Administration, 168
Navy, Brazilian, 142
Navy, Dutch, 142
Navy, Royal (GB), 15, 46
Navy, United States, 6, 8, 10, 14, 16, 17, 18, 22, 34, 38, 40, 41–47, 50, 53, 54, 66, 76, 86, 115, 119, 120, 139, 142, 148, 169, 170–79, 181, 182, 183, 184, 192, 193, 195, 230
Nazis, 18, 19, 27, 56, 70, 75, 160, 193, 209, 223
Netherlands, 4, 32, 46, 48, 102, 106, 122, 127, 129, 132, 146, 160, 177, 178, 203, 193–96, 208, 209, 221
Neuland, Operation (German), 141, 142
New Zealand, 226
Newfoundland, 27, 29, 47, 48, 50, 51, 92, 194
Nicaragua, 8, 63, 66
Norway, 140, 158, 221, 226
Núñez, Frank, 157

Oahu, Hawaii, 39
Office of Strategic Services (OSS), 95
Ohio, 52
Oil, 22, 33, 38, 41, 88, 95, 153, 154, 160, 166, 191, 196, 223
Oklahoma, 23
Oldendorf, Jesse, 52, 59
Oligopoly, 226
Olmstead, R. W., 60
Omaha, Nebraska, 30
O'Reilly, Camp, 115
Organization of American States, 55
Orlando, Florida, 255
Ortiz, Benjamín, 227, 228, 230
Orvieto, Italy, 248
Oscar, Chapman, 90, 110
Oxford, Balliol College, 31, 56

Pablin, 129, 137
Pacific, 8, 12, 13, 15, 27, 29–32, 34, 38, 43, 45, 46, 47, 51, 56, 58, 91, 113, 152, 193, 248, 256

Padelford, Norman J., 8, 24
Padín, José, 63, 106
Padrón, Lino, 167
Pagán, Bolívar, 71, 72, 79, 80, 91, 94, 98, 108, 109, 150, 155, 167, 204, 205, 206
Panama, 8, 158
Pan American Airways, 17
Panay, USS, 3
Pantojas García, Emilio, 199, 200, 213, 215
Paraguay, 221, 223
Paris, France, 220
Partido Popular Democrático, 72, 74, 77, 80, 82, 171, 188, 201, 213, 252
Pastor Ruiz, Justo, 175, 185
Paukenschlag, Operation, 139, 140, 141
Pava Publishing Company, 59
Pearl Harbor, 38, 39, 51, 58, 88, 92, 139, 149, 159, 175, 223
Pennsylvania, 105, 225
Pensacola, Florida, 17, 39, 40, 43
Percy, Celphil Alric, 214, 216
Pérez, Melanie Kinch, 212
Perkins, Dexter, 15, 26
Perloff, Harvey S., 123, 126, 135
Perón, Juan, 233, 242
Perú, 221
Petrograd, Russia, 63
Philadelphia, Pennsylvania, 25, 51, 105, 164, 256
Philippines, 6, 13, 38, 52, 63
Philips, Sarah T., 102, 105, 106
Picó, Rafael, 12, 126, 137, 176, 185, 209, 210, 217
Piñero, Jesús T., 66, 73, 77, 80, 102, 107, 110, 120, 161, 168, 210, 234–40, 243
Plummer, Jacqueline, 59
Polanco, Vicente Géigel, 185
Poland, 113
Ponce, Puerto Rico, 19, 64, 70, 99, 104, 115, 132, 138, 162, 165, 168, 172, 189, 208, 229, 234, 239, 252
Ponce Massacre, 64, 104
Popular Democratic Party, 12, 72, 74, 77, 80, 82, 84, 113, 121, 122, 127, 162, 171, 188, 213,

220, 225, 234. *See also* Partido Popular
    Democrático
Port-au-Prince, Haiti, 55, 209
Portland, Oregon, 30
Porto Rico General Telephone Company,
    221
Portugal, 32, 45, 47, 221, 226
PRACO, 177, 178, 179, 186
PRERA, 64, 214
Presidio, 251, 256, 258
PRIDCO, 147
Proof Gallon, 125, 126
Prostitution, 182
Public Works Administration (WPA), 113
Puerto Rico, 27, 35, 36, 57, 61, 110, 166, 177,
    218, 219, 220, 221, 224, 225, 226, 227, 229,
    232, 234, 235, 236, 239, 240, 243, 263
Puerto Rico Agricultural Company
    (PRACO), 177, 178, 179, 186
Puerto Rico Development Bank, 132, 133,
    171, 178, 237
Puerto Rico Emergency Relief Administra-
    tion (PRERA), 64, 214
Puerto Rico Reconstruction Administra-
    tion (PRRA), 64, 83, 85, 89, 103, 112, 113,
    116, 135, 214
Puerto Rico Telephone Company (PRTC),
    101, 219, 220, 221, 224, 226–39, 243
Puertorriqueños, 79, 136, 257

Quebec, Canada, 29
Queensland, 58
Quiñones, Samuel R., 109, 227, 236, 237
Quirós, Julio, 240

Racism, 119, 120
Raleigh, USS, 19
Ramey Air Field, 241
Regimiento 65 de Infantería, 255, 256, 258
Resettlement Administration, 225
Reuther, Walter, 104
Rice, 87, 152, 155, 157, 161, 163, 164, 165, 167,
    208

Riggs, Francis Elisha, 63, 64, 65
Rippy, Fred, 11, 25, 255
Rivas Rodríguez, Maggie, 257
Robbins, Carl, 200
Robert, Georges, 48, 53, 54
Rockefeller, Nelson A., 224
Rockwell, Kent, 80
Rodman Board Report, 14, 15
Rodney, George Brydges, 36
Rodríguez Bou, Ismae, 241
Rome, Italy, 248
Rommel, Erwin, 122
Roosevelt, Eleanor, 83, 90, 99, 106, 107
Roosevelt, Franklin D., 3, 6, 8, 11, 18, 22, 23,
    27, 28, 31, 44, 58, 61, 64–70, 75, 76, 78, 82,
    83, 85, 86, 87, 88, 89, 91–98, 100, 109, 112,
    113, 114, 116, 119, 122, 135, 142, 143, 149, 156,
    159, 160, 167, 192, 193, 197–201, 204, 205,
    214, 219, 222, 223, 224, 229, 230, 231, 232,
    234, 236, 238, 240, 242, 263; administra-
    tion, 4, 73, 88, 90, 91, 93, 100, 103, 114, 116,
    122; relationship with Ickes, 88; relation-
    ship with Tugwell, 83
Roosevelt, James, 20
Roosevelt, Theodore, 63
Roosevelt Corollary, 15
Roosevelt Roads Naval Base, 112, 118, 121,
    241
Ruiz, Justo Pastor, 175, 185
Rumania, 226
Russell, George, 221
Russia, 196

Saint Kitts, 191
Saint Lucia, 6, 48, 114, 194, 213
Samaná, 19, 36, 48, 57, 58
Samoa, 20, 38
Sampson, Anthony, 223, 240, 241, 242
San Andrés, 58
San Antonio, Texas, 251
San Cristóbal, Fort, 53, 114
San Diego, California, 39, 247
San Felipe del Morro, Fort, 114

San Francisco, California, 40, 251, 258
San Gabriel Valley, 254
San Jerónimo, Fort, 114
San Juan, Puerto Rico, 2, 4, 8, 9, 16, 17, 19, 26, 27, 28, 35, 36, 37, 39, 40, 42, 49, 53, 54, 57, 64, 65, 66, 68, 73, 77, 78, 79, 80, 84, 88, 89, 93, 94, 95, 97, 100, 102, 104, 109, 110, 112, 114, 115, 121, 131, 134–38, 142, 143, 146, 148, 149, 150, 151, 152, 153, 158, 161–68, 181, 183, 184, 186, 187, 214, 215, 216, 220, 229, 234, 241, 242, 243, 244, 247, 252, 256, 258, 261–64
San Martín, Ramón Grau, 239
San Pedro, California, 254
San Pedro de Macorís, 55, 209
San Rafael, California, 256
Sandino, Augusto César, 63
Santiago de Cuba, 55, 66, 137, 209; Punta Santiago, 135; Santiago de Chile, 19
Santibáñez, José, Ramírez, 73, 74
Santo Domingo, Dominican Republic, 8, 19, 20, 28, 36, 55, 160, 161, 209, 250
Santurce, 168, 185
Sao Paulo, 27
Saratoga, USS, 43
Schellenberg, Walter, 223
Schlesinger, Arthur M., Jr., 82, 102, 103, 104
Schroder, Kurt von, 223
Schroder, Roy, 185
Seabees, 183
Seoul, Korea, 252
Serrana Key, 58
Shanghai, China, 221
Silverman, Irvin W., 187
Smith, Gaddis, 139, 160
Soil Conservation Service, 167
Spanish-American War, 4, 22, 24, 34, 52, 66, 114, 249
Spruance, Raymond A., 52, 53
Social Security Service (SSS), 157
Stark, Harold Rainsford, 44
Stefansson, Vilhyjalmur, 80
Sudetenland, 5

Sullivan, Mark, 127
Sulzberger, C. L., 136
Surinam, 48, 52, 190
Swanson, Claude, 15, 135
Sweden, 221, 226
Switzerland, 204, 221, 223, 226
Swope, Guy, 113, 137

Tehuantepec, Mexico, 8
Tió, Juan Ángel, 175
Truesdell, Leon E., 164
Tugwell, Rexford G., 82, 83, 85, 86, 87, 89, 91–95, 97, 98, 99, 101, 103, 105, 107, 109, 111, 117, 134, 137, 162
Tydings, Millard, 63, 104

U-boats, 50, 51, 54, 59, 95, 96, 114, 122, 124, 132, 136, 139, 140, 141, 142, 144, 150, 157, 158, 160, 168, 170, 194, 196, 208, 262
United Kingdom, 44, 45, 188, 214, 256, 261
United Nations, 87, 162, 256
United States, 3, 4, 5, 7, 8, 9, 12, 13, 14, 15, 17, 18, 19, 21, 22, 24–28, 31, 34, 35, 36, 38, 40–48, 50, 51, 53–56, 60, 65, 70, 73, 82, 87, 89, 93, 94, 108, 110, 111, 113–16, 118, 119, 120, 122, 124, 128, 136, 137, 139, 141, 142, 143, 144, 145, 147, 148, 151, 155, 156, 158, 159, 161, 162, 168, 169, 170, 175, 176, 179, 181, 182, 186, 188–203, 206–22, 229, 233, 234, 235, 241, 248, 250, 251, 253, 257, 258, 264
Upshur, William P., 20
Uruguay, 18, 221, 225, 226

Valdés, Alfonso, 247
Valdés, Luis V., 247
Vargas, Getulio, 19
Venezuela, 8, 26, 30, 33, 47, 48, 52, 58, 196, 222
Vichy Government, 48, 52, 53, 54, 66, 151, 164
Vieques, 19, 34, 36, 48, 115, 117, 118, 120, 121, 134, 135, 136, 169, 170–87, 221, 261, 262
Vietnam, 246, 249, 256

Vilella, Roberto Sánchez, 236, 237, 243, 262
Virgin Islands, 4, 5, 6, 8, 11, 12, 13, 14, 16, 19,
    20, 22, 33, 34, 35, 36, 39, 50, 54, 55, 57, 61,
    94, 122, 124, 126, 137, 147, 152, 166, 176, 179,
    185, 186, 190, 192, 195, 220, 222
Virginia, 39, 40, 53

Wallace, Henry, 88, 100, 105, 224
West Indies, 10, 11, 25, 30, 31, 32, 35, 36, 38, 55,
    57, 59, 60, 93, 94, 164, 190, 195, 213, 214,
    215, 261
Wharton, School of Business, 225
Whiskey, 124, 129, 162, 170
Whitham, Charlie, 215
Wickard, Claude A., 156
Wilson, Woodrow, 56, 58, 86
Winship, Blanton, 11, 20, 22, 28, 63–80, 85,
    90, 103, 104, 113, 198, 262
Wisconsin, 81
WKAQ, 221
Works Progress Administration (WPA),
    113, 122, 134, 135
WPB, 147

Yerxa, Donald, 13, 25

www.ingramcontent.com/pod-product-compliance
Lightning Source LLC
Chambersburg PA
CBHW030610230426
43661CB00053B/1925